Managing the Multibusir

CW00556519

All multibusiness companies need to be able to justify the ownership of the businesses in the group. The corporate-level strategy must therefore show how and why the corporate parent adds value to the businesses. Classic strategic issues, which are addressed in this book, include the allocation of resources between businesses, the creation of synergy through linkages amongst the businesses and the choices faced when creating a corporate portfolio.

This selection of readings, which includes writings by leading business authorities, has been organized around the major issues outlined above. In Part I the readings concern the basic justification for the existence of multibusiness companies. Parts II and III concentrate much more on advice for the managers of these companies about how to handle the difficult strategic issues they face. Part IV offers empirical evidence on how diversified companies have performed, which leads to the penultimate part's selection of readings examining the nature of the influence that corporate parents actually exercise over their businesses, for good or ill. Part VI looks at the process for developing an effective corporate-level strategy.

Although the strategic issues that multibusiness companies confront will remain challenging and difficult, this book provides up-to-date thinking about how to approach them, and reveals that a robust framework for dealing with them is beginning to emerge.

Michael Goold is a director of the Ashridge Strategic Management Centre. Previously he was a Senior Fellow at the London Business School and a Vice President of the Boston Consulting Group. He has an MBA from Stanford Business School. **Kathleen Sommers Luchs** is an Associate at Ashridge Strategic Management Centre. She has an MBA from the London Business School and a PhD from Yale University.

Managing the Multibusiness Company

Strategic Issues for Diversified Groups

Edited by Michael Goold and
Kathleen Sommers Luchs

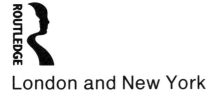

London and New York

First published 1996
by Routledge
11 New Fetter Lane, London EC4P 4EE

Simultaneously published in the USA and Canada
by Routledge
29 West 35th Street, New York, NY 10001

Typeset in Garamond by Datix International Limited, Bungay, Suffolk

Printed and bound in Great Britain by T J Press (Padstow) Ltd, Padstow, Cornwall

British Library Cataloguing in Publication Data
A catalogue record for this book is available from the British Library

Library of Congress Cataloging in Publication Data
A catalogue record for this book has been requested

ISBN 0–415–13268–1 (hbk)
ISBN 0–415–13269-X (pbk)

Contents

Figures, tables and exhibits

FIGURES

TABLES

EXHIBITS

Notes on sources

Chapter 1 Williamson, Oliver E. (1975) *Markets and Hierarchies*, New York: Free Press, pp. 8–10; 39–40; 132; 137–8; 141–51; 156–62; and references. Reprinted with the permission of the Free Press, a Division of Simon & Schuster Inc. from *Markets and Hierarchies: Analysis and antitrust implications* by Oliver E. Williamson. Copyright © 1975, 1983 by The Free Press.

Chapter 2 Teece, David J. (1982) 'Towards an Economic Theory of the Multiproduct Firm'. Reprinted from *Journal of Economic Behaviour and Organization*, 3, pp. 39–63, 1982, with kind permission from Elsevier Science B.V., Amsterdam, The Netherlands.

Chapter 3 Peteraf, Margaret A. (1993) 'The Cornerstones of Competitive Advantage: A Resource Based View', *Strategic Management Journal*, (14): 179–91. Reprinted by permission of John Wiley & Sons Ltd.

Chapter 4 Grant, Robert (1991) *Contemporary Strategy Analysis*, Oxford: Blackwell. pp. 340–4 + diagram p. 345.

Chapter 5 Reimann, Bernard C. (1988) "Managing for the Shareholders: An Overview of Value-Based Planning", *Planning Review*, 16(1): 10–22, January/February. This article is reprinted from *Planning Review*, 1988, with permission from The Planning Forum, The International Society for Strategic Management and Planning.

Chapter 6 Collis, David J. 'What is a "Related" Corporate Strategy?' unpublished paper, 1995.

Chapter 7 Haspeslagh, Philippe C. and Jemison, David B. (1991) *Managing Acquisitions: Creating Value Through Corporate Renewal*, New York: The Free Press, pp. 18–37. Reprinted with the permission of the Free Press, a Division of Simon & Schuster Inc. Copyright © 1991 by The Free Press.

Chapter 8 Porter, Michael (1985) *Competitive Advantage*, New York: Free Press. pp. 317–19; 323–63; and References. Reprinted with the permission of The Free Press, a Division of Simon & Schuster Inc. Copyright © 1985 by Michael E. Porter.

Chapter 9 Prahalad, C. K. and Hamel, Gary (1990) 'The Core Competence of the Corporation', *Harvard Business Review*, pp. 79–91, May–June.

Chapter 10 Kanter, Rosabeth Moss (1989) *When Giants Learn to Dance*, London: Simon & Schuster, pp. 100–16 and notes. Reprinted with the permission of Simon and Schuster.

Chapter 11 Ramanujam, Vasudevan and Varadarajan, P. Rajan (1989) 'Research on Corporate Diversification: A Synthesis', *Strategic Management Journal* 10 (6), 523–51, November–December. pp. 525; 526 (Figure only); 531–4; 535; 537–43; 545–51 (selected references). Reprinted by permission of John Wiley & Sons Ltd.

Chapter 12 Porter, Michael. E. (1987) 'From competitive advantage to corporate strategy', *Harvard Business Review* 65 (3): 43–59.

Chapter 13 Jensen, Michael C. (1989) 'Eclipse of the public corporation', *Harvard Business Review*, pp. 61–74, September–October.

Chapter 14 Chandler, Alfred D., Jr (1991) 'The Functions of the HQ Unit in the Multibusiness Firm', *Strategic Management Journal* 12: 31–50. Reprinted by permission of John Wiley & Sons Ltd.

Chapter 15 Campbell, Andrew, Goold, Michael and Alexander, Marcus (1995) 'The Value of the Parent Company', *California Management Review*, 38 (1), Fall.

Chapter 16 Prahalad, C. K. and Bettis, Richard A. (1986) 'The dominant logic: a new linkage between diversity and performance', *Strategic Management Journal*, 7: 485–501. Reprinted by permission of John Wiley & Sons Ltd.

Chapter 17 Goold, Michael., Campbell, Andrew and Alexander, Marcus (1994) *Corporate-Level Strategy: Creating Value in the Multibusiness Company*, New York: John Wiley & Sons, Inc. pp. 291–318. Copyright © 1994 M. Goold, A. Campbell and M. Alexander. Reprinted by permission of John Wiley & Sons Ltd.

Introduction

During the last forty years, an important shift has taken place in corporate strategies. Until the 1950s, the vast majority of companies were functionally organized and focused their activities around a single dominant business. Today, divisional structures are far more common, and most medium and large sized companies operate in a number of separate businesses. The emergence of companies that own and manage several different businesses, multibusiness companies, has been a striking feature in all developed industrial economies.

Multibusiness companies include not only the classic conglomerates, such as Hanson or ITT. The term also applies to the much larger number of companies which certainly do not see themselves as conglomerates, but whose operations nevertheless extend over more than one distinct business. Such companies include Dupont and ICI, Exxon and Shell, Procter & Gamble and Unilever, Banc One and Barclays, as well as a whole host of smaller companies organized around separate divisions or profit centres. These companies are all multibusiness companies, and, as such, face distinctive strategic issues.

All multibusiness companies need to be able to justify their ownership of their multiple businesses. They need to be able to show that the influence they exercise on their businesses as corporate parents is beneficial, and that the businesses perform better as part of the corporate portfolio than they would as separate, independent entities. This is the basic challenge for multibusiness companies; a corporate-level strategy that is no more than the aggregation of a collection of individual business strategies is seriously inadequate. The corporate-level strategy must show how and why the corporate parent adds value to its businesses, and must address issues such as the allocation of resources between the businesses, the creation of synergy through linkages amongst the businesses, and choices concerning the businesses that should make up the corporate portfolio. These are the classic strategic issues for multibusiness companies that are addressed in this book.

THE DEVELOPMENT OF MULTIBUSINESS COMPANIES

Alfred Chandler, the eminent business historian, has shown how the divisionalized, multibusiness company first emerged in the years before and during the Second World War.[1] In Chandler's view, companies like General Motors, Dupont, and Standard Oil were forced to adopt a divisional structure because they had grown too large and complex to be managed with their previous functional organizations. These companies had been drawn into a wider and wider range of products and markets to exploit the opportunities arising from their base businesses and competences, and found that the only way to avoid overload at the centre was by decentralization. Divisional structures were therefore introduced, which separated day-to-day management responsibilities for the businesses from corporate strategy and resource allocation. These divisional structures recognized, for the first time, a distinction between business-level decisions, which were now the primary responsibility of management within the division, and corporate-level strategy, which was the responsibility of the corporate centre.

The success of companies such as GM led to increased popularity for divisional structures. Richard Rumelt's *Strategy, Structure and Economic Performance* estimates that the percentage of divisionalized companies in the Fortune 500 rose from 24 per cent in 1949 to 51 per cent by 1959 and to 80 per cent by 1969.[2] In many cases, divisionalization was coupled with, or led on to, moves into new businesses to supplement the original, core business. The logic for these diversifications was that they could spread the company's risks, utilize its management skills, and, with new businesses that were related to the base businesses, provide opportunities for synergy.

By spreading risks across a variety of different businesses and countries, corporate managements believed they could reduce the volatility of their companies' performance and their dependence on individual markets or technologies. Although financial theorists now argue that investors should not value corporate diversification as a means of risk spreading, since they can diversify their risks more efficiently by selecting a portfolio of different investments,[3] many corporate managers have continued to be attracted by diversifications that reduce their exposure to a single, dominant business.

The ability to utilize management skills and competences more fully is a second, long established argument in favour of entering new businesses. From the 1950s onwards, writers like Peter Drucker were beginning to put forward the proposition that good managers needed to master certain general principles of management that were applicable in any business setting.[4] Given a belief in general management skills, it was not a great leap to conclude that 'professional managers' might be able to use their skills in a variety of different business areas.[5] At one extreme, conglomerates such as Litton, ITT, and Textron sought growth by entering a wide range of different businesses. The top managers of these conglomerates believed that they possessed distinctive general management skills, and that, by applying them to a large number of different businesses, they could grow profitably. But many other, more traditional industrial companies also diversified during the 1960s and 1970s. In particular, where the companies' base businesses were maturing, corporate managers looked for growth opportunities in new areas. Diversification was attractive to such companies as a means of leveraging corporate competences and resources, and thereby meeting corporate growth objectives. Typically, the diversifications were not in 'unrelated' areas, as with the true conglomerates, but were in 'related' businesses, which had some links with the base business.

Diversifications into related businesses could be justified both by the fuller utilization of management skills or competences and by a belief in synergy. Igor Ansoff, for example, advised firms to analyse their capabilities in areas such as manufacturing, marketing and general management, and to identify new product-markets where these capabilities could be exploited to achieve synergies.[6] Rumelt's research on diversification suggests that, by 1969, 44 per cent of the Fortune 500 companies had diversified into related businesses, while only 12 per cent had diversified into unrelated areas.[7]

For all these reasons, the growth and popularity of diversified, multibusiness companies continued unabated through the 1970s. By the 1980s, however, many diversified, multibusiness companies were encountering performance problems, and widespread scepticism about the ability of companies to manage and add value to multibusiness portfolios gained ground. Raiders such as Carl Icahn, T. Boone Pickens, Kohlberg Kravis and Roberts, and Hanson demonstrated that they could acquire even the largest companies, break them up, and realize huge profits. The takeover activity of the 1980s prompted a rethinking both of the role of the corporate centre and of the kinds of strategies which were appropriate in multibusiness companies. Moreover, consultants and academics, such as Tom Peters, Robert Hayes and Michael Porter, were less and less favourable towards diversification, with several studies showing that diversifications and acquisitions had generally performed poorly, and advocating a renewed focus on selected core businesses.[8] During the 1980s, corporate restructuring in the USA began to reverse the trend of the previous three decades, and the percentage of diversified firms declined among the Fortune 500.[9]

In the 1990s, many multibusiness companies therefore face an increasing need to improve their performance and sharpen their strategies.

Though multibusiness companies continue to account for a high proportion of economic activity in the developed economies, they are under increasing pressure to show that their corporate strategies create value, and that they should not be broken up into their constituent parts.

STRATEGIC ISSUES FOR MULTIBUSINESS COMPANIES

Although many corporate managers recognize the need to re-evaluate their corporate strategies, they confront contradictory advice on how this should be achieved. Multibusiness companies are advised to 'stick to the knitting' and focus on one or a few closely related core businesses, but are also told to exploit their strengths in new businesses to ensure corporate renewal and growth. They are told to downsize and delayer, but also exhorted to search for synergies and build the corporation's core competences. Some advisors portray portfolio changes such as demergers or acquisitions as opportunities to increase shareholder value, while others criticize such moves as accounting tricks. Sorting through such conflicting approaches, and distinguishing between passing fads and more enduringly valuable thinking about corporate strategy, is not an easy task.

This book of readings is designed to help managers and students of corporate strategy to identify concepts and frameworks that can help them to deal with the distinctive strategic issues faced by multibusiness companies. The purpose of the book is to highlight and make more accessible the main themes and ideas that writers and researchers on corporate-level strategy have put forward, and to provide the reader with an overview of current thinking. In selecting the readings, we have aimed to identify theoretical, empirical and practical approaches to corporate-level strategy that together provide a sound basis for addressing the major issues in this field.

The readings have been organized around six major issues faced by all multibusiness companies:

- What is the basic economic justification and rationale for bringing different businesses together under the common ownership of a single corporate entity?
- How should resources be allocated among the businesses in the corporate portfolio, what businesses are suitable for inclusion within the corporate portfolio, and what criteria should guide acquisitions and divestments?
- How should linkages and synergy between businesses be analysed and facilitated?
- How well have diversified, multibusiness companies performed, and

what are current trends in diversification?

- How do corporate parents in fact influence their businesses, and under what circumstances do they create or destroy value through their influence?
- What process should be adopted for developing a convincing and powerful corporate-level strategy for a multibusiness company?

Figure Intro.1 provides an overview of the topics covered and the readings included in the book.

The first set of readings, in Part I, concerns the basic justification for the existence of multibusiness companies. These readings are more concerned with economic theory than with practical managerial issues, but they attempt to provide a fundamental underpinning for the multibusiness organizational form. The transaction cost thinking developed by Oliver Williamson, the theory of specialized resources and market failures stressed by David Teece, and the whole resource-based theory of the firm summarized by Margaret Peteraf each give basic insights into why and how multibusiness firms can, in some circumstances, be more economically efficient than single business firms. These readings contain some hints for corporate strategists concerned with the management of multibusiness companies, but their main focus is on theory building, not practical advice.

The next two parts, by contrast, concentrate much more on advice for multibusiness company managers about how to handle difficult strategic issues that they face. In Part II, questions of resource allocation and portfolio development are addressed. What businesses should the company be in, and how should it allocate resources amongst them? In Part III, the topic is the search for synergy. How can the businesses be made to collaborate in ways that mean that 2 and 2 will add up to more than 4?

Resource allocation across a variety of different businesses has always been both a vital and a difficult role for multibusiness companies. Robert Grant summarizes the portfolio planning techniques which became so widely used for this purpose during the 1970s, and Bernard Reimann explains the techniques of value-based planning that have gained popularity more recently. Though both these approaches to resource allocation have shortcomings, their use in multibusiness companies has been widespread. David Collis concentrates more on portfolio development and Philippe Haspeslagh and David Jemison on acquisitions. Both these readings draw explicitly on the resource-based theory of the firm, and attempt to show its practical implications for multibusiness company managers.

The readings in Part III concern synergy, which many writers, including David Teece, believe should be the main rationale for multibusiness companies. Michael Porter, who supports this view of the importance of

THEORY

I Economic justification for the multibusiness firm

Williamson, *Transaction costs and market failure*

Teece, *Economic theory of the multiproduct firm*

Peteraf, *Resource-based theory*

ADVICE

II Resource allocation and portfolio composition

Grant, *Portfolio planning*

Reimann, *Value-based planning*

Collis, *Related corporate portfolios*

Haspeslagh and Jemison, *Creating value in acquisitions*

III The quest for synergy

Porter, *Interrelationships across businesses*

Hamel and Prahalad, *The core competence of the corporation*

Kanter, *Achieving synergies*

RESULTS

IV Diversification, performance and restructuring

Ramanujam and Varadarajan, *Research on diversification*

Porter, *Corporate strategy*

Jensen, *Eclipse of the public corporation*

PRACTICE

V How corporate parents influence their businesses

Chandler, *Functions of headquarters*

Campbell, Goold and Alexander, *Value of the parent company*

Prahalad and Bettis, *Dominant logic*

FRAMEWORK

VI Developing a corporate strategy

Goold, Campbell and Alexander, *Developing a corporate strategy*

Figure Intro. 1 Overview of the book

synergy for multibusiness companies, shows how detailed value chain analysis can be used for identifying potential synergies, and discusses the benefits and costs of different sorts of linkages between businesses. C. K. Prahalad and Gary Hamel propose that successful multibusiness companies should aim to develop selected core competences and share them across as many of their businesses as possible. Rosabeth Moss Kanter offers practical guidance on how to bring synergies about.

Part IV moves away from prescriptive advice to managers of multibusiness companies, and concentrates on the empirical evidence concerning how diversified companies have performed. Vasudevan Ramanujam and P. Rajan Varadarajan summarize the extensive research on whether 'related' diversifiers have done better than 'unrelated' diversifiers or single business firms, and show that no conclusive patterns emerge. There is little evidence to suggest that the theoretical advantages of related diversifiers have in practice been realized. Michael Porter's research shows that most acquisitions of new businesses appear not to be successful. The most negative assessment of multibusiness companies' records is given by Michael Jensen, who argues that most diversifications waste shareholders' money and are made only to satisfy management's aspirations. As a result, he foresees the eclipse of the public corporation, at least in more mature sections of the economy.

Despite the theoretical advantages of the multibusiness company, and the range of prescriptive advice available to managers, the performance of many multibusiness companies has therefore been disappointing. Part V consequently sets out to re-examine the nature of the influence that corporate parents actually exercise over their businesses, for good or ill. Alfred Chandler examines corporate experience in the USA and the UK, and argues that it is only if the role played by the corporate-level management fits with the nature and needs of the businesses that value will be created. Otherwise, performance will suffer. Andrew Campbell, Michael Goold and Marcus Alexander identify the main ways in which corporate parents both create and destroy value through their influence. They show how easy it is to damage performance rather than enhance it, and identify the limited conditions under which corporate parents do add value. C. K. Prahalad and Richard Bettis maintain that most corporate centres operate with a single dominant management logic that they apply across all their businesses; in multibusiness companies with a diverse range of businesses, this logic is often unsuitable for several of the businesses. All these readings, therefore, help to explain the poor performance of many multibusiness companies and point out the circumstances in which positive value will actually be created by multibusiness companies. The essential requirement is that the nature of the influence that the corporate parent exercises should fit well with the needs and opportunities in the businesses.

The final section, Part VI, addresses the process for developing a corporate-level strategy. All too often, the corporate-level strategy is no more than the aggregate of the business-level strategies, and there is no separate process or framework for examining the corporate strategy as such. Goold, Campbell and Alexander, however, propose a process that focuses on identifying the characteristics, resources and skills of the corporate parent, and assessing the extent to which they fit with the needs and opportunities in the businesses. This framework is consistent with the resource-based theory of the firm, but also acknowledges the practical difficulties that corporate parents face in adding value to multiple businesses. It places particular emphasis on determining a value creating role for the corporate parent, as the central issue in corporate-level strategy for multibusiness companies.

Until recently, the topic of corporate-level strategy for multibusiness companies has received far less attention than business-level strategy. Whereas business strategists have been able to make use of a large and developing body of theoretical and practical guidance to assist them, corporate strategists have been less well served. Furthermore, such advice as has been available has often been incomplete and contradictory. The readings in this book do, however, show that the strategic issues facing multibusiness companies are now being brought into focus. Although the writers represented draw on different traditions and emphasize different issues, there is evidence of a convergence of views around certain themes. In a broad sense, the resource-based theory of the firm provides both a theoretical and a practical grounding for the multibusiness company. It shows how, in principle, multibusiness companies may be able to enhance the collective performance of a suitably chosen group of businesses. Furthermore, a concern with the resources, skills and other characteristics of the corporate parent, and with their fit to the needs and opportunities in the businesses, is beginning to provide both an explanation of the mixed performance records of multibusiness companies and a basis for analysing and developing corporate strategies.

Although the strategic issues that multibusiness companies confront will remain challenging and difficult, we hope that this book shows that some robust frameworks for addressing them are beginning to emerge.

NOTES

1 Chandler, Alfred D., Jr. (1962) *Strategy and Structure*, Cambridge, Mass.: MIT; re-issued 1982.
2 Rumelt, Richard P. (1974) *Strategy, Structure and Economic Performance*, Boston, Mass.: Harvard Business School.
3 Brealey, Richard and Myers, Stewart (1991) *Principles of Corporate Finance*, 4th edn, New York: McGraw-Hill.
4 Drucker, Peter (1955) *The Practice of Management*, London: William Heinemann

Ltd, re-issued Pan Books, 1968; Koontz, Harold (1961) 'The Management Theory Jungle', *Academy of Management Journal*, 4(3): 174–88, December; Koontz, Harold (1969) 'A Model for Analyzing the Universality and Transferability of Management', *Academy of Management Journal*, 12(4): 415–30, December.

5 Katz, Robert L. (1955) 'Skills of an Effective Administrator', *Harvard Business Review*, 33–42, January–February.

6 Ansoff, Igor (1965) *Corporate Strategy*, New York: McGraw-Hill; London: Penguin Books, 1968.

7 Rumelt, Richard P. (1974) *Strategy, Structure and Economic Performance*, Boston, Mass.: Harvard Business School.

8 Porter, M. E. (1987) 'From Competitive Advantage to Corporate Strategy', *Harvard Business Review*, 65(3): 43–59; Peters, Thomas J. and Waterman, Robert H. (1983) *In Search of Excellence*, New York: Free Press; Hayes, Bob and Abernathy, Bill (1980) 'Managing Our Way to Economic Decline', *Harvard Business Review*, 67–77, July/August.

9 Markides, Constantinos C. (1991) 'Back to Basics: Reversing Corporate Diversification', *Multinational Business*, 4: 12–25.

Part I

Economic justification for the multibusiness firm

A fundamental question for multibusiness firms is, why should they exist at all? Why should separate businesses be brought into common corporate ownership, rather than have direct relationships to external investors and providers of capital? Is there any economic justification for Hanson to own businesses as diverse as tobacco, timber and coal or for Unilever's ownership of cosmetics, chemicals and ice cream businesses?

Historically, a popular managerial justification for diversification has been based on notions of risk spreading and balance. According to this thinking, a firm can avoid marked fluctuations in performance and better secure its future if it includes businesses spread across different industries with different risk characteristics and subject to different economic cycles. Poor performance of some businesses in the corporate portfolio will be balanced by the good performance of other businesses, thus smoothing out yearly earnings. Financial theorists, however, have discredited this conventional justification for diversification.[1] They argue that investors can easily diversify their portfolios themselves by spreading their investments across different sectors and companies. Unit trusts and mutual funds can provide investors with well-balanced portfolios, and the administrative costs of such funds should be much lower than the cost of corporate overheads in a diversified company. There is no economic role for the multibusiness company in diversifying risk for the owners. Despite the popularity of the risk spreading view, it does not provide a convincing rationale for multibusiness companies.

Another explanation for the existence of multibusiness firms is based on the notion of market power. In this view, firms seek growth and diversification in order to gain control of markets and thereby enhance their profits.[2] As a result, criticisms of diversification were widespread in the 1950s and 1960s, when large, diversified companies were often viewed with suspicion. Given these criticisms, and questions of public policy which they raised, Oliver Williamson's work on the underlying economic rationale for multibusiness firms has proved of seminal importance. Williamson's book, *Markets and Hierarchies: Analysis and Antitrust Implications*,[3] was published in 1975, and a selection from this book is included here. Williamson's work deserves (and requires) careful reading, because his ideas on why firms exist have become increasingly influential in the field of corporate strategy

Williamson builds on the work of R. H. Coase, who described markets and firms as alternative means of organizing transactions, and argued that firms exist because some transactions can be conducted more efficiently within a firm than in a market.[4] In the economic model developed by Williamson, the basic unit of analysis is the transaction. Transactions can be accomplished through different governance structures, ranging from markets at one end of a continuum to hierarchies, or firms, at the opposite end. The purpose of markets, firms and hybrid organizational forms is the same: to facilitate transactions. Economic efficiency is maximized when transactions are aligned to the governance structure which minimizes their costs. Williamson explores the kinds of transactions that are difficult or impossible to conduct in a market. For example, a manufacturing firm may require a highly specialized component for one of its products. The market solution would be for the firm to contract with an external supplier for the component, but suppliers may themselves need specialized equipment to produce the component, and they will require contractual guarantees to protect their investment. If the costs of establishing such contracts are high, a firm may choose to produce the component internally. The firm may not realize manufacturing economies of scale, but it will none the less be better off if the transaction costs of internal production are lower than those of contracting with external suppliers. In short, Williamson argues that firms exist because managerial hierarchies are more efficient than markets in conducting certain types of transactions.

Transaction cost analysis can be used to explain many facets of economic life, including the existence of multibusiness firms. According to Williamson, multibusiness firms economize on transaction costs by intervening between individual businesses and the capital markets. By using devices such as internal audits and managerial incentives, they are able to allocate resources more efficiently than would be the case if each business dealt directly with the external capital market. This provides a fundamental rationale for the existence of multibusiness companies.

In the next chapter, David Teece examines two issues in more detail: why do firms enter new product areas, and when is such diversification economically efficient? Teece argues that a business may generate excess resources, such as production capacity or knowhow. One option is for the business to sell its surplus resources in a market. For example, a firm might rent out idle machinery to another business, or sell some of its researchers' time to a university or to another firm. However, if the firm's resources are highly specialized or indivisible, such market-based transactions may be difficult or against the firm's interests. The effectiveness of a researcher may depend on the support he receives from a team, and therefore his services are more valuable within the firm than to any external buyer, or buyers of the firm's surplus resources may gain valuable information about its products or processes, and thus undermine the firm's position. In these circumstances, a firm may seek to exploit its resources internally by diversifying into new product areas. Teece thus argues that diversification occurs because it can be the most efficient means of exploiting a firm's resources.

The thinking of economists such as Williamson and Teece has influenced business and corporate strategists in recent years, and contributed to the development of the resource-based theory of the firm.[5] Resource-based theory draws on the economic concepts of transaction costs and market failure, but the focus of the work is on why firms pursue different strategies and achieve different results. Proponents of resource-based theories of the firm see firms as bundles of resources. These resources include physical assets, such as plant and machinery, but also assets such as know-how and competences. Firms differ because they accumulate different bundles of resources, and it is these resource bundles which determine the kinds of strategies which a firm can pursue successfully. According to resource-based theory, successful companies accumulate unique bundles of resources, which rivals cannot easily acquire or imitate, and these unique resources are the source of competitive advantage. This theory is relevant to firm scope, or the issue of diversification. Resources may have multiple uses, or support the production of a variety of products. If a firm accumulates resources which are not fully utilized in its current activities, it may simply sell its unused resources. High transaction costs or market failure, however, may mean that it is more efficient for the firm to find ways to exploit its resources internally, by diversifying into new product-markets. According to resource-based theory, multibusiness companies arise in order to exploit fully a firm's resources. Margaret Peteraf, in Chapter 3, explains the economic thinking underpinning the resource-based theory of the firm, and shows how this theory contributes to our understanding of both business-level and corporate-level strategy.

The authors included in the first part of the book draw on and develop economic theory to explain the circumstances under which multibusiness firms may develop and prosper. Concepts such as transaction costs, market failure and resource bundles may be unfamiliar to most managers, or seem too abstract to be relevant to the corporate strategist. They do, however, have important implications for corporate strategy. Most importantly, economic theory poses a basic test for a successful corporate strategy: the performance of a multibusiness company must be better than the alternative of independent businesses conducting transactions in the market, or there is no economic logic for the existence of the company. The multibusiness company must create some value over and above the value that is created by the individual businesses it owns in order to justify itself.

NOTES

1 Brealey, Richard and Myers Stewart (1991) *Principles of Corporate Finance*, 4th edn, New York: McGraw-Hill.
2 Scherer, Frederick (1990) *Industrial Market Structure and Economic Performance*, 3rd edn, Boston, Mass: Houghton Mifflin (first published 1970); for a summary of the various motives for diversification (i.e., risk spreading, market power) see Grant, Robert, (1991) *Contemporary Strategy Analysis*, Oxford: Blackwell Publishers: 306–10.
3 Williamson, Oliver E. (1975) *Markets and Hierarchies: Analysis and Antitmist Implications*, New York: Free Press.
4 Coase, Ronald H. (1937) 'The Nature of the Firm', *Economica N.S.*, 4: 386–437; reprinted in *The Nature of the Firm*, Williamson, Oliver E. and Winter, Sidney G. (eds) (1991) Oxford: Oxford University Press.
5 Grant, Robert (1991) 'The Resource-Based Theory of Competitive Advantage', *California Management Review*, 33(3): 114–35, Spring; Conner, Kathleen R. (1991) 'A Historical Comparison of Resource-Based Theory and Five Schools of Thought Within Industrial Organization Economics: Do We Have a New Theory of the Firm?' *Journal of Management*, 17(1): 121–54; Barney, J. B. (1991) 'Firm Resources and Sustained Competitive Advantage', *Journal of Management*, 17(1): 99–120; Teece, David J., Pisano, Gary and Shuen, Amy (1990) 'Firm Capabilities, Resources, and the Concept of Strategy', Consortium on Competitiveness & Cooperation, CCC Working Paper No. 90–8, December; Wernerfelt, B. (1989) 'From Critical Resources to Corporate Strategy', *Journal of Management*, 14: 4–12.

ADDITIONAL READING

Barney, J. B. (1991) 'Firm Resources and Sustained Competitive Advantage', *Journal of Management*, 17(1) 99–120.
A comparison of the resource-based model with other models of strategy, including Michael Porter's five forces framework.
Coase, Ronald H. (1937) 'The Nature of the Firm', *Economica N.S.*, 4: 386–437; reprinted in *The Nature of the Firm*, Williamson, Oliver E. and Winter, Sidney G. (eds) (1991) Oxford: Oxford University Press.
The development of the concept that firms and markets are alternative means of organizing economic transactions.
Conner, Kathleen R. (1991) 'A Historical Comparison of Resource-Based Theory and Five Schools of Thought Within Industrial Organization Economics: Do We Have a New Theory of the Firm?' *Journal of Management*, 17(1): 121–54.
Examines how the resource-based theory differs from other theories of the firm, including transaction cost theory.

Grant, Robert (1991) 'The Resource-Based Theory of Competitive Advantage', *California Management Review*, 33(3): 114–35, Spring.
  Explains the fundamental principles of resource-based theory and the impact of the theory on strategy formulation, with a focus on business-level strategy.
Teece, David J., Pisano, Gary and Shuen, Amy (1990) 'Firm Capabilities, Resources, and the Concept of Strategy', Consortium on Competitiveness & Cooperation, CCC Working Paper No. 90–8, December.
  Development of resource-based theory, and question of firm diversification.
Wernerfelt, B. (1989) 'From Critical Resources to Corporate Strategy', *Journal of General Management*, 14: 4–12.
  Explanation of some of the major concepts of resource-based theory, and their implications for strategy.
Williamson, Oliver E. (1991) 'Strategizing, Economizing, and Economic Organization', *Strategic Management Journal*, 12: 75–94.
  Comparison of transaction cost analysis with other concepts of corporate strategy.

Chapter 1

Transaction costs and market failure

Oliver Williamson

EDITORS' NOTE

The following selections from Markets and Hierarchies *by Oliver Williamson focus on topics especially relevant to diversified companies. In the first section, Williamson argues that markets and hierarchies are alternative means of conducting transactions, and discusses when hierarchies, or firms, have advantages over market-based transactions. In the following sections, Williamson examines the internal organization of the multidivisional firm and how this contributes to transactional efficiency, and then considers the economic purpose of conglomerate organization.*

THE ORGANIZATIONAL FAILURES FRAMEWORK

The general approach to economic organization employed here can be summarized compactly as follows: (1) Markets and firms are alternative instruments for completing a related set of transactions; (2) whether a set of transactions ought to be executed across markets or within a firm depends on the relative efficiency of each mode; (3) the costs of writing and executing complex contracts across a market *vary with the characteristics of the human decision makers who are involved with the transaction on the one hand, and the objective properties of the market on the other*; and (4) although the human and environmental factors that impede exchanges between firms (across a market) manifest themselves somewhat differently within the firm, the same set of factors apply to both. A symmetrical analysis of trading thus requires that we acknowledge the transactional limits of internal organization as well as the sources of market failure. Basic to such a comparative analysis is the following proposition: Just as market structure matters in assessing the efficacy of trades in the marketplace, so likewise does internal structure matter in assessing internal organization.

The markets and hierarchies approach attempts to identify a set of *environmental factors* which together with a related set of *human factors* explain the circumstances under which complex contingent claims contracts will be costly to write, execute, and enforce. Faced with such difficulties, and considering the risks that simple (or incomplete) contingent claims contracts pose, the firm may decide to bypass the market and resort to hierarchical modes of organization. Transactions that might otherwise be handled in the market are thus performed internally, governed by administrative processes, instead.

The environmental factors that lead to prospective market failure are uncertainty and small-numbers exchange relations. *Unless joined, however, by a related set of human factors, such environmental conditions need not impede market exchange.* The pairing of uncertainty with *bounded rationality* and the joining of small numbers with what I shall refer to as *opportunism* are especially important.

Consider first the pairing of bounded rationality with uncertainty. The principle of bounded rationality has been defined by Herbert Simon as follows: "*The capacity of the human mind for formulating and solving complex problems is very small compared with the size of the problems whose solution is required for objectively rational behavior in the real world*" (1957, p. 198, emphasis in original). It refers to neurophysiological limits on the one hand and language limits on the other. If, in consideration of these limits, it is very costly or impossible to identify future contingencies and specify, *ex ante*, appropriate adaptations thereto, long-term contracts may be supplanted by internal organization. Recourse to the latter permits adaptations to uncertainty to be accomplished by administrative processes in a sequential fashion. Thus, rather than attempt to anticipate all possible contingencies from the outset, the future is permitted to unfold. Internal organization in this way economizes on the bounded rationality attributes of decision makers in circumstances in which prices are not "sufficient statistics" and uncertainty is substantial.

Explicating the relation between opportunism and a small-numbers exchange condition is somewhat involved. Suffice it to observe here that (1) opportunism refers to a lack of candor or honesty in transactions, to include self-interest seeking with guile; (2) opportunistic inclinations pose little risk as long as competitive (large-numbers) exchange relations obtain; (3) many transactions that at the outset involve a large number of qualified bidders are transformed in the process of contract execution, so that a small-numbers supply condition effectively obtains at the contract renewal interval; and (4) recurrent short-term contracting is costly and risky when opportunism and transactions of this latter kind are joined.

In consideration of the problems that both long- and short-term contracts are subjects to – *by reason of bounded rationality and uncertainty in the first instance and the pairing of opportunism with small-numbers relations in the second* – internal organization may arise instead. Issues here are dealt with as they arise rather than in an exhaustive contingent-planning fashion from the outset. The resulting adaptive, sequential decision-making process is the internal organizational counterpart of short-term contracting and serves to economize on bounded rationality. Opportunism does not pose the same difficulties for such internal sequential supply relations that it does when negotiations take place across a market because (1) internal divisions do not have pre-emptive claims on profit streams (but more nearly joint profit maximize instead); and (2) the internal incentive and control machinery is much more extensive and refined than that which obtains in market exchanges. The firm is thereby better able to take the long view for investment purposes (and hence is more prepared to put specialized plant and equipment in place) while simultaneously adjusting to changing market circumstances in an adaptive, sequential manner.

But whichever way the assignment of transactions to firm or market is made initially, the choice ought not to be regarded as fixed. Both firms and markets change over time in ways that may render inappropriate an initial assignment of transactions to firm or market. The degree of uncertainty associated with the transactions in question may diminish; market growth may support large-numbers supply relations; and information disparities between the parties often shrink. Also, changes in information processing technology may occur which alter the degree to which bounded rationality limits apply, with the result that a different assignment of activities between markets and hierarchies than was selected initially becomes appropriate later. Thus, we ought periodically to reassess the efficacy of completing transactions by one mode rather than another.

At the risk of oversimplification, the argument can be summarized by the schematic in Figure 1.1. The main pairings are shown by the heavy double-headed arrows which associate bounded rationality with uncertainty/complexity on the one hand and opportunism with a small-numbers exchange relations on the other. Information impactedness is a derived condition, mainly due to uncertainty and opportunism, which in turn can give rise to a small-numbers result. That exchange takes place within a trading atmosphere is denoted by the broken line that surrounds the human and environmental factors which appear in the organizational failures framework.

To recapitulate, the advantages of internal organization in relation to markets are:

1 In circumstances where complex, contingent claims contracts are infeasible and sequential spot markets are hazardous, internal organization facilitates adaptive, sequential decision making, thereby to economize on bounded rationality.

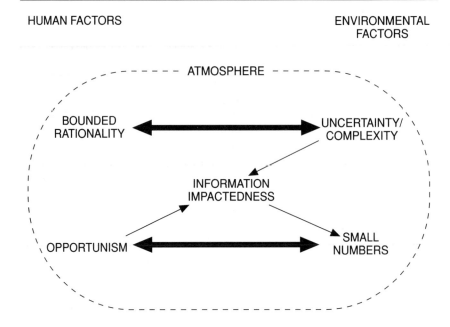

Figure 1.1 The organizational failures framework

2 Faced with present or prospective small-numbers exchange relations, internal organization serves to attenuate opportunism.
3 Convergent expectations are promoted, which reduces uncertainty.
4 Conditions of information impactedness are more easily overcome and, when they appear, are less likely to give rise to strategic behavior.
5 A more satisfying trading atmosphere sometimes obtains.

The shift of a transaction or related set of transactions from market to hierarchy is not all gain, however. Flexibility may be sacrificed in the process and other bureaucratic disabilities may arise as well.

EDITORS' NOTE

In his book, Williamson goes on to explore in detail the circumstances under which transactions may be conducted more efficiently through internal organization, or within a firm, than in a market. Simple, functionally organized hierarchies, or U-form (Unitary form) organizations and vertically integrated firms emerge because of transactional difficulties in product markets. As we noted in the introduction to this part, a firm producing a multicomponent product can either purchase the individual components in a market, or make the components itself. If there are many suppliers, then the cost of buying in the component will be low, and market transactions will be efficient. Buying in may be less efficient – or more costly – if a firm requires specialized components for its products. There may be only a few, or even one, supplier, and opportunism means that a supplier may demand too high a price. It may be more efficient for a firm to organize such transactions internally, with one production unit making the component for another production unit in the firm. In such a "unitary form" (U-form) organization, the authority of the firm's hierarchy helps overcome the problems of opportunism in the transaction.

Williamson goes on to investigate increasingly complex organizational forms – multidivisional (M-form) and conglomerate firms. In the selection included here, Williamson argues that these organizational forms arise because of inefficiencies in capital markets, and he explores the economic advantages of diversified firms.

MULTIDIVISION STRUCTURE

The characteristics and advantages of the M-form innovation can be summarized in the following way (Williamson 1970, pp. 120–1):

1 The responsibility for operating decisions is assigned to (essentially self-contained) operating divisions or quasifirms.
2 The élite staff attached to the general office performs both advisory and auditing functions. Both have the effect of securing greater control over operating division behavior.
3 The general office is principally concerned with strategic decisions, involving planning, appraisal, and control, including the allocation of resources among the (competing) operating divisions.
4 The separation of the general office from operations provides general office executives with the psychological commitment to be concerned with the overall performance of the organization rather than become absorbed in the affairs of the functional parts.
5 The resulting structure displays both rationality and synergy: the whole is greater (more effective, more efficient) than the sum of the parts.

In relation to the U-form [unitary] organization of the same activities, the M-form organization of the large, complex enterprise served both to economize on bounded rationality and attenuate opportunism. Operating decisions were no longer forced to the top but were resolved at the divisional level, which relieved the communication load. Strategic decisions were reserved for the general office, which reduced partisan political input into the resource allocation process. And the internal auditing and control techniques, which the general office had access to, served to overcome information impactedness conditions and permit fine tuning controls to be exercised over the operating parts.

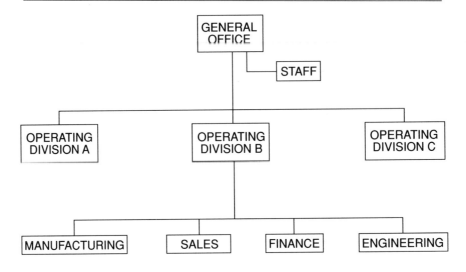

Figure 1.2 Multidivision form

COMPETITION IN THE CAPITAL MARKET

Frictionless capital markets

Advocates of received microtheory are loath to concede that capital markets may fail to operate frictionlessly. Partly for this reason, the fiction that managers operate firms in fully profit maximizing ways is maintained. Any attempt by managers to opportunistically promote their own goals at the expense of corporate profitability would occasion intervention through the capital market. Effective control of the corporation would be transferred to those parties who perceived the lapse; profit maximizing behavior would then be quickly restored.

Parties responsible for the detection and correction of deviant behavior in the firm would, of course, participate in the greater profits which the reconstituted management thereafter realized. This profit participation would not, however, be large. For one thing, incumbent managements, by assumption, have little opportunity for inefficiency or malfeasance because any tendency toward waywardness would be quickly detected and costlessly extinguished. Accordingly, the incremental profit gain occasioned by takeover is small. In addition, since competition among prospective takeover agents is presumably intensive, the gains mainly redound to the stockholders.

Peterson's sanguine views on corporate behavior are roughly of this kind. He characterizes the latitude of managers to disregard the profit goal as "small" (1965. p. 11) and goes on to observe: "Far from being an ordinary election, a proxy battle is a *catastrophic* event whose mere possibility is a threat, and one not remote when affairs are in *conspicuous* disarray." Indeed, even "stockholder suits . . . may be provoked by evidence of *serious* self-dealing." On the principle that the efficacy of legal prohibitions is to be judged "not by guilt discovered but by guilt discouraged," he concludes that such suits, albeit rare, may have accomplished much in helping to police the corporate system (ibid., p. 21; emphasis added).

While I do not mean to suggest that such deterrence has been unimportant, Peterson's observations appear to me to be consistent with the proposition that traditional capital markets are beset by serious problems of information impactedness and incur nontrivial displacement costs if the incumbent management is disposed to resist the takeover effort. Why else the reference to catastrophic events, conspicuous disarray, and serious self-dealing? Systems that are described in these terms are not ones for which a delicately conceived control system can be said to be operating As recent military history makes clear[1] controls that involve a discrete shock to the system are appropriate only when an offense reaches egregious proportions. The limits of opportunism are accordingly wider than Peterson seems prepared to concede.

The reasons, I submit, why traditional capital market controls are relatively crude are because an information impactedness condition exists with respect to internal conditions in the firms and, because of sorting out difficulties, the risk of opportunism on the part of would-be takeover agents is great. Given information impactedness, outsiders can usually make confident judgements that the firm is not adhering to profit maximizing standards only at great expense. The large firm is a complex organization and its performance is jointly a function of exogenous economic events, rival behavior, and internal decisions. Causal inferences are correspondingly difficult to make, and hence, opportunism is costly to detect. Moreover, once detected, convincing interested stockholders that a displacement effort ought to be supported encounters problems. Inasmuch as time and analytical capacity on the part of stockholders are not free goods, which is to say that their information processing limits must be respected, the would-be takeover agent cannot simply display all of his evidence and expect stockholders to evaluate it and reach the "appropriate" conclusion. Rather, any appeal to the stockholders must be made in terms of highly digested interpretations of the facts. Although this helps to overcome the stockholder's bounded rationality problem, it poses another: how is the interested stockholder (or his agent) to distinguish between *bona fide* and opportunistic takeover agents.

The upshot of these remarks is that the transaction costs associated with *traditional* capital market processes for policing management, of the sort described by Peterson, are considerable. Correspondingly, the range of discretionary behavior open to incumbent managements is rather wider than Peterson and other supporters of the frictionlessness fiction concede.[2]

The M-form firm as a miniature capital market

In a general sense, the most severe limitation of the capital market is that it is an *external* control instrument. It has limited constitutional powers to conduct audits and has limited access to the firm's incentive and resource allocation machinery. One should not, however, conclude that mere divisionalization, by itself, is sufficient to correct the inefficiencies and goal distortions that the large U-form firm develops. To emphasize this, the limits of the holding company form of organization are examined below. Attention is thereafter shifted to consider strategic controls of the sort appropriate to an M-form enterprise.

Holding company

What is referred to here as a holding company form of organization is a loosely divisionalized structure in which the controls between the headquarters unit and the separate operating parts are limited and often unsystematic. The divisions thus enjoy a high degree of autonomy under a weak executive structure.[3]

Perhaps the least ambitious type of divisionalization to consider within the holding company classification is that in which the general office is essentially reduced to a clerical agency for the assembly and aggregation of earnings and other financial reports. The holding company in these circumstances serves as a risk-pooling agency, but in this respect is apt to be inferior to a mutual fund. The transaction costs associated with altering the composition of the portfolio of the holding company, by selling off existing divisions and acquiring new operating companies, will ordinarily exceed the costs that a mutual fund of comparable assets would incur by its trading of common stocks (or other securities) so as to adjust its portfolio. Little wonder that those academics who interpret the conglomerate as being a substitute mutual fund report that it has inferior diversification characteristics to mutual funds themselves (Smith and Schreiner 1969; Westerfield 1970).

Moreover, it is not clear that just a little bit of additional control from the general office will lead to results that are superior to those that would obtain were the various divisions of the holding company to be freestanding firms in their own right. Being part of a holding company rather than an independent business entity easily has umbrella effects. Ii the holding company serves as a collection agency for unabsorbed cash flows and uses these to shore up the ailing parts of the enterprise, the resulting insularity may encourage systematic distortions (of a managerial discretion sort) among the divisional managements. Being shielded from the effects of adversity in their individual product markets, slack behavior sets in.

This is not, of course, a necessary consequence. The general management might consciously refuse to reinvest earnings but mainly pay these out as dividends. Alternatively, it might scrutinize reinvestment decisions every bit as well as the unassisted capital market could. Indeed, because it enjoys an *internal* relationship to the divisions, with all of the constitutional powers that this affords, the general management might be prepared to assume risks that an *external* investor ought properly to decline. (Thus, the general management can ordinarily detect distortions and replace the divisional management at lower cost than can an external control agent similarly detect and change the management of a comparable, free standing business entity. The holding company, in this respect, is less vulnerable to the risks of what might be referred to as managerial moral hazard.) Given, however, that the holding company is *defined* to be a divisionalized firm in which the general office does not involve itself in strategic controls of the sort described below, it is unclear that the holding company form of organization is socially to be preferred to an arrangement in which the various divisions are each set up as fully independent enterprises instead. Holding companies certainly cannot be expected reliably to yield results that compare favorably with those which I impute to the M-form structure.

Strategic controls in the M-form firm

If indeed the firm is to serve effectively as a miniature capital market, which in many respects is what the M-form structure ought to be regarded,[4] a more extensive internal control apparatus than the holding company form of organization possesses is required. This gets to the core issues. Manipulation of the incentive machinery, internal audits, and cash flow allocation each deserve consideration.

Closer adherence to the goals of the general management can be secured if the special incentive machinery to which internal organization uniquely has access to is consciously exercised to favor operating behavior that is consistent with the general management's objectives. Both pecuniary and nonpecuniary awards may be employed for this purpose.

That salaries and bonuses can be adjusted to reflect differential operating performance, assuming that such differentials exist and can be discerned, is a familiar application of the incentive machinery. That nonpecuniary rewards, especially status, can also be adjusted for this purpose should be evident from earlier arguments.

Of course, sometimes a change of employment, or at least of position, may be altogether necessary. The division manager may not have the management capacities initially ascribed to him, conditions may change in ways that warrant the appointment of a manager with different qualities, or he may be managerially competent but uncooperative (given, for example, to aggressive subgoal pursuit in ways that impair overall performance). Changes made for either of the first two reasons reflect simple functional assessments of job requirements in relation to managerial skills. By contrast, to replace a division manager for the third reason involves the deliberate manipulation of the incentive machinery to produce more satisfactory results. The occasion to intervene in this way will presumably be rare, however, if the conditional nature of the appointment is recognized from the outset. Rather, the system becomes self-enforcing in this respect once it is clear that the general management is prepared to replace division managers who regularly defect from general management's goals.[5]

Although the general office does not ordinarily become directly involved in the exercise of the incentive machinery within the operating divisions, its indirect influence can be great. The decision to change (replace, rotate) a division manager is often made for the incentive effects this has on lower-level participants. Employment policies – including criteria for selection, internal training procedures, promotions and so forth – can likewise be specified by the general office in ways that serve to ensure closer congruence between higher-level goals and the behavior of the operating parts. A more pervasive incentive impact on lower-level participants who are not directly subject to review by the general office can in these ways be effected.

Adjusting the incentive machinery in any fine tuning sense to achieve reliable results requires that the changes be made in an informed way. A backup internal audit that reviews divisional performance and attempts to attribute effects to the several possible causes – distinguishing especially between those outcomes that are due to changes in the condition of the environment from those that result from managerial decision-making is useful for this purpose.[6] As Churchill, Cooper, and Sainsbury observe: ". . . to be effective, an audit of historical actions should have, or at least be perceived as having, the power to go beneath the apparent evidence to determine what in fact did happen" (1964, p. 258). Of particular importance in this connection is the recurrent nature of this auditing process. Thus, although current variations of actual from projected may sometimes be "accounted for" in plausible but inaccurate ways, a persistent pattern of performance failure can be explained only with difficulty.

The advantages of the general office over the capital market in auditing respects are of two kinds. First, division managers are subordinates; as such, both their accounting records and backup files are appropriate subjects for a review. Stockholders, by contrast, are much more limited in what they can demand in the way of disclosure. Even relatively innocent demands for a list of the stockholders in the corporation, much less the details of internal operating performance, may be resisted by the management and disclosed only after a delay and by court order.

Second, the general office can expect knowledgeable parties to be much more cooperative than can an outsider. Thus, whereas disclosure of sensitive internal information to an outsider is apt to be interpreted as an act of treachery,[7] internal disclosure is unlikely to be regarded opprobriously. Rather, internal disclosure is affirmatively regarded as necessary to the integrity of the organization and is rewarded accordingly. Disclosure to outsiders, by contrast, commonly exposes the informant to penalties[8] albeit that these may be subtle in nature.

Not only are internal audits useful for ascertaining causality, they also serve as a basis for determining when operating divisions could benefit from assistance. The general management may include on its staff what amounts to an internal management consulting unit – to be loaned or assigned to the operating divisions as the need arises. Partly the occasion for such an assignment may be revealed by the internal audit. Thus, although the general management ought not routinely to become involved in operating affairs,[9] having the capability to intervene prescriptively in an informed way under exceptional circumstances serves to augment its credibility as an internal control agent.[10] Self-regulatory behavior by the operating division is thereby encouraged.

In addition to the policing of internal efficiency matters, and thereby securing a higher level of adherence to profit maximization than the unassisted capital market could realize (at comparable cost), the general management and its support staff can perform a further capital market function – assigning cash flows to high yield uses. Thus, cash flows in the M-form firm are not automatically returned to their sources but instead are exposed to an internal competition. Investment proposals from the several divisions are solicited and evaluated by the general management. The usual criterion is the rate of return on invested capital.[11]

Moreover, because the costs of communicating and adapting internally are normally lower than would be incurred in making an investment proposal to the external capital market, it may be practicable to decompose the internal investment process into stages. A sequential decision process (in which additional financing is conditional on prior stage results and developing contingencies) may thus be both feasible and efficient as an internal investment strategy. The transaction costs of effectuating such a process through the capital market, by contrast, are apt to be prohibitive.

In many respects, *this assignment of cash flows to high yield uses is the most fundamental attribute of the M-form enterprise* in the comparison of internal with external control processes, albeit that the divisionalized firm is able to assign cash flows to only a fairly narrow range of alternatives at any one point in time. Even if the firm is actively acquiring new activities and divesting itself of old, its range of choice is circumscribed in relation to that which general investors, who are interested in owning and trading securities rather than managing real assets, have access to. What the M-form firm does is trade off breadth for depth in this respect.[12] In a similar context, Alchian and Demsetz explain: "Efficient production with heterogeneous resources is a result not of having *better* resources but in knowing more *accurately* the relative productive performances of those resources" (1972, p. 29).

OPTIMUM DIVISIONALIZATION

The M-form structure is thoroughly corrupted when the general management involves itself in the operating affairs of the divisions in an extensive and continuing way. The separation between strategic and operating issues is sacrificed in the process; the indicated internalization of capital market functions with net beneficial effects can scarcely be claimed. Accountability is seriously compromised; a substitution of enterprise expansion for profitability goals predictably obtains.

Effective divisionalization thus requires the general management to maintain an appropriate distance. Moreover, this holds for the support staff on which the general management relies for internal auditing and management consulting services. Overinvolvement upsets the rational allocation of responsibilities between short-run operating matters and longer-run planning and resource allocation activities. What March and Simon refer to as Gresham's Law of Planning – to wit, "Daily routine drives out planning" (1958, p. 185) – takes effect when operating and strategic functions are mixed. While the arguments here are familiar and their implications for organizational design reasonably clear, maintaining a separation between these two activities apparently poses severe strain on some managements. A desire to be comprehensively involved is evidently difficult to resist.

Optimum divisionalization thus involves: (1) the identification of separable economic activities within the firm; (2) according quasi-autonomous standing (usually of a profit center nature) to each; (3) monitoring the efficiency performance of each division; (4) awarding incentives; (5) allocating cash flows to high yield uses; and (6) performing strategic planning (diversification, acquisition, and related activities) in other respects. The M-form structure is one that *combines* the divisionalization concept with an internal control and strategic decision-making capability. The general management of the M-form usually requires the support of a specialized staff to discharge these functions effectively. It bears repeating, however, that care must be exercised lest the general management and its staff become over-involved in operating matters and fail to perform the high-level planning and control functions on which the M-form enterprise relies for its continuing success.

Whether and how to divisionalize depends on firm size, functional separability, and the state of information technology (Emery 1969). Also, it should be pointed out that the reference here to optimum is used in comparative institutional terms. As between otherwise comparable unitary or holding company forms of organization, the M-form structure would appear to possess significant advantages. It cannot, however, be established on the basis of the argument advanced here that the M-form structure is the best of all conceivable structures. Organizational innovations may even now be in the making that will obsolete it in part – but which academics will identify as noteworthy only after several years. A keener sensitivity to organizational innovations and their economic importance than has existed in the past should nevertheless help to avoid the long recognition lags that have transpired before the significance of the M-form structure and its conglomerate variant became apparent.

Lest, however, these remarks lead to an underevaluation of the merits of the M-form structure, I hasten to add that, while evolutionary change is to be expected, the hierarchical decomposition principles on which the M-form is based are very robust. In his discussion of adaptive corporate organization, Beer observes: "The notion of hierarchy is given in cybernetics as a necessary structural attribute of any viable organism. This is not surprising to us, although its theoretical basis is profound, because all viable systems do in fact exhibit hierarchical organizations" (1969, p. 399). Moreover, not only does Simon's review of the properties of complex biological, physical, and social systems reaffirm this, but he emphasizes that hierarchies commonly factor problems in such a way that "higher frequency dynamics are associated with the subsystems, the lower frequency dynamics with the larger systems, . . . [and] intra-component linkages are generally stronger than inter-component linkages" (1962, p. 477). Hierarchical systems of this sort may be referred to as near-decomposable (Simon 1962). It is not merely fortuitous that the M-form structure factors problems very much in this way.

THE "M-FORM HYPOTHESIS"

Although the M-form structure was initially devised and imitated as a means by which to correct local conditions of inefficiency and subgoal pursuit, it has subsequently had pervasive systems consequences. These systems effects are partly attributable to competition in the product market; unadapted firms have found it necessary, as a survival measure, to eliminate slack so as to remain viable. But the effects of takeover threats from the capital market are also important. The conglomerate variant on the M-form structure is of particular interest in this connection – which is the subject of the next section. Focusing, however, strictly on direct effects, which is sufficient for our purposes here, the argument comes down to this: *The organization and operation of the large enterprise along the lines of the M-form favors goal pursuit and least-cost behavior more nearly associated with the neoclassical profit maximization hypothesis than does the U-form organizational alternative.*[13]

But more than mere divisionalization is needed for these effects to be realized. It is also necessary that a separation of operating from strategic responsibilities be provided. The former are assigned to the operating divisions while the latter are made the focus of the general management. Moreover, such a partitioning does not, by itself, assure strategic effectiveness; for this to obtain requires that the general management develop an internal control apparatus, to assess the performance of the operating divisions, and an internal resource allocation capability, which favors the assignment of resources to high yield uses.

EDITORS' NOTE

Having described the essential characteristics of multidivisional firms and arguing that such firms can be more efficient than external capital markets, Williamson explores further the economic rationale for diverse, multidivisional conglomerate firms. In the following section, he examines why conglomerates may be more efficient at allocating resources and controlling corporate behaviour.

CONGLOMERATE ORGANIZATION

An understanding of the conglomerate phenomenon is impeded if all conglomerates are treated as though they were indistinguishable one from another. Some types may pose genuine public policy problems, others have had an invigorating competitive influence, and still others have had essentially neutral effects. Those that combine mixtures of the first two types pose the most troublesome public policy issues.

The main emphasis here is on conglomerates of the revitalizing kind – by which I mean divisionalized firms that are provided with the strategic planning and internal control capability described previously and are diversified in sufficient degree to warrant assignment to the conglomerate category.[14]

The reason for focusing on conglomerates that have attractive internal efficiency characteristics is that, over the long pull, their superior viability properties should manifest themselves in terms of differential survival. Those conglomerates that rely on loophole exploitation, "irregular" security issues, follow-the-crowd fadishness, accounting chicanery and the like for their successes will eventually exhaust the well and be sorted out as loopholes are closed[15] and the test of continuing viability is faced. Although the earnings reported in any one year can be altered greatly by choosing judiciously among a wide variety of "defensible" accounting procedures,[16] the test of earnings over several successive periods is less subject to cosmetic adjustment in this way. The problems associated with the issue of special debt and equity instruments are likewise revealed over time as maturities become due and/or changes in the condition of the environment require the firm to face adversity. Conglomerate structures that lack financial and structural rationality and want for sound management will – as a group at least, although there will be individual exceptions – decline relatively. If the selection mechanism is working well, they will be required to adapt appropriately, shrink relatively, or face extinction.[17] Accordingly, attention is directed from the outset toward an examination of those types of conglomerates that are believed to have sound structural and management properties.

COMPETITION IN THE CAPITAL MARKET

Internal organization has an influence on competition in the capital market in three respects. First, divisionalized firms (of the appropriate kind) more assuredly assign cash flows to high yield uses. The arguments here are already familiar from the preceding section. Second, the divisionalized firm is well-suited to serve as a takeover agent. Acquired firms that might otherwise run slack are thereby made to operate more efficiently. Third, when the background threat of takeover exceeds threshold probabilities, prospective target firms are induced to take self-corrective measures.

Internal resource allocation

The capital market in an environment of U-form firms was earlier regarded as a less than efficacious surveillance and correction mechanism for three reasons: its external relation to the firm places it at a serious information disadvantage: it is restricted to nonmarginal adjustments; it experiences nontrivial displacement costs. The general office of the M-form organization has superior properties in each of these respects. First, it is an internal rather than external control mechanism with the constitutional authority and expertise to make detailed evaluations of the performance of each of its operating parts. Second, it can make fine-tuning as well as discrete adjustments. This permits it both to intervene early in a selective, preventative way (a capability which the capital market lacks altogether), as well as to perform *ex post* corrective adjustments, in response to evidence of performance failure, with a surgical precision that the capital market lacks (the scalpel versus the ax is an appropriate analogy). Finally, the costs of intervention by the general office are relatively low. Altogether, therefore, a profit-oriented general office in an M-form enterprise might be expected to secure superior performance to that which the unassisted capital market can enforce. The M-form organization might thus be viewed as capitalism's creative response to the evident limits which the capital market experiences in its relations to the firm, as well as a means for overcoming the organizational problems which develop in the large U-form enterprise when variety becomes great.[18]

Takeover

The argument can be carried a step further by considering the effects of the M-form innovation on capital market displacement efforts. *Ceteris paribus* displacement is more likely the greater the unavailed profit opportunities in the target firm and the lower the costs of effecting displacement. In relation to the U-form enterprise, the M-form innovation enhances the attractiveness of making displacement efforts in both respects.

The realization of operating economies by reconstituting a large U-form enterprise along M-form lines represents a source of potential profit gain which, in the absence of reorganization, is unavailable. The resulting economies are due to more effective resource allocation (between divisions and in the aggregate), better internal organization (a reduction in technical control loss), and the attenuation of subgoal pursuit. Unitary form organizations for which either (1) divisionalization is difficult (the natural unit is the integrated form)[19] or (2) the prevailing attitudes and distribution of power among the incumbent management make self-reorganization difficult, are natural takeover candidates.

Existing M-form enterprises are probably the most effective instruments for achieving displacement. For one thing, they are apt to have superior inference capabilities; the élite staff of the M-form structure may even have as one of its principal assignments the discovery of potential takeover candidates. In addition, such firms are already experienced in the organizational advantages that this structure offers.

Systems consequences

Unitary form enterprises that anticipate takeover efforts may attempt to shrink the potential displacement gain by making appropriate internal changes: subgoal pursuit may be reduced or, possibly, self-reorganization along M-form lines may be initiated. Such forestalling efforts are not apt to be common, however, until the probability of a takeover attempt has reached a nontrivial value. Except in U-form enterprises which have been specifically targeted for takeover, this may require that there be a relatively large number of multidivision enterprises actively surveying takeover opportunities. With only a few multidivision firms performing this function, the probability that any one unitary form enterprise will be the object of a takeover attempt is too small to warrant *ex ante* adaptation. Once the number of multidivision firms becomes sufficiently large, however, the effect on unitary form enterprises that are otherwise shielded from product market pressures is equivalent to an increase in competition in so far as subgoal pursuit is concerned. Selection on profits is thereby enhanced; the effects indeed may be pervasive. The argument thus reduces to the following proposition: internal organization and conventional capital market forces are complements as well as substitutes; the two coexist in a symbiotic relationship to each other.

But adaptive responses of a protective rather than a corrective kind might also appear. Although such protective responses serve the interests of incumbent managements, they are apt to be dysfunctional from the standpoint of the system as a whole. Cary (1969–70) enumerates the corporate devices used to insulate management from attack as follows: (1) amending the certificate of incorporation, including the abolishment of cumulative voting and the specification of super-majority requirements (for example, an eighty percent rule) to approve a merger; (2) acquiring a firm with products similar to those of the takeover agent, in order to produce antitrust problems; (3) placing additional stock in friendly hands by making a stock acquisition of another firm; (4) restricting loan agreements by including an unacceptable change of management clause; (5) buying off a raider by using corporate funds to purchase his stock; (6) making a tender offer to its own stockholders, so as to drive up the price of its stock above the existing tender offer value; (7) raising the dividend and splitting the shares for a similar purpose; (8) applying for an injunction by claiming that rival tender offers are misleading; and (9) applying to the securities commission of a state to change requirements for tender offers in such a way as to obtain relief. That these tactics are not merely hypotheticals, but in fact have been devised as defenses to the takeover threat posed by the conglomerate, should be noted.[20]

Special relevance of the conglomerate

If the M-form firm is to perform the capital market policing functions described above and if, simultaneously, antimerger policies with respect to horizontal and vertical acquisitions are to remain tough, preserving the conglomerate acquisition option may be essential. Otherwise, the threat of a takeover to firms operated by moribund managements will be rendered effete; bringing every form of market organization – including the conglomerate – under antitrust attack would have the unfortunate and presumably unintended consequence of impairing what Manne (1965) refers to as the "market for corporate control."

But why M-form firms or conglomerates? Under conventional assumptions that more choices are always preferred to fewer, ought not the banking system have superior resource allocation properties? Put differently, why should a miniature capital market ever be preferred to the real thing? Similarly, ought not individual banks, were they so inclined, be able to intervene actively in the internal affairs of firms – even to include the displacement of managements should the need arise?

There are three problems with such arguments: bounded rationality considerations are suppressed; crucial differences between internal and external controls are overlooked; and adaptive responses (given the prevailing institutional rules of the game) are neglected. Thus, were it that decision makers could be easily apprised of an ever wider range of alternatives and choose intelligently among them, there would be little reason to supplant the traditional market. But it is elementary that, where complex events have to be evaluated, information-processing capacities are quickly reached. As a result, expanding the range of choice may not only be without purpose but can have net detrimental effects. A tradeoff between breadth of information, in which respect the banking system may be presumed to have the advantage, and depth of information, which is the advantage of the specialized firm, is involved. The conglomerate can be regarded as an intermediate form that, ideally, optimizes with respect to the breadth-depth tradeoff.[21]

The failure to distinguish clearly between internal and external control processes is an equally serious defect in the banking argument. The powers of internal organization are, by definition, unavailable to an external control agent – whether he be a purchaser (as in the case of the military services), a supplier (such as a bank), or a regulatory commission. Access to internal information is strictly limited and difficult, without first-hand experience, to evaluate. It is thus unrealistic for the external control agent to attempt to make fine-tuning adjustments in anticipation of prospective market developments; even *ex post* audits are subject to severe limitations. The control instruments that the external agent commands are likewise limited. Control over the screening-selection-promotion process is mainly denied to outsiders; indeed, extensive interference by outsiders in internal personnel matters is apt to be thoroughly disruptive and have demoralizing effects.

Finally, were the banks to attempt aggressively to reallocate resources among sectors, large corporations could be expected to adapt defensively. Greater reliance on internal financing could be expected. Firms might even develop pools that bypassed the banking system.[22]

NOTES

1 Atomic weapons, with their catastrophic consequences, are ill-suited to support military campaigns involving even half a million men.

2 Smiley concludes his study of tender offers as follows (1973, pp. 124–5):

> Based on our most accurate estimating procedure, per share transaction costs are approximately 14% of the market value of the shares after a successful offer. We feel that this cost level is such as to inspire skepticism about the efficacy of the tender offer in constraining managers to act in the best interests of their shareholders. Another finding was that the equity of firms that have been tendered has lost half of its market value (in the 10 years prior to the tender offer) relative to what the equity would have been worth, had the management operated the firm in an optimal fashion.

3 That this is a somewhat special use of the term, holding company, ought to be appreciated. (I considered referring to this as the federal form of organization but decided that that posed at least as many problems.) Essentially what I am after is a category which, for reference purposes, represents divisionalization of a very limited sort.

4 The argument is developed more extensively in Williamson (1970, pp. 138–50, 176–7). For somewhat similar views, see Drucker (1970), Heflebower (1960), and Weston (1970).

5 This assumes that there are no property rights (academic tenure, civil service, and so forth) associated with positions.

6 In principle, the superior inference capability of an internal audit, as compared with the relatively crude powers of the capital market in this respect, commends internal organization as a substitute for the capital market not merely because discretionary behavior may thereby be attenuated but also because division managers may be induced to accept risks which in a free-standing firm would be declined. Too often, as Luce and Raiffa observe: ". . . the strategist is evaluated in terms of the outcome of the adopted choice rather than in terms of the strategic desirability of the whole risky situation" (1957, p. 76). This tendency to rely on outcomes rather than assess the complex situation more completely is especially to be expected of systems with low powers of inference. Managers of free-standing firms, realizing that outcomes rather than decision processes will be evaluated, are naturally reluctant to expose themselves to high variance undertakings. *Ceteris paribus*, the low cost access of internal organization to a wider range of sophisticated inference techniques encourages more aggressive risk-taking.

Whether the potential advantages of the divisional structure in auditing respects actually induce more aggressive risk-taking, however, is uncertain. Woods identified a strong conservative bias in the firms that he studied, where the companies were "rewarding the manager whose investment performance exceeds his original forecast and penalizing the one whose performance falls below the forecast" (1966, p. 93).

7 "Kings may vary in the tolerance they show to vices such as incompetence or laziness, but there is no tolerance of treason. Giving damaging information to the press or betraying plans to a rival are the actions of an enemy . . .: these are unpardonable offenses" (Jay 1971, p. 266). The disclosure of damaging inside information to the press or to a prospective takeover agent is regarded by the firm's leadership to be of this treacherous kind.

8 The disclosure of cost overruns on the C-5A by an employee of the Pentagon (A. Ernest Fitzgerald) resulted in his being fired. But for subsequent intervention by Senator Proxmire and others, his reemployment was unlikely. [See Mollenhoff (1973).] Such intervention is, of course, unusual and does not assure that the career expectations of the informant will be unimpaired.

9 The reasons for avoiding operating involvement have been given elsewhere. A recent comparative study by Allen of two divisionalized firms broadly supports the general argument. Allen observes that, of the two firms, the high-performing firm had a "fairly simple but highly selective set of organizational devices to maintain control over its division,' while the management of the low-performing firm became "over-involved," in relation to its capacity, in the affairs of its operating division (1970, p. 28).

10 This internal management consulting unit would ordinarily be made available at the request of the operating divisions as well as the behest of the general management. Such a unit would presumably possess scarce expertise of a high order. It would be uneconomical for each operating division to attempt to replicate such a capability.

11 For a discussion of a sophisticated internal resource allocation model in the International Utilities Corporation, see Hamilton and Moses (1973).

12 For a somewhat similar discussion of the internal resource allocation effects of M-form divisionalization, see Drucker (1970). Also of relevance in this connection are the treatments by Heflebower (1960) and Weston (1970).

Certain work at the Harvard Business School also relates to these issues, [see Bower (1971) and the references therein; also Allen (1970)].

13 It will be noted that the argument has been developed in comparative terms. It could therefore, be as easily expressed instead as a U-form hypothesis: namely, the organization and operation of the large enterprise along the lines of the U-form favors goal pursuit and cost behavior more nearly associated with the managerial discretion hypothesis than does the M-form organizational alternative. This equivalent statement makes evident an underlying symmetry that some may find disconcerting: if one accepts the affirmative argument on behalf of the M-form organization advanced above, a tacit acceptance of managerial discretion theory (in the context of U-form organization, may also be implied. That is, if the M-form organization has, for the reasons given, the superior efficiency, motivational, and control properties that have been imputed to it, then presumably the organization and operation of the large enterprise along the lines of the traditional (U-form) structure contributes to control loss and utility-maximizing behavior of the sort described in Williamson (1964). To the extent, therefore, that the coincidence of large, unitary form structures and nontrivial opportunity sets (mainly by reason of favorable product market conditions) is observed in the economy, utility-maximizing behavior (and its attendant consequences) is to be expected.

14 On some of the problems of defining diversification in requisite degree to warrant the conglomerate appellation, see Markham (1973, pp. 7–19).

15 The necessary expertise for dealing with loophole closure of these types is possessed by specialists on Internal Revenue and matters related to the Securities and Exchange Commission. Inasmuch as the emphasis here is on antitrust, and since antitrust enforcement is poorly suited to deal with defects in the tax and securities laws, these matters will not be pursued here.

16 For an interesting discussion, see; "What are Earnings? The Growing Credibility Gap," *Forbes*. May 15, 1967, pp. 29–34, 39–41.

17 See Winter (1971). He summarizes the general assumptions needed for the selection argument to go through as follows: (1) firms have decision rules that are adjusted in accordance with the satisficing principle: and (2) profitable firms add to capacity and expand relatively. If, in addition, "persistent search and the innovating remnant serve to eliminate as possible equilibrium positions situations in which possible but untried decision rules would yield higher profits than those currently utilized," long-run profit maximization will obtain (1971, pp. 247–8).

   Extinction may, however, take the form of management displacement, through competition in the capital market, if competition in the product market operates slowly.

18 The conjunction of these two consequences in a single organizational innovation should probably be regarded as fortuitous. Thus, the emergence in the late 1800's of large, single-product multifunctional (vertically integrated) enterprises along U-form lines presumably permitted transactional and possibly technical scale economies to be realized (as well, perhaps, as monopoly power), but the organizational innovations in this instance served to weaken capital market controls. That organizational innovations in the future should favor internal efficiency is reasonably to be expected; that, however, they should also enhance capital market controls is not at all obvious.

19 Even though the natural unit may be integrated, it may be possible to replicate several of these natural units; for example, several parallel product divisions might be created. The long delay in divisionalizing very large steel firms thus is not to be explained entirely in terms of the intrinsic requirements of vertical integration. Vertical integration within operating divisions, but quasi-autonomy between them (subject, probably, to rules governing coordinated marketing), is normally feasible in the larger of these firms – which greatly exceed minimum scale requirements for technically efficient production (Bain 1956)

20 See the chronology of the Northwest Industries attempt to take over B. F. Goodrich and the defensive responses that this set in motion . . . as reported in Williamson (1970, pp. 100–2).

21 Alchian and Demsetz (1972) interpret internal organization in a somewhat similar fashion. For a study of the use of the computer to extend the firm's capacity to deal effectively with a wider set of investment alternatives, see Hamilton and Moses (1973).

22 In consideration of these disabilities, the banking system would appear to be a poor substitute for the conglomerate. But what explains then the apparent success of the Japanese *Zaibatsu* form of organization? As Bronfenbrenner notes, the *Zaibatsu* has the characteristics of a giant conglomerate in which "there is a commonality of ownership between borrowing firm and its primary lending bank, with *Zaibatsu* banks and their officers investing heavily in the stock of their *Zaibatus* affiliates" (1970, p. 151). A much more extensive *integration* between banking and the operating affiliates thus constitutes one part of the answer. Funds are not really available for unrestricted investment but are allocated to particular bidders – to the disadvantage of the unaffiliated businesses (ibid., p. 152). In addition, the Japanese system may be culture-specific in important respects. For one thing, the Japanese Ministry of International Trade and Industry performs a wide range of "extra-legal expansive, regulatory, and protective functions" (ibid., p. 153) that many Americans would find objectionable. In addition, as Bronfenbrenner puts it, "important for an understanding of the Japanese economy . . . are certain elements of economic sociology" (ibid., p. 154) – low mobility, a high degree of paternalism, extensive employment security, and an unusually high propensity to save. The *Zaibatsu* is partly dependent for its success on the continuation of these conditions. That these conditions may not continue is suggested by the recent emergence of labor problems that have hitherto been absent in the Japanese economy.

REFERENCES

Alchian, A. A. and H. Demsetz, "Production, Information Costs, and Economic Organization," *American Economic Review, 62*: 777–95, December 1972.

——, "The Property Rights Paradigm." *Journal of Economic History, 33*: 16–27, March 1973.

Alchian, A. A. and R. A. Kessel, "Competition, Monopoly, and the Pursuit of Pecuniary Gain." *Aspects of Labor Economics*. Princeton: Princeton University Press, 1962.

Allen, Stephen A., III, "Corporate Divisional Relationships in Highly Diversified Firms," in Jay W. Lorsch and Paul R. Lawrence, eds.,

Studies in Organization Design. Homewood, Ill,: Richard D. Irwin, Inc., 1970, pp. 16–35.

Angyal, A., "A Logic of Systems," in F. E. Emery, ed., *Systems Thinking.* Middlesex. England: Penguin Books Ltd., 1969, pp. 17–29.

Beers, S., "The Aborting Corporate Plan: A Cybernetic Account of the Interface Between Planning and Action," in E. Jantsch, ed., *Perspectives of Planning.* Paris, 1969, pp. 397–422.

Bower, Joseph L., "Management Decision Making in Large Diversified Firms," draft, October 1, 1971.

Bronfenbrenner, Martin, "Japan's Galbraithian Economy," *Public Interest, 21*: 149–57, Fall 1970.

Cary, William, "Corporate Devices Used to Insulate Management from Attack," *Antitrust Law Journal,* (1) *39*: 318–33, 1969–70.

Churchill, N. C., W. W. Cooper and T. Sainsbury, "Laboratory and Field Studies of the Behavioral Effects of Audits," in C. P. Bonini, Robert K. Jaedicke and Harvey M. Wagner, eds., *Management Controls: New Directions in Basic Research.* New York: McGraw-Hill Book Company, 1964, pp. 253–67.

Drucker, Peter F., "The New Markets and the New Capitalism," *The Public Interest* No. 21: 44–79, Fall 1970.

Emery, J. C., *Organizational Planning and Control Systems: Theory and Technology.* New York: The Macmillan Company, 1969.

Hamilton, W. F. and M. A. Moses. "An Optimization Model for Corporate Financial Planning," *Operations Research, 21*: 677–92, May/June 1973.

Heflebower, R. B., "Observations on Decentralization in Large Enterprises," *Journal of Industrial Economics, 9*: 7–22, November 1960.

Jay, A., *Corporation Man,* New York: Random House, Inc., 1971.

Luce, R. D. and H. Raiffa, *Games and Decisions,* New York: John Wiley & Sons, Inc., 1957.

Manne, Henry G., "Mergers and the Market for Corporate Control," *Journal of Political Economy, 73*: 110–20, April 1965.

March, J. G. and H. A. Simon, *Organizations.* New York: John Wiley & Sons, Inc., 1958.

Markham, J., *Conglomerate Enterprise and Public Policy.* Boston: Division of Research, Harvard Graduate School of Business Administration, 1973.

Mollenhoff, Clark, "Presidential Guile," *Harpers,* 38–42, June 1973.

Peterson, S., "Corporate Control and Capitalism." *Quarterly Journal of Economics. 79*: 1019, February 1965.

Simon, H.A., *Models of Man.* New York: John Wiley & Sons. Inc., 1957.

——, "The Architecture of Complexity," *Proceedings of the American Philosophical Society, 106*: 467–82, December 1962.

Smiley, Robert. *The Economics of Tender Offers.* Unpublished Ph.D. dessertation. Stanford University, 1973.

Smith, K. V., and J. C. Schreiner. "A Portfolio Analysis of Conglomerate Diversification." *Journal of Finance. 24*: 413–29, June 1969.

Westerfield, Randolph, "A Note on the Measure of Conglomerate Diversification," *Journal of Finance, 25*: 904–14, 1970.

Weston, J. Fred, "Diversification and Merger Trends," *Business Economics. 5*: 50–7, January 1970.

Williamson, O. E. *The Economics of Discretionary Behavior: Managerial Objectives in a Theory of the Firm.* Englewood Cliffs, N.J.: Prentice-Hall, 1964.

——, *Corporate Control and Business Behavior.* Englewood Cliffs, N.J.: Prentice-Hall, Inc., 1970.

Winter, Sidney, "Satisficing Selection and the Innovating Remnant," *Quarterly Journal of Economics, 85*: 237–61, May 1971.

Woods, Donald H., "Improving Estimates that Involve Uncertainty," *Harvard Business Review, 44*: 91–8, July 1966.

Chapter 2

Towards an economic theory of the multiproduct firm

David J. Teece

INTRODUCTION

'Of all outstanding characteristics of business firms, perhaps the most inadequately treated in economic analysis is the diversification of their activities' [Penrose (1959, p. 104)]. Little progress has been made since Penrose registered her dismay. Accordingly, the theory of the firm has yet to accommodate one of the principal features of the modern business enterprise – its multiproduct character. The mission of this paper is to outline how this deficiency might be rectified. To accomplish this objective it turns out to be necessary to modify the neoclassical theory of the firm to emphasize the distinctive properties of organizational knowledge and the transactions cost properties of market exchange. It is also necessary to make an analytical separation between a theory of diversification and a theory of growth since growth and diversification are not inextricably linked. A central issue for a theory of multiproduct organization is to explain why firms diversify into related and unrelated product lines rather than reinvesting in traditional lines of business or transferring assets directly to stockholders.

An earlier paper [Teece (1980)] argued that the multiproduct firm could not be explained by reference to neoclassical cost functions. Panzar and Willig (1975 p. 3) have argued that economies of scope explain multiproduct organization.[1] While economies of scope explain joint production, they do not explain why joint production must be organized within a single multiproduct enterprise. Joint production can proceed in the absence of multiproduct organization if contractural mechanisms can be devised to share the inputs which are yielding the scope economies. Whereas the earlier paper had the limited objective of exploring the relationship between economies of scope and the scope of the enterprise, the objective here is more ambitious – to outline a theory of multiproduct enterprise.

As mentioned earlier, the existing literature has failed to grapple successfully with the multiproduct firm. Some theories depict the multi-product firm, particularly when created by mergers and acquisitions, as a manifestation of managerial discretion. Other explanations emphasize how taxes and regulations provide the driving force for diversification. Managers and business policy researchers often explain that value maximization through the capturing of 'synergies' lie at the heart of the incentive to diversify. (Rarely, however, are the nature of the efficiencies generating 'synergies' spelled out in a convincing fashion.) All of these factors undoubtedly help explain in part the ubiquity of multiproduct firms. The purpose here, however, is to focus on those incentives most likely to be operative in an economy which is dynamically competitive in the Schumpetarian sense, and which are consistent with profit seeking behavior by business firms. This focus is chosen partly because it traverses an essentially unexplored theoretical niche, but also because the perspective holds promise of explaining a good deal of observed behavior in modern industrial economies, a mission which orthodox theorizing has failed to accomplish.

SOME TRADITIONAL PERSPECTIVES

The neoclassical firm and multiproduct organization

The neoclassical theory of the firm generally assumes profit maximizing entities operating in competitive product and capital markets exhibiting zero transactions costs and competitive equilibrium. Under these assumptions, it is virtually impossible to erect a theory of the multiproduct firm. For instance, consider a cost function displaying scope economies (operating 'synergies'). Irrespective of the source of these economies, there is no compelling reason for firms to adopt multiproduct structures since in a zero transactions cost world, scope economies can be captured using market contracts to share the services of the inputs providing the foundations for scope economies [Teece (1980)].

Nor are 'financial synergy' arguments compelling within the classical framework. Thus, define for a firm both a mean return μ, and a probability distribution of returns described entirely by the variance σ^2. Statistical theory establishes that if the returns to independent firms are non-correlated, the creation of a single diversified firm leads to a reduction in the variance of total cash flow.[2] But within the context of the capital asset pricing model (CAPM), this need not reduce stockholder risk since all gains from this kind of amalgamation should have already been achieved by stockholders, all of whom are able to diversify away unsystematic risk. The argument clearly only has merit if the stock market is imperfect in some way, or if all stockholders are not following the precepts of the CAPM.

Nor does multiproduct organization increase the value of the firm by reducing default risks. While bondholders' risk and – hence the costs of debt – can be reduced through diversification, Galai and Masulis (1976) point out that since the value of the firm is simply the sum of the constituent parts, the value of the equity of the merged firm will be less than the sum of the constituent equity values and the value of debt will be higher. Options pricing theory indicates that increased variability increases the value of options and conversely. Since equity is an option on the face value of debt outstanding, its value will fall with a decrease in volatility [Black and Scholes (1973)]. 'What is taking place . . . is that the bondholders receive more protection since the stockholders of each firm have to back the claims of bondholders of both companies. The stockholders are hurt since their limited liability is weakened' [Galai and Masulis (1976, p. 68)]. Hence a pure diversification rationale for the multiproduct firm is not valid within the context of orthodox theories of financial markets. Reducing the risk to bondholders represents a redistribution of value from shareholders, leaving the total value of the firm unchanged.

Thus multiproduct firms can emerge within an economy operating under neoclassical competitive assumptions, but they must do so only by accident. Whether firms are organized along specialized or multiproduct lines is economically irrelevant since market arrangements and internal organization are perfect substitutes. Thus divesting multiproduct firms or diversifying specialized ones is a transformation lacking economic significance in the context of a neoclassical economy.

Managerial explanation

Another class of theories used to explain diversification are based on managerialism. Marris (1966) and Mueller (1969) have made important contributions which are illustrative of this literature. In Marris's growth maximizing managerial enterprise, managers not only bring the existing supply of resources and the demands upon them into line, but also their future rates of growth. Thus the equating of the growth of supply of resources and growth of demand upon them is an equilibrium condition. In identifying the main determinants of the growth of demand, Marris recognizes that firms are usually multiproduct and that diversification into new products is the main engine of corporate growth. Thus in order to grow any faster than the rate of growth of the markets in which the firm establishes itself, it must carry out further successful diversification.[3] However, there are significant costs attached to successful diversification and these costs of diversification all reduce the firms' rate of return on capital. The growth of demand is thus an inverse function of the rate of return on capital because faster growth of demand via more rapid diversification either requires a lower profit margin, which lowers the return on capital, or leads to a higher capital–output ratio, which also lowers the return on capital, or both.

The core of Mueller's (1969) theory is that managers are motivated to increase the size of their firms further. He assumes that the compensation to managers is a function of the size of the firm and he argues therefore that managers adopt a lower investment hurdle rate. The lower investment hurdle rate prompts the managers of older, larger, mature firms to invest more heavily than they would if they were confronted with a higher hurdle, and represents a basic motivation for diversification.[4] However, the basic premise of the theory – that compensation is a function of the size of the firm – is problematic. In a study critical of earlier evidence, Lewellen and Huntsman (1970) present findings that managers' compensation is significantly correlated with the firm's profit rate, not its level of sales. Thus Mueller's theory has to fall back on the non-pecuniary benefits – such as status and visibility in the business community – which managers may obtain from managing larger enterprises. Nor are the basic facts of diversification via merger supportive of Mueller's theory. The larger acquirers during the 1954–68 period were about 1/10 the average size of the larger, more mature non-acquirers [Bock (1970)]. Thus the initial size of the active conglomerate acquirers was small, not large as Mueller's theory suggests.

This is not to say that managerialist theories are entirely without merit. Managerial motives may well explain a portion of observed diversification activity. However, diversification can also be efficiency driven, as this paper will seek to demonstrate. The nature of possible efficiencies are delineated, thereby providing the foundations for an efficiency-based theory of the multiproduct firm. This theoretical exploration is of relevance to managers and policy analysts since a framework is developed within which it is possible to assess the likelihood that economies can be captured through corporate diversification strategies. Within this framework the firm is conceptualized as a structure designed to organize the employment of various assets which have greater value when employed under the internal control apparatus of a firm than under the external control apparatus of a market.

NATURE OF THE FIRM

In microtheory textbooks, and in much contemporary research, it is accepted practice 'to represent the business enterprise abstractly by the productive transformations of which it is capable, and to characterize these productive transformations by a production function or production set regarded as a datum' [Winter (1982, p. 58)].[5] Furthermore, production functions and hence firms can be eliminated or replicated with amazing alacrity, as when prices a whisker above competitive levels attract new entrants. New entry in turn drives profits back down to equilibrium levels. Embedded in this conceptualization is the notion that a firm's knowhow is stored in symbolic form in a 'book of blueprints'. Implicit in this commonly used metaphor is the view that knowledge can be and is articulated. Following Winter (1982), and Nelson and Winter (1980; 1982), the appropriateness of this abstraction is examined below, and the implications for multiproduct organization explored.

Individual and organizational knowledge

Polanyi has stressed, in obvious contradiction to the book of blueprints metaphor, that individual knowledge has an important tacit dimension, in that very often knowhow and skills cannot be articulated. It is a 'well known fact that the aim of a skillful performance is achieved by the observance of a set of rules which are not known as such to the person following them'[6] [Polanyi (1958, p. 49)]. In the exercise of individual skill, many actions are taken that are not the result of considered choices but rather are automatic responses that constitute aspects of the skill.[7]

Similarly, in the routine operation of an organization such as a business firm, much that could in principle be deliberated is instead done automatically in response to signals arising from the organization or its environment. Articulation of the knowledge underlying organizational capabilities is limited in the same respects and for the same reasons as in the case of individual capabilities though for other reasons as well, and to a greater extent. This routinization of activity in an organization itself constitutes the most important form of storage of the organization's specific operational knowledge. In a sense, organizations 'remember by doing'. Routine operation is the organizational counterpart of the exercise of skills by an individual [Nelson and Winter (1982, quoted in part from an earlier draft)].

Thus routines function as the basis of organizational memory. To utilize organizational knowledge, it is necessary not only that all members know their routines, but also that all members know when it is appropriate to perform certain routines. This implies that the individual must have the ability to interpret a stream of incoming messages from other organizational members and from the environment. Once received and interpreted, the member utilizes the information contained in a message in the selection and performance of an appropriate routine from his own repertoire.[8] Thus to view organizational memory as reducible to individual member memories is to overlook, or undervalue, the linking of those individual memories by shared experiences in the past, experiences that have established the extremely detailed and specific communication system that underlies routine performance. [Nelson and Winter (1982, p. 105).]

While there is abundant reason to believe that remembering-by-doing may in a wide range of circumstances surpass symbolic storage in cost effectiveness, one circumstance where complications arise is where the knowledge is to enter market exchange for subsequent transfer to a different organizational context. The transfer of key individuals may suffice when the knowledge to be transferred relates to the particulars of a separable routine. The individual in such cases becomes a consultant or a teacher with respect to that routine. However, only a limited range of capabilities can be transferred if a transfer activity is focused in this fashion. More often than not, the transfer of productive expertise requires the transfer of organizational as well as individual knowledge.[9] In such cases, external transfer beyond an organization's boundary may be difficult if not impossible, since taken out of context, an individual's knowledge of a routine may be quite useless.

Fungible knowledge

Another characteristic of organizational knowledge is that it is often fungible to an important degree. That is, the human capital inputs employed by the firm are not always entirely specialized to the particular products and services which the enterprise is currently producing. This is particularly true of managerial talent, but it is also true for various items of physical equipment and for other kinds of human skills as well. Of course, various items of capital may have to be scrapped or converted if an organization's product mix is changed but these costs may in fact be quite low if the opportunity cost of withdrawing the equipment from its current use is minimal.

Accordingly, the final products produced by a firm at any given time merely represent one of several ways in which the organization could be using its internal resources [Penrose (1959)]. As wartime experience demonstrated, automobile manufacturers suddenly began making tanks, chemical companies began making explosives, and radio manufacturers began making radar. In short, a firm's capability lies upstream from the end product – it lies in a generalizable capability which might well find a variety of final product applications. Economies of specialization assume a different significance when viewed from this conceptual vantage point, as specialization is referenced not to a single product but to a generalized capability. (It might be 'information processing' rather than computers, 'dairy products' rather than butter and cheese, 'farm machinery' rather than tractors and harvesters, and 'time measurement' rather than clocks and watches.) The firm can therefore be considered to have a variety of end products which it can produce with its organizational technology. Some of these possibilities may be known to it and some may not. What needs to be explained is the particular end product or configuration of end products which the firm chooses to produce.

This view of the nature of the firm turns the neoclassical conceptualization on its head. Whereas the neoclassical firm selects, according to factor prices, technologies off the shelf to manufacture a given end product, the organization theoretic firm depicted here selects an end product configuration, consistent with its organizational technology, which is defined yet fungible over certain arrays of final products. In short, the firm has end product as well as technological choices to confront.

DYNAMIC CONSIDERATIONS

General

Whether the firm's knowhow is embedded in a book of blueprints or in individual and organizational routines will not explain its multiproduct scope unless other dimensions of the neoclassical model of firms and markets are modified. Thus following Schumpeter (1950) and others, the competitive process is viewed as dynamic, involving uncertainty, struggle, and disequilibrium. In particular, two fundamental characteristics of a dynamic competitive system are recognized: (a) firms accumulate knowledge through R&D and learning, some of it incidental to the production process, (b) the market conditions facing the firm are constantly changing, creating profit opportunities in different markets at different times. Furthermore, the demand curve facing a specialized firm is rarely infinitely elastic, as is assumed in the perfectly competitive model.

Learning, teaching and 'Penrose-effects'

Edith Penrose (1959) has described the growth processes of the firm in a way that is both unconventional and convincing. According to Penrose, at any time a firm has certain productive resources, the services of which are used to exploit the production opportunities facing the firm. Opportunities for growth exist because there are always unused productive services which can be placed into employment – presumably in new as well as existing lines of business. Unused resources exist not only because of indivisibilities, but also because of the learning which occurs in the normal process of operating a business. Thus, even with a constant managerial workforce, managerial services are released for expansion without any reduction in the efficiency with which existing operations are run. Not only is there continuous learning, but also as each project becomes established so its running becomes more routine and less demanding on managerial resources. The managerial workforce can also be expanded, at least within limits. Existing managers can teach new managers. However, the increment to total managerial services provided by each additional manager is assumed to decrease the faster the rate at which they are reoriented (the 'Penrose-effect').

A specialized firm's generation of excess resources, both managerial and technical, and their fungible character is critical to the theory of diversification advanced here. What has to be explained, however, is (1) why diversification is likely to lead to the productive utilization of 'excess' resources, and (2) the sequence in which this assignment is likely to occur.

Demand conditions

A specialized firm's excess resources can of course be reinvested in the firm's traditional business. Indeed, if the firm confronts a perfectly elastic demand curve, has a distinctive capability (lower costs) in its traditional business, and markets elsewhere are competitive, it has incentives to reinvest in its traditional line of business, both at home and abroad. Assume, however, that at some point competitive returns can no longer be obtained through reinvestment at home or abroad, either because of a secular decline of demand due to life cycle considerations [Grabowski and Mueller (1975); Mueller (1972)], or because the firm is facing a finite degree of elasticity to its demand curve, in which case reinvestment and expansion will serve to lower prices and profits. Confronted with this predicament, a profit seeking firm confronts three fundamental choices:

1 It can seek to sell the services of its unused assets to other firms in other markets.
2 It can diversify into other markets, either through acquisition or *de novo* entry.
3 If the unused resource is cash, it can be returned to stockholders through higher dividends or stock repurchase.

A theory of diversification for a profit seeking enterprise emerges when conditions are established under which the second option appears the more profitable. The first option involves the use of markets for capturing the employment value of the unused assets. Multiproduct diversification (option 2) will be selected by profit seeking firms over the market alternative (option 1) when transactions cost problems are likely to confound efficient transfer. Accordingly, an assessment of the efficiency properties of factor and financial markets is warranted.

Market failure considerations: physical and human capital

If excess resources are possessed by a single product firm, there is the possibility of disposal in factor markets, i.e., sale and transfer to other specialized firms. This strategy permits standard specialization economies to be obtained, and if transaction costs are zero, ought to usurp incentives for diversification. Consider, therefore, whether efficient employment of these resources is likely to involve multiproduct organization. Assume, furthermore, that the excess resources are either individisible or fungible, so that scope economies exist.[10] Four classes of scope economies are identified and analyzed.

Class I   Indivisible but *non-specialized* physical capital as a common input into two or more products.

Scope economies may arise because some fixed item of capital equipment is indivisible. It may be a machine – such as heavy gauge sheet metal shears – which is needed occasionally in the production process for product A but is otherwise idle. Assume that the machine could be used to manufacture both products A and B. Even if this is the case it need not indicate that an efficient solution is for the manufacturer of A to diversify into the manufacture of B. There are at least two other options. The manufacturer of A could rent the services of another firm's machine, or it could acquire its own machine and lease access to it when it would otherwise remain idle.

To the extent that there is not a thin market for the services of the machinery in question – which will often be the case – there does not appear to be a compelling reason for diversification on account of the hazards of exposure to opportunism [Williamson (1975); Klein, Crawford and Alchian (1978)]. Market solutions would appear to be superior.[11]

Class II   Indivisible *specialized* physical capital as a common input to two or more products.

Assume that the piece of equipment is specialized but not entirely so. Assume specifically that it can only be used for making products A and B, that there is some idle capacity if it is only used to manufacture A, and that the market for A and B will only support a small number of producers. In these circumstances there may be incentives for the manufacturer of A to also manufacture B because of the transactional difficulties which might otherwise be encountered in the small numbers markets assumed. Since the fixed asset is highly specialized, and the number of potential leasees is assumed to be quite small, markets for the services of the fixed assets will be thin. Bilateral monopoly situations can then arise in which leasees may attempt to extract the quasi-rents associated with the utilization of the leasor's fixed and specialized asset.[12]

[Williamson (1975, 1979); Klein, Crawford and Alchian (1978); Monteverde and Teece (1982a, b).] In order to avoid these hazards, intrafirm trading – that is, multiproduct diversification   can be substituted for market exchange. Internal trading changes the incentives of the parties and enables the firm to bring managerial control devices to bear on the transaction, thereby attenuating costly haggling and other manifestations of non cooperative behavior. Exchange can then proceed more efficiently because of lower transactions costs.

Class III   Human capital as a common input to two or more products.

To the extent that knowhow has fungible attributes, it can represent a common input into a variety of products. Knowhow may also display some of the characteristics of a public good in that it may be used in many different non-competing applications without its value in any one application being substantially impaired. Furthermore, the marginal cost of employing knowhow in a different endeavor is likely to be much less than the average cost of production and dissemination (transfer). Accordingly, the transfer and application of proprietary information to alternative production activities is likely to generate important economies.

However, internal organization (multiproduct enterprise) is generally needed for these economies to be realized. Markets do not work well as the institutional mode for trading knowhow. One reason is that an important component of organizational knowledge is tacit. As discussed above, the transfer of tacit knowledge from one enterprise to another is likely to be difficult and costly. A temporary if not permanent transfer of employees may be needed, especially if the technology involved is state of the art and has not as yet been stabilized and formalized. If this is the case, multiproduct organization is likely to have appeal because it provides a more efficient technology transfer mode.

Besides the logistical problems surrounding the transfer of tacit knowledge, technology transfer must confront an important class of transactions cost problems. These can be summarized in terms of (1) recognition, (2) disclosure, and (3) team organization [Teece (1980); Williamson and Teece (1982)]. Thus consider a firm which has accumulated knowhow which can potentially find application in the fields of industrial activity beyond its existing product line(s). If there are other firms in the economy which can apply this knowhow with profit, then according to received microtheory, trading will ensue until Pareto Optimality conditions are satisfied. Or, as Calabresi has put it, 'if one assumes rationality, no transactions costs, and no legal impediments to bargaining, all misallocations of resources would be fully cured in the market by bargains' [Calabresi (1968)]. However, one cannot in general expect this result in the market for proprietary knowhow. Not only are there high costs associated with obtaining the requisite information but there are also organizational and strategic impediments associated with using the market to effectuate transfer.

Consider, to begin with, the information requirements associated with using markets. In order to carry out a market transaction it is necessary to discover who it is that one wishes to deal with, to inform people that one wishes to deal and on what terms, to conduct negotiations leading up to the bargain, to draw up the contract, to undertake the inspection needed to make sure that the terms of the contract are being observed, and so on [Coase (1960, p. 15)]. Furthermore the opportunity for trading must be identified. As Kirzner (1973, pp. 215–16) has explained:

> for an exchange transaction to be completed it is not sufficient merely that the conditions for exchange which prospectively will be mutually beneficial be present; it is necessary also that each participant be aware of his opportunity to gain through exchange . . . It is usually assumed . . . that where scope for (mutually beneficial) exchange is present, exchange will in fact occur . . . In fact of course exchange may fail to occur because knowledge is imperfect, in spite of conditions for mutually profitable exchange.

The transactional difficulties identified by Kirzner are especially compelling when the commodity in question is proprietary information, be it of a technological or managerial kind. This is because the protection of the ownership of technological knowhow often requires suppressing information on exchange possibilities. For instance, by its very nature industrial R&D requires disguising and concealing the activities and outcomes of R&D establishment. As Marquis and Allen (1966, p. 1055) point out, industrial laboratories, with their strong mission orientation, must

> cut themselves off from interaction beyond the organizational perimeter. This is to a large degree intentional. The competitive environment in which they operate necessitates control over the outflow of messages. The industrial technologist or scientist is thereby essentially cut off from free interaction with his colleagues outside of the organization.

Except as production or marketing specialists within the firm perceive the transfer opportunity, transfer may fail by reason of non-recognition.

Even where the possessor of the technology recognizes the opportunity, market exchange may break down because of the problems of disclosing value to buyers in a way that is both convincing and does not destroy the basis for exchange. A very severe information impactedness problem exists, on which account the less informed party (in this instance the buyer) must be wary of opportunistic representations by the seller. If, moreover, there is insufficient disclosure, including veracity checks thereon, to assure the buyer that the information possesses great value, the 'fundamental paradox' of information arises: 'its value for the purchaser is not known until he has the information, but then he has in effect acquired it without cost' [Arrow (1971, p. 152)].

Suppose that recognition is no problem, that buyers concede value, and are prepared to pay for information in the seller's possession. Occasionally that may suffice. The formula for a chemical compound or the blueprints for a special device may be all that is needed to effect the transfer. However, more is frequently needed. As discussed above, knowhow has a strong tacit and learning-by-doing character, and it may be essential that human capital in an effective team configuration accompany the transfer. Sometimes this can be effected through a one-time contract (a knowhow agreement) to provide a 'consulting team' to assist start-up. Although such contracts will be highly incomplete, and the failure to reach a comprehensive agreement may give rise to dissatisfaction during execution, this may be an unavoidable, which is to say irremediable, result. Plainly, multiproduct organization is an extreme response to the needs of a one-time exchange. In the absence of a superior organizational alternative, reliance on market mechanisms is thus likely to prevail.

Where a succession of proprietary exchanges seems desirable, reliance on repeated contracting is less clearly warranted. Unfettered two-way communication is needed not only to promote the recognition and disclosure of opportunities for information transfer but also to facilitate the execution of the actual transfer itself. The parties in these circumstances are joined in a small numbers trading relation and as discussed by Williamson, such contracting may be shot through with hazards for both parties [Williamson (1975, 1979)]. The seller is exposed to hazards such as the possibility that the buyer will employ the knowhow in subtle ways not covered by the contract, or the buyer might 'leap frog' the licensor's technology and become an unexpected competitive threat. The buyer is exposed to hazards such as the seller asserting that the technology has better performance or cost reducing characteristics than is actually the case; or the seller might render promised transfer assistance in a perfunctory fashion. While bonding or the execution of performance guarantees can minimize these hazards, they need not be eliminated since costly haggling might ensue when measurement of the performance characteristics of the technology is open to some ambiguity. Furthermore, when a lateral transfer is contemplated and the technology has not therefore been previously commercialized by either party in the new application, the execution of performance guarantees is likely to be especially hazardous to the seller because of the uncertainties involved [Teece (1977)]. In addition, if a new application of a generic technology is contemplated, recurrent exchange and continuous contact between buyer and seller will be needed. These requirements will be extremely difficult to specify *ex ante*. Hence, when the continuous exchange of proprietary knowhow between the transferor and transferee is needed, and where the end use application of the knowhow is idiosyncratic in the sense that it has not been accomplished previously by the transferor, it appears that something more than a classical market contracting structure is required. As Williamson notes 'The non-standardized nature of (these) transactions makes primary reliance on market governance hazardous, while their recurrent nature permits the cost of the specialized governance structure to be recovered' [Williamson (1979, p. 250)]. What Williamson refers to as 'relational contracting' is the solution; this can take the form of bilateral governance, where the autonomy of the parties is maintained; or unified structures, where the transaction is removed from the market and organized within the firm subject to an authority relation [ibid., p. 250]. Bilateral governance involves the use of 'obligational contracting' [Wachter and Williamson (1978); Williamson (1979)]. Exchange is conducted between independent firms under obligational arrangements, where both parties realize the paramount importance of maintaining an amicable relationship as overriding any possible short-run gains either might be able to achieve. But as transactions become progressively more idiosyncratic, obligational contracting may also fail, and internal organization (intrafirm transfer) is the more efficient organizational mode. The intrafirm transfer of knowhow avoids the need for repeated negotiations and ameliorates the hazards of opportunism. Better disclosure, easier agreement, better governance, and therefore more effective execution of knowhow transfer are likely to result. Here lies an incentive for multiproduct organization.

The above arguments are quite general and extend to the transfer of many different kinds of proprietary knowhow. Besides technological knowhow, the transfer of managerial (including organizational) knowhow, and goodwill (including brand loyalty) represent types of assets for which market transfer mechanisms may falter, and for which the relative efficiency of intrafirm as against interfirm trading is indicated.

Class IV   External economies:
George Stigler has cast the Coase theorem [Coase (1960)] in the following form:

> Under perfect competition and any assignment of property rights, market transactions between a firm producing a nuisance and one consuming it will bring about the same composition of output as would have been determined by a single firm engaged in both activities. That is, market transactions will have the same consequences

as internal management no matter what the property structure, *provided transactions costs are negligible.*

[Stigler (1966, p. 113, emphasis added)]

The converse of this is that external economies – which can generate economies of scope – will dictate multiproduct organization when there are significant transaction costs.

External economies in the production of various goods are quite common. For instance, there are locational externalities if a new airport opens up a previously remote area and stimulates tourism [13] There are also externalities if a cost saving innovation in one industry lowers costs in another. If these externalities can be captured at low cost by common ownership, then multiproduct organization is suggested.

Of course there are limits to the economies which can be captured through diversification. If diversification is based on scope economies, then there will eventually be a problem of congestion associated with accessing the common input. For instance, if the common input is knowhow, then while the value of the knowhow may not be impaired by repeated transfer, the costs of accessing it may increase if the simultaneous transfer of the information to a number of different applications is attempted. This is because knowhow is generally not embodied in blueprints alone; the human factor is critically important in technology transfer. Accordingly, as the demands for sharing knowhow increase, bottlenecks in the form of over-extended scientists, engineers and managers can be anticipated.[14] Congestion associated with accessing common inputs will thus clearly limit the amount of diversification which can be profitably engaged. However, if the transfers are arranged so that they occur in a sequential fashion, then the limits imposed by congestion are relieved, at least in part [Teece (1977)].

Control loss considerations may also come into play. However, the establishment of a decentralized divisionalized 'M-Form' [Williamson (1975)] structure is likely to minimize control loss problems. In fact Chandler argues that the M-Form innovation made diversification a viable strategy [Chandler (1969)]. It is also important to note that diversification need not represent abandonment of specialization. It is simply that a firm's particular advantage is defined not in terms of products but in terms of capabilities. The firm is seen as possessing a specialized knowhow or asset base from which it extends its operations in response to competitive conditions. This element of commonality simplifies the control problem, at least compared to other forms of diversification.

Market failure considerations and financial capital

Suppose that cash is the only excess capacity possessed by a specialized firm. Assuming, for the moment, that taxation of dividends and capital gains is unimportant, I wish to investigate whether allocative efficiency and/or a firm's market value can possibly be improved by diversification if financial markets are 'efficient'. Oliver Williamson, among others, has postulated that multidivisional firms can establish internal capital markets with resource allocation properties superior to those obtained by the (external) capital market. In particular, he postulates 'a tradeoff between breadth of information, in which respect the banking system may be presumed to have the advantage, and depth of information, which is the advantage of the specialized firm' [Williamson (1975, p. 162)]. Inferior access to inside information and the weak control instruments exercised by financial intermediaries and the stock market provides the foundation for Williamson's assertion that the 'miniature capital market' within the firm has distinctive efficiency properties.

Financial theorists, however, are often quick to reply that since the financial markets have been shown to be 'efficient', no improvement in allocative efficiency or market value can possibly derive from managers usurping the role of financial markets. Myers (1968), Schall (1972), and Mossin (1973) have all argued that value is conserved (value additivity obtains) under the addition of income streams, as would occur with diversification by merger. However, the notions of 'efficiency' as used by financial theorists are highly specialized and do not accord with the concept of allocative efficiency used in welfare economics. Nor does it deny that stockholder wealth can be improved through the operations of the firm's internal capital markets. These issues are critical to the analysis to follow and so are examined below.

In the finance literature, the term 'efficient markets' has taken on a specialized and misleading meaning. One widely employed definition refers to informational efficiency. For example, according to Fama (1970, p. 383) 'A market in which prices fully reflect available information is called "efficient"',[15] and according to Jensen (1978) 'A market is efficient with respect to information set Θ_t if it is impossible to make economic profits by trading on the basis of information set Θ_t'. The other widely employed definition is what can be called mean-variance efficiency. The market is mean-variance efficient if capital market prices correspond to an equilibrium in which all individuals evaluate portfolios in terms of their means and variances, about which they all have identical beliefs. Unfortunately, these concepts have nothing to do with allocative efficiency. As Stiglitz (1981) has shown, neither informational efficiency or mean variance efficiency are necessary or sufficient conditions for the Pareto optimality of the economy. In short, 'there is no theoretical presumption simply because the financial markets appear to be competitive, or "pass" the standard finance literature tests concerning efficiency, that they are efficient' [ibid., p. 237].

One reason for this result is that it is costly to obtain and transmit information about investment opportunities. Since managers are obviously more informed about investment opportunities available to the firm, they must somehow convey this information to potential investors if efficient outcomes are to be obtained solely through utilization of the (external) capital market. However, 'capital markets in which it is costly to obtain and transmit information look substantially different from those in which information is assumed to be perfect, and they fail to possess the standard optimality properties' [ibid., p. 244].

The capital market clearly does not fully reflect all information – which is what is necessary for Pareto optimality to obtain.[16] If markets were perfectly efficient in transmitting information from the informed to the uninformed, informed individuals wouldn't obtain a return on their investment in information; thus the only information which can, in equilibrium, be efficiently transmitted is costless information. With costly information, markets cannot be fully arbitraged [Grossman and Stiglitz (1976, 1980)].

The above considerations indicate why a useful economic function can be performed by the internal allocation of capital within the firm. If managers have access to an information set which is different from investors, and if it is difficult and costly to transmit the content of this information set to investors, then managers may be able to increase stockholder wealth by making investment decisions on behalf of the stockholders. In the process, resource allocation is likely to be improved over a situation in which all earnings are returned to stockholders who then make all reinvestment decisions. The transactions cost properties of such an arrangement render it absurd in most circumstances. Accordingly, the existence of internal capital markets and the (partial) internalization of the capital allocation process within the firm appear to possess a compelling rationale – both in terms of stockholder wealth enhancement and allocative efficiency.

In this context it is possible to recognize that if a specialized firm possesses financial resources beyond reinvestment opportunities in its traditional business, there are circumstances under which both stockholder wealth and allocative efficiency can be served if managers allocate funds to new products. However, the domain within which an efficiency gain is likely swings on empirical factors, and is likely to be quite narrow, given the relative efficiencies within which managers and stockholders can scan investment opportunities. It is generally only with respect to related businesses – businesses related functionally, technologically and geographically – that a relative advantage seems likely. It is for those investment opportunities in which the firm has a decided information advantage that managers are likely to possess such an advantage. Broader investment opportunities are better assessed by mutual funds which specialize in that function and can make portfolio investments at low transactions costs.

Nevertheless, financial theory provides insights into other ways by which stockholder wealth might be changed through diversification. In particular, the Capital Asset Pricing Model (CAPM)[17] provides a framework for assessing the rate of return the capital market expects an individual asset to earn. According to the CAPM, this rate of return is a function of the asset's level of systematic risk, the market portfolio rate of return, and the risk-free rate of return. A security's systematic risk, measured in the marketplace, depends on the degree of correlation between its return and the market's return. Defined as cash income plus capital appreciation over one time period, these 'returns' are equivalent to a security's cash flow over its lifetime. Focusing on cash flow allows systematic risk to be decomposed into the systematic risk of the current-period cash flow, and the systematic risk arising from future cash flows. Whereas current cash flow is fixed in timing and size, the future cash flow component of systematic risk is not fixed. It has a variable time horizon and the possibility of growth, and its estimated size is affected by changing investor expectations. The effect of varying the time horizon and growth of cash flow on present value is obvious; an increase in either results in more cash in absolute terms at some future date, and consequently a greater present value.

In the context of the CAPM, multiproduct organization can increase stockholder wealth by (1) increasing the income stream, (2) improving forecast reliability, or (3) decreasing the systematic risk by an amount greater than could be obtained by creating a portfolio investment in specialized firms. Economies of scope, where the economies would not be captured by a set of contracts amongst specialized firms, is a case in point. In addition, stockholder wealth could be increased if diversification assists the creation of free cash flows that have a negligible relationship to the level of activity of the economy, or improved investor confidence about future cash flows, since these developments would lead to reduced systematic risk. Outcomes of this kind seem possible, in that a distinctive attribute of internal organization is that it enables physical and human resources to be transferred, using powers of fiat, from one kind of business to the other, at low cost and with considerable speed. This flexibility, if exploited, might in fact provide the foundation for enhanced stockholder wealth. Businesses could be assembled in a fashion which enables the low cost and timely transfer of resources from one to another.

RELATED ISSUES

Slack and managerial discretion

The concept of excess resources used here and in Penrose (1959) bears certain similarities with the concept of slack found in the organization theory literature, excellently summarized by Bourgeois (1981). For in stance, slack has been variously defined as: '[The] disparity between the resources available to the organization and the payments required to maintain the coalition' [Cyert and March (1963, p. 36)]; the 'supply of uncommitted resources' [ibid., p. 54]; 'The margin or surplus (perform-ance exceeding "satisficing" levels) which permits an organization's dominant coalition to adopt structural arrangements which accord with their own preferences' [Child (1972, p. 11)]; 'The difference between existing resources and activated demand' [March and Olsen (1976, p. 87)]; 'since organizations do not always optimize, they accumulate spare resources and unexploited opportunities which then become a buffer against bad times.' Although the buffer is not necessarily intended, slack produces performance smoothing, reducing performance during good times and improving it during bad times [March (1979, p. 17)];

> organizational slack is that cushion of actual or potential resources which allows an organization to adapt successfully to internal pres-sures for adjustment or to external pressures for change in policy, as well as to initiate changes in strategy vis-à-vis the external environment.
>
> Bourgeois (1981).

While definitions abound, the concept of slack has, unfortunately, never been successfully operationalized. Part of the problem is that it can perform many functions; it can be a technical buffer, an inducement mechanism to attract and sustain organizational numbers [Barnard (1938)], a resource for conflict resolution, or a facilitator of strategic behavior [Bourgeois (1981)].

As used here, the concept of excess resources refers to the services of factor inputs available once managerial goals and the requirements for the long-run profitable operation of a production process have been met. In short, it refers to excess factor services over and above what is needed to meet managers requirements for organizational slack. As such, the concept is consistent with both satisficing and maximizing theories of the firm, as excess resources, as defined, can emerge in business firms no matter the behavioral rules it is following. Thus, if the desired level of organizational slack is zero, all redundant factor services become excess resources.

De novo entry vs. acquisition or merger

The appropriate vehicle for diversification is an issue upon which the theory is not silent. If an enterprise has excess or slack internal resources, and market failure considerations dictate internal utilization, then the choice of *de novo* entry or acquisition will depend upon the amount of slack, the time period over which it is available and the complementary resources which can be accessed through acquisition. Thus, if the slack appears gradually over a long period of time, *de novo* entry is likely to provide an effective entry vehicle. This is because *de novo* entry can be tailored as an incremental approach to diversification. If, on the other hand, slack resources are expected to emerge suddenly – due, for instance, to a sudden surge in technological innovation or due to an adverse change in demand which suddenly throws internal resources into unemployment – then merger or acquisition is likely to be the most favored route. Merger or acquisition will also be preferred if complementary resources can thereby be acquired.

Another consideration will be the relationship between the firm's internal valuation and the market value of the takeover candidate. Since the acquired firm possesses, by assumption, complementary resources which will work with the acquiring firm's slack resources, then the lower the price of the acquired firm relative to the market price of the individual resources which it possesses, then the greater the attractiveness of the takeover alternative. Hence, a depression in the stock market coupled with buoyant factor markets may change the relationship between the market value of the complementary resources purchased as a 'team' and their value if purchased in factor markets. This differential – which reflects the difference between the value of a firm as a 'going concern' and the value of its underlying assets when disaggregated – will help determine whether acquisition or *de novo* entry is the preferred route. Thus, as firm specific or economy wide factors depress the market value of a firm, the firm will appear more attractive as a takeover target to other firms which wish to diversify into its product line(s). Furthermore, the faster internal resources are released, the more attractive does the acquisition strategy become.

A curious implication of this analysis is that viewed on this framework, an active takeover market not only provides discipline for the acquired firm, thereby serving to minimize managerial discretion [Williamson (1975, Ch. 9)] but it may also function as a vehicle for channelling the internal resources of the acquiring firm into productive use. Hence, it appears that mergers and acquisitions may serve to minimize slack in both the acquiring and acquired firms, thereby generating a positive contribution to economic efficiency.

Lateral vs. conglomerate diversification

A robust theory of the multiproduct enterprise should ideally be able to explain the richness of diversified enterprises existing on the industrial landscape. At least two different types of diversification can be identified: lateral or 'related' diversification in which the different physical capital and technical skills of business or products bear an important element of commonality; and conglomerate diversification, where the physical capital and technical skills requirements are quite disparate.

The above analysis supports an efficiency rationale for the lateral integrated (diversified) enterprise. The efficiency rationale for the conglomerate is much more circumscribed. The only skill likely to be common to 'unrelated' businesses is management, but except in those circumstances where the market for managerial services is subject to high transactions costs, it is doubtful whether the scope economies arising from transferring managerial resources are large enough to provide compelling efficiencies.

A firmer foundation for conglomerates can be built by examining the operation of the internal capital market. Conglomerate firms may be able to develop distinctive capabilities in assessing investment opportunities in disparate businesses. As compared to banks, operating companies can often bring industrial experience to the assessment of acquisition candidates. Furthermore, with the appropriate internal governance structure, disparate businesses can be managed efficiently. For these and other reasons, Williamson concludes 'a transactional interpretation of the conglomerate, in which the limitations of capital markets in corporate control respects are emphasized, reveals that conglomerate firms (of the appropriate kind) are not altogether lacking in social purpose' [ibid., p. 175]. The Williamson conglomerate with its own internal capital market is superior to the unassisted capital market in its ability to identify and direct cash to high yield investment.

Some historical observations

The economic theory of the multiproduct firm outlined above has firms adopting multiproduct features due to the coupling of market failures and the emergence of excess capacity. Implicit in the analysis is a conviction that this model explains a substantial portion of the diversification activity which has occurred in the American economy. To demonstrate this convincingly would involve a major empirical effort. I settle here for a more limited objective – to establish that the historical trends appear broadly consistent with the theory.

Diversification has unquestionably made for great changes in the profile of American industry during the last half century [Chandler

(1969, p. 247)]. Furthermore, the Depression apparently triggered the trend towards diversification. Historians point out that the purpose of diversification was not to reduce portfolio risk or to pursue managerial motives, but rather to put slack resources to work. Furthermore, it was the technologically sophisticated firms which led the way. As Chandler (ibid., p. 275) observed:

> Precisely because these firms had accumulated vast resources in skilled manpower, facilities, and equipment, their executives were under even greater pressure than those of smaller firms to find new markets as the old ones ceased to grow. In the 1920's, the chemical companies, each starting from a somewhat different technological base, began to widen their product lines into new industries. In the same decade, the great electrical manufacturers – General Electric and Westinghouse – which had concentrated primarily on the manufacture of light and power equipment, diversified into production of a wide variety of household appliances. They also entered electronics with radios and X-ray equipment. During the Depression General Motors (and to a lesser extent other firms in the auto industry) moved into diesels, appliances, tractors, and airplanes. Some makers of primary metals, particularly aluminum and copper, turned to consumer products like kitchenware and household fittings, while rubber firms developed the possibilities of rubber chemistry to compensate for declining tire sales. In the same period food companies employed their existing distribution organizations to market an increasing variety of products.

Whereas the Depression triggered diversification by generating excess capacity, the Second World War stimulated the demand for new products because the world market for many raw materials was severely disrupted while the war effort generated demand for a wide range of military products. The synthetic rubber program caused both rubber and petroleum firms to make far greater use of chemical technologies than they had ever done before. Similarly, the demand for radar and other electronic equipment carried the electrical, radio and machinery firms farther into this new field, and the production of tanks, high-speed aircraft and new drugs all created skills and resources [ibid., p. 275]. Once these capabilities were created, they were applied, where possible, in the production of civilian goods for the peace time economy. Thus, 'the modern diversified enterprise represents a calculated rational response of technically trained professional managers to the needs and opportunities of changing technologies and markets' [ibid., p. 279].[18]

IMPLICATIONS AND CONCLUSIONS

Recent contributions to the transactions costs and market failures literature [Williamson (1975, 1979); Klein, Crawford and Alchian (1978);

Teece (1980)], and to the literature on the nature of the firm [Nelson and Winter (1982)] have made it possible to outline a theory of the multi-product firm. Important building blocks include excess capacity and its creation, market imperfections and the peculiarities of organizational knowledge, particularly its fungibility and tacit character. Further research on each of these elements, and how they relate to incentives for diversification, is likely to assist in the construction of a robust theory of the multiproduct firm. The successful completion of this mission could provide the foundation for a discriminating approach towards mergers and acquisitions.

NOTES

1 Economies of scope exist when for all outputs y_1 and y_2, the cost of joint production is less than the cost or producing each output separately [Panzar and Willig (1975)]. That is, it is the condition, for all y_1 and y_2: $C(y_1, y_2) < [C(y_1, 0)] + C(0, y_2)$.

2 This can be most easily illustrated by considering the merger of two firms with identical pre-merger μ and σ^2. The expected return, μ_m, of the merged firm is, of course, 2μ. The variance of these returns is given by $\sigma_m^2 = \sigma_i^2 + \sigma_j^2 + 2r_r\sigma_i\sigma_j$, where i and j refer to the pre-merger firms and m to the merged firm. r is the coefficient of correlation between the two profit streams, and can take values between $+1$ and -1. If $r = 1$ then a positive or negative deviation in firm i returns is paralleled by an identical variation in the profits of firm j. In this case $\sigma_m^2 = 4\sigma^2$. This means that the expected returns to the merged firm are exactly the sum of the expected returns of the constituent firms, and the spread of returns (measured by the standard deviation σ_m has also doubled. There has been no reduction in the variability of the earnings stream expressed as a ratio of the average return. (This measure is the coefficient of variation, a normalized measure of variability.) However, for $r < 1$ it is clear that $\sigma_m^2 < 4\sigma^2$. Specifically when $r = 0$, i.e., the two profit streams are completely independent of each other, $\sigma_m^2 = 2\sigma^2$. So the return has doubled, but the standard deviation increases by only $\sqrt{2}$, so the coefficient of variation diminishes by a factor of $1/\sqrt{2}$. Finally if $r = -1$ the two streams move in precisely opposite directions: a positive deviation in firm i is exactly offset by a negative deviation in firm j. In this unlikely case, the variance of the returns falls to zero. Obviously in all cases where $r < 1$, a merger reduces the variability of profits.

3 Thus $g_D = f_i(d)$ where g_D is growth of demand and $\hat{d}$ is the rate of successful diversification.

4 The Mueller theory must also confront efficient market theory. If managers are making investment decisions using a hurdle rate below the market equilibrium rate and therefore below the alternative returns available to stockholders, stockholders will shift their investment to firms offering higher rates of return. Capital market forces will not permit different firms to follow a 'two-tier' investment hurdle rate policy, at least not in the long run.

5 In modern general equilibrium theory [Arrow (1951); Arrow and Debreu (1954); Debreu (1959)]

commodity outputs in amounts represented by $q = (q_1, \ldots, q_m)$ may or may not be producible from input commodities in amounts represented by $X = (x_1, \ldots, X_n)$. If q is producible from x, then the input/output pair (x, q) is 'in the production set'. Whatever is known or considered plausible as a property of the structure of technical knowledge is treated as a postulate about the properties of the production set.

[Winter (1982, p. 63)]

6 'The premises of a skill cannot be discovered focally prior to its performance, not even understood if explicitly stated by others, before we ourselves have experienced its performance, whether by watching it or engaging in it ourselves' [Polanyi (1958, p. 1962)].

7 Polanyi illustrates this point by discussing how a bicyclist keeps his balance:

I have come to the conclusion that the principle by which the cyclist keeps his balance is not generally known. The rule observed by the cyclist is this. When he starts falling to the right he turns the handlebars to the right, so that the course of the bicycle is deflected along a curve towards the right. This results in a centrifugal force pushing the cyclist to the left and offsets the gravitational force dragging him down to the right. This maneuver presently throws the cyclist out of balance to the left which he counteracts by turning the handlebars to the left; and so he continues to keep himself in balance by winding along a series of appropriate curvatures. A simple analysis shows that for a given angle of unbalance the curvature of each winding is inversely proportional to the square of the speed at which the cyclist is proceeding. But does this tell us exactly how to ride a bicycle? No. You obviously cannot adjust the curvature of your bicycle's path in proportion to the ratio of your unbalance over the square of your speed; and if you could you would fall off the machine, for there are a number of other factors to be taken into account in practice which are left out in the formulation of this rule.

[Polanyi (1958, pp. 49–50)]

8 An organizational member's repertoire is the set of routines that could be performed in some appropriate environment [Nelson and Winter (1982)].

9 Over the years an individual may learn a piece of the company puzzle exceptionally well and he may even understand how the piece fits into the entire puzzle. But he may not know enough about the other pieces to reproduce the entire puzzle.

[Lieberstein (1979)]

10 As a general matter

economies of scope arise from inputs that are shared, or utilized jointly without complete congestion. The shared factor may be imperfectly divisible, so that the manufacture of a subset of the goods leaves excess capability in some stage of production, or some human or physical capital may be a public input which, when purchased for use in one production process, is then freely available to another.

[Willig (1979, p. 346)]

11 A related example would be the provision of air services between points A and B. An airport will be needed at both A and B and in the absence of complete congestion, service can also be provided from both points to C (which has an airport) once airport terminals A and B are constructed.

Hence $C(AB, BC, AC) < C(AB, 0, 0) + C(0, BC, 0) + C(0, 0, AC)$. While economies of scope exist, it need not imply that one airline ought to provide services AB, BC, and CA. Individual airlines could specialize on each route and access to terminals (the source of the assumed indivisibility) could be shared via contracts. Only in the extent to which transactional difficulties can be expected in writing, executing, and enforcing contracts will common ownership be necessary to capture the scope economies.

12 The quasi-rents will be the difference between the asset value it the equipment is used to produce multiple products and its value when it is used to produce the single product.

13 Common ownership may also be needed if the external economies are in the form of skills. Suppose firm X_1 is a monopolist in industry A. A new industry Y emerges which requires labor skills developed in industry X. Because of the transactional difficulties which confront X_1 in appropriating the skills with which it has imbued its employees, X_1 may generate an externality in industry Y. Diversification of X_1 into Y enable the externality to be internalized.

14 The 'Penrose-Effect' discussed earlier focuses on this problem with respect to managerial resources.

15 Fama (1970, 1976) actually defines three types of efficiency, each of which is based on a different notion of the type of information understood to be relevant in the phrase "prices fully reflect available information". Specifically, he recognizes:

1 *Weak-form efficiency* No investor can earn excess returns if he develops trading rules based on historical price or return information. In other words, the information in past prices or returns is not useful or relevant in achieving excess returns.

2 *Semistrong-form efficiency* No investor can earn excess returns from trading rules based on any publicly available information. Examples of publicly available information are: annual reports of companies, investment advisory data such as 'Heard on the Street' in *The Wall Street Journal*, or ticker tape information.

3 *Strong-form efficiency* No investor can earn excess returns using any information, whether publicly available or not.

Obviously, the last type of market efficiency is very strong indeed. If markets were efficient in their strong form, prices would fully reflect all information even though it might be held exclusively by a corporate insider. Suppose, for example, he knows that his company has just discovered how to control nuclear fusion. Even before he has a chance to trade based on the news, the strong form or market efficiency predicts that prices will have adjusted so that he cannot profit.

16 Strong form efficiency, defined in the previous footnote, would be necessary for Pareto optimality to hold.

17 The CAPM was developed almost simultaneously by Sharpe (1963, 1964), and Treynor (1961), while Mossin (1966), Lintner (1965, 1969) and Black (1972) made important extensions.

18 While Chandler's original focus was on managerial and technological considerations, his more recent writings indicate that he has been able to identify additional sources of underutilized resources—such as marketing and purchasing knowhow—which could also provide the foundation for an efficient diversification strategy. In the years after the First World War,

'many American companies . . . added lines that permitted them to make more effective use of their marketing and purchasing organizations and to exploit the by-products of their manufacturing and processing operations' [Chandler (1977, p. 473)].

REFERENCES

Arrow, K. J., 1951, 'An extension of the basic theorems of classical welfare economics,' in: J. Neyman, ed., *Proceedings of the Second Berkeley Symposium on Mathematical Statistics and Probability* (University of California Press, Berkeley, CA) 507–32.

Arrow, K. J. 1971, *Essays in the theory of risk bearing* (Markham Publishing Co., Chicago, IL and North-Holland Publishing Co., Amsterdam-London).

Arrow, K. J. and G. Debreu, 1954, 'Existence of equilibrium for a competitive economy,' *Econometrica* 22, July, 265–90.

Barnard, Chester I., 1938, *Functions of the executive* (Harvard University Press, Cambridge, MA).

Black, F., 1972, 'Capital market equilibrium with restricted borrowing,' *Journal of Business*, July, 1972, 444–55.

Black, F. and Myron Scholes, 1973, 'The pricing of options and corporate liabilities,' *Journal of Political Economy*, May/June, 657–9.

Bock, B., 1970, *Statistical games and the '200 largest' industrials: 1954 and 1968* (The Conference Board, New York).

Bourgeois, L. J., 1981, 'On the measurement of organizational slack,' *Academy of Management Review* 6, no. 1 Jan.

Calabresi, G., 1968, 'Transactions costs, resource allocation and liability rules: A comment,' *Journal of Law and Economics*, April.

Chandler, A., 1969, 'The structure of American industry in the twentieth century: A historical review,' *Business History Review*, Autumn.

——, 1977, *The visible hand* (Harvard University Press, Cambridge, MA).

Child, John, 1972, 'Organizational structure, environment and performance: The role of strategic choice,' *Sociology* 6 no. 1, 2–22.

Coase, R. H., 1960, 'The problem of social cost,' *Journal of Law and Economics* Oct., 1–44.

Cyert, Richard and James E. March, 1963, *A behavioral theory of the firm* (Prentice Hall Englewood Cliffs, NJ).

Debreu, G., 1959, *Theory of value* (Wiley, New York).

Fama, E. F., 1970, 'Efficient capital markets: A review of theory and empirical work,' *The Journal of Finance*, May, 383–417.

——, 1976, *Foundations of finance* (Basic Books, New York).

Galai, D. and R. W. Masulis, 1976, 'The option pricing model and the risk factor of stock,' *Journal of Financial Economics*, Jan./March, 53–82.

Grabowski, H. and D. Mueller, 1975, 'Life cycle effects of corporate returns of retentions,' *Review of Economics and Statistics*, Nov.

Grossman, S. J. and J. E. Stiglitz, 1976, 'Information and competitive price systems,' *American Economic Review* 66, May, 246–53.

Jensen, M. C., 1978, 'Some anomalous evidence regarding market efficiency,' *Journal of Financial Economics* 6, June/Sept., 95–101.

Kirzner, I., 1973, *Competition and entrepreneurship* (University of Chicago Press, Chicago, IL).

Klein, B., R. G. Crawford and A. A., Alchian, 1978, 'Vertical intergration appropriable rents and the competitive contracting process,' *Journal of Law and Economics* XXI, no. 2, Oct., 297–326.

Lewellen, W. G. and B. Huntsman, 1970, 'Managerial pay and corporate performance,' *American Economic Review*, Sept., 710–20.

Lieberstein, S. H., 1979, *Who owns what is in your head* (Hawthorn Publishers, New York).

Lintner, J., 1965, 'The valuation of risk assets and the selection of risky investments in stock portfolios and capital budgets,' *The Review of Economics and Statistics*, Feb., 13–37.

———, 1969, 'The aggregation of investor's diverse judgments and preferences in purely competitive security market,' *Journal of Financial and Quantitative Analysis*, Dec., 347–400.

March, James, 1979, Interview in Stanford GSB (Graduate School of Business, Stanford University, Stanford, CA).

March, James and John Olsen, 1976, *Ambiguity and choice in organisations* (Universitets-forlaget, Bergen).

Marquis, D. and T. Allen, 1966, 'Communication patterns in applied technology,' *American Psychologist* 21.

Marris, Robin, 1966, *The economic theory of managerial capitalism* (Macmillan, London).

Monteverde, K. M. and D. J. Teece, 1982a 'Supplier switching costs and vertical integration,' *Bell Journal of Economics*, Spring.

———, 1982b 'Appropriable rents and quasi vertical intergration.' *Journal of Law and Economics*. Oct.

Mossin, J., 1966, 'Equilibrium in capital assets market,' *Econometrica*, Oct., 768–83.

———, 1973, *Theory of financial markets* (Prentice-Hall, Englewood Cliffs, NJ).

Mueller, D. C., 1969, 'A theory of conglomerate mergers,' *Quarterly Journal of Economics*, Nov., 643–59. (See also comment by Dennis E. Logue and Phillipe A. Naert, Nov., 1970, 663–67; comment by David R. Kanerschen, 668–73, and reply by Dennis C. Mueller, 674–9.)

———, 1972, 'A life cycle theory of the firm,' *Journal of Industrial Economics*, July.

Myers, S. C., 1968, 'Procedures for capital budgeting under uncertainty,' *Industrial Management Review*, Spring, 1–19.

Nelson, Richard R. and Sidney G. Winter, 1980, 'Firm and industry response to changed market conditions: An evolutionary approach,' Economic Inquiry, April.

———, 1982, *An evolutionary theory of economic change* (Harvard University Press, Cambridge, MA).

Panzar, John and R. Willig, 1975, 'Economics of scale and economics of scope in multioutput production,' Unpublished working paper (Bell Laboratories, Murray Hill, NJ).

Penrose, Edith T., 1959, *Theory of the growth of the firm* (Blackwell, Oxford).

Polanyi, Michael, 1958, *Personal knowledge: Towards a post-critical philosophy* (University of Chicago Press, Chicago, IL).

Schall, L. D., 1972, 'Asset valuation, firm investment, and firm diversification,' *Journal of Business*, Jan., 11–28.

Schumpeter, Joseph A., *Capitalism, socialism, and democracy* (Harper and Brothers, 1950, New York).

Sharpe, W. F., 1963, 'A simplified model for portfolio analysis,' *Management Science*, Jan., 277–93.

——, 1964, 'Capital assets prices: A theory of market equilibrium under conditions of risk' *Journal of Finance*, Sept., 425–42.

Stigler, George, 1966, *The theory of price* (Macmillan, New York).

Stiglitz, Joseph E., 1981. 'The allocation role of the stock market,' *Journal of Finance*, no. 2, May.

Teece, David J., 1979, 'Technology transfer by multinational firms: The resource cost of transferring technological knowhow,' *Economic Journal* 87, June.

——, 1980, 'Economies of scope and the scope of the enterprise,' *Journal of Economic Behavior and Organization* 1, no. 3, 223–47.

Treynor, J., 1961, 'Towards a theory of the market value of risky assets,' Unpublished manuscript.

Wachter, M. and O. Williamson, 1978, 'Obligational markets and the mechanics of inflation,' *Bell Journal of Economics*, Autumn.

Williamson, Oliver E., 1975, *Markets and hierarchies* (Free Press, New York).

——, 1979, 'Transactions costs economics: The governance of Contractual Relations,' *Journal of Law Economics*.

Williamson, Oliver E., and D. J. Teece, 1982, 'European economic and political integration: The markets and hierarchies approach' in: Pierre Salmon, ed. *New approaches to European integration*, forthcoming.

Willig, Robert, 1979, 'Multiproduct technology and market structure,' *American Economic Review*, May.

Winter, Sidney G., 1982, 'An essay on the theory of production,' in: S. H. Hymans, ed., *Economics and the world around it* (The University of Michigan Press, Ann Arbor, MI).

Chapter 3

Resource-based theory

Margaret A. Peteraf

INTRODUCTION

In recent years, a model of how firms compete, which is unique to the field of strategic management, has begun to emerge. Known as the 'Resource-Based View', it is regarded by some as having momentous potential as a paradigm for our field. Others wonder whether this emergent model provides much additional insight over traditional understandings. Admittedly, resource-based work is consistent with and rooted squarely in the policy research tradition. The notion that firms are fundamentally heterogeneous, in terms of their resources and internal capabilities, has long been at the heart of the field of strategic management. The classic approach to strategy formulation, for example, begins with an appraisal of organizational competencies and resources (Andrews 1971). Those which are distinctive or superior relative to those of rivals, may become the basis for competitive advantage if they are matched appropriately to environmental opportunities (Andrews 1971; Thompson and Strickland 1990).

Those ideas may be thought of as the basic principles upon which resource-based research continues to build. While the model is still in the developmental stage, it has deepened our understanding regarding such topics as how resources are applied and combined, what makes competitive advantage sustainable, the nature of rents, and the origins of heterogeneity.[1] The work of Penrose (1959) is considered a very influential force. Other notable contributions include Lippman and Rumelt (1982), Teece (1980, 1982), Nelson and Winter (1982), Rumelt (1984, 1987), Wernerfelt (1984), Barney (1986, 1991), Dierickx and Cool (1989), Castanias and Helfat (1991), Conner (1991), and Mahoney and Pandian (1992). This research stream is an impressive one. And while many agree that there is a need for greater rigor and richness of detail, the work that has been done provides a strong foundation and an inspiration for work to come.

In reviewing this work, one encounters numerous strands of research on a series of closely related topics. While each paper offers a distinct contribution, there is also considerable overlap of ideas. To the uninitiated this may be confusing. In part, this is because subtle variations in terminology across papers have made communication more difficult. But in addition, the underlying model seems somewhat disjoint, as if the ideas of these disparate authors have not fully coalesced into an integrated whole. While there is general agreement as to the basic insights of the model, there are small disagreements over minor points.

The purpose of this paper is to develop a general model of resources and firm performance which at once integrates the various strands of research and provides a common ground from which further work can proceed. My aim is to build consensus for a parsimonious model, clarify basic issues, suggest possible implications, and, in so doing, facilitate the continuing dialogue among scholars.

In the first section, a resource-based model of the theoretical conditions which underlie competitive advantage is presented. There are four such conditions, all of which must be met. The first of these is *resource heterogeneity*, from which come Ricardian or monopoly rents. *Ex post limits to competition* are necessary to sustain the rents. *Imperfect resource mobility* ensures that the rents are bound to the firm and shared by it. *Ex ante limits to competition* prevent costs from offsetting the rents. Each of these conditions is described in turn.

The model is intended to aid our theoretical understanding of superior firm performance as well as to inform management practice.

In the final section, some applications and implications of the model are described. In particular, the application of resource-based work to single-business strategy, as well as to multibusiness corporate strategy, in all of its forms, is discussed.

A MODEL OF COMPETITIVE ADVANTAGE

Heterogeneity

A basic assumption of resource-based work is that the resource bundles and capabilities underlying production are heterogeneous across firms (Barney 1991).[2] One might describe productive factors in use as having intrinsically differential levels of "efficiency." Some are superior to others. Firms endowed with such resources are able to produce more economically and/or better satisfy customer wants.

Heterogeneity implies that firms of varying capabilities are able to compete in the marketplace and, at least, breakeven. Firms with marginal resources can only expect to breakeven.[3] Firms with superior resources will earn rents.[4]

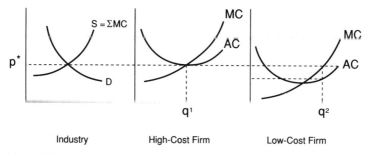

Figure 3.1 Scarcity rents with heterogeneous factors
Key: P* = Equilibrium price. □ = Rents to efficient producer

Ricardian rents

Heterogeneity in an industry may reflect the presence of superior productive factors which are in limited supply. They may be fixed factors which cannot be expanded. More often, they are quasi-fixed, in the sense that their supply cannot be expanded rapidly. They are scarce in the sense that they are insufficient to satisfy demand for their services. Thus, inferior resources are brought into production as well.

This is the familiar Ricardian argument.[5] It may be understood most clearly by assuming that firms with superior resources have lower average costs than other firms.[6] (See Figure 3.1.) These low cost firms have somewhat inelastic supply curves, in that they cannot expand output rapidly, regardless of how high the price may be. High prices, however, do induce other less efficient firms to enter the industry. Such firms will enter and produce so long as price exceeds their marginal cost (MC). In equilibrium, industry demand and supply are in balance, high-cost firms breakeven (P = AC), and low-cost firms earn supranormal profits in the form of rents to their scarce resources (P > AC).

Note that this model is consistent with competitive behavior in the product market. Firms are price takers and produce at the point where price equals marginal cost. The high returns of efficient firms cannot be attributed to an artificial restriction of output or to market power. Neither do they depend upon uniqueness or even rarity in the absolute sense. It is theoretically possible for the rents to be earned by a number of equally efficient producers, so long as an efficiency differential remains between them and other producers. What is *key* is that the superior resources remain *limited* in supply. Thus, efficient firms can sustain this type of competitive advantage only if their resources cannot be expanded freely or imitated by other firms.

Consider what happens if this is not so. (See Figure 3.2.) Increased production by additional efficient producers will shift the supply curve out. This will drive down the equilibrium price, forcing marginal firms

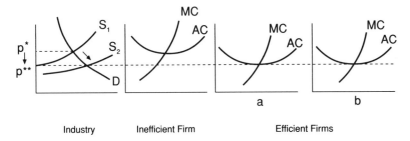

Figure 3.2 Imitation (expansion) of low-cost firms causes rents to dissipate and high-cost firms to exit
Key: P** = New equilibrium price

to leave the market. Remaining firms will produce at the point where price equals both marginal cost and average cost. As a result, rents will be dissipated and only normal returns will be earned by efficient (now homogeneous) producers.

The Ricardian model is often thought of with respect to resources which are strictly fixed in supply. But it may be applied as well to quasi-fixed resources, which are of much greater importance. These are resources which, while limited in the short run, may be renewed and expanded incrementally within the firm that utilizes them.[7] Utilization of such resources may in fact augment them.

Prahalad and Hamel (1990) describe how core competencies, particularly those which involve collective learning and are knowledge-based, are enhanced as they are applied. Such resources may provide both the basis and the direction for the growth of the firm itself. For example, there may be a natural trajectory embedded in a firm's knowledge base.[8] Current capabilities may both impel and constrain future learning and investment activity.[9] Incremental growth and renewal of such limited resources, however, is not inconsistent with a Ricardian view of rent and competitive advantage.

Monopoly rents

The condition of heterogeneity is equally consistent with models of market power and monopoly rents as it is with the Ricardian story. What distinguishes monopoly profits from Ricardian rents is that monopoly profits result from a deliberate restriction of output rather than an inherent scarcity of resource supply.

In monopoly models, heterogeneity may result from spatial competition or product differentiation.[10] It may reflect uniqueness and localized monopoly. It may be due to the presence of intra-industry mobility barriers which differentiate groups of firms from one another (Caves and

Porter 1977.) It may entail size advantages and irreversible commitments or other first mover advantages.[11] There are numerous such models. What they all have in common is the supposition that firms in favorable positions face downward sloping demand curves. These firms then maximize profits by consciously restricting their output relative to competitive levels. These are models of market power. Unlike Ricardian models, many are 'strategic' in that firms take into account the behavior and relative position of their rivals.

Apparently homogeneous firms may also earn monopoly rents. Cournot behavior exhibited by identical rivals, for example, may yield prices in excess of marginal costs. So may collusive behavior, tacit or otherwise. But these kinds of behaviors are facilitated by fewness of numbers and therefore depend on barriers to entry. Asymmetries must exist between incumbent firms and potential entrants. In this case, the heterogeneity occurs across these two groups of firms.

Ex post limits to competition

Regardless of the nature of the rents, sustained competitive advantage requires that the condition of heterogeneity be preserved. If the heterogeneity is a short-lived phenomenon, the rents will likewise be fleeting. Since strategists are primarily concerned with rents over a longer term, the condition of heterogeneity must be relatively durable to add value. This will be the case only if there are in place *ex post* limits to competition as well. By this I mean that *subsequent* to a firm's gaining a superior position and earning rents, there must be forces which limit competition for those rents. Competition may dissipate rents by increasing the supply of scarce resources. Alternatively, it might undermine a monopolist's (or oligopolist's) attempts to restrict output. Figure 3.2 illustrates how *ex post* competition makes the industry supply curve more elastic and erodes Ricardian rents. *Ex post* competition erodes monopoly rents as well, by increasing output or by making individual demand curves more elastic.

Resource-based work has focused on two critical factors which limit *ex post* competition: imperfect imitability and imperfect substitutability.[12] Substitutes reduce rents by making the demand curves of monopolists or oligopolists more elastic. This is one of Porter's (1980) classic "five forces." Much greater attention, however, has been given to the condition of imperfect imitability.

Rumelt (1984) coined the term 'isolating mechanisms' to refer to phenomena which protect individual firms from imitation and preserve their rent streams. These include property rights to scarce resources and various quasi-rights in the form of lags, information asymmetries, and frictions which impede imitative competition (Rumelt 1987). Of particular interest is the notion of causal ambiguity (Lippman and Rumelt 1982). This refers to uncertainty regarding the causes of efficiency differences among firms. Causal ambiguity prevents would-be-imitators from knowing exactly what to imitate or how to go about it. Coupled with nonrecoverable costs, such uncertainty may limit imitative activity, thus preserving the condition of heterogeneity.

Other isolating mechanisms include producer learning, buyer switching costs, reputation, buyer search costs, channel crowding, and economies of scale when specialized assets are required (Rumelt 1987).[13]

Rumelt (1984) describes isolating mechanisms as an analog of Caves and Porter's (1977) mobility barriers, which are themselves an extension of Bain's (1956) concept of entry barriers.[14] Mobility barriers, however, serve to isolate groups of similar firms in a heterogeneous industry, while entry barriers isolate industry participants from potential entrants.

Yao (1988) has distilled a set of factors more basic than the list of entry barriers suggested by Porter (1980) and Bain (1956). He contends that failures of the competitive market are due more fundamentally to production economies and sunk costs, transaction costs, and imperfect information.

Ghemawat (1986) suggests a different categorization, with more of a firm than a market orientation. He argues that inimitable positions derive from size advantages, preferred access to either resources or customers, and/or restrictions on competitors' options.

Dierickx and Cool (1989) offer a unique perspective on the topic of limits to imitation. They focus on factors which prevent the imitation of valuable but nontradeable asset stocks. They maintain that how imitable an asset is depends upon the nature of the process by which it was accumulated. They identify the following characteristics as serving to impede imitation: time compression diseconomies, asset mass efficiencies, interconnectedness of asset stocks, asset erosion, and causal ambiguity.

Dierickx and Cool's (1989) paper is a particularly important piece of work because it focuses precisely on those kinds of resources and capabilities which are of central concern to resource-based theory: nontradeable assets which develop and accumulate within the firm. Such assets tend to defy imitation because they have a strong tacit dimension and are socially complex. They are born of organizational skill and corporate learning. Their development is 'path dependent' in the sense that it is contingent upon preceding levels of learning, investment, asset stocks, and development activity.[15] For such assets, history matters. Would-be-imitators are thwarted by the difficulty of discovering and repeating the developmental process and by the considerable lag involved. Importantly, assets of this nature are also immobile and thus bound to the firm. Factor immobility, or imperfect mobility is another key requirement for sustainable advantage.

Imperfect mobility

Resources are perfectly immobile if they cannot be traded. Dierickx and Cool (1989) discuss several examples of this sort. Resources for which property rights are not well defined or with "bookkeeping feasibility" problems fall into this category (Dierickx and Cool 1989; Meade 1952; Bator 1958). So do resources which are idiosyncratic to the extent that they have no other use outside the firm. (See Williamson, 1979.)

Other kinds of resources may be described as imperfectly mobile. These are resources which are tradeable but more valuable within the firm that currently employs them than they would be in other employ. Resources are imperfectly mobile when they are somewhat specialized to firm-specific needs.[16]

Montgomery and Wernerfelt (1988) use the concept of switching costs to discuss how firm-specific investments may cement the trading relationship between a firm and the owners of factors employed by the firm. These investments by the resource owners may be regarded as a sunk cost (nonrecoverable cost) which may inhibit the factor's exit from a firm. These costs give the firm a greater claim on the resource in question.

Cospecialized assets may be another case in point (Teece 1986). These are assets which must be used in conjunction with one another or which have higher economic value when employed together. To the extent that they have no other equivalent uses (they are transaction specific) and to the extent that at least one of the assets is firm-specific, their mobility is limited.

Other resources may be imperfectly mobile simply because the transactions costs associated with their transfer are exceedingly high (Williamson 1975; Rumelt 1987.)

Because immobile or imperfectly mobile resources are nontradeable or less valuable to other users, they cannot be bid away readily from their employer. They remain bound to the firm and available for use over the long run. Thus, they can be a source of sustained advantage.[17] Furthermore, the opportunity cost of their use is significantly less than their value to the present employer. This is an important point and one which will be developed further in the next section. It implies that any Ricardian or monopoly rents generated by the asset will not be offset entirely by accounting for the asset's opportunity cost.

I use opportunity cost, here, in a sense slightly different from the conventional use of the term. Conventionally, it refers to the value of a resource in its next best use. Here, I mean it to refer to the value of the resource to its second-highest valuing potential-user. (See Klein, Crawford and Alchian 1978.) The use to which the potential user may wish to put it may be exactly the same.

This difference between the value of a resource to a firm and its opportunity cost is also a form of rent. Pareto rents, also called quasi-rents, are the excess of an asset's value over its salvage value or its value in its next best *use*. Following Klein *et al.* (1978), I use the term 'appropriable quasi-rents' or 'A-Q rents' to refer to the excess of an asset's value over its value to the second-highest valuing potential user or bidder for the resource. Klein *et al.* (1978) demonstrate that it is entirely possible for a resource to generate A-Q rents in the absence of either Ricardian or monopoly rents. Resources need not be rare or inimitable for them to be differentially valuable to possible users. Thus the presence of A-Q rents is not a sufficient indicator of competitive advantage. There must be monopoly or Ricardian rents generated as well.

A-Q rents are appropriable in the sense that they need not be paid out to the resource for the user to retain its services (ibid.). Were the user to appropriate the whole of the A-Q rents, the resource could earn no more elsewhere.[18]

It may be more accurate, however, to recognize that the rents will be shared between the factor owners and the firm employing them. First, one might as easily view the firm as tied to the use of specialized factors, since it cannot substitute generic factors at equal cost. This implies that the situation might be characterized best as a bilateral monopoly, in which the distribution of rents is indeterminate. Secondly, it should be recognized that the rents are in fact *jointly* produced and are as much due to the firm as to the factor. A specialized factor cannot be so productive apart from the firm. Therefore, its super-productivity is attributable as much to the context and other elements of the firm as to the factor itself. The firm and the factor are, in essence, a team. Caves (1980) states that rents are not entirely passed on to factors which are not traded on the open market. In a similar vein, Rumelt (1987) has argued that 'the rent on (specialized) factor(s) is not logically or operationally separable from the profits of the firm' (p. 143).

These two facts – that imperfectly mobile resources will remain available to the firm and that the rents will be shared by the firm – are the key features of imperfect factor mobility (see Wernerfelt 1989). They, in turn, make imperfect factor mobility a necessary condition for sustainable competitive advantage. In addition, imperfect factor mobility is a particularly important component of the model because such resources are less likely to be imitable than other kinds.[19] Furthermore, the opportunity cost of such assets, as defined above, does not offset the rents. But even together with heterogeneity and *ex post* limits to competition, imperfect factor mobility is not yet sufficient for sustained competitive advantage.

Ex ante limits to competition

One last condition must be met for a firm to have competitive advantage. There must be *ex ante* limits to competition as well. By this I mean that, prior to any firm's establishing a superior resource position, there must be limited competition for that position. This may be best explained by illustration. Suppose it is perceived, *a priori*, by equally endowed firms that by occupying certain choice locations they can gain an inimitable resource position over their rivals. What will ensue is fierce competition for those locations to the point that the anticipated returns are, in essence, competed away. A superior location could only be a source of above normal returns if some firm had the foresight or good fortune to acquire it in the absence of competition. This is the point brought out by Barney (1986) in arguing that the economic performance of firms depends not only on the returns from their strategies but also on the cost of implementing those strategies. Without imperfections in strategic factor markets, where the resources necessary to implement strategies are acquired, firms can only hope for normal returns. Rumelt (1987) makes a similar point in noting that unless there is a difference between the *ex post* value of a venture and the *ex ante* cost of acquiring the necessary resources, the entrepreneurial rents are zero. Profits come from *ex ante* uncertainty.

While only tradeable resources can be acquired in strategic factor markets, the argument can be extended to immobile and imperfectly mobile resources as well, as both Dierickx and Cool (1989) and Barney (1989) have noted. *Ex ante* competition to develop imperfectly mobile resources, such as the good will of clients, can also dissipate expected returns. While it is less likely that the full value of such resources will be anticipated or that firms will be equally efficient in accumulating such resources, it is important to recognize that imperfect resource mobility is not sufficient unto itself. There must be limits to *ex ante* competition as well.

The cornerstones of competitive advantage

In sum, four conditions must be met for a firm to enjoy sustained above-normal returns. Resource heterogeneity creates Ricardian or monopoly rents. *Ex post* limits to competition prevent the rents from being competed away. Imperfect factor mobility ensures that valuable factors remain with the firm and that the rents are shared. *Ex ante* limits to competition keep costs from offsetting the rents. The model is summarized in Figure 3.3.

This model is intended to highlight the importance of each of these conditions, as distinct from one another, and to explicate the particular

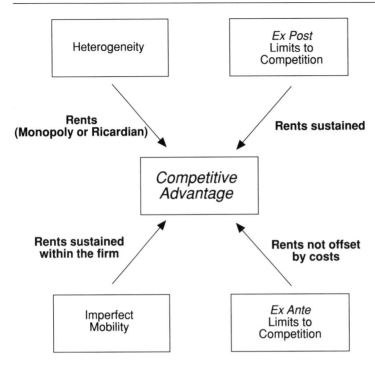

Figure 3.3 The cornerstones of competitive advantage

role that each plays in creating and sustaining rents. It is not meant to imply, however, that these four conditions are entirely independent of one another. They are, in fact, related conditions.

Heterogeneity is the most basic condition. It is the *sine-qua-non* of competitive advantage and has long been a fundamental concept of strategic management. For these reasons it deserves special emphasis. The model tells us that heterogeneity is necessary for sustainable advantage, but not sufficient. For rents to be sustained, we required *ex post* limits to competition *as well*. One can imagine heterogeneity without *ex post* limits to competition. Firms may have short-lived and unsustainable readily-imitated differences. It takes a greater stretch of the imagination to conceive of *ex post* limits to competition without heterogeneity. (Perhaps a regulator enforcing a pricing cartel among numerous homogeneous trucking firms.) For the most part, *ex post* limits to competition imply heterogeneity, although heterogeneity does not imply *ex post* limits to competition.

Heterogeneity underlies the condition of imperfect mobility as well. Again heterogeneous resources need not be imperfectly mobile. But it is hard to imagine any imperfectly mobile resources which are not also heterogeneous in nature. Resources which are immobile because of their idiosyncratic or firm-specific nature are certainly heterogeneous. Resources which are immobile due to ill-defined property rights or the lack of a market might possibly be homogeneous (pollution rights, for example?) Once again, however, imperfect mobility, for the most part, implies heterogeneity as well.

Finally, it is important to recognize that the productivity of superior resources depends upon the nature of their employment and the skill with which a strategy based on resource superiority is implemented.

APPLICATIONS OF THE RESOURCE-BASED MODEL

A major contribution of the resource-based model is that it explains long-lived differences in firm profitability that cannot be attributed to differences in industry conditions. Indeed, there is considerable evidence to show that such differences are not well explained by industry participation (Schmalensee, 1985; Mueller, 1986; Wernerfelt and Montgomery, 1988; Hansen and Wernerfelt, 1989; Rumelt 1991). There is less agreement on the relative magnitude of firm effects, but several studies have indicated that these effects are substantial (Mueller, 1986; Hansen and Wernerfelt, 1989; Rumelt, 1991). The resource-based model is a theoretical complement to this work.

On the practical side, the model may prove useful to managers seeking to understand, preserve, or extend their competitive advantage. While the model itself is freely available to all, its strategic implications depend on a firm's specific resource endowment. Barney (1986) argues that a firm may gain expectational advantages by analyzing information about the assets it already controls. So long as its assets are imperfectly mobile; inimitable, and nonsubstitutable, other firms will not be able to mimic its strategy. Thus, application of the model will not increase competition for available rents. It will only ensure that each firm optimizes the use of its own specialized resources.

Because of its focus on imperfectly mobile resources, for which the transactions cost of market exchange are high, resource-based theory has important implications for corporate strategy and issues regarding the scope of the firm as well as single business strategy. Some applications in each of these areas are discussed in turn.

Single business strategy

At the single business level, the model may help managers differentiate between resources which might support a competitive advantage from other less valuable resources (Barney 1991). For example, a brilliant, Nobel prize winning scientist may be a unique resource, but unless he has firm-specific ties, his perfect mobility makes him an unlikely source of sustainable advantage. Managers should ask themselves if his productivity has to do, in part, with the specific team of researchers of which he is a part. Does it depend on his relationship with talented managers who are exceptionally adept at managing creativity? Does it depend on the spirit of the workers or the unique culture of the firm?

A resource-based perspective may also help a firm in deciding whether to license a new technology or whether to develop it internally. If the technology is imperfectly mobile in the sense that its potential value cannot be well communicated to others because of the risk of revealing proprietary information, it might best be developed internally. Alternatively, its marketability might depend upon cospecialized assets such as long established relationships with vendors who are reluctant to switch to other suppliers. If the cospecialized assets are held by the firm and are themselves immobile, internal development may still make sense. If the innovation is perfectly mobile, the innovators could do no better than to license the technology.

Decision-making would also be enhanced by considering how imitable the innovation is. If the innovation is no more than a clever and complex assembly of relatively available technologies, then no wall of patents could keep opponents out. Recognizing this vulnerability, a manager might want to think more carefully about the length of the expected entry lag and whether or not there may be some advantage possible due to firm-specific learning or asset mass efficiencies. He might consider trying to use his head start to build other cospecialized resources that are less available (say a reputation for service on the new technology). This might be possible if the secondary resource is time path dependent or if his expectational advantage inhibits competition from developing the secondary resources.

The general point is that by analyzing his resource position, a manager would have a clearer understanding of whether his situation meets necessary conditions for a sustainable advantage. Fewer strategic mistakes would be made. But in addition, it might help him to utilize his expectational advantage in looking ahead.

Amit and Schoemaker (1993) draw upon resource-based theory in developing a behavioral view of strategic assets and offer some prescriptive advice on how to target, develop and deploy them. Wernerfelt (1989) proposes some guidelines to help managers identify their critical resources and decide how to apply them.

In some cases causal ambiguity may make it impossible for a firm to evaluate its resources or even to identify them (see Lippman and Rumelt 1982). While such resources may be the basis for competitive advantage, the causal ambiguity involved leaves little room for strategy. Firms owning the resources have no informational advantage over other firms and little ability to leverage these resources further since there is uncertainty regarding their dimensions and/or their value.

Other resources can more easily be identified as value-creating resources, but their reproduction may be highly uncertain. Resources
which are strongly time-path dependent or which are socially complex
fit this category, (See Barney 1991.) While these resources may be
difficult to reproduce or extend, the firm owning the assets is likely to
have a strong advantage in extending them over other firms. In part,
this advantage is informational, based on complex and tacit understandings, not easily accessible to outsiders. But also it's because the production of a socially complex resource is likely to require firm specific
cospecialized assets which cannot be duplicated in other settings. The
resource-based view would help managers to understand that such
resources can be an important basis for competitive advantage. And, by
highlighting the value of these resources, it might help managers see
that, despite the difficulty, they should consider leveraging these resources further.

Corporate strategy

The resource-based model is fundamentally concerned with the internal
accumulation of assets, with asset specificity, and, less directly, with
transactions costs. Thus it lends itself naturally to the consideration of
questions regarding boundaries of the firm. A number of researchers
have utilized a resource-based view to analyze issues regarding the scope
of the firm.

Barney (1988), for example, has addressed the issue of whether bidding
firms may realize abnormal returns from strategically related acquisitions.
His resource-based framework provides the answer that it depends upon
how rare and inimitable is the resulting combination of resources.

Montgomery and Hariharan (1991) have shown that firms with broad
resource bases tend to pursue diversification. (See Penrose 1959, as
well.) In doing so, firms tend to enter markets where the resource
requirements match their resource capabilities.

More generally, the prevailing theory of diversification can be characterized as resource-based. (See, for example, Teece 1982; Wernerfelt
1984; Williamson 1985; Wernerfelt and Montgomery 1986; Montgomery
and Wernerfelt 1988.) This theory characterizes the kinds of resources
which support diversification as quasi-fixed, yet inherently fungible: that
is, they can support a variety of products. Other resources may possess a
property of public goods, in that their use in one application does not
diminish their availability for other uses. A brand name, for example,
may be used without being 'used up' in the process. The crux of the
theory is that diversification is the result of excess capacity in resources
which have multiple uses and for which there is market failure.[20]
Without market failure, due to high transactions costs or imperfect

mobility, the firm could simply sell the services of their redundant resources. In that case, single business firms could operate more efficiently than a diversified firm, even if there are economies of scope (Teece 1980, 1982).

One issue, which has been inadequately addressed, is the paradox of how 'excess capacity' in resources may lead to 'scarcity rents' for resource holders. Certainly, these notions are incompatible if the resource has but a single use, since inferior resources would be driven from the market[21] (See Figure 3.2). Recall, however, that the price of a resource is determined by the condition of supply and demand in the factor market. Factor demand, in turn, is derived from the demands of *all* products which it can be used to produce. If, at the equilibrium price, heterogeneous factors are employed across the markets, then superior factors will earn rents, regardless of whether their availability surpasses the needs of a single-product market. They are still scarce relative to total demand for their usage. In this way, excess capacity of a resource in a single-product market is compatible with its ability to command scarcity rents. Similarly, resources with public good characteristics may earn rents, despite their availability for multiple employment. Since, after some point, there are limits to the expansion of these resources, perhaps because of a fixed supply of cospecialized assets within the firm, such resources may still be scarce relative to total demand for their services.

Eastman Kodak is an example of a firm that has diversified on the basis of excess capacity in its core capability in photographic technology. Its ability to expand in certain markets was limited by its high market share and antitrust considerations. In the mid-70s, its market share for film was estimated at 90 percent; it was estimated at 85 percent for cameras.[22] In order to more fully utilize its prodigious R&D capabilities Kodak had to seek opportunities outside its original markets. This was possible because the potential for photographic technology applications was quite broad, encompassing movie films and equipment, medical and industrial X-ray films and equipment, audiovisual products, microfilm, etc. In 1975, Kodak had a market share of just 38 percent of the total US market for amateur photographic products. In this sense, its resources were 'scarce' relative to total demand for their use over all applications, despite excess capacity relative to particular markets.

A second issue which needs further attention is the question of why firms do not expand more fully in initial markets before they enter additional ones. It may be that the competitive model is inadequate to characterize product markets. Or it may be that, in general, both resources and market conditions may be better represented in a dynamic model, changing incrementally over time (Montgomery and Hariharan 1991).

Montgomery and Wernerfelt (1989), employ a framework which characterizes resources by their 'specificity' or range of application. Diversification is viewed as a result of matching a firm's resources to the set of market opportunities. These two conditions together determine both the range of strategic options and the profitability of a firm. For example, the high specificity of expertise in glass technology would constrain a firm from diversifying far afield on the basis of this resource. And, since specialized resources also tend to be relatively scarce, the model would predict higher rents for narrow diversifiers.

In contrast, firms with generalizable resources may face a much wider opportunity set. So, for example, a firm with expertise in cost cutting, embodied in a team of managers and firm-specific routines, might diversify quite widely. Lower rents would be expected, however, since these skills might be in greater supply. This does not imply that there is no scarcity value to such resources, but simply that they are relatively less scarce than more specialized resources. What is important is that heterogeneous managerial resources are heterogeneous and superior managers are less than perfectly mobile.

Although the authors do not say so, the model also implies an optimal extent of diversification. Since the returns in each added market diminish due to resource efficiency loss, diversification will cease when rents in the final added market are zero. See Figure 3.4.

Dosi, Teece, and Winter (1990) address the issue of the degree of relatedness among a firm's products – what they term 'coherence' in its business activities. The authors draw on concepts from organizational economics to explain the connection between a firm's core competencies and the degree of coherence among its parts. According to this theory, variations in the speed of learning, the breadth of the path dependencies, the degree of asset specialization and the nature of the selection environment explain the nature and extent of the scope of the firm. This work, although it is preliminary, appears to make a very fruitful start. In addition, it highlights the rich use that may be made of evolutionary

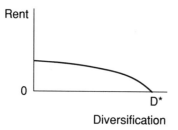

Figure 3.4 The determination of the extent of diversification
Key: D* = Extent of diversification. Space below the line = Accumulated rents

economics, in particular, toward explaining phenomena of central interest to researchers taking a resource-based view of strategy.

As these examples demonstrate, resource-based theory, clearly, has power and implications for many important questions regarding corporate scope. It is a unifying theory which allows us to view both related and unrelated diversification through a common lens. It addresses diversification extent as well as type. It goes further than competing theories in simultaneously explaining the differences in profitability which are observed across firms, while also offering an explanation about why all firms do not and cannot pursue strategies which in the aggregate offer the highest returns. Instead, firms are seen as adopting strategies which their resources can support. Just as all resources supporting single business strategies do not have equal profit generating potential, neither do the resources supporting various diversification strategies. For an individual firm, whether it is a single-line business or widely diversified, the critical task is to use its available resources to the greatest end they can support.

In sum, this emerging theory may prove to be a paradigm capable of elucidating and integrating research in all areas of strategy. Despite the need for further work, it has already shown itself to be a robust and integrative tool. It has strong implications for single-business strategy, for corporate strategy, for theorists and practitioners alike. Importantly, it is the only theory of corporate scope which is capable of explaining the range of diversification, in all its richness, from related constrained to the conglomerate form. This is the crucial mark of a robust theory of diversification (Teece, 1982). It is an area ripe for research, which has already demonstrated its fruitfulness and deserves the concentrated efforts of this community of scholars.

NOTES

1 This is not meant to suggest that the contributions of resource-based work have been limited to these topics.
2 See Nelson (1991) and Williams (1992) for discussions on why firms are different.
3 In equilibrium, industry demand and supply conditions determine the minimum efficiency level required to breakeven
4 Earnings in excess of breakeven are called rents, rather than profits, if their existence does not induce new competition.
5 See Ricardo (1817) and Rumelt (1987).
6 Note, however, that superior resources do not necessarily lead to a low cost position. This is simply the most tractable example.
7 See Nelson and Winter (1982) and Wernerfelt (1989).
8 This is a notion attributable to organizational economics. See Teec
9 See Dosi, Teece, and Winter's (1990) discussion of core capabl
dependencies and learning.

10 See Schmalensee (1978).
11 See Ghemawat (1986) and Lieberman and Montgomery (1988). Consider also models of dominant firm behavior.
12 See Barney (1991) and Dierickx and Cool (1989).
13 These topics and other related ones have received much attention in modern industrial organization literature as well.
14 For further discussion, see Mahoney and Pandian (1992).
15 See, Barney (1991) and Dosi, Teece, and Winter (1990).
16 Williamson (1985) discusses such assets and their implications for efficient firm boundaries extensively.
17 On the other hand, such assets may make a firm less responsive and flexible in the face of environmental or technological changes which upset a previously held advantage. Specialization is a two-edged sword.
18 Note that, in a multiperiod model, human resources would be reluctant to invest in firm-specific attributes if they expected the firm to appropriate the rents generated.
19 Dierickx and Cool (1989) contend that nontradeability is required to ensure that an asset remains fixed in supply.
20 For some empirical evidence on this point, see Chatterjee and Wernerfelt (1991).
21 In this country [USA] antitrust constraints typically limit market share. For this reason, inferior resources may well remain in the market despite excess capacity in single-use superior resources.
22 See 'Polaroid-Kodak', HBS case # 376–266.

REFERENCES

Amit, R. and P. J. Schoemaker. (1993). 'Strategic assets and organizational rent', *Strategic Management Journal*, **14**, pp. 33–46.
Andrews, K. R. (1971). *The Concept of Corporate Strategy*, Irwin, Homewood, IL.
Bain, J. (1956). *Barriers to New Competition*, Harvard University Press, Cambridge, MA.
Barney, J. B. (1986). 'Strategic factor markets: Expectations, luck and business strategy', *Management Science*, **42**, pp. 1231–41.
——, (1988). 'Returns to bidding firms in mergers and acquisitions: Reconsidering the relatedness hypothesis', *Strategic Management Journal*, **9**, pp. 71–8.
——, (1989). 'Asset stocks and sustained competitive advantage: A comment', *Management Science*, **35**, pp. 1511–13.
——, (1991). 'Firm resources and sustained competitive advantage', *Journal of Management*, **17**, pp. 99–120.
Bator, F. (1958). 'The anatomy of market failure', *Quarterly Journal of Economics*, pp. 351–79.
Castanias, R. and C. Helfat. (1991). 'Managerial resources and rents', *Journal of Management*, **17**, pp. 155–71.
Caves, R. E. (1980). 'Industrial organization, corporate strategy and structure', *Journal of Economic Literature*, **18**, pp. 64–92.
Caves, R. E. and M. Porter. (1977). 'From entry barriers to mobility barriers: Conjectural decisions and contrived deterrence to new competition', *Quarterly Journal of Economics*, **91**, pp. 241–62.
Chatterjee, S. and B. Wernerfelt. (1991). 'The link between resources and type of diversification: Theory and evidence', *Strategic Management Journal*, **12**, pp. 33–48.

Conner, K. (1991). 'A historical comparison of resource-based theory and five schools of thought within industrial organization economics: Do we have a new theory of the firm?', *Journal of Management*, **17**, pp. 121–54.

Dierickx, I. and K. Cool. (1989). 'Asset stock accumulation and sustainability of competitive advantage', *Management Science*, **35**, pp. 1504–11.

Dosi, G., D. Teece, and S. Winter. (1990). 'Toward a theory of corporate coherence: Preliminary remarks', Working paper.

Ghemawat, P. (Sept.–Oct. 1986). 'Sustainable advantage', *Harvard Business Review*, pp. 53–8.

Hansen, G. and B. Wernerfelt. (1989). 'Determinants of firm performance: The relative importance of economic and organizational factors', *Strategic Management Journal*, **10**, pp. 399–411.

Klein, B., R. Crawford, and A. Alchian. (1978). 'Vertical integration, appropriable rents, and the competitive contracting process', *Journal of Law and Economics*, **21**, pp. 297–326.

Lieberman, M. and D. Montgomery. (1988). 'First mover advantage', *Strategic Management Journal*, **9**, Special issue, pp. 41–58.

Lippman, S. A. and R. P. Rumelt. (1982). 'Uncertain imitability: An analysis of interfirm differences in efficiency under competition', *The Bell Journal of Economics*, **13**, pp. 418–38.

Mahoney, J. and J. R. Pandian. (1992). 'The resource-based view within the conversation of strategic management', *Strategic Management Journal*, **13**, pp. 363–80.

Meade, J. (1952). 'External economies and diseconomies in a competitive situation', *Economic Journal*, pp. 56–67.

Montgomery, C. A. and S. Hariharan. (1991). 'Diversified expansion by large established firms', *Journal of Economic Behavior*, pp. 71–89.

Montgomery, C. A. and B. Wernerfelt. (1988). 'Diversification, Ricardian rents, and Tobin's q', *Rand Journal*. pp. 623–32.

Mueller, D. (1986). *Profits in the Long Run*. Cambridge University Press, Cambridge, MA.

Nelson, R. (1991). 'Why do firms differ and how does it matter', *Strategic Management Journal*, **12**, pp. 61–74.

Nelson, R. R. and S. G. Winter. (1982). *An Evolutionary Theory of Economic Change*, Belknap Press, Cambridge, MA.

Penrose, E. T. (1959). *The Theory of Growth of the Firm*, Basil Blackwell, London.

Porter, M. E. (1980). *Competitive Strategy: Techniques for Analyzing Industries and Competitors*, The Free Press, New York.

Prahalad, C. K. and G. Hamel. (May–June 1990). 'The core competence of the corporation', *Harvard Business Review*, pp. 79–91.

Ricardo, D. (1965, Original 1817). *The Principles of Political Economy and Taxation*, Reprinted, J. M. Dent and Son, London.

Rumelt, R. P. (1984). 'Toward a strategic theory of the firm', In R. Lamb (ed.), *Competitive Strategic Management*, Prentice Hall, Englewood Cliffs, NJ, pp. 556–70.

——, (1987). 'Theory, strategy, and entrepreneurship', In D. Teece, (ed.), *The Competitive Challenge*, Ballinger, Cambridge, MA, pp. 137–58.

——, (1991). 'How much does industry matter?', *Strategic Management Journal*, **12**, pp. 167–86.

Schmalensee, R. (1978). 'Entry deterrence in the ready-to-eat breakfast cereal industry', *Bell Journal of Economics*, **9**, pp. 305–27.

——, (1985). 'Do markets differ much?', *The American Economic Review*, **75**, pp. 341–50.

Teece, D. J. (1980). 'Economics of scope and the scope of the enterprise', *Journal of Economic Behavior and Organization*, **1**, pp. 223–47.

——, (1982). 'Toward an economic theory of the multiproduct firm', *Journal of Economic Behavior and Organization*, **3**, pp. 39–63.

——, (1986). 'Firm boundaries, technological innovation, and strategic management', In L. G. Thomas, III, (ed.), *The Economics of Strategic Planning*, Lexington, Lexington, MA, pp. 187–99.

——, (1990). 'Contributions and impediments of economic analysis to the study of strategic management', In J. W. Fredrickson (ed.), *Perspectives on Strategic Management*, Harper Business, New York, pp. 39–80.

Thompson, A. A. and A. J. Strickland. (1990). *Strategic Management: Concepts and Cases*, Irwin, Homewood, IL.

Wernerfelt, B. (1984). 'A resource based view of the firm', *Strategic Management Journal*, **5**, pp. 171–80.

Wernerfelt, B. (1989). 'From critical resources to corporate strategy', *Journal of General Management*, **14**, pp. 4–12.

——, and C. A. Montgomery. (1986). 'What is an attractive industry?', *Management Science*, **32**, pp. 1223–9.

——, (1988). 'Tobin's q and the importance of focus in firm performance', *American Economic Review*, **78**, pp. 246–50.

Williamson, O. (1975). *Markets and Hierarchies*, Free Press, New York.

——, (1979). 'Transaction-cost economics: The governance of contractual relations', *Journal of Law and Economics*, **22**, pp. 233–61.

——, (1985). *The Economic Institutions of Capitalism*, Free Press, New York.

Williams, J. (1992). 'Strategy and the search for rents: The evolution of diversity among firms.' Working Paper, Carnegie Mellon University.

Yao, D. (1988). 'Beyond the reach of the invisible hand: Impediments to economic activity, market failures and profitability', *Strategic Management Journal*, **9**, pp. 59–70.

Part II

Resource allocation and portfolio composition

Decisions about what businesses to include in the corporate portfolio and how to allocate resources among the businesses are key corporate strategy issues for all multibusiness companies. We have seen, in Part I, that transaction cost theory suggests that multibusiness companies should be able to allocate resources among their businesses more efficiently than the external capital markets; and that the resource-based theory of the firm implies that valuable corporate resources which cannot be readily traded can none the less be leveraged through entry to new businesses that can benefit from these resources. In theory, resource allocation and portfolio composition decisions should be major sources of corporate value added.

However, resource allocation and portfolio building decisions are never easy for practising managers. Joseph Bower, in his 1970 study of capital budgeting procedures in large companies, showed that corporate hurdle rates for new investments did not provide much guidance on resource allocation because, in practice, business managers only proposed projects which met the required rate of return.[1] How should choices be made between investment proposals from different businesses that face different opportunities, different competitive conditions and different strategic issues? What new business entry, acquisition and divestment decisions will achieve a coherent, manageable and successful group of businesses? These are vital practical issues, on which pure economic theory offers limited guidance. Consultants and business school academics have, however, offered advice on these matters.

Two of the most popular practical tools that have been put forward to help managers with resource allocation decisions are portfolio planning and value-based planning. Portfolio planning techniques, initially developed in the 1970s by General Electric/McKinsey and by the Boston Consulting Group (BCG)[2] provide corporate managers with common frameworks to compare the strategies and investment requirements of a variety of different businesses. Each business is placed on a portfolio matrix or grid, which reflects the underlying competitive position and market prospects of the business. Businesses in different quadrants of the matrix (cash cows, stars, question marks and dogs in BCG's terminology) should be expected to have different strategies, profitability levels and investment needs. Guidelines on resource allocation between the businesses, therefore, follow. These frameworks have been especially valued by companies with numerous businesses in different sectors, where the problems of comparing the merits of investment proposals from different businesses are most acute. In an extract from his book, *Contemporary Strategy Analysis*, Robert Grant describes and discusses the McKinsey and BCG portfolio planning approaches.

Portfolio planning gained widespread acceptance during the 1970s and, by 1979, 45 per cent of the Fortune 500 were using some form of the technique.[3] During the 1980s, however, several companies became disillusioned with portfolio planning, believing that it provided too simplistic a view of resource allocation choices, and tempted companies to enter unfamiliar businesses for which they had few relevant management skills.[4]

Value-based planning represents a different approach to resource allocation. Whereas portfolio planning assumes that a company must have a mix of businesses generating and requiring cash in order to balance its overall cash flow, with value-based planning, the crucial judgement for each business is whether it will generate discounted cash flow returns on equity that beat the cost of capital. Businesses with investments that will beat the cost of capital hurdle rate should be resourced fully, but businesses whose investments will not beat the cost of capital should receive no new resources. There are several variants of this basic approach, and many different consulting groups offer their own version of it. Bernard Reimann, in the article included here, gives an overview of these approaches.[5]

With a more active market for corporate control, and increasing attention to shareholder returns, many companies have adopted value-based planning in the late 1980s and 1990s. As an extension of well-established DCF project appraisal techniques, it is hard to fault as a quantitative criterion for resource allocation choices. The power of the technique is that it forces companies to concentrate resources on only those businesses that can deliver the level of returns expected by shareholders. This discipline has led to sharper choices in many companies. But value-based planning offers no guidance on what sorts of businesses and investments are most likely to be able to beat the cost of capital or, indeed, on which businesses' forecasts are likely to prove optimistic or pessimistic.

The widespread acceptance of portfolio planning and value-based planning among large corporations is evidence that corporate-level managers, recognizing the importance of resource allocation in diversified companies, have readily accepted practical approaches that address this key issue. However, both approaches have their critics, who point

out that they can encourage superficial consideration of resource allocation issues, since they are not based on any concept of how the
corporate centre adds value to its businesses.

Recent work on resource allocation and portfolio composition has
aimed to make a more explicit and practical link to corporate added
value via the resource-based theory of the firm. David Collis, a specialist
in multibusiness company strategy at Harvard Business School, has been
at the forefront of this movement. In his article, "What is a 'Related'
Corporate Strategy?" he argues that multibusiness companies should
build their portfolios around businesses that have common "roots" in
that they can draw off the main resources of the corporation. Such
resources may concern familiar areas such as technology, patents, brand
names or facilities. But they also cover managerial resources (KKR) or
even cartoon characters (Disney). Collis examines how managers can use
the concept of corporate resources in its widest sense to make sound
decisions about what businesses to include in the corporate portfolio, as
well as to identify businesses which do not fit.

Many writers have offered advice on acquisitions, though by no
means all concentrate on the need for the acquiring company to be able
to add some value through its acquisition initiatives. Among the most
useful books are Malcolm Salter and Wolf Weinhold's *Diversification
through Acquisition* and Philippe Haspeslagh and David Jemison's *Managing Acquisitions*.[6] Haspeslagh and Jemison, in the selection included here,
emphasize the important contribution acquisitions can make to corporate
development and renewal, while reminding managers that many, if not
most acquisitions actually destroy value. They explore the implications
of resource-based thinking for acquisitions, urging managers to view
acquisitions as an opportunity to expand the firm's capabilities, and
providing a framework for different types of capability transfers. The
authors also argue that firms need to create an acquisition process that
focuses on integrating these new capabilities into the firm.

The importance of resource allocation decisions has meant that practical tools and techniques are desperately needed to assist multibusiness
companies that are struggling with the complex issues raised. But these
tools and techniques need to be grounded in fundamental thinking
about the role and value added by corporate management. Amongst the
most promising developments are recent attempts to convert the economic theories underpinning the resource-based theory of the firm into
practically useful advice for managers.

NOTES

1 Bower, Joseph L. (1970) *Managing the Resource Allocation Process: A Study of
Corporate Planning and Investment*, Boston: Harvard Business School Press.

2 Hedley, Barry (1977) "Strategy and the 'Business Portfolio'", *Long Range Planning*, 10: 9–15, February.
3 Haspeslagh, Philippe (1982) "Portfolio Planning: uses and limits", *Harvard Business Review*, pp. 58–73, January–February; Hamermesh, Richard (1986) *Making Strategy Work*, New York: John Wiley & Sons.
4 Hamermesh, Richard G. and White, Roderick E. (1984) "Manage Beyond Portfolio Analysis", *Harvard Business Review*, pp. 103–9, January–February; Hayes, Bob and Abernathy, Bill (1980) "Managing Our Way to Economic Decline", *Harvard Business Review*, July/August.
5 See also Copeland, Tom, Koller, Tim and Murrin, Jack (1990) *Valuation: Measuring and Managing the Value of Companies*, New York: John Wiley & Sons, Inc., 2nd edn 1994; Rapaport, Alfred (1986) *Creating Shareholder Value*, New York: The Free Press; McTaggart, James M., Kontes, Peter W. and Mankins, Michael C. (1994) *The Value Imperative: Managing for Superior Shareholder Returns*, New York: The Free Press.
6 Salter, Malcolm and Weinhold, Wolf A. (1979) *Diversification Through Acquisition: Strategies for Creating Economic Value*, New York: The Free Press; Haspeslagh, Philippe C. and Jemison, David B. (1991) *Managing Acquisitions: Creating Value Through Corporate Renewal*, New York: The Free Press.

ADDITIONAL READING

Bower, Joseph L. (1970) *Managing the Resource Allocation Process: A Study of Corporate Planning and Investment*, Boston: Harvard Business School Press. A classic study of the capital budgeting process and guidance on managing the process.

Copeland, Tom, Koller, Tim and Murrin, Jack. (1990) *Valuation: Measuring and Managing the Value of Companies*, New York: John Wiley & Sons, Inc., 2nd edn 1994.
Techniques of value-based planning and their application, including the valuation of the activities of corporate centres, acquisitions and divestitures. The authors are McKinsey consultants.

Hamermesh, Richard. (1986) *Making Strategy Work*, New York: John Wiley & Sons.
A discussion of the merits and defects of portfolio planning, including a number of case examples.

Hamermesh, Richard G. and White, Roderick E. (1984) "Manage Beyond Portfolio Analysis", *Harvard Business Review*, pp. 103–9, January–February.
Discussion of some of the problems of portfolio planning, and how top management should cope with businesses with different strategic characteristics.

Haspeslagh, Philippe, (1982) "Portfolio Planning: uses and limits", *Harvard Business Review*, pp. 58–73, January–February.
A survey of the extent of use of portfolio planning techniques, and a discussion of their value and limitations.

Hayes, Bob and Abernathy, Bill (1980) "Managing Our Way to Economic Decline", *Harvard Business Review*, July/August.
A critical article on many American management approaches, including portfolio planning.

Hedley Barry, (1977) "Strategy and the 'Business Portfolio'" *Long Range Planning*, 10: 9–15, February.
A good description of the basic BCG portfolio matrix.

McTaggart, James M., Kontes, Peter W. and Mankins, Michael C. (1994) *The Value Imperative: Managing for Superior Shareholder Returns*, New York: The Free Press. The authors are with Marakon Associates, a leading consulting firm in value-based management. Their book provides a framework for the management of shareholder value.

Rapaport, Alfred (1986) *Creating Shareholder Value*, New York: The Free Press. Explanation of the difference between accounting and economic measures of performance, and of how discounted cash flow can be used to evaluate business strategies.

Salter, Malcolm S. and Wienhold, Wolf A. (1979) *Diversification Through Acquisition: Strategies for Creating Economic Value*, New York: The Free Press. Explores frameworks that can help managers identify how diversification can create value and suggests guidelines for value-creating acquisitions.

Chapter 4

Portfolio planning

Robert Grant

PORTFOLIO PLANNING MODELS

Portfolio analysis is probably the best known and most widely applied technique of strategy analysis ever to be developed. The basic idea is to represent the businesses of the diversified company within a simple graphic framework that can assist in four areas of strategy formulation:

- allocating resources;
- formulating business unit strategy;
- setting performance targets;
- analyzing portfolio balance.

Allocating resources Portfolio analysis examines the position of a business unit in relation to the two primary sources of profitability – industry attractiveness and competitive position – thus enabling its investment attractiveness to be compared with that of other business units.

Formulating business unit strategy On the basis of a business unit's location in relation to the same basic variables – industry attractiveness and competitive position – portfolio analysis yields simple and straightforward strategy recommendations. For example, the McKinsey matrix offers three recommendations: grow, hold, or harvest. Further analysis may generate more sophisticated recommendations, for instance, suggesting how a poorly-positioned business may be developed into a more attractively-positioned business.

Setting performance targets To help establish performance targets for individual businesses, standardized procedures based upon a limited number of key environmental and strategic variables can be used to estimate what kind of profit performance can reasonably be expected for such a business.

Analyzing portfolio balance A single diagrammatic representation of the positions of the different businesses within the company is a valuable means of representing the overall balance, cohesiveness, and performance potential. Portfolio analysis can assist in examining several dimensions of portfolio balance:

- cash flow;
- continuity;
- risk.

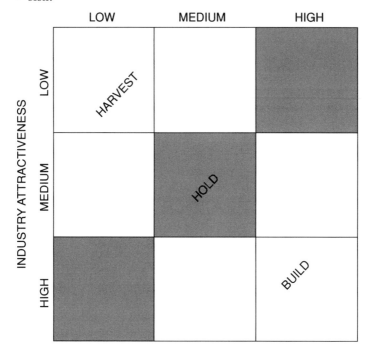

BUSINESS UNIT POSITION

The Criteria

Industry attractiveness
1 Market size.
2 Market growth (real growth rate over 10 years).
3 Industry profitability (3-year av. ROS of the business and its competitors.
4 Cyclicality (av. annual percent trend deviation of sales).
5 Inflation recovery (ability to cover cost increases by higher productivity and increased prices).
6 Importance of overseas markets (ratio of international to US market).

Business unit position
1 Market position (av. US market share; av. international market share; market share relative to three major competitors).
2 Competitive position (superior, equal, or inferior to competitors with regard to quality, technology, manufacturing and cost leadership, distribution and market leadership).
3 Relative profitability (SBU's ROS less av. for 3 main competitors).

Figure 4.1 The McKinsey–General Electric portfolio analysis matrix

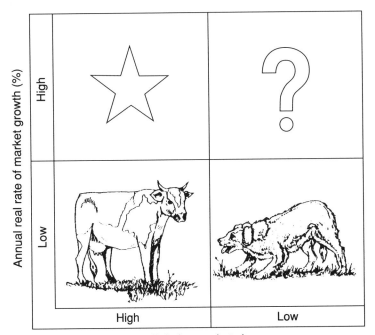

Figure 4.2 The BCG growth-share matrix
Note that relative market share measures the market share of the business relative to the market share of the largest competitor, e.g., if a business has a market share of 10 percent, while the largest competitor has 20 percent, relative market share is 0.5.

Diversified companies often seek independence from the external capital market by achieving a balanced cash flow within the company. This requires that businesses which generate a surplus cash flow finance businesses which are in their growth phases and which are net absorbers of cash.

To maintain the company over the long term, companies frequently seek a portfolio which is composed of businesses in different stages of their life cycle. As older businesses decline and die, they are replaced by younger, growing businesses.

Managing risk may involve risk reduction through spreading the firm's activities over businesses whose returns are imperfectly correlated.

The McKinsey matrix

One of the fruits of General Electric's collaboration with McKinsey and Company was the portfolio analysis matrix shown in Figure 4.1. The two axes of the matrix are familiar: They are the two basic sources of

		High	Low
Annual real rate of market growth (%)	**High**	**Earnings:** high, stable, growing **Cash flow:** neutral **Strategy:** invest for growth	**Earnings:** low, unstable, growing **Cash flow:** negative **Strategy:** analyze to determine whether business can be grown into a star, or will degenarate into a dog
	Low	**Earnings:** high, stable **Cash flow:** high, stable **Strategy:** milk	**Earnings:** low, unstable **Cash flow:** neutral or negative **Strategy:** divest

Relative market share

Figure 4.3 Predictions and recommendations of BCG's growth-share matrix

superior profitability for a firm – industry attractiveness and competitive advantage. In the case of the McKinsey matrix the axes are composite variables. Figure 4.1 also show the individual variables which together determine the levels of industry attractiveness and competitive position for a business unit. The strategy recommendations derived from the matrix are quite simple:

- business units which rank high on both dimensions have excellent profit potential and should be "grown";
- those which rank low on both dimensions have poor prospects and should be "harvested";
- in between business are candidates for a "hold" strategy.

The value of this technique is its simplicity. Even for a highly complex and diverse company such as General Electric, which in 1980 comprised 43 SBUs, the positions of all the firm's SBUs can be combined into a single display. Thus, while the matrix may be simplistic, its power lies in its ability to display the businesses of the whole company and to compress a large amount of data into two dimensions.

The Boston Consulting Group's growth-share matrix

The BCG matrix follows a similar approach: It combines market attractiveness and competitive position to compare the situation of different

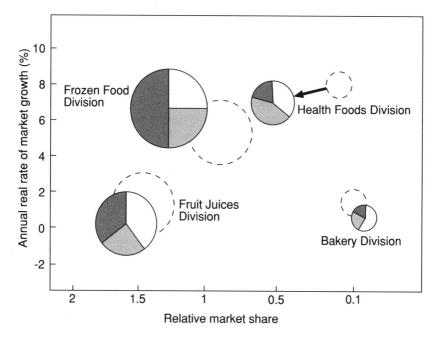

Figure 4.4 Application of the BCG matrix to BM Foods Inc.
Note: (a) the continuous circles show the position of each division in 1987, the broken circles show the position in 1984; (b) the sizes of the circles are proportional to sales revenue *at 1987 prices*; (c) the vertically-shaded segments show sales to supermarket chains, the horizontally-shaded segments show sales to other retailers, the unshaded segments show sales to wholesalers and caterers.

SBUs and to draw strategy prescriptions. It differs from the McKinsey matrix in that the two axes measure single variables: *Market growth rate* and *relative market share* (i.e., the business unit's market share relative to that of the largest competitor). This choice of variables reflected BCG's view, first, that growth is the primary determinant of industry attractiveness, and, secondly, that competitive position is primarily determined by market share (because of its link, through the experience curve, with relative cost position). Figure 4.2 shows how a company's business units may be plotted upon the axes of the BCG matrix.

The BCG matrix provides clear predictions as to the pattern of profit earnings and cash flow associated with the different cells (see Figure 4.3). It also provides recommendations as to appropriate strategies: Milk the cows, invest in the stars, divest the dogs, and analyze the question marks to determine whether they can be grown into stars or will degenerate into dogs.

The BCG's growth-share matrix is even more elementary than the McKinsey matrix and at best it can provide only a rough, first-cut analysis. Corporate strategy decisions should never be taken by the mechanistic application of such a framework. The major weaknesses of the analysis include:

* its focus upon just two determinants of business unit performance,
* the positioning of a business unit in terms of market growth and market share depend critically upon how the market is defined;
* the ambiguous and contentious relationship between each of the variables (market growth and market share), and profitability;
* the assumption that each business is entirely independent and that interdependencies between business units can be ignored.

But in spite of these limitations, the BCG matrix has been widely used and has been found useful even by some of the most sophisticatedly-managed companies in America and Europe. It is the very simplicity of the analysis which is its strength.

* As with other portfolio analyses, all the business units of the firm can be displayed within a single diagram.
* Because information on only two variables is required, the analysis can be prepared easily and quickly.
* It assists senior managers in cutting through vast quantities of detailed information to reveal key differences between the positioning of individual business units.
* The analysis is versatile – in addition to comparing the position of different business units, the framework can be used to examine the performance potential of different products, different brands, different regions, different distribution channels, and different customers.
* It provides a useful point of departure for more detailed analysis and discussion of the competitive positions and strategies of individual business units.

Some of this more detailed analysis can be incorporated within the framework of the BCG matrix. For example, the movement over time in the positions of different businesses can be plotted, and additional descriptive information can be added (see Figure 4.4).

Chapter 5

Value-based planning

Bernard C. Reimann

The traumatic moments of free fall during the October 1987 market plunge shocked everyone who spends his or her career creating value for shareholders. These calamitous events may also have convinced many top managers that they are relatively powerless to affect the way the market values their firms' stock. This is ironic because for much of this decade CEOs have been experimenting with the new technology of stock price management – techniques for enhancing shareholder value.

As recently as 1984, a Louis Harris poll revealed that the majority of top executives of more than 600 companies felt that the market did not value their companies' stock fairly. While only 2 percent felt that their stock was overvalued, 60 percent thought that the market undervalued their shares. Since the thunderous crash in stock prices in October 1987 returned many shares to levels close to those in 1984, it is fair to assume that the majority of CEOs still feel that their companies' shares are undervalued. And if they are, will there be a second season for the takeover tycoons?

After all, what incumbent managers see as an unfair valuation by the market often looks like an opportunity to discover shareholder value to people like T. Boone Pickens or Sir James Goldsmith. The successful "raiders" all have one thing in common (besides a lot of money): They can spot true value – like a favorable ratio of a firm's equity and debt to the real replacement value of its assets.

This means that it's absolutely essential for corporate managers to learn to look at their organizations in the same way a potential raider would. To do this, top management needs to become familiar with the new techniques and concepts of value-based planning and value-based strategic management.

The various value-based approaches are all aimed explicitly at the goal of structuring and managing a corporation in a way that will create more value for its shareholders. However, a number of specific approaches to this common end have gained acceptance in the last decade or so. While all of these approaches share some common key elements, they also differ from one another in some more or less subtle ways. This article highlights important similarities and differences among some of the more popular approaches to value-based planning and outlines the latest trends in their practical application.

WHAT'S NEW ABOUT VALUE-BASED PLANNING?

Value-based planning got its start in the late 1970s, when it was becoming apparent that many otherwise successful corporations were not creating much value for their shareholders. A number of strategy consulting firms and academics began to deal with this problem by modifying the then popular portfolio planning techniques to focus on the goal of creating economic value for the corporation's shareholders.

Just how does value-based planning differ from traditional approaches? Its most significant contribution is the explicit introduction of the perspective of current as well as prospective shareholders into the strategic planning and performance measurement process. Proponents of this new approach recognize that since value is "in the eye of the investor", it must be measured from the investor's point of view.

One reason that so many companies have let themselves get undervalued is that their managers have been measuring corporate performance against standards that have too little to do with market valuation – performance indicators like EPS, ROE or ROI. These accounting-based financial ratios are simply not up to the task of measuring the economic value that sooner or later determines stock price. The reason for this is that they don't look at what really counts – the way investment choices are actually made. When all is said and done, it is the investors' and the capital market's assessment of the relative prospects of a firm that really establish the market value of a company's securities.

All value-based planning methods seek to increase the value investors put on all the businesses of a corporation. For a firm whose securities are traded in the capital markets, this investment value is simply its current stock price. However, since the individual businesses in a corporate portfolio do not have markets for their own securities, and their valuation is not nearly as straightforward, value-based planners are forced to make an analysis that is part calculation and part a set of assumptions about how investors would assign value to a business unit if it were a free-standing company. That is, what performance measures would the investor select to estimate the value of a business, and its strategy, in the corporate portfolio?

The main contrasts between the different approaches to value-based planning center around the assumptions underlying the investor decision process. More precisely, they diverge in the way they address the following investor concerns:

THE "CAPM"

The CAPM (capital asset pricing model) assumes that an investor expects to be compensated in direct proportion to the degree of risk inherent in a security's future cash flows. The simplest version of the model assumes that the investor adds a risk premium to the interest rate of a virtually risk-free security, such as a government bond. The risk premium, in turn, is a function of the expected variability of the future yields of a given investment.

In pricing common stocks, for example, the risk premium would depend on the risk of the stock market average, adjusted by the beta coefficient. This beta coefficient reflects the volatility of a stock's price, relative to that of the market as a whole. If its beta is greater than one, a stock is more volatile, and therefore riskier than the market. A beta less than one is below average in risk, while a beta of zero would imply a risk-free security. Services like Value Line regularly publish betas for publicly traded stocks, based on the variability of their past prices.

The market risk premium would be determined from the difference between the average return on the market (e.g., for the S&P 500) and the risk-free rate. For example, if the current rate on long-term government bonds were 7.0 percent and the average return from the S&P 500 were 12.0 percent, the market risk premium would be 5.0 percent. A stock with a beta of 1.5 (i.e., 50 percent more variable than the market average) would have a cost of capital of 14.5 percent, calculated as follows:

COC = Risk-Free Interest Rate + Beta × Market Risk Premium
COC = 7% + 1.5 × 5% = 7% + 7.5% = <u>14.5%</u>

- How risky is the investment relative to other opportunities?
- How much cash is the investment expected to return?
- Over what period of time will the returns be forthcoming?

RISK AND THE COST OF CAPITAL

An investor's assessment of the relative riskiness of an investment is reflected in the corporation's (or the business unit's) cost of capital (COC). The COC is the minimum, or threshold return that will induce an investor to buy a given security. For an explanation of how COC is calculated see CAPM box.

Measures like EPS and ROI don't reflect any changes in risk or cost of capital for the underlying investment that generated the reported earnings. This can make these rate-of-return measures quite deceiving, as illustrated by the fact that many firms who reported steady increases in EPS or ROE over the last decade failed to create much, if any, economic value. It may well be that their capital costs were rising even more rapidly than their returns.

A PIONEERING APPROACH

Marakon Associates is one of the pioneers of the value-based approach to portfolio planning. This consulting firm was among the first to call attention to the importance of the cost of capital in assessing business performance. Marakon emphasizes that firms cannot create value unless they invest in projects where rates of return exceed capital costs.

Therefore, Marakon urges its clients not to look at ROE alone, but to focus on the "spread" between return on equity and the cost of capital of the SBUs in the corporate portfolio. Investment in the growth of positive-spread businesses is advisable since this growth will contribute to shareholder value. Units with negative spreads must either be "turned around" toward higher profitability or "sacrificed". That is, growth may have to be sacrificed to improve the profitability spread, or to minimize the impact of a negative spread between ROE and COC. If a negative spread persists, divestiture is the only way to avoid the erosion of shareholder value.

The equity-spread approach is intuitively appealing, because of its apparent simplicity, and because it promises to work wonders in improving a corporate portfolio that has been "undervalued" by the stock market. Equity-spread performance measures seem to make it relatively easy to identify the value-creating "stars" and destructive "dogs" in the portfolio and take the appropriate actions. Corporate restructuring by the reallocation of resources from value-destroying units (those with negative spread) to the more profitable value creators can, indeed, result in some dramatic improvements of stock prices. Not surprisingly, Marakon's methodology has been quite well received by corporate strategists and portfolio managers. Top corporations that have adopted this approach to measuring performance include Atlantic Richfield, Levi Strauss, Owens-Illinois, Sun, Union Oil of California, and Westinghouse.

While the equity spread can be effective in identifying extreme under- or over-performers, it may not be sensitive enough to "fine tune" the corporate portfolio strategy. First of all, the size of spread is affected by the way debt and risk are assigned to a particular business. Second, the equity spread only reflects the potential value contribution from profitability, ignoring other important sources of value, such as deferred taxes and the terminal value of the business at the end of the planning period. Finally, the spread improperly compares an economic, market-determined value (cost of equity) with an accounting value (ROE).

THE IMPORTANCE OF CASH FLOW: THE "R" FACTOR

The real question is: What do sophisticated investors look at when they search for a place to park their funds? Certainly not accrual-accounting-based numbers like ROE or ROI! According to Joel Stern, of Stern Stewart & Company, investors are only interested in cash, and accounting conventions just muddy the waters. Among those conventions that create the most serious distortions are depreciation and capitalization policies, inventory valuation (LIFO vs. FIFO), and amortization of goodwill.

One of Stern Stewart's answers to the problem has been to develop a measure of return on capital employed (R) that has been corrected for accounting distortions. The numerator of R is NOPAT (operating profit, before financing charges and before bookkeeping entries having no effect on cash, but after taxes actually paid). In the denominator is total capital employed to operate the business, including all interest-bearing debt and total shareholders' equity, as well as any equity equivalents such as deferred taxes and LIFO reserves. (See Stern Stewart's R and EVA box.)

From an investor's perspective, this cash-based return measure has some advantages over ROE as an indicator of value creation. First of all, it looks at the actual cash flows rather than at accounting profits. Second, R explicitly recognizes the fact that debt and equity are both equally viable ways of financing an investment. Finally, the spread between R and the cost of capital (C) does not compare economic with accounting measures.

Stern Stewart combines this cash-based version of the spread with the level of capital invested to come up with an indicator of the value-creation potential of a business. Their EVA (economic value added) is simply the product of the spread (R-C) and total capital employed in the business. They suggest three alternative means to increase shareholder value, based on a business unit's EVA:

- Increase the economic earnings derived from the existing capital base. This would mean improving the efficiency of business units without increasing their size.
- Grow only those businesses whose economic returns exceed their capital costs (or risks) – that is, those with positive spreads.
- Reduce the drag on the value of uneconomic, negative-spread businesses by shrinking them and diverting capital to positive-spread units. Or, improve the spread by selling or closing the least efficient parts.

Actually, Stern Stewart's recommendations are strikingly similar to Marakon's – to turn around, shrink, or even divest business units with

STERN STEWART'S R AND EVA
Example Business Income Statement for 1987
(with Adjustments to Cash Equivalents)

Net Sales	$20,000
Cost of Goods Sold	12,000
Selling, General and Administrative	6,000
Net Operating Profit	2,000
Other Income	120
Earnings Before Interest and Taxes	2,120
Cash Operating Taxes*	927
NOPAT	$1,193

* Cash Taxes Computed as follows:

Provision for Taxes	$975
Increase in Deferred Taxes	(35)
Cash Taxes Actually Paid	940
Tax Shield of Interest Expense	42
Tax on Interest Income	(55)
Cash Operating Taxes	$927

Selected Balance Sheet Information

Capital Employed:	
Net Working Capital	2,500
Net Property, Plant and Equipment	3,500
Other Assets (e.g., Deferred Taxes)	337
Total Capital Employed (TCE)	$6,337
Increase in Capital over 1986 (I)	634
Net Cash Flow (NOPAT − I)	$559

Calculation of Stern Stewart's EVA:

Cost of Capital (C) =	15%
R = NOPAT/TCE =	18.83%
"Spread" = (R − C) =	3.83%
EVA = (R − C)*TCE =	$242

negative spreads and reallocate capital to growing positive-spread units. This should come as no surprise, since the two approaches are similar in concept and differ only in their application. That is, both assume that value depends on a combination of returns and growth; however,

Marakon looks at equity only, while Stern Stewart considers total capital and adjusts the accounting numbers to a cash-flow basis.

Marakon and Stern Stewart should come up with similar recommendations in many cases since ROEs tend to be highly correlated with cash flows. However, in those situations where accounting conventions introduce substantial distortions, the two approaches can result in very different conclusions. And these, in fact, may be just what the corporate raiders are looking for. Successful takeover artists are known to have an exceptional "nose" for value. Their secret is their ability to look beyond the reported (accounting) numbers and sniff out the real cash-generating capacity of the business in a corporate portfolio.

DISCOUNTING FUTURE CASH FLOWS

This brings us to another limitation of the spread approaches – even if based on cash returns. Investors worry not only about the size but also about the timing of expected cash returns. This is especially true for raiders and LBO specialists, since they usually take on a lot of debt that must be repaid out of the anticipated stream of cash flows from the purchased businesses. The spread approaches described above do not explicitly consider this time dimension. In particular, they fail to take into account the terminal (or residual) value of a business unit at the end of its planning horizon.

Typically, less than a third of the present (economic) value of a business can be attributed to its expected cash flows for the next five to ten years. The bulk of its value comes from the future value of the business as a going concern at the end of the planning horizon. The full economic return generated by a business unit's strategy depends on the estimated cash flows during the planning period, plus the projected terminal value of the business. Therefore, the returns and cash flow during the planning period may not be a complete indicator of a business unit's economic value. In fact, high cash flows during the planning period may come at the expense of a firm's future value, while low, or even negative cash flows may simply be the result of heavy front-end investment in building the business.

This problem of future value can be handled by applying basic capital budgeting techniques to business-unit valuation. Not surprisingly, most value-based planning approaches rely heavily on DCF (discounted cash flow) techniques to determine the net present value (NPV) or internal rate of return (IRR) of business units.

The major drawback of this DCF valuation is its complexity. The added complications come from several sources. First of all, a firm's accounting data must be translated into cash flows. Second, a series of cash flows must be projected over a future planning period. Third, an

DCF VALUATION
EXAMPLE BUSINESS

	Current 1987	Forecast → 1988	1989	1990	1991	1992
NOPAT	$1,193	1,312	1,444	1,588	1,747	1,922
Capital Investment	634	697	767	844	928	1,021
Net Cash Flow	559	598	640	685	733	784
Residual Value (1992)*						12,811
Present Value Factor		0.870	0.756	0.658	0.572	0.497
Present Value of Cash Flow		520	484	450	419	390
Total PV of Cash Flows		2,264				
PV of Residual Value		6,369				
Total Present Value		$8,633				

ASSUMPTIONS:
Discount Rate = 15%
Growth Rate = 10%

* Perpetuity: Residual Value = NOPAT/Discount Rate = $1,922/.15.

appropriate cost of capital must be determined for discounting the projected cash flows to their present value. Finally, the investment value of a business must be estimated at the beginning and end of the planning period.

DECISION SUPPORT FOR VALUE-BASED PLANNERS

One popular solution to the complexities of DCF valuation has been the development of computer models to facilitate or automate the necessary calculations. Many companies have developed their own customized models with mainframe-based decision-support software like IFPS, or PC-based spreadsheet products like Lotus 1–2–3. Some strategy consulting firms have even come out with their own proprietary software designed to facilitate the application of their particular approach to value-based planning.

A good example is the versatile and relatively easy to use decision-support package provided by The Alcar Group for IBM-compatible PCs. Alcar's "The Value Planner" is particularly useful for calculating the value-creation potential of alternative business strategies. It consists of two main parts: "The Forecaster," for projecting pro forma financial statements; and "The Valuator," for assessing the impact of various financial variables on the economic (DCF) value of a business or strategy.

A software package like Alcar's has a number of benefits for managers attempting to implement value-based planning. First of all, it is designed to accept readily available accounting information and automatically translate it into the numbers needed for value-based planning calculations. Secondly, it takes the user through the major steps and assumptions required by the DCF process. This not only makes the results easier to understand (and to explain to others), it actually helps educate the user in the financial accounting relationships and concepts that underlie the value-based planning framework. Finally, this type of software enables managers to simulate different scenarios and test the sensitivity of value to changes in inputs, or "value drivers," such as revenues, profit margins and asset turnover.

As might be expected, the Alcar software does reflect a particular approach to value-based planning – that of its developers, Alfred Rappaport and Carl Noble. Rappaport is probably the leading authority and writer on the subject of shareholder value creation. He has described his approach in a number of articles, as well as in a recent book: *Creating Shareholder Value* (New York: Free Press, 1986).

Although he is an accountant by training, Rappaport is clearly among the most enthusiastic proponents of the economic, cash-based approach to measuring shareholder value. Where he departs from some of the other proponents of value-based planning is in his determination of the investment values of a business at the beginning and end of the planning period.

THE PROBLEM OF BUSINESS VALUATION

This problem of establishing the true value of a business as a going concern is one of the most critical and controversial in applying the value-based planning approach. In fact, a key difference among the approaches centers around the way this problem is handled.

The difficulty is that we have no direct and reliable method for assigning a market value to an individual business unit. One exception would be a newly acquired business whose market value would simply be the total price paid for it. Obviously, an equivalent investment valuation is much more difficult to establish for a business that is already in the corporate portfolio. Many analysts simply look at the book value of total assets. Yet, over time, this book value can diverge considerably from the true economic value of a business. For one thing, such accounting conventions as depreciation may not accurately reflect the true change in the value of the assets over time. For another, the book value does not reflect the potential earning power of a business.

For these reasons, others have chosen to base their assessment on cash flow, capitalized at the investor's cost of capital. The rationale is that investors assign value to a security in proportion to its expected cash returns. They adjust for risk by capitalizing the expected earnings stream by their capital cost (which is the return they require to compensate them for the riskiness of the investment). This is the popular "perpetuity" assumption that treats the investment like an annuity with perpetual cash payments equivalent to the projected annual after-tax earnings.

Rappaport favors this perpetuity method of valuation for both his beginning "pre-strategy" and ending "post-strategy" business values. This means that the investment value of the business at the start of the planning period is calculated by capitalizing its after-tax operating profit in the previous year. (Or, if profits were too erratic, a "normalized" or trend value for several years might be used.)

Similarly, the value of the business at the end of the planning horizon is determined by capitalizing the final year's operating profit after tax. Here, the rationale is that the business will have reached a point where the returns on any further investment will have been driven down to the cost of capital (due to an inevitable deterioration of its competitive situation). Therefore, any further investment would not add or detract from the value of the business, resulting in the equivalent of a perpetual annuity equal to the free cash flow of the business.

This perpetuity assumption greatly simplifies the valuation process and is probably satisfactory in a great many situations. In fact, many consultants and practitioners of the shareholder value approach, including Stern Stewart, use the perpetuity assumption in their DCF valuation models. On the other hand, a number of experts in value-based planning have criticized this assumption as not being warranted in many cases.

MARKET VALUE MULTIPLES

Another valuation method that has gained wide acceptance by practitioners is based on the use of market multiples. The idea is to find a business-level equivalent of the market/book multiple. To establish such a multiple, we must find the indicators, or "drivers," of market value that can be measured at the business as well as at the corporate level.

The proponents of this approach have developed models to predict stock prices and have tested them on historical data. A number of research studies have demonstrated that the combination of returns and growth have tracked stock prices very well over extensive time periods. Researchers from SPI (Strategic Planning Institute) found that two additional variables improved the relationship still further: R&D expenditures, and times interest earned (this was based on multiple regression analysis of the PIMS data). The implications of these results are both interesting and logical. R&D expenditures suggest that a firm has long-term orientation, and interest coverage is an indicator of its financial risk.

"PERPETUITY"

A "perpetuity" of after-tax earnings is perhaps the most popular and convenient assumption for assigning value to a going concern. The expected earnings from a business are assumed to behave like a perpetual annuity, so they can be capitalized (i.e., divided by the cost of capital). The perpetuity assumption applies to a business that is only able to invest at its cost of capital for the foreseeable future. The total asset value of such a business will remain unchanged "in perpetuity." Any capital investment would just be enough to keep the current asset base constant (i.e., equal to depreciation). The after-tax earnings can then be treated like a constant, perpetual annual cash flow.

The perpetuity assumption greatly simplifies the valuation process, and is appropriate for many businesses with relatively predictable earnings. The best candidates are businesses whose product markets have reached or are approaching maturity, like corn flakes or Coca-Cola.

However, this assumption can give misleading readings for short-lived or cyclical products like hula-hoops or couch potatoes. Clearly the assumption of stable earnings would not apply here. The assumption may also be less than satisfactory for a business with a strong, sustainable competitive advantage, particularly if its market(s) enjoy excellent long-term growth prospects as well. Such a business should have no problem investing above the cost of capital over the longer term. Some examples are Merck in pharmaceuticals, Genentech in biotechnology, and Microsoft in computer software. On the other hand, some businesses may actually be forced to invest below their cost of capital in the long run. Many examples could be found in depressed industries like steel and autos, as well as among public utilities, especially those with nuclear power plants.

Whether a basic two-variable model or a more complex one is used to simulate the market, the multiple approach works as follows. First, the model is calibrated to yield an M/B multiple of 1.0 for an "average" business unit. This business would have a simulated market value equal to its book value. Businesses scoring relatively high on the combination of value drivers would have multiples greater than 1.0, while lower scores would result in multiples below 1.0.

The matrix in Table 5.1 illustrates this method by giving asset multiples for different combinations of return on assets and growth in assets. It is based on a model that computes the present value of future cash flows presupposed by projected returns and growth. (Since this matrix was derived for a discount rate of 15 percent, another would have to be used for different discount rates.) If, for example, a business with a return on net assets (RONA) of 18 percent were growing at a rate of 5 percent, its M/B multiple would be 1.27 (see Table 5.1). The same

---

VALUE-BASED PLANNING AT THE COCA-COLA COMPANY

Some recent actions of the Coca-Cola Company provide good illustrations of the VBP approach. A value-based portfolio analysis revealed that its Entertainment Business Sector was not contributing its fair share to corporate value. A key reason was that the business was very different in nature from Coke's other endeavors. In particular, its performance was much more volatile, resulting in greater risk and, therefore, a relatively high cost of capital. Top management decided to spin the entertainment business off as a separate unit, by combining it with its 38.6 percent-owned Tri-Star Pictures Inc. Coca-Cola will keep only a minority financial interest in the new company, to be called Columbia Pictures Entertainment, Inc. Since this move will reduce the Coca-Cola Company's risk considerably, the stock market reacted very favorably to the news.

However, Coca-Cola used the VBP approach not only to decide which businesses to divest or acquire but also for fixing poorly performing individual businesses. The VBP analysis uncovered a rather surprising fact: its mainstay soda fountain business was actually destroying shareholder value at a worrysome rate. This discovery came as quite a shock, since the business had always been regarded as highly profitable. After all, there weren't a lot of bottles or cans to fill, transport, and store. What management had not realized was that, over time, the business had become quite capital intensive. The return on capital was only 12.5 percent, while the company's cost of capital was estimated to be 16 percent. Thus, every dollar invested in this business was dissipating shareholder value.

The main culprit turned out to be an expensive five-gallon stainless steel container used to transport the Coke syrup. The business switched to disposable bag-in-a-box containers and to 50-gallon containers for large customers. Its return on capital rose to 17 percent and, by increasing its leverage, the company was able to reduce its cost of capital to 14 percent. Suddenly the business was turned into a strong contributor to shareholder value.

---

growth rate for a business with an RONA of 10 percent would give a multiple of only 0.62.

The fact that this multiple is less than one should be expected, since the spread between RONA and the cost of capital (15 percent) is negative. In fact, a lower growth rate should yield a better multiple, since the drag on value of a negative spread would be lessened. This is borne out by the multiple of 0.65 for RONA 10 percent and growth 2 percent.

The value-creation trade-offs between profitability and growth can also be illustrated by a diagram, such as the one shown in Figure 5.1 Here, the simulated market-to-book (assets) multiples are shown as a function of the spread between returns on assets and the cost of capital. The diagram dramatizes the fact that growth is a two-edged sword in its

Table 5.1 Table of asset multiples for different combinations of returns and growth (Discount Rate = 15%)

		Asset Growth (Annual Rate)				
		2%	3%	4%	5%	6%
Return on Assets	10%	0.65	0.64	0.63	0.62	0.61
	11%	0.72	0.72	0.71	0.70	0.70
	12%	0.79	0.79	0.79	0.79	0.78
	13%	0.87	0.87	0.87	0.87	0.87
	14%	0.94	0.94	0.94	0.95	0.95
	15%	1.01	1.02	1.02	1.03	1.03
	16%	1.08	1.09	1.10	1.11	1.12
	17%	1.15	1.17	1.18	1.19	1.20
	18%	1.23	1.24	1.25	1.27	1.28
	19%	1.30	1.32	1.33	1.35	1.37
	20%	1.37	1.39	1.41	1.43	1.45

effect on shareholder value. Business units A and D, for example, are both growing at a 20 percent rate. However, the negative spread of business D will result in a substantial loss of value. The corporate portfolio would clearly be better off if investment capital were reallocated away from D and C to positive-spread businesses such as A or B.

This market value multiple lends itself very well to simulating both the beginning and ending market values of a business unit on the basis of the book value of its assets. For the beginning value, the multiple is determined from the value drivers of the business (e.g. return and growth) and applied to its current book value. This is naturally a bit more difficult to determine for the terminal value, since both book assets and value drivers must be projected to the end of the planning period.

However, a key advantage of this multiple approach is that its validity can readily be tested with historical data. This is exactly what the SPI researchers did with a sample of 600 firms from the Compustat data base. They found that value-creation estimates based on multiples of either investment (assets) or sales correlated much more closely with actual shareholder value creation (i.e., stock price appreciation plus dividends) than did accounting measures of ROS, ROI, and EPS, or capitalized earnings (whether normalized or not).

THE Q RATIO

Still another way to simulate the investor's perspective on value is to focus on the amount that investors actually put at risk initially and adjust that amount to its current value. As with any alternative investment

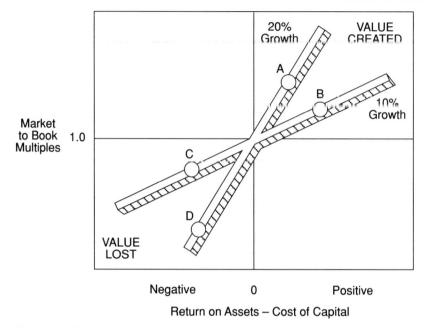

Figure 5.1 Market to book multiples as a function of the "spread" between return on assets and capital cost
Source: Adapted from Bernard C. Reimann, *Managing for Value*, Oxford, Ohio: The Planning Forum, 1987

such as a bond, what investors originally put in must be adjusted for inflation to be compared to what they actually get back.

CMA (Callard, Madden & Associates) and HOLT Planning Associates are consulting and research firms who take this position. They focus on the real value of the assets employed by a business unit by adjusting the original investment for inflation. Tobin's Q ratio plays a central role in this approach. This Q ratio compares the market value of a firm's equity and debt to the real (inflation adjusted) value of its net assets. Thus this Q ratio is a market to book (M/B) multiple with the book value of net assets in the denominator adjusted for the effects of inflation. (See Tobin's Q Box, p. 114.)

To apply the Q ratio concept to corporate strategic planning, an internal equivalent of the current market value of individual business units is needed. Both HOLT and CMA estimate the present value of a unit with a DCF technique such as the ones described earlier. Where the Q ratio approach departs from traditional DCF methods is in that returns, asset growth, and discount rates are all adjusted for inflation. The rationale is that investors adjust their expected returns for anticipated inflation when pricing alternative investments. Therefore the true, or "real," value of a business must also reflect this inflation factor.

The numerator of the Q ratio (present value of a business unit) is calculated by discounting the unit's expected stream of net cash receipts over the planning horizon, including its residual value at the end of the planning period. HOLT and CMA do not make simplifying assumptions such as a post-horizon "perpetual" cash flow. A business unit's real ROI is expected to follow a normal life cycle and approach the S&P 400 average of about 7 percent over the long term, with a real asset growth rate of about 3 percent. The residual value (or "asset release") is estimated as a function of future real ROI and growth, which are assumed to fall (or rise) from the values projected to the end of the planning horizon toward these long-term industrial averages.

Businesses with Q ratios greater than one are value creators, while those whose ratios fall below one are destroying shareholder value. Once these Qs have been determined, the application is essentially similar to other value-based approaches. That is, resources are to be reallocated away from low Q businesses to units with the highest Q ratios. The Q ratio also is useful in developing executive compensation plans. For example, CMA's data base can provide the Q ratios of various publicly held firms which can be used as a basis for comparing company performance to that of a selected "peer" group.

THE INVESTOR'S DISCOUNT RATE

Another value-based planning controversy centers around the definition and determination of the appropriate investor's discount rate or cost of capital. By far the most popular approach is the capital asset pricing model (CAPM). (See CAPM box.) However, the validity of the CAPM method for determining the discount rate recently has come under serious attack. For example, CMA's research shows that the CAPM-based discount rate, even after adjusting for inflation, differed considerably from that determined empirically for the S&P 400 over the period from 1948 to 1981. CMA researchers offer two major reasons for this discrepancy:

- The CAPM model tends to overestimate risk.
- It does not take into consideration the impact of personal taxes on investors.

A recognition of the inadequacy of the CAPM model has resulted in the search for a better model. One that has gained some notoriety recently is based on arbitrage pricing theory (APT). The APT model is actually just an extension of the CAPM, in that it simply offers a further breakdown of the two components of the riskless rate and market risk premium. The risk premium is considered to be a function of both the risk itself and of the term of the risk exposure. Similarly, the riskless rate

TOBIN'S Q

The Q ratio, developed in the early 1960s by the Nobel Prize winning economist James Tobin, is a ratio of the market value of a company's physical assets to the cost of replacing those assets in current dollars. Q is the economist's way of explaining how the level of stock market prices affects capital spending. A Q ratio greater than one means the stock market values a company's assets more than their actual cost, while a ratio less than one means the exact opposite. With a high Q (greater than one), corporations have a strong incentive to invest in new plant and equipment since the market values each dollar of investment at over a dollar. Conversely, Qs less than one reduce the incentive for capital investment but encourage acquisition via stock purchases. Tobin and his colleagues have demonstrated a strong correlation between the Q ratio and the level of fixed nonresidential investment for US nonfinancial corporations.

The Q ratio makes a particularly good indicator of whether stocks are over- or undervalued. It is interesting to note that the average Q ratio for the top 500 US corporations has been estimated to have sunk as low as 0.50 in 1981. This means that an investor ("raider") could buy the productive assets of the average large corporation for as little as 50 cents on the dollar. And, since the 50 percent figure was only an average, the *Fortune* 500 must have included some real bargains! No wonder shrewd "prospectors" like T. Boone Pickens were so successful in finding tempting takeover targets!

Of course, the rash of takeovers and LBOs, along with the strong bull market helped to bring the Q ratio well over the 1.0 mark by the summer of 1987. This fact should have served as a warning that the market was getting over-valued. Those who really believed in Q and took appropriate actions must have saved some serious losses or even profited from last October's crash!

The financial research and consulting firm of Callard, Madden and Associates (CMA) pioneered the application of this Q ratio concept to the microeconomic problem of measuring the shareholder value creation potential for individual firms. CMA's Q is defined as the ratio of the firm's market value of equity plus debt to the real value of securityholder net assets (total assets less non-debt liabilities). CMA has presented empirical evidence that an inflation-adjusted spread between cash returns and the cost of capital correlates much more strongly with the real market value to book ratio (i.e., the Q ratio) than the nominal, accounting-based equivalent.

At the business level we have no way to determine a direct market value of equity and debt. Therefore, CMA calculates the present value of the projected cash flows (adjusted for expected inflation), discounted by the real cost of capital.

To summarize, the Q ratio is calculated as follows:

At the Corporate Level:

$$Q = \frac{\text{Market Value of Equity and Debt}}{\text{Inflation-adjusted Assets}}$$

At the Business Unit Level:

$$Q = \frac{\text{Present Value of Real Cash Flows}}{\text{Inflation-adjusted Assets}}$$

is composed of a basic real rate plus an adjustment for risks of current and expected inflation. However, empirical research so far has not demonstrated that the APT model is superior enough to the CAPM to warrant its added complexity.

CMA and HOLT have dealt with the inadequacy of the CAPM discount rate in a different way. Instead of trying to come up with a better theory, they use an empirical approach to come up with a "market derived" real investor discount rate. This real discount rate is calculated from actual stock prices and the "warranted" prices based on the present value of anticipated net cash receipts.

The market derived discount rate is that rate which will discount a company's projected net cash returns, expressed in current dollars (the warranted stock price), to the current market price. That is, this discount is equivalent to the IRR (internal rate of return) which will make the present value of future cash flows just equal to the actual market price of the investment. When applied to the whole market (e.g., the S&P 500), this IRR represents the average expected return, or cost of capital, for all stock market investors. (This is also how analysts calculate bond yields, based on the anticipated coupon returns and current bond prices.)

VALUE-BASED PLANNING IN PRACTICE

The discussion to this point has demonstrated some of the complex variety of the approaches to value-based planning. The variety reflects the uncertainties inherent in trying to simulate investor behavior – and, to some degree, the efforts of consultants and researchers in this area to differentiate their work from that of others.

Which of the approaches is best? Each method has something going for it. Marakon's and Stern Stewart's are the simplest, Alcar's has the best software support, and CMA and HOLT's have the strongest empirical evidence. Finally, SPI's multiples approach to valuation makes the most strategic sense since it explicitly considers the importance of the business unit's competitive position.

In actual practice, however, the significance of the methodological differences tends to be dwarfed by the very real difficulties of implementing the shareholder value approach. There is little doubt that more complex methods, including such refinements as inflation adjustment and additional variables, improve the accuracy of the valuation process. What is open to debate is whether the added accuracy compensates for the increase in complexity. One reason for the popularity of Marakon's equity spread method is its ease of application. The same can be said for the controversial simplifying assumption of perpetuity cash flows in business valuation.

But even the best value-based plans won't score big gains if those charged with carrying them out drop the ball. It doesn't really matter which technique is chosen. The important issue is that it must be understood and accepted by the managers of the business units – the people whose actions actually create value. Therefore, the successful implementation of value-based planning techniques requires both appropriate support systems, and effective incentive systems.

Software like Alcar's can help business managers learn to appreciate how their units contribute (or fail to contribute) to the shareholder value created by the corporation as a whole. This understanding, coupled with their active involvement in the value-based planning process, can help motivate these executives to choose strategies and actions that will create shareholder value. A top management review process focused on these goals can further reinforce this motivation.

However, the real key to motivating executives is an effective compensation system. No value-based planning effort is complete without executive incentives focused on value creation. Actually, one of the most popular incentives for senior executives is very closely tied to shareholder value – stock options. However, stock options have only very limited value as incentives at the business level, which is simply too far removed from the action in the stock market. Even for top-level corporate executives, stock options have their limits as incentives, since the payoff is affected by a number of variables – such as market conditions and inflation rates – that are beyond their control.

The contribution of value-based techniques is that they provide business-level performance measures that simulate market value creation. This makes it possible to design incentives based on business-level targets for value drivers. Stern Stewart, for example, has developed executive compensation plans based on the EVA measure; Alcar focuses on such value drivers as growth and return on sales; and CMA uses the Q ratio.

AVOIDING NUMBER BLINDNESS

Value-based planning can provide major benefits for firms who apply the technique. The list of companies who have restructured and repositioned their businesses with the guidance of value-based planning includes some major success stories. Nevertheless, the apparent success of value-based planning methods has a downside too.

A particularly serious danger is that the quantitative and sophisticated nature of the methods may divert attention from the equally important, but less tangible, qualitative aspects of strategy. Managers must be extremely wary of a natural tendency not to look past their computer-generated numbers. They must not forget that the value-based output numbers are highly sensitive to variations in the value driver inputs. This sensitivity can be illustrated with a market value multiple matrix like the one shown in Table 5.1. It demonstrates that a change of just one percentage point in return can result in a change of 8 percent or more in the asset multiple.

Since shareholder value creation is so sensitive to its business-level drivers, it is vital that the latter be projected as accurately as possible. Yet, in practice, these very inputs are often the Achilles heel of the value-based planning process. This is because corporate management must rely on its business-level managers' predictions of the returns and growth of their units. These predictions may be inaccurate for a variety of reasons. First of all, the executives may simply do a poor job of assessing their business situation, or conditions may change in some unexpected fashion.

However, executives may also exaggerate the expected performance to make themselves look better and get a larger share of corporate resources. Or, if they want to avoid goals that are difficult to reach, they may want to paint a more pessimistic picture.

To help avoid these kinds of inaccuracies, value-based techniques must be complemented with a heavy dose of qualitative strategic analysis. Business managers must be encouraged to provide qualitative descriptions of their business strategies and competitive situations. One way some firms have accomplished this is by educating their executives in competitive analysis using a framework like Michael Porter's. General managers are then expected to defend their performance projections with qualitative as well as quantitative information about such strategic factors as trends in their market environments and their specific competitive advantages.

QUALITATIVE VALUE-BASED PLANNING

Another useful framework is that provided by the PIMS (profit impact of market strategy) methodology. A product of the Strategic Planning

Institute in Cambridge, Mass., PIMS is based on an extensive data base of the characteristics, both financial and strategic, of some 3,000 business units. A particularly useful service offered by SPI is the PAR ROI report. (See PIMS PAR ROI box.)

PIMS can contribute to value-based planning in at least three major ways. First, the business unit's Par ROI can provide a benchmark value for a "reality test" of performance projections. A wide discrepancy will require justification or further investigation. The PIMS variables also act as a useful checklist for variables or characteristics that are important in the strategic analysis of a business. Finally, a sample of look-alike, or peer, businesses can be used to simulate the impact of various changes in strategy.

Empirical research with the PIMS data base has also yielded some useful guidelines for reviewing business-level value-based planning projections. One recent longitudinal study revealed, for example, that businesses starting out with a strong competitive position are far more likely to increase shareholder value over the ensuing five-year period than those with a weak position. While this finding is not a big surprise, it does provide empirical verification of the improbability of the "hockey stick forecast." A manager who projects high value creation for a poorly positioned business would have to provide some strong strategic arguments to show why and how that business can beat the odds.

THE POTENTIAL OF VALUE-BASED PLANNING

If value-based planning techniques share one major flaw, it is their strong identification with the discipline of finance and its associated emphasis on complex equations, esoteric theories, and number crunching. This rigorous complexity has undoubtedly stood in the way of their effective application in many firms who could have benefited from a shareholder value orientation. On the one hand, a great many firms or business units simply wanted nothing to do with value-based planning because of its very complexity. On the other, many of the firms who made a serious effort to implement the approach became so involved in the method, that "number blindness" set in and distracted managers from the vital job of more basic, qualitative strategic analysis of environmental trends, competitive advantages, etc.

So far, the contribution of value-based planning has been most visible in the typical corporate portfolio restructuring strategy, where business units with a poor fit (or spread) are divested or even liquidated, businesses with good profit and growth prospects are acquired, while the businesses remaining in the portfolio are reorganized for greater efficiency. This type of restructuring can have a substantial and immediate impact on shareholder value. However, these benefits tend to be short-lived. A corporation can keep buying and divesting businesses just

---

PIMS PAR ROI

THE PIMS PAR ROI REPORT: The PIMS model gives an expected value of the returns for a business unit, given its strategic position and market/industry situation. This expected performance is based on a complex statistical regression analysis of all the businesses in the PIMS data base. This model explains over 70 percent of the variance in ROI among these businesses. A "Par ROI Report" lists the 28 most important factors from the PIMS data and their relative impact on profitability. It also provides a summary of the impact on the Par ROI of the four major categories of these 28 factors. A sample of such a summary for a hypothetical business is reproduced below:

Par ROI Summary for Business ABC:	FACTOR IMPACT (pct. points)
● COMPETITIVE POSITION (Market Share, Quality, etc.)	− 0.7
● LIFE-CYCLE STAGE (Growth Rate, R&D, New Products, etc.)	+ 0.5
● MARKETING ENVIRONMENT (Concentration, Marketing Intensity, etc.)	+ 1.2
● CAPITAL AND PRODUCTION STRUCTURE (Investment, Productivity, etc.)	− 2.8
Total Impact	− 1.8
+ Average ROI (PIMS Businesses)	20.2%
'Par' Return on Investment for this Business	18.4%

PIMS as a Guide to Management Action: The PIMS Par ROI Report can give some clues for management actions to be taken for improving profitability. The PIMS variables reflect four categories of factors found to be important to business profitability:

● Competitive position.
● Stage of life cycle.
● Marketing environment.
● Capital and production structure.

The most serious strategic problem of the hypothetical business unit illustrated above is its relatively poor capital and production structure. This weakness, combined with its slightly inferior competitive position are "costing" this business a total of 3.5 percentage points (− 2.8 and − 0.7%) in profitability relative to the PIMS mean. On the other hand, this business is above the PIMS average in the attractiveness of its market environment (+ 1.2%) and life cycle stage (+ 0.5%). Thse positive factors partially offset its internal weaknesses to give a net negative impact of 1.8 percentage points.

so long; at some point it must begin to manage the remaining businesses themselves in a way that will contribute to economic value.

Value-based planning methods have the potential to play an even more important role in the on-going process of long-term shareholder value creation. They can provide reliable and valid rulers for measuring business unit performance as well as for evaluating alternative strategies. Value-based planning methods also give management the means to measure the business-level drivers of value, such as profit margins, growth, and asset management. This is particularly important in developing an effective executive incentive plan focused on business value creation. It also provides a way for business-level managers to appreciate their units' contribution to shareholder value creation.

TOWARD VALUE-BASED STRATEGIC MANAGEMENT

However, one serious stumbling block in the decentralization of strategic decisions is top management's fear that autonomous business units might pursue strategies that run counter to major corporate interests, such as the creation of shareholder value. Such fears help to explain the enormous popularity of portfolio planning techniques, which allow corporate management to dictate which business units will be grown, harvested, or divested. Yet, value-based planning methods provide a more rational framework for linking the business strategy directly with its contribution to shareholder value. This approach enables business-level managers to evaluate their alternative competitive strategies in terms of their contribution to corporate value-creation goals.

Nevertheless, it is vital that the financially oriented value-based techniques be balanced by, and integrated with, more qualitative strategic analysis. This balance between financial valuation and strategic thinking and analysis at the business level lies at the heart of an evolving approach to value-based strategic management. Here, the emphasis is on the industry environment and competitive advantages of the business unit. At this point, value-based methodology can provide the glue that binds the individual business strategies together to form a cohesive corporate strategy. The focus on the competitive situation of the businesses ensures that unit managers don't lose sight of the fact that value is created by the sustainable advantages their businesses can achieve over competitors in their industries. At the same time, value-based performance targets help to keep all business managers' eyes on the common corporate goal of shareholder value creation.

It's too soon to tell whether this value-based approach to strategic management is having a beneficial impact – after all, its real contribution will only be felt over the longer term. However, more and more

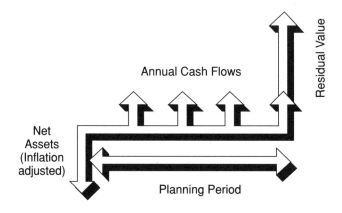

Figure 5.2 Q-ratio valuation model

companies are moving beyond the original, purely financial approach to value-based planning by increasing their emphasis on the more qualitative aspects of strategy. They are introducing programs to educate their managers in the finer points of powerful, qualitative tools like Porter's competitive analysis and PIMS. They are also beginning to implement new long-term executive incentive plans pegged, in part, on the achievement of shareholder-value targets. At the moment, the future for value-based methods looks both promising and challenging.

Chapter 6

Related corporate portfolios

David J. Collis[1]

What do hotels, cartoons and ice hockey have in common? Nothing, until you add the magic word ... Disney! Then it becomes readily apparent that those very different businesses have a great deal in common, not the least of which is Mickey Mouse and the other Disney cartoon characters (Collis 1988, 1994a). This simple example illustrates the very basic and vitally important lesson for corporate strategy that the relatedness of businesses in a corporate portfolio should have little to do with product market relatedness and much to do with how those businesses leverage the unique resources of the corporation – in this case Disney's library of highly recognizable animated characters.

Much empirical research demonstrates the value of related corporate strategies and so confirms the intuition that "relatedness" creates synergy through the sharing of activities, or transferring of skills among businesses (see, for example, the original work of Rumelt 1974; the various extensions and qualifications in Montgomery and Hariharan 1991 and Porter 1986, and recent summaries in Montgomery 1994 and Ramanujam and Varadarajan 1989). The implication of this has recently been reaffirmed in the widely advocated notions of "sticking to your knitting" (Peters and Waterman 1985) and "refocusing" the corporation on its core businesses (Hoskisson and Hitt 1994). We absolutely agree with the concept of relatedness as a critical part of good corporate strategy, our concern is with the commonly held notion of the knitting. Good corporate strategies do not necessarily cluster in industries within the same broad product category. Good corporate strategies cluster in industries which share similar resource bases, strategic characteristics, and managerial requirements.

THE NEED FOR EFFECTIVE CORPORATE STRATEGY

In the 1980s America's large multibusiness corporations faced a threat to their very existence. Activities in the capital markets in the form of leveraged buyouts, hostile takeovers, and corporate raiders challenged the role of such entities in modern society, questioning whether the traditional corporate hierarchy remained the most appropriate vehicle for controlling and coordinating industrial activity (Jensen 1989, 1993). In particular the capital market's emphasis on shareholder value focused attention on whether or not the large corporation, as we know it, added economic value to its constituent business units (Copeland *et al.* 1990; MacTaggart *et al.* 1994; Goold *et al.* 1994). Corporations, therefore, began divesting the businesses they had, in many instances, hastily acquired.

While the excesses of the capital markets in the 1980s are unlikely to be repeated soon, and while the most pathological corporate portfolios of the time have since been rectified, experience to date in the 1990s suggests that corporations are not yet off the hook. If anything, the pressure to demonstrate that large corporations can create value is even more compelling now, since this time the threat is not from outsiders but insiders – the Board of Directors and large institutional shareholders. In turn, many of the giants of corporate America have seen their top executives held accountable for the performance of their corporate strategy as never before. General Motors, Kodak, IBM, American Express, Westinghouse – the list of companies whose Boards, either independently or under duress from activist shareholders, have disciplined CEOs whose attempts at corporate strategy have failed to create value, reads like a roster of the corporate élite of only five or ten years ago.

Our research indicates that this is no surprise (Collis and Montgomery 1996). We went in search of state of the art corporate strategy practice, visiting some of America's premier companies, but we were surprised to find that when we got there, there was, in the words of Gertrude Stein, "No there, there."[2] The simple fact is that many of America's large, well thought of corporations are hard pressed to articulate how they create value from their multibusiness activities.

The reasons for this are simple. On ascending to the office, CEOs inherit a set of businesses that few are able to understand. As a consequence many CEOs run their corporations on momentum, retaining businesses simply because they are part of the portfolio, rather than because a carefully formulated corporate strategy justifies their continuing ownership. Indeed, the decision to divest a business will involve a diminution of the CEO's responsibility and status, as well as the abandonment of colleagues and employees to whom the CEO may feel a personal commitment. In addition, misconceptions about corporate level strategy still abound. The heritage of previous dogmas, such as the benefit of risk reduction through diversification; the merit of having three legs to a corporation to smooth earnings; and the portfolio approach replete with cash cows, dogs, and stars (Henderson 1979), still adorn corporate offices. So, unfortunately, does the simple executive desire for self-aggrandizement with its corollary of wasteful corporate perks and a desire for size for the sake of size itself.

Corporations managed this way are protected from the discipline of the capital market because of the premium acquirors must pay in a hostile takeover. This premium – on the order of 20 percent (Jensen and Ruback 1983), along with transaction costs of 2 percent – make it unrealistic for any acquiror to step in and attempt to remedy corporate underperformance until that performance falls below 78 percent of what is perceived as feasible.

A FRAMEWORK FOR CORPORATE STRATEGY

Drawing on the work of researchers on the resource based view of the firm (Wernerfelt 1984; Barney 1986, 1991; Dierickx and Cool 1989; Peteraf 1993; Collis and Montgomery 1995), a framework is, however, emerging which articulates an approach to corporate strategy that will allow America's largest and potentially strongest corporations to realize the full value of their resources. This framework does not identify three or four, or even a typology of good corporate strategies. Rather we have seen that a successful corporate strategy is an internally consistent set of three elements – *resources*; *businesses*; and *organization structure, systems and processes* – which when motivated by a vision and supported by a set of well defined short-term goals and objectives, generates a corporate advantage. This advantage – analogous to a competitive advantage at the business unit level – justifies the ownership of multiple business units when (as suggested by Goold and Campbell 1992):

- The ownership of each business unit creates value somewhere in the corporation.
- The value added compensates for the expense of the corporate overhead. (Corporate office costs now run at about 1 percent of sales or 1.2 percent of assets, compared to a mutual fund which charges about 0.5 percent of assets (Copeland *et al.* 1990; Goold and Young 1993.)
- The corporation adds more value to the business unit than any other possible owner.

This framework views an effective corporate strategy like a tree (see also Prahalad and Hamel 1990, 1994). The corporation's resources are the roots of the tree that nurture its growth. The set of businesses in the corporate portfolio are the branches the tree has grown. And the organization structures and processes are the tree's shape and biological processes that maintain the efficient functioning of the entire system (Figure 6.1)

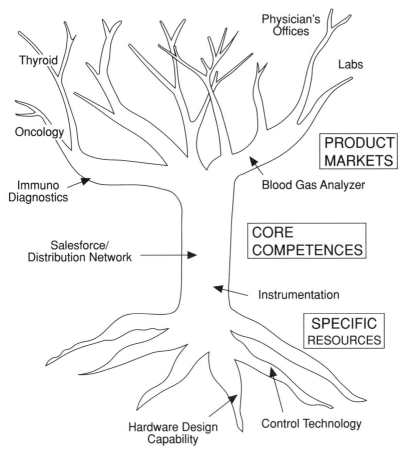

Figure 6.1 Medical diagnostics company

At the root of an effective corporate strategy are the resources of the corporation. Other authors have used different names to describe this set of assets. Prahalad and Hamel refer to them as core competences (Prahalad and Hamel 1990, 1994), Stalk *et al.* (1992) as capabilities, while the original treatment of Andrews and others at Harvard in the 1960s called them distinctive competences (Andrews 1971). We prefer the term resources because it refers to a body of theory within the strategic management field, and because it necessarily embodies a much broader concept than competences or capabilities alone (Collis and Montgomery 1995).

Resources are the collection of tangible and intangible assets that companies have acquired over their histories. They include physical assets, such as plant and distribution channels; intangible assets, such as

A new perspective is emerging in the strategic management literature under the name of the Resource Based View of the Firm (RBV)
which describes firms as unique bundles of durable assets that
have been accumulated over time (Wernerfelt 1984, Barney 1989
and 1991, Dierickx and Cool 1989, Conner 1992, Amit and Schoemaker 1993, Peteraf 1993). The advantage of this perspective is that
it explains sustainable competitive advantage. While traditional
strategic analysis – industry analysis, the value chain, and generic
strategies (see in particular the work of Porter 1980 and 1985) –
demonstrated how firms could achieve a competitive advantage,
that perspective's focus on revenue and expenditure flows could
not explain the durability of any advantage. The RBV, with its
emphasis on asset stocks, complements traditional strategic analysis by identifying the characteristics of resources which make any
position of competitive advantage sustainable, as rarity, inimitabil-
ity, appropriability, and nonsubstitutability. While many of a company's resources will be pedestrian, those resources which are
durable and competitively superior, can be the source of sustainable competitive advantage in multiple markets, and so can be the
basis of an effective corporate strategy. (For a further explanation
of how the RBV applies to corporate strategy see Collis and Montgomery 1995.)

brand names and technological knowledge; and also organizational
capabilities, such as rapid product development, or the innovation and
marketing of branded national consumer packaged goods. Like the roots
of a tree these resources have been accumulated over time, are often intertwined and overlapping, and at their ends are thin and narrowly defined.

Previous descriptions of competences and capabilities have treated a
corporation's critical resources more like the tree trunk – a single broad
and thick asset. We have found that analyzing a corporation's resources
at the level of the trunk is easy to do – it is after all very visible – but
ultimately unrewarding. The level of aggregation of the trunk is too
high to be able to derive real strategic insights. Instead we must dig to
uncover the tree's roots if we are to really understand the source of the
corporation's vitality. Knowing that 3M is good at coating technology,
does little to identify the actionable programs it can undertake either to
reinforce its coating technology, or to suggest which businesses to enter.
Indeed, many corporations that have rushed to embrace core competence
because it is so intuitive, have come up short when trying to apply its
lessons. The analysis of a corporation's resources must take place at the
disaggregated level of the roots, and not at the immediately obvious
level of the trunk.

If resources are the roots which are the ultimate source of value in the
corporation, the businesses are its branches. These grow from the roots
and are nurtured and supported by the roots. Thus, metaphorically and

literally, all businesses which the corporation can justify owning – can demonstrate they add value to – must be derived from the unique resources the corporation possesses.

In many successful corporations the linkages among businesses are as apparent as the branches of a tree and have evolved as natural extensions of earlier branches in the corporate portfolio. The chart of 3M's technological evolution tracks the expansion of its businesses, as they gradually branched out from one another (Figure 6.2). At Disney, children's cartoons led to children's live action movies, led to adult entertainment movies, led to the Disney channel on cable TV, led to . . . (Figure 6.3). However, unlike trees, corporations can also *acquire* entirely new branches. Yet for the strategy to be successful, even acquired businesses must also derive strength – competitive advantage – from the company's resource roots.

Finally the organization structure, systems and processes used to control and coordinate the corporation must fit with the resources it is leveraging across markets. Again the analogy to the tree is useful. All trees share the same biological processes of photosynthesis and nutrient extraction, yet observation reveals how widely the various species differ in every form and function. Even so, the physical structure of each species is optimized for its common needs and habitat: trees with deep roots grow tall; evergreens have thin needles filled with pitch to survive the winter; leaf shapes are coordinated with branch structures to ensure the maximum absorption of light. Similarly, all companies have budgeting, capital expenditure, compensation systems, even though their exact details differ enormously. Yet, just as those structures and processes are optimized for each species of tree, so the organizational structures, systems and processes for each corporation must be optimized according to the nature of the firm's resources and the set of businesses in which it competes.

A detailed account of how the corporate structure and systems must fit with the overall corporate strategy (the contingency view of organizational design, Lawrence and Lorsch 1967; Lorsch and Allen 1973) is beyond the scope of this article. Here it is sufficient to say that we have identified three basic roles for the corporate office (in addition to the public company functions of tax and financial reporting, etc.) that, like the differences between evergreen and deciduous trees, lead to aggregate differences among organizational forms, even though the particulars within each category will still differ somewhat. The requirements for implementing each of these three roles – establishing the context for decentralized decision making, provision of a central resource, and coordinating activities among business units – determine, at an aggregate level, the elements of organization design that make up the administrative context of the corporation.

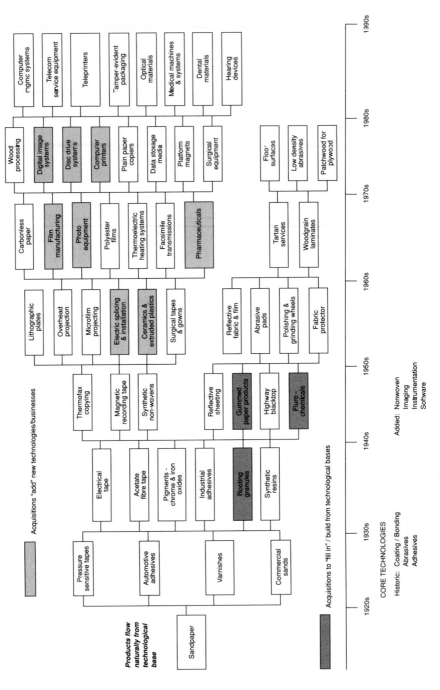

Figure 6.2 Technology evolution at 3M

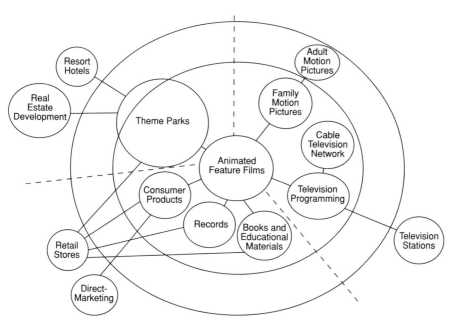

Figure 6.3 The Walt Disney Company

RELATEDNESS IN CORPORATE STRATEGY

If the corporate strategy is to be successful, if it is to possess a corporate advantage that creates value from the ownership of multiple businesses, the three elements of corporate strategy – resources, portfolio of businesses, and organization structure, systems and processes – must be aligned. Just as strategy at the business level requires the alignment of functional activities, (Andrews 1971), so strategy at the corporate level must develop an internally consistent set of the three elements.

This requirement for the internal consistency of the three elements is the key to our notion of relatedness. Relatedness is not defined by any characteristics of the product market, but rather by whether the businesses leverage the same resources, and can be controlled and coordinated with the same systems and by the same corporate managers. The "relatedness" of businesses is, therefore, determined by the "fit" with the other two elements of the corporate strategy, and not by the degree of similarity among the products or services. The tree metaphor suggests that the notion of relatedness defines the domain of businesses in which any particular corporate strategy thrives.

Consider as an example what has probably been the most successful corporate strategy of the 1980s on any one of many dimensions – growth, profitability, shareholder value: Kohlberg, Kravis and Roberts

(KKR). If you are surprised to see KKR listed as the best example of corporate strategy, you should remember that in less than fifteen years it has built an entity (albeit privately, rather than publicly held) with annual sales over $40 billion, and during that time has earned an average of over 40 per cent p.a. for equity participants (Kovaleff 1993; Anders 1992). Whatever we may think of the way KKR has accumulated this portfolio, its success is unquestionable.

But what businesses is KKR the owner of today? Cigarettes, cookies, dog treats, insurance, publishing, etc. An apparent hodgepodge of unrelated products and services. Yet beneath the facade of diversity there is a common theme which KKR, and in fact all the other successful LBO firms, recognize. All these businesses are in mature, low growth, low technology, basic needs industries which face very little uncertainty, and all the companies they own are branded market leaders, or dominant players in a narrow niche. It is critical that their businesses meet these criteria because the only resource LBO partnerships contribute to create value in their businesses is a governance structure, and because they have a simple organization design that employs only basic internal control processes and a few financially trained managers (Baker and Montgomery 1994).

LBOs create economic value by improving the operational efficiency of their acquisitions and by ending the dissipation of free cash flow on projects or perks that are destroying economic value (Kaplan 1989). They do this by introducing a governance structure that is a combination of the stick and the carrot. The stick is high leverage which commits managers to generate the cash flow to service the interest and principal payments. The carrot is equity participation which provides the incentive for managers to increase the value of the business. This combination of penalties and rewards motivates managers and resolves the principal–agent conflict inherent in large corporations when managers who control the purse strings do not have their interests aligned with those of shareholders (Jensen and Meckling 1976; Jensen 1989).

LBOs are organized with minimal intervention from the LBO partnership, which even at KKR only employs about seventy-five people. The incentive scheme is the main method of controlling businesses, and operating managers are given enormous autonomy in the running of their own businesses. In fact the LBO partners are well advised to stay away from running the businesses since they know nothing about how to run a large company. The only other organizational design tool LBOs use is personnel selection. Great care is taken in selecting the top two or three people for each of the businesses, and the response to underperformance at a company is usually to replace the senior management team.

Under what circumstances will this very simple sort of control mechanism and value adding approach work? First, it requires that LBOs acquire companies which have slack and inefficient use of assets. These are typically companies in mature industries which face little competition and as a consequence are able to perform below their potential without being competitively threatened. Secondly it requires simple, easy to understand businesses which LBO partners with very little practical experience can easily get their hands around; again this suggests mature, basic needs, low technology industries. Thirdly it requires that cash flow generation is a good measure of strategic performance. Since so much emphasis, and nearly all the control is placed around cash flow, when that is not an accurate reflection of strategic performance, the business will slowly be run into the ground. This is why it is so important for LBOs to avoid high growth, high technology industries (and why LBO partnerships, like Forstmann Little, that are now investing there are venturing at their own risk, or must be anticipating changing the resources and the way they create value), and why they are rightly accused of having a short-term mentality. Cash flow is a short-term measure, but in the set of businesses in which KKR and other successful LBOs compete, it is not a bad measure of how well the company performed that year. KKR is a success because its corporate strategy is internally consistent, and its businesses are related in the sense that they fit with the corporate resources and organization.

To make the notion of relatedness more concrete for practitioners, its conditions can be framed in terms of each of the three elements of corporate strategy.

Resource relatedness

With respect to resources, a business is related when:

- The valuable corporate resources contribute to sustainable competitive advantage in the business, matching the key success factors in the business.
- The corporate resources can be transferred into, or mobilized within the business.

The concept of resource relatedness refers to this match between a given set of resources and the requirements for value creation in a particular business. As Porter observed, corporations do not directly create value, they only create value through their impact on product market competition (Porter 1986). Thus, the corporate resources must always contribute directly to the competitive advantage of businesses in the portfolio. If they do not, the business does not benefit from corporate ownership and that ownership cannot be justified.

As KKR's governance structure created value in its businesses, so other examples of resources creating value can be found in all the categories of assets that we identified earlier as potential sources of corporate advantage.

With respect to physical assets, for example, the cable companies and the local telephone companies in the US possess a valuable resource in the form of the wire that runs to the house. Having this wire in place is an enormous competitive advantage in the new interactive multimedia business because the single wire can carry video, voice and data communications, and because the cost to anyone else of laying a cable (even if they could get the right of way) might approach $2,000 per household.

The Newell Company's unique competence – its trunk – is its distribution channel (Collis 1994b). For over twenty years it has built a unique relationship with the discount retailers. Over 80 percent of its sales are to twenty chains including Walmart, Kmart, Target and Home Depot. While it helps to grow with the most successful US retail format, Newell's 20 percent compound growth in sales and 15 percent growth in earnings per share over the last twenty years has been achieved by acquiring over fifteen companies whose very different products it then distributes through this channel. Its original business was drapery hardware, the next business pots and pans, the next glassware, the next pens, the next hair accessories. . . . All seemingly unrelated products which are tied together by the competitive advantage they receive from sharing the same distribution channel.

The resources that were the roots of Newell's strategy – from which it derived competitive advantage – were built over time. Newell was an early investor in information technology. Today over 80 percent of its sales are conducted through the paperless invoicing of electronic data interchange (EDI). This not only gives Newell itself cost savings, but also matches the requirements of discount retailers which benefit from the reduced cost and faster delivery of EDI. All Newell acquisitions are, therefore, put on the corporate EDI systems, and their own computer or manual order processing and MIS systems are replaced by the central computer system. This gives them an immediate advantage over competitors, most of whom are smaller, single business entities.

Newell has also developed unique merchandising capabilities for its distribution channels and the everyday, low technology, low cost products it sells. A common characteristic of such items is that customers choose to buy these at a certain retail outlet, rather than search for a particular brand. If one manufacturer can provide the complete set of price points for a product that customers might want, it is advantageous both to the retailer and the manufacturer to have a single source of supply. Recognizing this, Newell has developed an approach to "good/better/best" merchandising that meets this need for a complete program of products within a particular category, and which encourages customers to trade up. This merchandising approach has been applied to all Newell's acquisitions with enormous success.

It is the competitive advantage that these resources can contribute that determines which businesses are "related" for Newell. However, those advantages are sufficiently limited that Newell will not be successful in every product you find on the shelf at Walmart. Indeed its success depends on recognizing its own limitations and very clearly setting boundaries that define the businesses it will not enter – seasonal, fashion oriented, non-durable, high technology – because its resources do not match the key success factors in those types of businesses.[3]

Under the organizational capabilities category of resources that can underpin corporate advantage, consider the corporate strategy of Philip Morris. At the trunk level of analysis, Philip Morris's corporate strategy is based on a capability in branded consumer product marketing. The original business in which these skills were developed was cigarettes, where it has been demonstrated that Philip Morris has a unique competence among the tobacco companies in the launching of new brands (Thomas 1989). After an initial diversification in a variety of directions, including real estate development, which it quickly realized had no relationship whatsoever to its core skills, Philip Morris concentrated on three businesses in succession – beer (Miller), soft drinks (7 Up), and food (Kraft General Foods).

Unlike the previous example which finds relationships among apparently dissimilar businesses, this is a story of differences among seemingly similar businesses. All three appear to meet the criteria of consumer branded products in which new product launch skills would be an important source of competitive advantage, but only two of those worked for Philip Morris. With Miller, Philip Morris took the seventh ranked brewer in the US into second place behind Anheuser-Busch on the strength of the successful introduction of the "lite beer" category. Kraft General Foods was also a great success as the company repositioned some brands, extended others and launched yet others. Yet Philip Morris failed in its endeavors to turn around 7 Up and ultimately sold off the business. Why was this?

While some of the explanation is competitive – Pepsi and Coke are just hard to compete with – the business was unrelated to the others in one critical dimension. Soft drinks, unlike beer and food, involve a franchised production and distribution network, yet Philip Morris had no experience in managing franchise relationships. Indeed, many of the actions it took, such as trying to proliferate product lines (which were appropriate in their direct marketed businesses) were in conflict with the franchisees who resented the overhead costs imposed by additional product lines. At the same time, they tried to substitute national advertising dollars for local franchisee promotional dollars, further estranging their relations with the most critical part of the distribution system. As a result of this failure Philip Morris narrowed its definition of relatedness to nationally marketed, branded consumer goods that did not rely on intermediaries, in order to more closely connect the key success factors in a business to its valuable resources.

Thus, the first aspect of resource relatedness, exemplified above, is the match between the corporate resources and the key success factors of the business. However it is equally important that the firm be able to deploy the resources in the new market. Unfortunately, the best corporate resources, which appear to offer the greatest potential for corporate advantage, are often the most specific and hardest to replicate in additional businesses. The UK retailer, Marks and Spencer, for example, took thirty years to make a success of its European operation because it took that long to create the reputation, supplier and employee relations, and market knowledge that underpinned its dominant position in the UK. In contrast, the most generalized resources, like general management skills, that can readily be transferred to new businesses, are usually those that are least likely to contribute to competitive advantage in a new business (Montgomery and Wernerfelt 1988).

Business relatedness

At the level of the portfolio of businesses, the notion of relatedness is that:

- The activities of the businesses are mutually reinforcing, and exploit economies of scope.
- Each business contributes to an expansion of, or an improvement to, the corporate resources.

As well as drawing on the corporate resources, businesses can also directly affect one another. It is, perhaps, this aspect of relatedness that is closest to that of product relatedness in the traditional sense because it is concerned with the existence of scope economies among businesses. These can arise on the cost side, as, for example, occurs when The Limited is able to leverage its presence in the malls as a diversified format speciality retailer – The Limited, Victoria's Secret, Abercrombie and Fitch, etc. – to benefit from lower rents. Or they can arise on the demand side, in the way that Newell is able to counter the power of discount retailers by virtue of its size and array of products. Whatever the specific source of the economies that multibusiness activity brings, there has to be some underlying production or customer commonality to create direct benefits from the sharing of activities. At the Harvard Business School, for example, the MBA program is directly supported by the executive education programs, which utilize the faculty when the MBA students are on vacation.

Competing in a business should also enhance the resources of the corporation. If the strategy is to be fully effective, businesses and resources should be mutually reinforcing, as the Harvard Business School further illustrates. The school's resources of reputation, faculty, case library and alumni network clearly give Harvard a competitive advantage in, what is now, a highly competitive management development industry. But its presence in executive education also enhances the school's resources. Graduates of the executive programs become alumni of the school whose future exploits enhance the Harvard name. They often offer sites for additional case writing and research, and teaching them ensures that the faculty stay at the forefront of management practice.

When a business contributes to the resources the corporation possesses, it both reinforces the competitive advantage of the existing businesses and opens the possibility of entering further businesses. Japanese firms are particularly cognizant of this interconnection between resources and businesses. The challenge they see in developing effective corporate strategy is to continually upgrade the corporate resources by pushing into those new businesses that both leverage existing resources, and develop additional resources.

Executives at Sharp, for example, talk of the interrelationship between seeds and needs – seeds are the technological resources the firm possesses, needs are the market demands. Indeed, Sharp made the successful transition from second tier assembler of radios and televisions in the 1950s, to the world leader in liquid crystal displays and a variety of derived electronics products today, by creating a virtuous circle of seeds and needs expansion (Collis 1993). The circle commenced with Sharp's entry into the calculator business in the early 1960s (Figure 6.4). To compete with low cost competitors by offering a very small size calculator, it chose to develop its own semiconductors and LCD displays. The success with those technologies supported an expansion into flat screen displays. The need for higher quality displays led Sharp to improve the technology to a level where it could offer screens for the Wizard personal organizer and laptop computers. Entry into these markets required developing flash memories. These memories will be an essential ingredient in all portable electronic equipment in the future, thus enabling Sharp, which now has alliances with Apple (for the Newton), and Intel (for flash memories), to build its position in an even broader range of products. In this case, and in many others, corporate resources and businesses grow together, enhancing one another, just as the tree's roots grow with its branches.

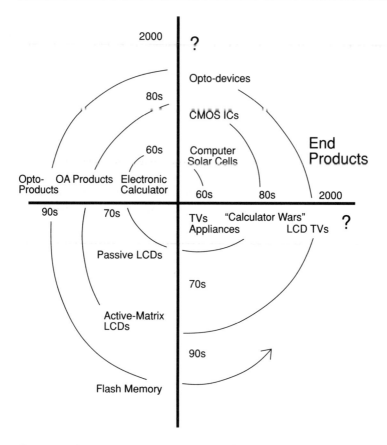

Figure 6.4 Sharp Electronic Components/Devices

Organizational relatedness

In businesses that are related in terms of their organizational requirements,

- The same corporate level organizational structure, systems and processes can be applied to manage the businesses.
- The "dominant logic" of corporate executives is relevant to the businesses.

The first requirement does not imply that all businesses in a corporation have the same pay structures, accounting systems, etc. Good corporate strategies can accommodate organizational differences within divisions. But the overall design framework that the corporation chooses to fulfil the three roles mentioned earlier, does have to be consistently applied across the set of businesses in the corporate portfolio. The same hands-off governance structure has to be applied by KKR to all its businesses, however different the actual systems and processes employed in the individual companies it owns must be. It is this necessity that determines the organizational relatedness of a business.

As an example of how organizational systems can determine which businesses are related consider Saatchi and Saatchi, where inconsistencies on this dimension contributed to the downfall of what was once the world's largest advertising agency (Collis 1992). Among its other deficiencies, Saatchi and Saatchi diversified into the consulting business. Originally this was done in a restrained manner, focusing on those consulting businesses which, like advertising, have a loyal base of repeat customers that can be retained after a takeover. Saatchi and Saatchi's initial foray into consulting was to buy the Hay Group whose main business is annual compensation audits for existing clients. Unfortunately, management could not restrain itself from letting the desire for growth overwhelm the strategy, and later acquisitions were of more traditional management consultants.

At the same time a consultant was put in charge of both the consulting and the advertising business. He imposed the consulting budgeting system onto the advertising agencies. This might not seem problematic until the very different nature of the two businesses is recognized. In management consulting, employees to a great extent generate their own business. Hire another employee and she can go out and hustle for business. Thus consulting firm budgets start from the personnel line, derive from that the office space required, and back into a revenue number. This was the system that Saatchi and Saatchi applied to its advertising agencies, where budgeting traditionally starts from the revenue expected from existing clients, and then works back to the number of employees required. If additional unexpected business arrives during the year, the agency will go out and hire additional employees. Imagine what happened when Saatchi and Saatchi imposed the consulting budgeting system on the advertising agencies. With a mandate to grow, they all went out and hired more employees, signed long-term leases on additional floor space and waited . . . for the downturn in the advertising business. To account for the unwanted lease obligations, Saatchi and Saatchi took a write-off of £150 million in 1992 and even that did not cover the total excess space.

At American Express the much vaunted "One Enterprise" strategy to build a financial supermarket foundered on the inability to develop structures and systems that encouraged corporate wide coordination. In turn, this was because of the very different organizational requirements in the investment banking, financial planning, credit card, and brokerage activities. While it is true that they are all part of the financial services industry, the set of compensation and reward schemes, for example, are so different that trying to establish a consistent policy to reward cross business cooperation was impossible to do without creating enormous resentment and conflict in at least one of the businesses.

Both these examples of problems of organizational relatedness come close to arising from differences in the "dominant logic" of the various businesses (Prahalad and Bettis 1986). This is the managerial paradigm, that partly reflects personality, education and corporate context, but also cumulates through managerial experiences. As one of the more important informal elements of organizational design, this cognitive perspective of senior executives biases the way they conduct business, the control systems they rely on (Simons 1994) and affects the repertoire of solutions they draw on when faced with a decision (Cyert and March 1963). It is often specific to a particular type of industry since the "industry recipes" (Spender 1988) for success that are required in different industry environments, differ (Collis 1993). Skilled managers from capital intensive commodity industries, for example, are often out of their depth in high technology environments. Those from engineering dominated firms are uncomfortable in consumer packaged goods industries. It is, therefore, vital that the dominant logic of the corporation's managers matches that required by the businesses in the corporate portfolio. When this does not happen, failure ensues.

Consulting is a different business to advertising, and a successful consulting executive could easily misunderstand the nature of the differences between the businesses. Similarly, at American Express, investment bankers compete in different ways from financial planners. Thus even if the product looks related, if the nature of the businesses – the ways to react to exogenous events, respond to competition, etc. – is different, the businesses cannot be treated as organizationally related.

UNRELATED BUSINESSES

The requirements for relatedness laid out above are demanding. It is, therefore, no surprise to find that many firms overestimate their capability to diversify, nor that between one-third and one-half of all acquisitions are divested (Porter 1986; Ravenscraft and Scherer 1987). When the three sets of conditions outlined above, most particularly that of resource relatedness which governs value creation, are not fulfilled for a particular business, the harsh lesson of the 1980s is that the corporation has two choices – to divest the business, or outsource the activity.

ICI is one company, which under the threat of a possible bid from Hanson, addressed the issue of relatedness (Owen and Harrison 1995). As a consequence, in June 1993, it split the company into two parts – a heavy chemicals company (which retains the ICI name), and a "light" pharmaceutical, biotechnology and specialized chemicals company (called

Zeneca). The decision recognized that the scope economies which used to tie ICI's businesses together, in particular the ability to leverage the company's research into its multiple end markets, were no longer present. While historically a development in seed fungicides might actually become a human drug, or a development in plastics might generate a new insulation business, going forward, ICI saw far less ability to realize the benefits of integration across a broad set of chemical and pharmaceutical businesses (Haspeslagh 1992). Moreover, the control systems and mechanisms appropriate for capital intensive businesses, whose important strategic decisions revolve around infrequent but very substantial investments in plants, were in no way appropriate for running a research intensive pharmaceuticals business, or even a marketing intensive consumer paints business. Accordingly, the bold move was made to split the company in two, even if the two halves remained essentially chemical companies.

Similarly, the outsourcing of activities is appropriate when the corporate resources simply do not provide for a competitive advantage in the business. Consider gardening at Harvard. None of the resources of the school, least of all the faculty, give Harvard an advantage in the gardening business. Thus Harvard contracts out that activity to specialists. Nor does outsourcing such an activity jeopardize the strategy of the school because competing in gardening does not in any way contribute to building those resources which are the source of the school's corporate advantage. The outsourcing of such ancillary corporate activities is increasingly common in corporate America, and, in our view, appropriately so.

CONCLUSION

Corporations are successful when they possess a unique set of resources – tangible and intangible assets and capabilities accumulated over time – and are organized in a way that effectively leverages those resources into their portfolio of businesses. The whole provides a consistent economic and organizational rationale to the corporation. Corporate management then develops an understanding and a set of control systems that form a "dominant logic" to the company. When businesses fit this alignment of the elements of corporate strategy, they are related and deserve to be in the corporate portfolio, regardless of how disparate they appear in product market terms. When businesses do not fit this alignment, they do not belong inside the corporation, regardless of how similar the products may be.

The best corporate strategies are indeed related – just not related in the traditional way of thinking.

NOTES

1 This paper could not have been written without many discussions with Cynthia Montgomery. Financial support from the Division of Research at the Harvard Graduate School of Business Administration is acknowledged.
2 This reference was suggested by Cynthia Montgomery.
3 A common finding in our research is that successful corporations define themselves as much by the businesses they will not go into, as by specifying exactly the ones they will go into. Simons refers to this as the boundary setting control system (Simons 1994). Its value at the corporate level is the discretion it leaves to divisional managers as to which businesses they enter, and the time and effort saved by having told them which ones it is not worth even thinking about.

REFERENCES

Amit, R. and Schoemaker, P. J. (1993) "Strategic assets and organizational rent," *Strategic Management Journal* 14, 33–46.
Anders, G. (1992) *Merchants of Debt: KKR and the Mortgaging of American Business*, New York: Basic Books.
Andrews, K. (1971) *The Concept of Corporate Strategy*, Homewood, IL: Dow Jones-Irwin.
Baker, G. P. and Montgomery, C. A. (1994) "Conglomerates and LBO associations: a comparison of organizational forms," Harvard Business School working paper.
Barney, J. B. (1986) "Organizational Culture: Can it Be a Source of Sustained Competitive Advantage?" *Academy of Management Review*, 11(2) 656–65.
——, (1989) "Asset stocks and sustained competitive advantage: a comment," *Management Science* 35: 1511–13
——, (1991) "Firm Resources and Sustained Competitive Advantage," Journal of Management 17(1): 99–120.
Collis, D. J. (1988) "The Walt Disney Company (A): Corporate Strategy," *HBS Case #2–388–147.*
——, (1992) "Saatchi and Saatchi Corporate Strategy," *HBS Case #792–056.*
——, (1993) "The Sharp Corporation: Technology Strategy," *HBS Case #793–064.*
——, (1994a) "The Walt Disney Company (B): Sustaining Growth," *HBS Case #794–129.*
——, (1994b) "Newell Company: Acquisition Strategy," *HBS Case #9–794–066.*
Collis, D. J. and Montgomery, C. A. (1995) "Competing on resources," *Harvard Business Review (forthcoming).*
——, (1996) *Corporate Strategy*, Homewood, IL: Irwin (forthcoming).
Conner, K. (1992) "A historical comparison of resource-based theory and five schools of thought within industrial organization economics: do we have a new theory of the firm?" *Journal of Management* 17: 121–54.
Copeland, T. E., Koller, T. and Murrin J. (1990) *Valuation: Measuring and Managing the Value of Companies*, New York: Wiley & Sons, Inc.
Cyert, R. and March, J. (1963) *A Behavioral Theory of the Firm*, Englewood Cliffs, NJ: Prentice-Hall.
Dierickx, I. and Cool, K. (1989) "Asset stock accumulation and sustainability of competitive advantage," *Management Science* 35: 1504–11.
Goold, M. and Campbell, A. (1992) "Parenting advantage," Ashridge Strategic Management Centre, mimeo.

Goold, M., Campbell, A. and Alexander, M. (1994) *Corporate-Level Strategy: Creating Value in the Multibusiness Company*, New York: John Wiley & Sons, Inc.

Goold, M. and Young, D. (1993) "Effective headquarters staff: A guide to the size, structure and role of the corporate headquarters staff," London: Ashridge Strategic Management Centre.

Haspeslagh, P. (1992) "ICI Plc." *INSEAD* Case *#392–088.*

Henderson, B. (1979) *Henderson on Corporate Strategy*, Cambridge, MA: Abt.

Hoskisson, R. and Hitt, M. (1994) *Downscoping: How to Tame the Diversified Firm*, Oxford: Oxford University Press.

Jensen, M. (1989) "Eclipse of the Public Corporation," *Harvard Business Review*, 67: 61–74.

——, (1993) "The modern industrial revolution, exit, and the failure of internal control systems," *Journal of Finance* (July): 831–80.

Jensen, M. and Meckling, W. (1976) "Theory of the Firm: Managerial behavior, agency costs, and capital structure," *Journal of Financial Economics*, 3: 305–60.

Jensen, M. and Ruback, R. S. (1983) "The Market for Corporate Control: The Scientific Evidence," Journal of Financial Economics, 11: 5–50.

Kaplan, S. (1989) "The effects of management buyouts on operating performance and value," *Journal of Financial Economics* (December): 191–212.

Kovaleff, T. P. (1993) Book review of G. Anders (1992) *Merchants of Debt: KKR and the Mortgaging of American Business*, in J. High (ed.) *Business History Review* (Spring 1993) Boston: Harvard Business School: 168–70.

Lawrence P. R., and Lorsch, J. W. (1967) *Organisations and Environment*, Boston: Harvard Business School.

Lorsch, J. W. and Allen, S. A. (1973) *Managing Diversity and Interdependence*, Boston: Harvard Business School.

McTaggart, J. M., Kontes, P. W. and Mankins, Michael C. (1994) *The Value Imperative: Managing for Superior Shareholder Returns*, New York: Free Press.

Montgomery, C. A. (1994) "Corporate diversification," *Journal of Economic Perspectives*: 8: 163–78.

Montgomery, C. A. and Harihuran, S. (1991) "Diversified expansion by large established firms," *Journal of Economic Behavior:* 15: 71–89.

Montgomery, C. A. and Wernerfelt, B. (1988) "Tobin's q and the Importance of Focus in Firm Performance," *American Economic Review* 78(1)

Owen, G. and Harrison, T. (1995) "Why ICI Chose to Demerge," *Harvard Business Review* 73: 133–42.

Peteraf, M. A. (1993) "The cornerstones of competitive advantage: a resource-based view," *Strategic Management Journal* 14: 179–91.

Peters, T. J. and Waterman, R. H., Jr, (1985) *In Search of Excellence: Lessons from America's Best-Run Companies*, New York: Warner Books.

Porter, M. E. (1980) *Competitive Strategy*, New York: Free Press.

——, (1985) *Competitive Advantage*, New York: Free Press.

——, (1986) "From competitive advantage to corporate strategy," *Harvard Business Review* 65: 43–59.

Prahalad, C. K. and Bettis, R. A. (1986) "The dominant logic: a new linkage between diversity and performance," *Strategic Management Journal* 7: 485–501.

Prahalad, C. K. and Hamel, G. (1990) "The core competence of the corporation," *Harvard Business Review* 68: 79–91.

——, (1994) *Competing For the Future*, Boston, MA: Harvard Business School Press.

Ramanujam, V. and Varadarajan, P. (1989) "Research on corporate diversification: a synthesis," *Strategic Management Journal* 10: 523–52.

Ravenscraft, D. and Scherer, F. M. (1987) *Mergers, Sell-offs, and Economic Efficiency*, Washington, DC: The Brookings Institution.

Rumelt, R. (1974) *Strategy, Structure, and Economic Performance*, Boston, MA: Harvard Business School Press.

Simons, R. (1994) *Levers of Control: How Managers Use Innovative Control Systems to Drive Strategic Renewal*, Boston, MA: Harvard Business School Press.

Spender, J. C. (1988) *Industry Recipes*, Cambridge, MA: Blackwell.

Stalk, G., Evans, P. and Schulman, L. E. (1992) "Competing on capabilities: the new rules of corporate strategy," *Harvard Business Review* 70: 57–69.

Thomas, L. G. (1989) "Which Brands Succeed?" Columbia University mimeo.

Wernerfelt, B. (1984) "A Resource-based view of the firm," *Strategic Management Journal* 5: 171–80.

Chapter 7

Creating value in acquisitions

Philippe Haspeslagh and *David Jemison*

INTRODUCTION

The rapid increase of acquisitive activity in all countries with market economies has heightened the debate among managers, academics, politicians, and regulators about acquisition activity, the roles of different players, the various motives for acquisitions, and the benefits they produce. Opinions on many of these topics are strongly held, but by no means universally accepted.[1] The crux of the arguments may lie in the difficulty in reconciling the clear benefits of an active market for corporate control, as enjoyed by countries like the United States and the United Kingdom, with the strategic investment behavior exhibited by firms in countries like Germany and Japan.

Most of this debate has focused on whether or not acquisitions lead to value creation. This has led to the neglect of equally important questions for managers and acquisitive firms: "How is value created in firms and how do acquisitions themselves contribute to value creation?" This chapter provides the conceptual foundation for our arguments by outlining an expanded view of how value creation takes place in firms and the role of acquisitions in that process.

In this chapter we explore the concept of value creation from different viewpoints. We then contrast value creation with value capture and show how firms can create value by transferring and applying strategic capabilities that lead to competitive advantage. Finally, we discuss the different ways in which acquisitions can contribute to value creation.

PERSPECTIVES ON CORPORATE VALUE

The concept of corporate value has different meanings for different constituents of the firm. Before examining corporate value from a managerial perspective, we will briefly review the question of what value is from two other perspectives: the capital markets view and a broader stakeholders perspective.

Capital markets view of value creation

The surge in acquisition activity worldwide and the rise of contested takeovers have highlighted the need to understand the criteria by which acquisitions should be judged. The capital markets perspective on this question asserts that the merits of an acquisition should be judged in terms of the immediate value created for the shareholders.[2] This view has attracted widespread support because its logic is derived from the tenets of the capitalist economic system in general and from the efficient markets hypothesis of financial economics in particular.[3] This view suggests that the market value of a firm's stock price reflects an unbiased estimate of all publicly available information about the firm's future cash flows and their related risks.

A natural extension of this view is that any acquisition that causes an immediate increase in market value (after adjustment for normal market fluctuations) is good, and one that causes an immediate decrease in market value is bad. Using this perspective, financial economists have concluded, after extensive research, that acquisitions on the average do not create value for shareholders of the acquiring firm. The same studies, however, reveal that, on the average, a significant premium accrues to the acquired firm's shareholders.[4]

In the aggregate the capital markets perspective argues that the entire economy benefits from the asset reallocation that results from acquisitions. In this market for corporate control, new owners pay a premium for a firm's shares and install different management.[5] The line of reasoning is that the new group of owners has been able to pay more for the firm because they believe the assets can be more productively utilized under the stewardship of management they choose. Former owners of the firm receive a premium for their shares and then reinvest the proceeds. When this premium plus the net change (positive or negative) in the value of the acquiring firm's shareholders' wealth is positive, acquisitions represent an overall creation of wealth, and the welfare of society is increased because assets have been allocated to more productive uses.[6]

While the capital markets perspective encourages a view of the firm that emphasizes optimal societal resource allocation, its relevance for managers is limited. In this view the firm is merely a bundle of assets; value is created when an acquisition either increases the income stream of those assets or decreases the variability.[7] But it does not address the *way* in which the income stream is created; it says only that it can be changed by reallocating the firm's portfolio among different sets of assets. Thus the source of firm performance remains unexplained and seems to result from rather mysterious activities that take place in a black box.

The capital markets perspective is elegant in its simplicity and important because of the number of managers and academics who subscribe to it. Perhaps its most salutary contribution is that it reminds us to put value creation ahead of managerial motives. Yet, because it focuses on the entire economy and not a firm, it provides little guidance for action-oriented managers who want to understand how they can create value in a particular situation.[8] Managers and scholars need to understand more about the ways in which firms create value and the role of acquisitions in that value-creation process.[9]

Other constituents' views

In a broader sense, a firm's value can also be seen from the perspective of several groups other than shareholders, each of whom considers the value or worth of the firm differently, e.g., employees, communities, customers, suppliers.[10] Employees value a firm for many reasons including employment, pride of association, and a means of achieving personal goals. Communities value firms for the benefits they provide, through employment, taxes, the types of people they attract to the area, and the involvement of the firms' employees in the life of the community. Customers find value in a firm's ability to meet their needs for products and services. Suppliers value relationships with firms not only because they are outlets for goods and services but also because they provide valuable market information.

Even in the United States, where the capital markets view is prevalent, a constituents' view of acquisitions is far from theoretical. When the Norton Corporation, Worcester, Massachusetts' largest employer, with a tradition of community involvement, faced a takeover bid from the British conglomerate BTR, a public outcry was heard. It was feared that BTR would move jobs away and end the community service role that Norton had sustained for over fifty years. After repeated public and corporate protests, as well as hurried state legislation, BTR withdrew its bid. BTR's bid was replaced by one from a French firm. Saint-Gobain not only offered a higher price for the firm's shares, but also guaranteed to keep plants, jobs and community involvement intact for at least the next five years.[11]

The view that managers' decisions should be guided by obligations broader than maximizing shareholder value is not as strongly held in countries with active markets for corporate control. Yet in some countries such as Japan, it has the same legitimacy that the capital markets view has in the United States and Great Britain. In other countries an amalgam of the two exists. In Germany, Switzerland and Holland, for example, management is expected to balance stockholders' interests with those of other stakeholders when solving problems.[12] But, beyond suggesting the need to include more interests in decision making, the stakeholders' perspective does not provide much guidance for managers seeking to create value.

A managerial perspective on value creation

Most managers strike a middle ground between these two perspectives. The executives we interviewed were uncomfortable with the premise that the real measure of performance was either the immediate stock market reaction to their firm's acquisitions or broad stakeholder support. These managers believed that the investments they were making (many of which were acquisitions) were consistent with their strategic vision for the firm and would add to the firm's capabilities and long-term competitive position. Both financial results and the ability to serve the needs of all its stakeholders were expected to flow from these commitments. The managers' confidence in their decisions did not result from hubris as much as from their best judgment, based on an understanding of the strategic, technological, and market opportunities facing their firm and their vision of how they would compete in the future. They could support this confidence with precise financial projections for some acquisitions. But for others they would have been hard pressed to clarify and quantify precisely the linkage between their acquisition decision and positive changes in their firm's income stream. Although they used discounted cash flow analysis as one way to evaluate acquisitions, these managers had confidence in "a strategic premium" that reflected their judgment of the long-term benefits of an acquisition, rather than estimates of cash flows.

Clear differences existed across national boundaries in the extent to which managers' judgments in these matters were linked to the immediate reaction of capital markets. The divergence in resulting investment behavior was most striking in some "industries of the future" such as advanced composite materials or ceramic materials. In such situations, up-front investment in leading technology segments (in this case military and civilian aerospace) were expected to bear fruit only over time in terms of bigger markets such as automotive applications. In these industries, the German, Swiss, Japanese, and some of the British companies that we studied were all committing themselves not only to acquisitions, but also to major subsequent investments. In contrast, many of the American firms were either selling or waiting out the industry evolution.[13]

Firms we studied held very different views of what they should focus on to accomplish the corporate purpose. Some management groups emphasized realizing financial results, others conquering market positions, and others building up corporate capabilities. All managers interviewed agreed that financial performance was the long-term yardstick, but managers in some firms shared a much more complex and multidimensional view of how to balance an acquisition's short-term financial performance with long-term strategic needs.

VALUE CAPTURE VERSUS VALUE CREATION

The current debate about shareholder value masks the fact that there are two fundamentally different ways of improving shareholder wealth with acquisitions.[14] One, *value capture*, involves shifting value from previous shareholders or other stakeholders to the acquiring firm's shareholders. Value capture tends to be a one-time event, largely related to the transaction itself. The other way, *value creation*, is a long-term phenomenon that results from managerial action and interactions between the firms. It embodies the outcome of what many people refer to as synergy. In our conception, synergy occurs when capabilities transferred between firms improve a firm's competitive position and consequently its performance. Value creation implies a different concept of the firm.

How is value created?

We believe that the most managerially relevant view of the value creation process is to see a firm as a set of capabilities (embodied in an organizational framework) which, when applied in the marketplace, can create and sustain elements of competitive advantage for the firm.[15] These elements of competitive advantage produce operating results for the firm (with an associated risk profile) and create value for its shareholders. Figure 7.1 outlines the dynamics in this process.

The advantage to both managers and researchers of this capabilities-based perspective over the financial assets perspective is that it segments the value-creation process and allows careful consideration of each of the steps involved.

This perspective also contrasts with the traditional notion of strategy in which firms strive to achieve a distinctive competence, something they can do uniquely better than other firms that will give them a unique and lasting competitive advantage.[16] In the competitive situations facing most firms, it is illusory to expect that a single dimension will provide a decisive competitive advantage or, even if it did, to expect it to be sustainable.[17] In this capabilities-based perspective that we suggest, a firm's competitive advantage results from the application of a wide range of capabilities and, in particular, of a set of core capabilities, which can be defined as those capabilities central to competitive advantage, that (1) incorporate an integrated set of managerial and technological skills, (2) are hard to acquire other than through experience, (3) contribute

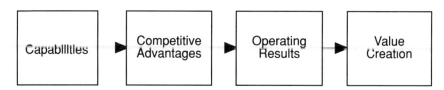

Figure 7.1 A capabilities-based perspective on value creation

significantly to perceived customer benefits, and (4) can be widely applied within the company's business domain.[18] But markets are sufficiently varied to provide room for different competitors with different capability profiles to coexist.[19] Thus the only real distinctive competence is in the ability to mobilize an organization to form new combinations of capabilities continually and to renew them.[20]

Conceptualizing a firm's competitive position as the result of a set of core capabilities leads to new insights. For example, the competitiveness of a firm like Canon, which competes in four broad product-markets (cameras, copiers, office equipment, and professional optics), can be better understood by regarding the company as a portfolio of capabilities, not businesses. These exist both upstream (quality manufacturing of small equipment, value engineering, and leading-edge technology in microelectronics, optics, and new materials) and downstream (mass merchandising, a dealer network, and a brand franchise).[21] A clear understanding of which capabilities are central to a firm's competitive success (and which are secondary) makes it possible to develop a corporate strategy for renewing such capabilities and a clearer picture of the options open to the firm. It is also central, as we shall argue, to developing an acquisitive strategy that will create value.

Renewing a firm's capabilities

Competition and other environmental changes naturally erode a firm's competitive advantages. Faced with a constant need to *renew* its competitive position, the firm seeks to add new capabilities or to change the product-markets where its existing capabilities are applied. These choices are not independent. Entry into new product-markets, which may be driven by the desire to exploit existing capabilities, usually brings with it the need for complementary new capabilities to compete effectively. Entry itself may add other new capabilities that can be deployed in one's existing product-markets or become the basis for further product-market diversification.

In this interactive process it is essential that the strategist keep the focus on which capabilities are core, i.e., central to competitive advantage in the companies' business domain, and which are secondary. That judgment is idiosyncratic, as every firm competes differently and has a unique set of capabilities.

One impediment to focusing strategic reflection on a firm's capabilities is that it is generally much easier to observe the renewal and change of the firm's businesses, product, or markets than the renewal of its capabilities. Yet the renewal of capabilities is central to long-term competitive strength. Firms compete on the basis of their relative ability to renew and deploy capabilities as much as they do on their ability to extract profits from product-markets.

This capabilities-based perspective of the firm also allows general managers to consider a variety of options for strategic renewal, including acquisitions, internal development, and joint ventures. The key is to focus on how the relative merits of each option contribute to the needed capabilities. We will focus our attention on how managers can use acquisitions effectively as a form of renewal, rather than on the trade-offs among these options.

How is value captured?

While the focus of this book is value creation, we must address value capture briefly because of its popularity among some groups of managers and scholars. In fact, value capture embodies most directly the prevailing views of the capital markets perspective we discussed above. Many acquisitions are driven by the desire to capture value by transferring it from one set of stakeholders to shareholders or managers of the acquiring firm. These transactions usually involve either corporate restructuring (by individual raiders or by acquisitive firms) or leveraged buy-outs. Value is captured by a variety of one-time, transaction-oriented means, including acquiring undervalued assets, tax benefits, increasing debt, and asset stripping. The seller, future owners, the government, and existing creditors are the common sources of such captured value.

Value can be captured from the *seller* by identifying and acquiring firms whose market prices may be undervalued. For example, Charlie Bluhdorn stated that his motive in creating Gulf & Western was his confidence in his ability to spot undervalued assets. Similarly, Boone Pickens's view at Mesa Petroleum is that he understands the oil business well enough to bid for the undervalued assets of firms like Gulf. The fact that the firm that first spotted the undervaluation does not always end up as the acquiring firm, does not mean that value capture did not take place. The discount at which the shares of a conglomerate or closed-end mutual fund sell is another example of undervaluation that can be released by simple breakup. Value capture from firms with undervalued assets is most commonly associated with multibusiness companies whose value is difficult for the stock market to assess or whose corporate managers do not pursue value-maximizing strategies. Even single-business firms may provide opportunities for value capture from the seller if some of their assets, e.g., buildings and other real estate, are not related to the cash-generating potential of the firm.

Value can also be captured *from future owners*, the shareholders of firms to whom a buyer intends to resell a portion of an acquired business. For example, a substantial part of the gains made by acquirers of conglomerate firms has been based on their ability to keep for themselves during negotiations a significant portion of the synergies that the industrial companies to which they resell individual businesses expected to achieve.

Hanson Trust, for example, acquired SCM in 1985 for $930 million. By the end of 1988 it had sold off SCM companies and assets for $1249.6 million, but it still owned Smith Corona, SCM Chemicals, and SCM Metals. It repeated this performance with the Imperial group, which it acquired in 1986 for $2.5 billion. After selling off Imperial assets for $2.247 billion by the end of 1988, it ended up owning Imperial Tobacco and a number of smaller businesses for a net price of $253 million. Again, in its 1987 acquisition of Kaiser Cement for $250 million, Hanson disposed of assets for $284.3 million and kept Kaiser's Northern California cement business for essentially no cost.[22]

The government is a favorite source of value capture for acquiring firms because they can take advantage of complexities and subtleties in the tax laws. Quite often, acquiring firms are able to reap substantial savings or reductions of tax liabilities through judicious application of tax loss carryforwards from the target firm, tax treatment of goodwill, or other special tax treatment of acquisitions.[23] In leveraged acquisitions the new owners also realize a transfer of value through an effective reduction in the cost of capital based on the tax deductibility of interest.

Finally, there may be some opportunities to transfer value to shareholders of the acquiring firm from the acquired firm's *existing creditors*.[24] One way is to increase the risk level of previous lenders by maintaining their old debt while significantly increasing post-acquisition indebtedness, especially through the use of so-called high-yield junk-bond financing. For example, when Campeau Corporation of Canada acquired Federated Department Stores in the United States in 1988, the market value of Federated's bonds fell by 17 percent because of the debt financing used by Campeau to complete the acquisition. In turnaround acquisitions, the acquisition may also provide a one-time opportunity to renegotiate downward the higher-risk debt of firms by providing guarantees that at least a portion of it will be repaid.

A firm's ability to *capture* value through acquisitions rests largely on the skills of a small but highly experienced cadre of legal and financial experts and operating managers with well-developed expertise in analysis and deal making. Above all, this ability rests on their judgment, their comfort with risk taking, and their ability to commit increasing sums of money to ever-larger takeovers that can contribute appreciably to the growing base of the firm.

Managers who are interested in value creation need to put the activity of value-capturing financial entrepreneurs in the proper perspective. Value capture is not a sufficient motive for strategic acquirers. Although the benefits of value capture can be very substantial for a particular acquisition opportunity, a solitary focus on value capture masks the need to focus on the managerially based process of true value creation. By the same token, we believe that strategic acquirers should also take full advantage of the opportunities to capture value in their acquisitions.

Through the acquisition of multibusiness firms in particular, a management team can gain access to individual business units that are of strategic interest to them for value creation and then capture value by reselling the rest, often paying less than it would have expected for the business of interest. For example, because ICI was willing to acquire all of Stauffer Chemical for $1.9 billion and then to resell part of these business activities to Akzo and Rhône-Poulenc, it was able to gain access to the agrochemical division it wanted at a net cost of less than $800 million.

Few firms are able to capture and create value in the same acquisition. Doing so requires both the quick decision making of the financial entrepreneur and the strategic view of the patient organization builder. Because our interest is on strategic acquisitions, we will concentrate on value creation.

STRATEGIC ACQUISITIONS IN A CAPABILITIES-BASED PERSPECTIVE

Although they share the underlying motivation of value creation, the acquisitions we call "strategic" differ by the type of capability they transfer, their relation to corporate strategy, and their contribution to business strategy.[25] Each of these distinctions emphasizes a dimension important in our capabilities-based perspective, and each has consequences for the nature of the acquisition decision-making process and for the challenges in the integration process. The remainder of this chapter develops these three ways to distinguish among strategic acquisitions.

Our first classification addresses the differences in the type of capability transfer that underlies value creation in acquisitions. Our second classification distinguishes among acquisitions in terms of how they relate to corporate strategy. Finally, some acquisitions may be a small ingredient in an internal development strategy, while others actually represent the business strategy. Thus our third set of considerations focuses on what the acquisition contributes to implementing a particular business strategy.

Acquisitions and the type of capability transfer

Acquisitions create value when the competitive advantage of one firm is improved through the transfer of strategic capabilities. To develop a practical understanding of how value creation will occur we must examine the specifics of what the exact source of capability transfer (in other words, of synergy) will be. Economists and business researchers have each developed categorization schemes and a language to look at the benefits flowing from acquisitions. Economists tend to focus on market power and cross-subsidization (neither of which they favor because of their anticompetitive nature), and economies of scale or scope, both of which they do like.[26] Management researchers have discussed a vast array of "synergies" typically related to different business functions: marketing synergies, manufacturing synergies, etc.[27]

Neither categorization corresponds well with the nature of the managerial task required for achieving synergies. The economist's notion of economies of scope, for example, may cover such disparate activities as incorporating a newly acquired company in one's planning and control system in such a way that operating units are little affected by their counterparts in the other organization, to cross-selling of products through each other's sales forces, which will require a great deal of coordination between both operating units. Popular managerial categories such as marketing synergies, on the other hand, cover anything from sales force rationalization to improved brand management, which represent very different sources of benefits and imply very different organizational tasks.

Our research suggests that four different categories of acquisition benefits can be distinguished. Each presents very different integration challenges: operational resource sharing, functional skill transfer, general management skill transfer, and combination benefits.[28] The first three involve strategic capability transfer. The fourth, combination benefits, refers to a number of advantages that are present in many acquisitions but do not require capability transfer. Many acquisitions involve all four types of benefits, but we will discuss them individually for the sake of clarity.

Combination benefits These accrue from some acquisitions and do not involve formal capability transfer. For example, market power and increased purchasing power come from the leverage that size itself allows over customers, suppliers, distribution channels, and smaller competitors.[29] Financial resources may be shared, leading to lower financing costs or greater financing capability. Greater stability may be achieved through diversity.[30] Even reputation may be enhanced; as the increase in size and stature resulting from the merger that created Dai-Ichi Kangyo Bank enabled it to attract more top-quality university graduates and improve its overall management capabilities.

These combination benefits have one aspect in common – they do not require a managerial process to transfer capabilities between the organizations. While they play a major role in some acquisitions, combination benefits are not at the heart of value creation in truly strategic acquisitions. It is in the three categories of resource sharing and the transfer of functional and general management skills that capability transfer takes place in value-creating acquisitions.

Resource sharing   This involves the combination and rationalization of some of the operating assets of both firms. Such rationalization can take place in one or more functions and leads to cost improvements that stem from economies of scale or scope. Economies of scale result when the combined unit volume allows the firm to operate at a lower unit cost. Economies of scope come about when the joint use of an asset results in a lower overall cost than the firms had when they operated independently. Sharing distribution channels and sales forces is a goal of acquirers seeking economies of scope. A major reason for the acquisition of Charles Schwab by Bank of America was to cross-sell each firm's products into the other's markets. Using the other firm's channels for related products would share the cost of establishing and maintaining customer relationships. Gaining the benefits from economies of scope sometimes requires eliminating duplication. For example, many of the benefits of Seagram's strategy of acquiring other brands like the French cognac Martell lie in eliminating sales force duplication.

Even intangible assets such as brands can be shared. For example, when Black and Decker acquired General Electric's small home appliance business, they planned to lever their own brand's reputation in power hand tools onto the former GE products.

Although the economics of resource sharing seem straightforward, in practice the combination of operating resources brings with it a "cost of compromise." The overall economic benefits of resource sharing need to be balanced against any loss of effectiveness in their use. When Esselte acquired Dymo, for example, there was a clear opportunity for resource sharing by combining Esselte's stationery supplies sales force with the sales force for Dymo's well-known embossing tool, as their products overlapped almost completely at the store level. Against the economic benefits gained by creating a single sales force, the firm had to weigh the differences in the sales skills required for the two products. Esselte's products, which were low margined, required primarily order-taking and pricing. Dymo's were high margined and required merchandising and demonstration.[31] In practice, the potential for resource sharing often has to be traded off against the next source of benefits: the possibility for skill transfer.

Functional skill transfer   This creates value when one firm improves its capabilities by bringing in, from another firm, functional skills that can help it to be more competitive. Examples included advanced manufacturing process skills in the merger of two manufacturing firms, detailed knowledge of a distribution channel in the merger of two consumer goods firms, or cutting-edge research in financial theory used to develop new products in mergers between brokerage firms. The common denominator among these is that one firm improves its competitive position by learning from another through the transfer of functional skills.

The very factors that make capabilities strategic, make value creation through skill transfer difficult. Skills are typically embedded in the activities, habits, and automatic responses of key people throughout the organization.[32] The less replicable the skill, the more difficult it is to imitate and the more effective it can be as a competitive weapon. In addition, the most valuable skills are often organizational routines for performing particular activities. These routines are learned over time, often by trial and error; their performance often becomes automatic when a particular situation occurs.

General management skill transfer   This occurs when one firm can make another more competitive by improving the range or depth of its general management skills. These capabilities range from the broad skills needed in setting corporate direction and leadership to more analytically oriented skills and systems, such as those needed for strategic planning, financial planning, control, or human resource management. For example, the Saga Corporation had developed general management skills in operating an institutional food services company. But its traditional markets in cafeteria management had stopped growing. To continue its growth, Saga targeted a series of small, high-potential restaurant chains. Its strategic logic was to enhance the growth of these chains by providing them with the benefit of Saga's general management skills.

The acquiring firm can also improve its own general management capabilities through acquisitions. For example, Esselte's acquisition of Dymo served another purpose besides providing a strong sales network. The Swedish stationery manufacturer had already made a series of loosely connected acquisitions in the stationery supplies field in Europe and had left each with its own systems intact. Another reason was that Dymo could bring management discipline and worldwide systems to these earlier, smaller acquisitions.

Sometimes firms make acquisitions to acquire good managers from other firms. This has occurred among building societies in Great Britain.[33] Because the building society industry had operated for many years with a highly protected, near-monopoly on making loans for home ownership, few individual societies had developed any general management talent in depth. In 1981 the Conservative government changed the rules of competition in the UK financial services industry. Building societies found themselves competing with banks and other financial institutions for deposits and home loan customers. This increased competition required general management talent that was more attuned to a competitive environment and different from that available in most societies. Several building society managers we interviewed conceded that a prime motive behind some of the mergers that had taken place had been a desire to acquire capable chief executives from other societies. Because of loyalty to their current society, they would not agree to become chief executive of another society unless the two were merged.

Every value-creating acquisition presents a potential mixture of the foregoing types of capability transfer. The important question is, which of these types a firm's management will choose to focus on. These decisions will depend in part on the strategic motivation behind the acquisition; its relation to corporate strategy forms the basis for our next distinction among acquisitions.

Acquisitions and corporate renewal

Our second categorization distinguishes acquisitions in terms of their contribution to corporate-level strategy. From a corporate perspective, acquisitions have to be seen in light of their relation to maintaining or changing the balance between the firm's existing domain and the renewal of its capabilities. Each company operates within a "domain" that encompasses the set of businesses within which it is competitive, the capabilities that underlie them, with which its top management is familiar, and to which its corporate organization is suited.[34]

Acquisitions can contribute to the corporate renewal process in three ways: they can deepen the firm's presence in an existing domain; they can broaden that domain in terms of products, markets, or capabilities; or they can bring the company into entirely new areas. In other words, acquisition can be domain strengthening, domain extending, or domain exploring. Each of these types of acquisitions is fairly distinct, and they have different implications for how to approach the decision-making process as well as the integration process.

Domain Strengthening   Domain-strengthening acquisitions augment or renew the capabilities underlying a firm's competitive position in an existing business domain.[35] They correspond to firms' proactive or defensive reactions to the industry restructuring process.[36]

Although the essence of a domain-strengthening acquisition is the desire to defend or fortify a company's business domain, some variation obviously exists within this category. The most straightforward is a completely horizontal acquisition of a competitor with the same products in the same markets, for example, the French tire manufacturer Michelin's acquisition of the number two French manufacturer, Kleber-Colomb, to prevent it from falling into the hands of Goodyear. National consolidations in the airline industry are another example of domain-strengthening acquisitions made to achieve economies of scope and scale. The desire of airlines to dominate a hub airport, to gain market share on a set of key routes, to spread fixed costs of corporate staff over a large volume, and to consolidate reservations systems so as to increase demand for their planes drives much of this activity.

Sometimes the overlap between the firms is less complete because they are selling different products to the same market. This was the case of Stauffer Chemical's Agrochemical business, which was retained by ICI's Agrochemicals division. Although the two companies were selling to the same regions in the United States, they had product ranges for different crops of the same farmers. Similarly, the merger of Hughes Tool Company and Baker International, two oil industry supply firms, brought Hughes's market position and reputation in drill bits together with Baker's reputation and expertise in oil field equipment to consolidate efforts in a severely distressed industry.

A third variant, often seen in the context of globalization are acquisitions of competitors with similar or overlapping products who cover different geographic markets. An example is the purchase of the American paint manufacturer Inmont by BASF, which gave the German company an important share of Detroit's big three, all-important in the global automotive paints business. Another example is the regional expansion of such US bank holding companies as NCNB, Wachovia, and BancOne.

Beyond the real forces driving domain-strengthening acquisitions, there is a lemming effect as the "urge to merge" spills over into areas where the economic benefits are less clear. Managers should be cautious in judging domain overlap with a potential partner. A common error is to focus more on the similarities than on the differences between the firms. For example, Louis Vuitton and Moët-Hennessey merged their luxury products firms in 1987 but soon discovered that their managerial concepts of luxury products were very different.

Domain Extension   Domain-extending acquisitions apply the firm's existing capabilities in new, adjacent businesses or bring new capabilities into the firm to apply in its existing businesses. The combined firms share the challenge of relating what is a new capability for one to what is a new business opportunity for the other.

Habitat's acquisition of Mothercare in the UK is a good example of an acquisition to apply a firm's existing capabilities in new product-market domains. Habitat, the UK furniture designer and retailer, had built its success on the ability to translate attractive, fashionable designs into reasonably priced home furnishings. Mothercare, a chain of retail shops that catered to expectant and new mothers, was well respected for its operating abilities. But because its maternity and baby clothing and accessories were perceived as dowdy and plain, it was beginning to lose fashion-conscious customers. Sir Terence Conran, Habitat's founder, transferred its design flair and fashion-conscious merchandising capability to Mothercare's product lines, stores, and catalogs, and Mothercare's sales and profitability both increased.

In an example of acquisitions intended to *add* capabilities, Computer Associates International became the largest independent software firm in the industry by making a series of acquisitions of software houses. Each of these acquisitions provided a new type of programming capability that contributed to Computer Associates International's ability to achieve its strategy of becoming a full-line software provider.[37]

Firms can also extend their capabilities by acquiring existing businesses. For example, the American automobile firms Ford and Chrysler bought free-standing financial service firms to augment their existing in-house financing arms. These moves have positioned them well for the future as the financial services industry deregulates. They also give the auto firms the ability to enhance their product offerings with coordinated financing packages and enable them to capture the profits from auto financing that formerly went to lenders. Ford's purchase of First Nationwide Savings is an interesting example of synergy in financial services. The savings arm is now able to match its shorter-term deposits with auto loan repayments rather than home mortgages, thus reducing the firm's interest rate risk on fixed-rate, long-term mortgages.

Domain Exploration   Domain-exploring acquisitions involve moves into new businesses that at the same time require new capability bases. These types of acquisitions are frequently driven by managerial motives such as the desire to use cash or to reduce risk. Contrary to managerial wisdom, value is not being created by risk reduction itself. Indeed, modern financial theory has shown that an investor can easily diversify his or her portfolio and thus achieve the same sort of systematic risk reduction as a conglomerate.[38]

Domain-exploring acquisitions can create value in two ways. In the first case the motive is a long-term concern about the core business. Here acquisitions may be a way to bring new capabilities or businesses into the firm that might at some point be relevant to existing businesses but cannot yet be incorporated in their current logic. An example of acquisitions that bring learning to a core domain was Ciba-Geigy's move into the consumer goods industry through a number of small acquisitions in the United States and Europe, particularly its acquisition of Airwick.[39] Although Airwick was divested in a subsequent portfolio restructuring, it did expose the Swiss pharmaceuticals and chemicals group to the culture and values of consumer marketing at a time when its core pharmaceuticals business was not ready to adopt the marketing culture needed to tackle the over-the-counter consumer market in that business.

Value can also be created by applying a firm's general management skills to foster a more rapid development or more disciplined management in unrelated acquired businesses without direct relevance to the core business. In such cases the host structure set up by the acquiring firm, over the acquisition performs a role akin to that of the corporate and group levels in a conglomerate. A domain exploration acquisition is British Petroleum's acquisition of Hendrix, a Dutch animal feed company, which BP nurtured into a Europe-wide nutrition business.

In some firms domain exploration involves acquiring a series of companies in a single new area and then clustering them to form a new business domain. One example is Lafarge New Materials, a new division set up by the French Lafarge Corporation, a leading cement manufacturer. The division has acquired a large number of small family firms clustered in three areas – facade surface materials, building material chemicals, and refractory products. These firms were only indirectly related to Lafarge's core businesses and to each other. But they could share a common management approach provided by the divisional umbrella.

Most often, however, the objective of domain exploration is to lever the industry-specific learning and the credibility from successful initial small acquisitions into a broader commitment to the acquisition and development of a more significant position in that industry. The early acquisitions by British Petroleum in the animal feed industry led not only to the nurturing of those companies but also to other acquisitions, including that of Purina Mills in the United States, which have made BP Nutrition the world's largest supplier in this industry.

Acquisitions and business strategy

A third useful distinction relates to an acquisition's contribution to a specific business strategy. We distinguish three broad types here: acquiring a specific capability, acquiring a platform, or acquiring an existing business position.[40] Our research has focused on the latter two, which, especially in the context of domain extension or exploration, present significantly different challenges to management.

Acquiring a Capability   Sometimes a firm will use a rifle-shot approach to acquire a specific capability it needs to implement a business strategy. We referred earlier to the software firm Computer Associates, which built a business by acquiring very small software houses, each specializing in a single type of system software programming. By pulling all the firms together, the firm acquired a broad-based capability to meet customers' evolving system software requirements.

Acquiring a Platform   We characterize acquisitions as platforms if they may have been viable before being acquired, but clearly will not be as part of the acquiring firm unless it commits to significant further investment. In that sense they represent a commitment to an investment strategy that far exceeds the initial purchase price.

British Petroleum's entry in advanced composite materials is a platform acquisition. When BP, after unsuccessful efforts in its central research lab, wanted to enter the advanced composite business, it first bought the small and relatively troubled British firm, Bristol Composites. After investing substantial resources in Bristol's turnaround and development, the sponsors of this investment, BP Ventures, used the know-how and credibility derived from this first investment to acquire Hitco, one of the leading US firms in this area.

Acquiring a Business Position   In acquisitions that involve an existing business position, the acquisition itself almost implements the strategy. Nestlé's acquisition of Carnation in the United States is a case in point, as are Ford's purchase of First Nationwide Savings and Habitat's purchase of Mothercare.

These three categories represent different management challenges, both in pre-acquisition decision making and in integration. Whether a firm should have an internal development strategy, augmented with some acquired capabilities, or base an acquisitive strategy on acquisition of a platform or the direct pursuit of an existing business position becomes an important choice.[41] This choice should be informed by a clear understanding of differences in how these acquisitions would be integrated and contribute to value creation.

SUMMARY

This chapter proposed an overall perspective on how acquisitions can contribute to value creation which managers can relate to their own unique circumstances. We set aside financial engineering acquisitions that concentrate on value capture and focused on the vast majority of strategic acquisitions that are intended to create value. From a managerial perspective we argued that value is created after the acquisition and it is the product of managerial action over time. It requires an outlook focused on the underlying capabilities that allow a firm to establish a competitive advantage that leads to financial performance.

This capabilities-based perspective provides the conceptual basis for examining the strategic role of acquisitions and distinguishing among different types of acquisitions. Focusing on the capabilities that underlie competitive advantage and on the capability transfer that is expected to flow from an acquisition allows managers to link the desired results (an improvement in competitive advantage) with the processes through which these results are achieved over time (the activities and interactions involved in capability transfer). These activities involve the challenges not only of acquiring these capabilities, but also of preserving them, transferring them to the appropriate setting, and applying them in expectation of improved competitive advantage.

These challenges lie at the heart of making acquisitions work and they should not be underestimated. The acquired capabilities and the contexts from which they come and to which they will be applied are rooted in the organizational and cultural context of the acquiring and acquired firms. The nature and difficulty of these integration challenges depend on the factors we have outlined in this chapter, namely:

- How does the acquisition relate to the company's business domain?
- What does the potential acquisition contribute to the firm's strategy?
- What is the type of the strategic capability to be transferred?

Understanding these issues is at the heart of developing an adequate acquisition justification during the acquisition decision-making process and of being able to begin the integration process afterwards.

NOTES

1 For a summary of the research on merger and acquisition activity from three perspectives – financial economics, strategic management, and organizational behaviour – see Haspeslagh, Philippe C. and David B. Jemison, *Managing Acquisitions: Creating Value Through Corporate Renewal*, New York: The Free Press, 1991, Appendix B.

2 See Rappaport (1986) and Salter and Weinhold (1979, Chapter 6) for a discussion of how firms are valued.

3 A summary of the capital asset pricing model based on the efficient market hypothesis is presented in Mullins (1982). To study the seminal papers in CAPM, along with a detailed treatment of the model, see Markowitz (1952), Sharpe (1964), and Lintner (1965), and the paper by Fama (1968). See Jensen (1972) for a compendium of important earlier papers.

4 The financial economics research on this issue is summarized well in Jensen and Ruback (1983). Their results suggest that shareholders of acquiring firms do not benefit or benefit only marginally, whereas shareholders of acquired firms enjoy substantial abnormal returns to their holdings. Jarrell, Brickley, and Netter (1988), who explore similar questions about the value-creating aspects of acquisitions made in the United States from 1980 to 1987, come to the same conclusions. Similar findings result from studies in other markets, including Australia (Dodd 1976), Belgium (Gagnon *et al.* 1982), Canada (Eckbo 1986), France (Eckbo and Langohr 1985; Husson 1986), and the United Kingdom (Franks *et al.* 1977). For an overview, see Husson (1987, pp. 53–81).

The conclusions of these studies may be somewhat attenuated because they neglect the size effect. On the average, acquired firms are significantly smaller than acquirers; hence their impact on the acquirer's stock price should be expected to be small. Asquith, Bruner, and Mullins (1983) found that "abnormal" returns to bidders depended on the relative size of the target firms. In general, the smaller the target, the lower the returns to the bidder.

Financial economists' studies use an "event study" methodology that examines the net "abnormal" returns associated with a particular security around an "event" such as an acquisition announcement. See Brown and Warner (1980) for an excellent discussion of this methodology and its strengths, weaknesses, and uses.

Magenheim and Mueller (1988, p. 190) suggest that studies of merger and acquisition results are "sensitive to both the choice of time intervals used and the choice of benchmark against which performance is measured." They suggest that

> . . . an acquisition is a sufficiently complex event that it might take the market more than a single month or year to form an accurate estimate of its future effect. These considerations suggest to us the need for a longer-run view of the consequences of acquisitions.

Roll (1986) suggests that, contrary to the assumption of economists that individuals make rational decisions, merger decisions are individual decisions. He suggests that the lack of gain to bidding firms is a result of hubris.

Industrial organization economists have a different perspective on the results of acquisition activity. For example, Ravenscraft and Scherer (1987) studied 5,822 mergers and acquisitions in the 1950–77 time period and concluded that "on average profitability declines and efficiency losses resulted from mergers of the 1960s and early 1970s" (pp. 211–12). Caves (1987) and Elwood (1987) offer reviews of the research in the area.

Several scholars from strategic management have addressed this question as well. Their interests are typically whether value creation differs by type of acquisition made and its relatedness. In general, the results here are mixed. Bettis (1981) found that related diversifiers outperformed unrelated diversifiers. Palepu (1985) found that related diversifiers performed better than unrelated diversifiers. Lubatkin (1987) found that related mergers did not create more value than unrelated mergers. Michel and Shaked (1984) found that when firms diversify into unrelated areas their performance is better than those with businesses that are related. Bettis and Mahajan (1985) found that related diversification aids in achieving a favorable balance between risk and return.

5 See Manne (1965) for the seminal article on the market for corporate control. Schleifer and Vishny (1988) suggests that managers can entrench themselves by investing in projects, facilities and other companies that complement their unique personal skills and abilities. A question does remain whether takeovers for purposes of efficiency in the market for corporate control are the result of internal management failure. Abuse of power by management is a matter of judgment and abuse becomes a vague criterion. To be sure, abuse does occur in some circumstances. But in many situations where the firm's stock price is depressed, more noble managerial motives may be present. In particular, a management team may sincerely believe that their approach, which may require more patience than the shareholders have, is best for the firm in the long term.

6 Note that the price of the acquiring firm's shares does not increase unless the market believes that the negotiated transaction price allows the acquiring firm to retain some of the expected synergy benefits.

7 See Salter and Weinhold (1979 pp. 41–2) for an excellent description of this.

8 The following vignette from a recent conference on corporate restructuring highlights the limited relevance of the financial assets perspective for acquisitions. Gregg Jarrell, at the time chief economist at the United States Securities and Exchange Commission, recounted some congressional testimony in which he argued for the need to allow acquisitions to continue without governmental restrictions. He said that he argued for the macroeconomic benefits of acquisitions to society and suggested that in the long run we are all better off when assets are redistributed to more productive uses. Jarrell said, "A senator looked down over the top of his spectacles at me and said, 'Son, there are no senators here from the state of Macroeconomics'" (Jarrell 1986).

We suggest that just as there are no senators from the state called "Macroeconomics," there are no managers from the firm of Macroeconomics, Inc.

9 The importance of understanding how value is created is recognized by many finance scholars. For example, Bradley, Desai, and Kim (1983) suggest that acquisitions via tender offers are attempts by bidding firms to exploit potential synergies.

10 The stakeholder perspective is well presented by Freeman (1984). Also see Summer (1980, Chapter 1) for a discussion of the variety of pressures general managers must balance in their decision making. Andrews (1970) discusses the responsibilities that general managers have to diverse constituencies.

Donaldson and Lorsch (1983, p. 7) found that in contrast to the view that maximization of shareholder wealth is the primary goal of managers:

their primary goal is the survival of the corporation in which they have invested so much of themselves psychologically and professionally. Therefore they are committed, first and foremost, to the enhancement of *corporate* wealth which includes not only the firm's financial assets reflected on the balance sheet but also its important human assets and its competitive positions in the various markets in which it operates.

11 See Dickson (1990, p. 6).
12 For a broad comparison of how the legal, regulatory, and cultural context of the market for corporate control differs across EEC countries, see Armstrong (1988). A full discussion of how Dutch corporate law formally embodies a stakeholder's perspective, holding managers responsible to broad "corporate interests" (in Dutch *het vennootschappelijke belang*) can be found in Fromm and Haspeslagh (1987).
13 Among transactions were ICI's acquisition of Fiberite, BP's acquisition of Hitco and BASF's acquisition of Celanese's advanced materials businesses. For a discussion of the industry, see the case "EHC and the Advanced Materials Business," written by Sarah Williams under the supervision of Professor Yves Doz and Associate Professor Philippe Haspeslagh, INSEAD, 1990.
14 See Haspeslagh and Jemison (1987) for an earlier discussion of the distinction between value capture and value creation.
15 Penrose's seminal work (1959) first raised the conception of the firm as a combination of capabilities embodied in an administrative framework. Recently other researchers have stressed more explicitly the importance of capabilities underlying such competitive advantage. Among the scholars developing a capabilities-based view from an analytical perspective are Wernerfeldt (1984), Barney (1986a, b), Jemison (1988a, b), and Dierickx and Cool (1989), and from an administrative perspective: Lenz (1980), Haspeslagh (1983), Bartlett and Ghoshal (1989), Doz (1986), Hamel and Prahalad (1989, 1990).

Porter (1985) encouraged a focus on the importance of competitive advantages as the basis for performance. Christensen and Fahey (1986) see two types of competitive advantages, one that increases demand for a firm's products and services and one that constrains supply. Demand-enhancing competitive advantages are the characteristics of a firm, its products, or services that cause them to be preferred over those of competitors. Competitive advantages that constrain supply do so by limiting market entry or expansion by a competitor.

Implicit in the writing of Pascale and Athos (1981) and Peters and Waterman (1982) was the presence of organizational and organizing capabilities that allow firms to be more effective competitors.
16 See Andrews (1970) and Selznick (1957) for a discussion of distinctive competence.
17 See Ghemawat (1986) and Dierickx and Cool (1989) for a discussion of sustainable competitive advantage.
18 See Jemison (1988b) for a discussion of how capabilities contribute to competitive advantage and how acquisitions can add capabilities to a firm. See Hamel and Prahalad (1990) for an initial discussion of the concept of core competencies.
19 This concept has been explored by strategic management scholars in light of the concept of strategic groups. See clinical work on strategic groups by Hunt (1972), their relationship to industrial organization economics by Porter (1980, Chapter 7), empirical work by Cool and Schendel (1988), and an extensive review and critique of the literature and concept by McGee and Thomas (1986).
20 Hamel and Prahalad (1989) provide an excellent discussion of this issue.
21 We are indebted to Yves Doz for this example. For a detailed discussion of Canon's organizational approach, see "Canon, Inc." written by Yoko

Ishikura under the supervision of Professor Michael Porter, Boston: HBS Case Services, Harvard Business School no. 9384151.

22 See "Hanson, Plc.," written by Dean Stone under the supervision of Associate Professor Philippe Haspeslagh, INSEAD, 1990. The importance of these value-capturing benefits does not take away from the fact that Hanson Trust actively pursues value creation in the units they retain, mainly through operating efficiencies that the company seeks through the imposition of tight controls and the provision of strong performance-oriented incentives.

23 There is some disagreement over the influence of tax benefits as an acquisition motive. In a study of 318 mergers and acquisitions between 1968 and 1983, Auerbach and Reishus (1987) found tax benefits to be significant enough to influence the merger decision in 20 percent of the situations they studied. In contrast, Jarrell, Brickley, and Netter (1988) argue that much of the takeover activity in the past twenty years has not been tax-motivated. Gilson, Scholes, and Wolfson (1988) explore the broad range of ways that tax policies and their alternatives can affect the market for corporate control.

24 The impact of restructuring transactions on the value of bondholders' claims on the firm has been the subject of a variety of empirical studies. Most of these have suggested that corporate restructuring does not significantly harm bondholders. See Dennis and McConnell (1986) for a study of mergers, and Hite and Owers (1983) and Schipper and Smith (1983) for studies of spin-offs. Kim, McConnell, and Greenwood (1977) did show evidence of significant bondholder losses in their study of captive finance subsidiaries. Taggart (1988), in a survey of junk bond financing, argues that while there have been individual cases of significant losses to bondholders, "transferring wealth from bondholders is [not] a primary motivation for issuing junk bonds."

25 There is no shortage of typologies to distinguish among acquisitions from a strategic perspective. Many of these typologies are broad categorizations based on how an acquisition relates to other businesses of the firm, such as Kitching's (1967) often-used distinction between horizontal mergers, vertical integration, market-relatedness, technology-relatedness, and unrelated acquisitions. Others clarify the motives that inspire them, such as Salter and Weinhold (1979), who distinguish between defensive and offensive acquisitions.

26 Panzar and Willig (1977) presented one of the earliest formulations of economies of scope. See also Panzar and Willig (1981).

27 See Chatterjee (1986) for an extensive discussion of synergy in acquisitions.

28 In an earlier publication, we used the term "automatic benefits" for the latter category. See Haspeslagh (1986a).

29 See Scherer (1970, pp. 267–95) for an excellent summary of the arguments about the relationships among industry concentration (market power) and industry and firm returns. Results on the extent of diversification and market power are mixed. Backaitis, Balakrishnan, and Harrigan (1984) found that firms pursuing related diversification had greater market power, while Montgomery (1985) did not find that market power led to profitability increases associated with diversification.

30 Although the capital asset pricing model implies that diversification does not create value *per se*, the use of the resulting greater operating stability in

countercyclical or otherwise strategic investment behavior may lead to value creation.

31 For a detailed description, see "Esselte-Dymo (A)(B)(C)" INSEAD case written by Andy Kodjamirian under the supervision of Associate Professor Philippe Haspeslagh and Professor Dominique Heau (INSEAD 1984).

32 The difficulties of transferring context-based knowledge or skills (also known as "tacit knowledge") have been explored by a variety of scholars. Polanyi (1962, p. 49) pointed out that "the aim of a skillful performance is achieved by the observance of a set of rules which are not known as such to the person following them." Arrow (1974) suggested that organizations use codes to convey information efficiently and that there are costs to changing the codes. Nelson and Winter (1982, pp. 81–2) observed that

> much operational knowledge remains tacit because it cannot be articulated fast enough, because it is impossible to articulate all that is necessary to a successful performance, and because language cannot simultaneously serve to describe relationships and characterize the things related.

From another perspective, Coase (1937) pointed out that information is not costless and Williamson (1975) argued that the use of information is difficult because of its impactedness. Teece (1980) suggests that internal organization may be preferred over markets in generating scope economies from embedded know-how. Itami (1987) refers to such skills as invisible assets. Lippman and Rumelt (1982) discuss how the difficulty in imitating an asset can enable a firm to earn abnormal returns in a competitive marketplace. Barney (1986b) discusses how certain inimitable assets like a firm's culture or history are sources of strategic advantage.

33 See the "Note on the Building Society Industry in Great Britain," Teaching Note S-BP-247N, by Associate Professor David B. Jemison, Stanford, CA: Graduate School of Business, Stanford University.

34 The issue of relatedness is central to the study of diversification in general and to acquisitions in particular. Wrigley's (1970) four categories of single product, dominant product, related product, and unrelated product were expanded by Rumelt (1974) to include nine categories within the original four groups. See Rumelt (1974, pp. 11–32) for an excellent discussion. Salter and Weinhold (1979, pp. 61–62) classified acquisitions in two broad categories, related and unrelated, with further subcategories of related-complementary and related-supplementary. Chandler (1962, p. 70) suggests ". . . that it is related effort that should be coordinated and not [merely] 'like things'." Singh and Montgomery (1987) suggest that relatedness is multifaceted with the target firm being valued by different other firms. Haspeslagh and Jemison (1987) suggest that in acquisitions value-creation activities come not from relatedness but from interdependence.

Although Rumelt's early categorizations refer to corporate-level relatedness, much of the strategic management literature on acquisitions has applied these categories to examine business-level relatedness, focusing on the linkage between an acquisition and the acquirer's existing businesses.

Another stream of research has focused on corporate-level relatedness and the overlap between business from a general management perspective. Normann (1977) used the notion of a company's "territory" as the niche in the environment in which the company's "business idea" is operative. Miles (1982) brings in the notion of a firm's domain, which may be conceptualized in terms of the services rendered, the population served, and the technology employed (Levine and White 1961; Thompson 1967). Haspeslagh (1985) has discussed the concept of a core competence domain and a business domain as one of the key elements of corporate strategy in a diversified firm. Prahalad and Bettis (1986) also emphasize the importance of general management. They examine relatedness with respect to the dominant logic, which they define as "a world view or conceptualization of the business and the administrative tools to accomplish goals and make decisions in the business" (p. 491). It is this corporate-level perspective that underpins the research design of this study.

35 Readers familiar with Miles (1982) may see our notion of domain strengthening as encompassing both Miles's domain defense and offense. Miles's domain creation is analogous to our domain exploring. Abell (1980) contends that defining the business is the most important strategic question that general managers face. He proposes a framework for business definition in terms of customer groups served, customer functions served, and technologies utilized.

36 Industry restructuring can be triggered by a variety of factors including:

- *Deregulation*, which removes historically artificial barriers to entry, exit, or competition. For example, the gradual decline of regulatory barriers in the global financial services industry is encouraging consolidation through acquisitions.
- *Technological change* has the same effects, because it can affect minimum scale economies, such as the introduction of digital switching in telecommunications, radial technology in tires, etc.
- *Globalization* through customer need or cost-driven factors. For example, in the automotive paint business the globalization of automotive companies and increasing R&D costs are driving paint suppliers to seek global presence and scale.
- *Competitor initiative*, which may set the industry off on a road to consolidation without strong external triggers. The KMPG merger, for example, has triggered another round of consolidation among the large accounting firms that are already opening worldwide.

37 See "Charles Wang and his thundering nerds," *Forbes*, July 11, 1988, 118–24.

38 See Mullins (1982), Bettis (1983), and Peavy (1984) for a discussion of this issue.

39 See Salter and Weinhold (1979, pp. 161–71) for a discussion of this case. See also "CIBA-Geigy (A)(B)." Boston, MA: HBS Case Services, Harvard Business School), (9–375–246), (9–375–247).

40 See Haspeslagh (1986b) and Haspeslagh and Jemison (1987).

41 The work of Dierickx and Cool (1989) offers insight into these choices between internal development and capability, platform, or position acquisitions. They provide an important theoretical treatment of a firm's competitive position conceptualized as "stocks" of assets in place at a particular time (analogous to the capabilities in our terminology). Changes in the level of these stocks, which are a function of the "flows" from managerial investment decisions, are necessarily gradual. While acquisitions offer the opportunity to increase the flow of new asset stocks into the firm, the result of the combination of some of these flows may not be time compressible. Acquisitions can be a quick solution to some firms' competitive problems. But, the logic of acquiring additional asset stocks or capabilities to help a

firm catch up with its competitors must address important practical questions of the compatibility of these new stocks.

REFERENCES

Abell, D. F. (1980). *Defining the Business: The Starting Point of Strategic Planning.* Englewood Cliffs, NJ: Prentice-Hall.

Andrews, K. R. (1970). *The Concept of Corporate Strategy.* Homewood, IL: Dow Jones-Irwin.

Armstrong, T., under the supervision of D. Neven and P. Haspeslagh. (1988). "Note on the Harmonisation of European Takeover and Merger Regulation." INSEAD.

Arrow, K. (1974). *The Limits of Organization.* New York: Norton.

Asquith, P. R., F. Bruner, and D. W. Mullins. (1983). "The Gains to Bidding Firms from Mergers." *Journal of Financial Economics* 11: 51–72.

Auerbach, A. J., and D. Reishus. (1987). "Taxes and the Merger Decision." In *Takeovers and Contests for Corporate Control,* edited by J. Coffee and L. Lowenstein, 157–87. Oxford: Oxford University Press.

Backaitis, N. T., R. Balakrishnan, and K. R. Harrigan. (1984). "The Dimensions of Diversification Posture, Market Power, and Performance: The Continuing Debate." Working Paper, Columbia University Business School.

Barney, J. B. (1986a). "Organizational Culture: Can It Be a Source of Sustained Competitive Advantage?" *Academy of Management Review* 11: 656–65.

———, (1986b). "Strategic Factor Markets: Expectations, Luck, and Business Strategy." *Management Science* 42: 1231–41.

Bartlett, C., and S. Ghoshal. (1989). *Managing Across Borders.* Boston: Harvard University Press.

Bettis, R. A. (1981). "Performance Differences in Related and Unrelated Diversified Firms." *Strategic Management Journal* 2: 379–94.

———, (1983). "Modern Financial Theory, Corporate Strategy, and Public Policy: Three Conundrums." *Academy of Management Review* 8: 406–15.

Bettis, R. A., and V. Mahajan. (1985). "Risk/Return Performance of Diversified Firms." *Management Science* 31: 785–99.

Bradley, M., A. Desai, and E. H. Kim. (1983). "The Rationale Behind Interfirm Tender Offers: Information or Synergy." *Journal of Financial Economics* 11: 182–206.

Brown, S. J., and J. B. Warner. (1980). "Measuring Security Price Performance." *Journal of Financial Economics* 8: 205–58.

Caves, R. E. (1987). "Effect of Mergers and Acquisitions on the Economy: An Industrial Organization Perspective." In *The Merger Boom,* edited by L. E. Browne and E. S. Rosengren, 149–68. Boston: Federal Reserve Bank of Boston.

Chandler, A. D. (1962). *Strategy and Structure: Chapters in the History of the American Industrial Enterprise.* Cambridge: MIT Press.

Chatterjee, S. (1986). "Types of Synergy and Economic Value: The Impact of Acquisitions on Merging and Rival Firms." *Strategic Management Journal* 7:119–40.

Christensen, H. K., and L. Fahey. (1986) "Resources, Distinctive Competence, and Competitive Advantage." Paper presented at the annual meeting of the Academy of Management, Chicago.

Coase, R. (1937). "The Nature of the Firm." *Econometrica* 4:386–405.

Cool, K., and D. E. Schendel. (1988). "Performance Differences Among Strategic Group Members." *Strategic Management Journal* 11:207–23.

Dennis, D. K., and J. J. McConnell. (1986). "Corporate Mergers and Security Returns." *Journal of Financial Economics* 16: 143–87.

Dickson, M. (1990). "A Little Local Difficulty." *Financial Times*, April 28, 6.

Dierickx, I., and K. Cool. (1989). "Asset Stock Accumulation and the Sustainability of Competitive Advantage." *Management Science* 35: 1504–11.

Dodd, P. (1976). "Corporate Takeovers and the Australian Equity Market." *Australian Journal of Management* 1: 15–35.

Donaldson, G., and J. W. Lorsch. (1983). *Decision Making at the Top*. New York: Basic Books.

Doz, Y. L. (1986). *Strategic Management in Multinational Companies*. Oxford: Pergamon Press.

Eckbo, B. E. (1986). "Mergers and the Market for Corporate Control: The Canadian Evidence." *Canadian Journal of Economics* 19(May): 236–60.

Eckbo, B. E., and H. Langohr. (1985). "Disclosure Regulations and Determinants of Takeover Premiums." Unpublished paper, University of British Columbia and INSEAD.

Elwood, J. W. (1987). "The Effects of Mergers and Acquisitions on the Governance of the Modern Corporation." In *Handbook of Modern Finance*, edited by D. E. Logue, 29B1–29B69. Boston: Warren, Gorham, and Lamont.

Fama, E. F. (1968). "Risk, Return, and Equilibrium—Some Clarifying Comments." *Journal of Finance* 23: 29–40.

Franks, J., J. Broyles, and M. Hecht. (1977). "An Industry Study of the Profitability of Mergers in the United Kingdom." *Journal of Finance* 32 (December): 1513–25.

Freeman, R. E. (1984). *Strategic Management: A Stakeholder Approach*. Boston: Pitman.

Fromm, D., and P. Haspeslagh. (1987). "The Dutch View of Hostile Takeovers." *Acquisitions Monthly* (September): 51–2.

Gagnon, J. M., P. Brehain, C. Broquet, and F. Guerra. (1982). "Stock Market Behaviour of Merging Firms: The Belgian Experience." *European Economic Review* 17 (February): 187–211.

Ghemawat, P. (1986). "Sustainable Advantage." *Harvard Business Review* (September–October): 53–8.

Gilson, R. J., M. S. Scholes, and M. A. Wolfson. (1988). "Taxation and the Dynamics of Corporate Control: The Uncertain Case for Tax-Motivated Acquisitions." In *Knights, Raiders, and Targets: The Impact of Hostile Takeovers*, edited by J. C. Coffee, L. Lowenstein, and S. Rose-Ackerman, 271–99. New York: Oxford University Press.

Hamel, G., and C. K. Prahalad. (1989). "Strategic Intent." *Harvard Business Review* (May–June): 63–76.

———, (1990). "The Core Competence of the Corporation." *Harvard Business Review* (May–June): 79–91.

Haspeslagh, P. C. (1983). "Portfolio Planning Approaches and the Strategic Management Process in Diversified Industrial Companies." Doctoral dissertation. Boston: Harvard Business School.

———, (1985). "Toward a Concept of Corporate Strategy for the Diversified Firm." Research Paper No. 816, Graduate School of Business, Stanford University.

———, (1986a). "Conceptualizing the Strategic Process in Diversified Firms: The

Role and Nature of the Corporate Influence Process." Working Paper No. 86/09, INSEAD.

——, (1986b). "Making Acquisitions Work." *Acquisitions Monthly*: 14–16.

Haspeslagh, P. C., and D. B. Jemison. (1987). "Acquisition: Myth and Reality." *Sloan Management Review* (Winter): 53–8.

Hite, G. L., and J. E. Owers. (1983). "Security Price Reactions Around Corporate Spin-Off Announcements." *Journal of Financial Economics* 12: 409–36.

Hunt, M. (1972). "Competition in the Home Appliance Industry 1960–70." Ph.D. diss., Harvard University.

Husson, B. (1986). "The Wealth Effect of Corporate Takeovers. An Empirical Investigation of a French Sample of Cash Tender Offers, Exchange Tender Offers and Controlling Block Trades." *Cahier de Recherche du Centre HECISA*, Jouy-en-Josas, France.

——, (1987). "La Prise de Controle des Entreprises." Paris: Presses Universitaires de France.

Itami, H. (with T. Roehe). (1987). *Mobilizing Invisible Assets*. Cambridge: Harvard University Press.

Jarrell, G. A. Comment at conference, sponsored by the Karl Eller Center at the University of Arizona, entitled "Corporate Restructuring Through Mergers, Acquisitions, and Leveraged Buyouts," December 1986.

Jarrell, G. A., J. A. Brickley, and J. M. Netter. (1988). "The Market for Corporate Control: The Empirical Evidence Since 1980." *Journal of Economic Perspectives* (2):21–48.

Jemison, D. B. (1988a). "Process Constraints on Strategic Capability Transfer in Acquisitions Integration." Working Paper 88/89 5–1, Graduate School of Business, University of Texas, Austin.

——, (1988b). "Value Creation and Acquisition Integration: The Role of Strategic Capability Transfer." In *Corporate Restructuring Through Mergers, Acquisitions, and Leveraged Buyouts*, edited by G. Liebcap, 191–218. Greenwich, CT: Jai Press.

Jensen, M. C. (1972). *Studies in the Theory of Capital Markets*. New York: Praeger.

Jensen, M. C., and R. S. Ruback. (1983). "The Market for Corporate Control: The Scientific Evidence." *Journal of Financial Economics* 11:5–50.

Kim, E. H., J. J. McConnell, and P. Greenwood. (1977). "Capital Structure Rearrangement and Me-First Rules in an Efficient Capital Market." *Journal of Finance* 32:789–810.

Kitching, J. (1967). "Why Do Mergers Miscarry?" *Harvard Business Review* (November–December):84–101.

Lenz, R. T. (1980). "Strategic Capability: A Concept and Framework for Analysis." *Academy of Management Review* 5(2):225–34.

Levine, S., and P. E. White. (1961). "Exchange as a Conceptual Framework for the Study of Interorganizational Relationships." *Administrative Science Quarterly* 5:583–601.

Lintner, J. (1965). "The Valuation of Risk Assets and the Selection of Risky Investments in Stock Portfolios and Capital Budgets." *Review of Economics and Statistics* 47:13–37.

Lippman, S. A., and R. P. Rumelt. (1982). "Uncertain Imitability: An Analysis of Interfirm Differences in Efficiency Under Competition." *Bell Journal of Economics* 13:418–38.

Lubatkin, M. (1987). "Merger Strategies and Stockholder Value." *Strategic Management Journal* 8:39–53.

Magenheim, E. B., and D. C. Mueller. (1988). "Are Acquiring-Firm Shareholders Better Off after an Acquistion?" In *Knights, Raiders, and Targets: The Impact of Hostile Takeovers,* edited by J. C. Coffee, L. Lowenstein, and S. Rose-Ackerman, 171–93. New York: Oxford University Press.

Manne, H. G. (1965). "Mergers and the Market for Corporate Control." *Journal of Political Economy* 73–4: 110–20.

Markowitz, H. (1952). "Portfolio Selection." *Journal of Finance* 7:77–91.

McGee, J., and H. Thomas. (1986). "Strategic Groups: Theory, Research, and Taxonomy." *Strategic Management Journal* 7:141–61.

Michel, A., and I. Shaked. (1984). "Does Business Diversification Affect Performance?" *Financial Management* 13(4):18–25.

Miles R. H., in collaboration with Kim S. Cameron. (1982). *Coffin Nails and Corporate Strategies.* Englewood Cliffs, NJ: Prentice-Hall.

Montgomery, C. A. (1985). "Product Market Diversification and Market Power." *Academy of Management Journal* 5:181–91.

Mullins, D. W., Jr. (1982). "Does the Capital Asset Pricing Model Work?" *Harvard Business Review* (January–February): 104–14.

Nelson, R. R., and S. G. Winter. (1982). *An Evolutionary Theory of Economic Change.* Cambridge: Harvard University Press.

Normann, R. (1977). *Management for Growth*: New York: John Wiley.

Palepu, K. (1985). "Diversification Strategy, Profit Performance, and the Entropy Measure." *Strategic Management Journal* 6:239–55.

Panzar, J. C., and R. D. Willig. (1977). "Economies of Scale and Economies of Scope in Multi-Output Production." *Quarterly Journal of Economics* 91:481–93.

Panzar, J. C., and R. D. Willig (1981). "Economies of Scope." *American Economic Review* 71:268–72.

Pascale, R. T., and A. Athos. (1981). *The Art of Japanese Management.* New York: Warner Books.

Peavy, J. W., III. (1984). "Modern Financial Theory, Corporate Strategy, and Public Policy: Another Perspective." *Academy of Management Review* 9:152–7.

Penrose, E. (1959). *The Theory of the Growth of the Firm.* London: Basil Blackwell.

Peters, T. J., and R. H. Waterman, Jr. (1982). *In Search of Excellence.* New York: Basic Books.

Polanyi, M. (1958). *Personal Knowledge: Towards a Post-Critical Philosophy.* Chicago: University of Chicago Press.

Porter, M. E. (1980). *Competitive Strategy.* New York: Free Press.

———, (1985). *Competitive Advantage.* New York: Free Press.

Prahalad, C. K., and R. A. Bettis. (1986). "The Dominant Logic: A New Linkage Between Diversity and Performance." *Strategic Management Journal* 7: 485–501.

Rappaport, A. (1986). *Creating Shareholder Value: The New Standard for Business Performance.* New York: Free Press.

Ravenscraft, D. J., and F. M. Scherer. (1987). *Mergers, Sell-offs, and Economic Efficiency,* Washington, DC: Brookings Institution.

Roll, R. (1986). "The Hubris Hypothesis of Corporate Takeovers." *Journal of Business* 59: 197–216.

Rumelt, R. P. (1974). *Strategy, Structure, and Economic Performance.* Boston: Division of Research, Graduate School of Business Administration, Harvard University.

Salter, M. S., and W. S. Weinhold. (1979). *Diversification Through Acquisition.* New York: Free Press.

Scherer, F. M. (1970). *Industrial Market Structure and Economic Performance.* Chicago: Rand McNally.

Schipper, K., and A. Smith. (1983). "Effects of Recontracting on Shareholder Wealth: The Case of Voluntary Spin-Offs." *Journal of Financial Economics* 12: 437–67.

Selznick, P. (1957). *Leadership in Administration.* Evanston, IL: Row, Peterson.

Sharpe, W. F. (1964). "Capital Assets Prices: A Theory of Market Equilibrium Under Conditions of Risk." *Journal of Finance* 19: 425–42.

Shleifer, A., and R. W. Vishny, (1988). "Management Buyouts as a Response to Market Pressure." In *Mergers and Acquisitions*, edited by A. J. Auerbach, 87–102. Chicago: University of Chicago Press.

Singh, H., and C. A. Montgomery. (1987). "Corporate Acquisition Strategies and Economic Performance." *Strategic Management Journal* 8: 377–86.

Summer, C. E. (1980). *Strategic Behavior in Business and Government.* Boston: Little, Brown.

Taggart, R. A., Jr. (1988). "The Growth of the 'Junk' Bond Market and Its Role in Financing Takeovers." In *Mergers and Acquisitions*, edited by A. J. Auerbach, 5–24. Chicago: University of Chicago Press.

Teece, D. (1980). "Economies of Scope and the Scope of the Enterprise." *Journal of Economic Behavior and Organization* 1: 223–47.

Thompson, J. D. (1967). *Organizations in Action.* New York: McGraw-Hill.

Wernerfeldt, B. (1984). "A Resource-based View of the Firm." *Strategic Management Journal* 5: 171–80.

Williamson, O. E. (1975). *Markets and Hierarchies: Analysis and Antitrust Implications.* New York: Free Press.

Wrigley, L. (1970): "Divisional Autonomy and Diversification." Doctoral dissertation. Boston: Harvard Business School.

Part III

The quest for synergy

The resource-based theory of the firm, discussed in Parts I and II, emphasizes the importance of a firm's tangible and intangible resources, and suggests that firms should diversify into new products and businesses in order to make full use of their resources. From a managerial perspective, the resource-based theory of the firm implies that a multibusiness firm should seek to achieve synergies across its businesses. The common ownership of a group of businesses may make it possible to share manufacturing facilities, sales forces, distribution channels or advertising among the businesses. Or a firm may possess specialized skills, such as research expertise or marketing to particular types of customers, and should seek to find ways to apply such skills in new businesses. In each case, the firm achieves synergies if the sharing of activities or skills enables each business to perform better than it would if it was an independent entity. Synergy means that a firm is more than simply the sum of its parts, and the achievement of synergy has been a goal of many corporate strategies.

Synergy is a powerful concept, and researchers have noted that managers almost always justify mergers, acquisitions and diversifications mainly in terms of the opportunities for synergies.[1] Michael Porter, one of the most notable writers on strategy, is a strong advocate of corporate strategies based on synergy. He argues that without synergy – which he defines as achieving interrelationships across a group of businesses, or 'horizontal strategy' – a diversified firm is little more than a mutual fund. Porter acknowledges that efforts to achieve synergy have by and large failed. He attributes this to a misguided commitment to decentralization which undermines linkages across businesses, and to managers' lack of understanding of the concept. In Porter's view, managers often appraise potential benefits too superficially, and he urges them to take a much more disciplined approach to assessing benefits from interrelationships across businesses. In the piece included here, Porter explains how value chain analysis can be used to identify activities and skills that can be shared across a group of businesses. His framework provides detailed guidance to managers on the potential for sharing in areas such as production, procurement and technology. Additionally, Porter details both the potential benefits and the costs of numerous types of sharing.

While Porter focuses on how businesses can profitably share activities and, in some cases skills, other writers have taken a somewhat different approach to the question of synergy. The Japanese academic, Hiroyuki Itami, focuses on a firm's intangible assets, which may be technological expertise or a brand name or customer knowledge. Such assets are particularly valuable because, unlike physical or financial assets, the value of invisible assets does not diminish with use. In his book, *Mobilizing Invisible Assets*, Itami argues that when a firm finds ways of using its invisible assets in new products or businesses, it gains a 'free ride', or synergy.[2]

The notion that the real strengths of a corporation are its skills and know-how, and that a firm should aim to exploit these assets in new areas, also underlies the work of many resource-based theorists. C. K. Prahalad and Gary Hamel, in their prize-winning article from the *Harvard Business Review*, 'The Core Competence of the Corporation', which is included here, argue that the key resources of a corporation are its core competences, or its expertise in particular technologies. Successful multibusiness companies, such as NEC and 3M, base their corporate strategies on developing and exploiting their core competences in different businesses. Although the end products of the different businesses can vary widely, the separate businesses share and contribute to the core competences of the corporation.[3] Prahalad and Hamel argue that this approach is the key to a successful corporate strategy.

Prahalad and Hamel, in common with Michael Porter, are critical of many of the current approaches to corporate strategy in Western companies. They argue that successful corporations should be more than mere collections of autonomous business units and that the task of managing a diversified company goes beyond allocating capital among discrete businesses. In their view, only by identifying and exploiting the opportunities for sharing activities or core competences across different businesses will managers achieve the goal of making the multibusiness company more than simply the sum of its parts.

For many companies, the approach to synergy advocated by Porter, Prahalad and Hamel demands significant changes in corporate structures, cultures and values, and such fundamental changes pose a real challenge for managers. Hence, the question of how to achieve synergy benefits is critical, and this is the focus of our third reading by Rosabeth Moss Kanter. A Harvard professor and consultant, Kanter has written several influential books on successful organizational approaches to innovation and change. In this selection, from her book *When Giants Learn to Dance*, she shows how many corporate practices, such as competition among business units or performance pay based solely on unit performance, hinder the development of profitable linkages across businesses. To overcome these problems, Moss Kanter calls for new organizational approaches that are geared to encouraging co-operation and exploiting opportunities for sharing resources among different businesses.

Kanter's argument that we need new kinds of organizations to exploit synergy opportunities is also supported by other authorities. For example, Christopher Bartlett and Sumantra Ghoshal in their book, *Managing Across Borders*,[4] argue that a new organizational type is emerging among multinational firms, which they call the transnational. A transnational is an interdependent web of businesses, where people, goods and resources flow freely between the different parts. Such an organizational structure facilitates the achievement of synergies. Although there are, as yet, very few fully developed transnational companies, Bartlett and Ghoshal argue that this organizational form will become increasingly important as multinational firms seek to make the most of their diverse operations and resources.[5]

The authors included in this chapter aim to provide managers with analytical techniques and practical approaches to synergy issues. In reality, however, many companies have found it difficult or even impossible to gain synergy benefits. Even the committed pursuit of synergies, such as that undertaken by American Express and other financial service firms during the 1980s, is no guarantee of success.[6] While synergy opportunities often promise substantial benefits, in many companies efforts to achieve synergies have added costs without providing significant benefits. Despite the advice available from academics and consultants, synergy remains an elusive goal for many companies.

NOTES

1 Reed, Richard and Luffman, George A. (1986) 'Diversification: the Growing Confusion', *Strategic Management Journal* 7: 29–35; Trautwein, Friedrich (1990) 'Merger Motives and Merger Prescriptions', *Strategic Management Journal*, 11: 283–95. One approach to measuring synergy effects is discussed in Buzzell, Robert D. and Gale, Bradley T. *The PIMS Principles: Linking Strategy to Performance*, New York: The Free Press, (1987) Chapter 12.

2 Itami, Hiroyuki (1987) *Mobilizing Invisible Assets*, Boston, Mass.: Harvard University Press.

3 For a fuller discussion of core competences see Prahalad, C. K. and Hamel, Gary (1994) *Competing for the Future*, Boston, Mass.: Harvard Business School Press.

4 Bartlett, Christopher A. and Ghoshal, Sumantra (1989) *Managing Across Borders: The Transnational Solution*, Boston, Mass.: Harvard Business School Press.

5 The synergy issues confronting multinational companies are also discussed in Prahalad, C. K. and Doz, Yves L. (1987) *The Multinational Mission*, London: Free Press.

6 Grant, Robert (1992) 'Diversification in the Financial Services Industry', in A. Campbell and K. Luchs (eds) *Strategic Synergy*, Butterworth Heinemann, pp. 203–42.

ADDITIONAL READING

Bartlett, Christopher A. and Ghoshal, Sumantra (1989) *Managing Across Borders: The Transnational Solution*, Boston, Mass.: Harvard Business School Press.
A study of both successful and unsuccessful efforts by multinational companies to leverage their resources in their worldwide operations. These authors argue that successful global companies are moving towards a new kind of organizational structure, the transnational, which is a network of interdependent units.

Buzzell, Robert D. and Gale, Bradley T. (1987) *The PIMS Principles: Linking Strategy to Performance*, New York: The Free Press.
Chapter 12, 'Integrating Strategies for Clusters of Businesses' considers some of the empirical evidence on synergy effects.

Campbell, Andrew and Luchs, Kathleen (1992) *Strategic Synergy*, Butterworth Heinemann,
A book of readings which provides a survey of the current literature on synergy and a discussion of the major issues. The book includes some detailed case studies of efforts to gain synergy benefits.

Itami, Hiroyuki (1987) *Mobilizing Invisible Assets*, Boston, Mass.: Harvard University Press.
Develops the concept of intangible resources, and argues that the aim of the strategist is to create synergy by building and using these resources.

Prahalad, C. K. and Doz, Yves L. (1987) *The Multinational Mission*, London: Free Press.
Study of the particular opportunities and challenges confronting multinational corporations aiming to achieve synergies, including a thorough discussion of the costs of interdependencies.

Prahalad, C. K. and Hamel, Gary (1994) *Competing for the Future*, Boston, Mass.: Harvard Business School Press.
The authors develop the concept of core competences, and how these should be the basis of successful multibusiness corporations.

Reed, Richard and Luffman, George A. (1986) 'Diversification: the Growing Confusion', *Strategic Management Journal*, 7: 29–35.
A critical assessment of the 'mystique' surrounding synergy and the way in which diversification and synergy have become virtually inseparable in management texts and in management thinking.

Trautwein, Friedrich (1990) 'Merger Motives and Merger Prescriptions', *Strategic Management Journal*, 11: 283–95.
An analysis of different theories of merger motives and the evidence supporting these theories. Argues that there is little evidence to support the 'efficiency theory' of mergers, whereby synergy benefits are realized. None the less, managers frequently justify mergers in terms of their synergies.

Chapter 8

Interrelationships across businesses

Michael Porter

As strategic planning theory and practice have developed, most firms have come to recognize two types of strategy: business unit strategy and corporate strategy. Business strategy charts the course for a firm's activities in individual industries, while corporate strategy addresses the composition of a firm's portfolio of business units. Reflecting this distinction, most major firms have divided their businesses into some type of strategic business units (SBUs), and instituted formal planning processes in which SBUs submit plans for review by top management on an annual or biannual basis. At the same time, corporate strategy has become increasingly viewed as portfolio management, typically using some variation of the portfolio planning techniques that were widely adopted in the 1970s.[1]

As these developments in formal planning have been occurring, the concept of synergy has become widely regarded as *passé*. The idea that combining different but related businesses could create value through synergy was widely accepted and used as a justification for the extensive diversification that took place in the United States in the 1960s and early 1970s. Statements describing hoped-for areas for synergy accompanied many merger announcements, and were common in annual reports. By the late 1970s, however, the enthusiasm for synergy had waned. Synergy, it seemed, was a nice idea *but rarely occurred in practice*. Instead of in synergy, the answer seemed to lie in decentralization where business unit managers would be given authority and responsibility and rewarded based on results. Recent popular business writing has identified decentralization as a foundation of many successful firms, and many major corporations now practice decentralization with near-religious reverence. Decentralization, coupled with disenchantment with synergy, has reinforced the view that portfolio management is the essential task of corporate strategy.

The failure of synergy stemmed from the inability of companies to understand and implement it, not because of some basic flaw in the concept. Firms often used it to justify actions taken for other reasons.

Ill-defined notions of what constituted synergy underlay many companies' acquisition strategies. Even in instances where companies possessed a genuine opportunity to harness synergy, they often failed because the tools for analyzing it were lacking or they could not overcome the substantial organization problems of implementation.

Compelling forces are at work today, however, that mean that firms must reexamine their attitude toward synergy. Economic, technological, and competitive developments are increasing the competitive advantage to be gained by those firms that can identify and exploit interrelationships among distinct but related businesses. These interrelationships are not the fuzzy notions of "fit" which underlay most discussions of synergy, but tangible opportunities to reduce costs or enhance differentiation in virtually any activity in the value chain. Moreover, the pursuit of interrelationships by some competitors is compelling others to follow suit or risk losing their competitive position.

These developments have made *horizontal* strategy, which cuts across divisional boundaries, perhaps the most critical item on the strategic agenda facing a diversified firm. Horizontal strategy is a coordinated set of goals and policies across distinct but interrelated business units. It is required at the group, sector, and corporate levels of a diversified firm. It does not replace or eliminate the need for separate business units and/or business unit strategies. Rather, horizontal strategy provides for explicit coordination among business units that makes corporate or group strategy *more* than the sum of the individual-business unit strategies. It is the mechanism by which a diversified firm enhances the competitive advantage of its business units.

Horizontal strategy is a concept of group, sector, and corporate strategy based on competitive advantage, not on financial considerations or stock market perceptions. Corporate strategies built on purely financial grounds provide an elusive justification for the diversified firm. Moreover, the benefits of even successful financial strategies are often temporary. Without a horizontal strategy there is no convincing rationale for the existence of a diversified firm because it is little more than a mutual fund.[2] Horizontal strategy – not portfolio management – is thus the essence of corporate strategy.

Strategically important interrelationships have long been present in many diversified firms. Little attention has been given to identifying and exploiting them systematically, however, and many interrelationships have remained untapped. Achieving interrelationships involves far more than simply recognizing their presence. There are a number of organizational barriers to achieving interrelationships in practice, which are difficult to surmount even if the strategic benefits are clear. Without organizational mechanisms to facilitate interrelationships that work in tandem with a decentralized corporate organizational structure, horizontal strategy will fail.

This chapter will provide a framework for analyzing interrelationships among business units and how they relate to competitive advantage. I will describe the three broad types of interrelationships among business units: tangible interrelationships, intangible interrelationships, and competitor interrelationships. Then I will discuss how each form of interrelationship leads to competitive advantage, and how interrelationships can be identified.

INTERRELATIONSHIPS AMONG BUSINESS UNITS

There are three broad types of possible interrelationships among business units: tangible interrelationships, intangible interrelationships, and competitor interrelationships. All three types can have important, but different, impacts on competitive advantage and are not mutually exclusive:

Tangible Interrelationships   Tangible interrelationships arise from opportunities to share activities in the value chain among related business units, due to the presence of common buyers, channels, technologies, and other factors. Tangible interrelationships lead to competitive advantage if sharing lowers cost or enhances differentiation enough to exceed the costs of sharing. Business units that can share a sales force, for example, may be able to lower selling cost or provide the salesperson with a unique package to offer the buyer. Achieving tangible interrelationships often involves jointly performing one value activity while in other cases it involves multiple activities. When sister business units cross-sell each other's product, for example, they are sharing both of their sales forces.

Intangible Interrelationships   Intangible interrelationships involve the transference of management know-how among separate value chains. Businesses that cannot share activities may nevertheless be similar in generic terms, such as in the *type* of buyer, *type* of purchase by the buyer, *type* of manufacturing process employed and *type* of relationship with government. For example, beer and cigarettes are both frequently purchased recreational products sold on the basis of image as well as taste, while trucking and waste treatment both involve the management of multiple sites.

Intangible interrelationships lead to competitive advantage through transference of *generic skills* or know-how about how to manage a particular type of activity from one business unit to another. This may lower the cost of the activity or make it more unique and outweigh any cost of transferring the know-how. For example, Philip Morris applied product management, brand positioning, and advertising concepts learned in cigarettes to the beer business, substantially changing the nature of competition and dramatically enhancing the competitive position of the Miller brand. It performed marketing activities for cigarettes and beer separately, but used expertise gained in managing activities in one industry to manage them more effectively in another.

Often intangible interrelationships are manifested in a firm's use of the same generic strategy in a number of business units, reflecting management's skills in executing a particular strategy. For example, Emerson Electric and H. J. Heinz compete by using cost leadership strategies in many of their business units. Emerson and Heinz have learned how to manage many activities to achieve low cost, and transfer this know-how to similar but separate value activities in many business units.

Competitor Interrelationships   The third form of interrelationship, competitor interrelationships, stems from the existence of rivals that actually or potentially compete with a firm in more than one industry. These *multipoint competitors* necessarily link industries together because actions toward them in one industry may have implications in another. While competitor interrelationships occur without tangible or intangible interrelationships being present and vice versa, the two often coexist because tangible and intangible interrelationships can provide the basis for diversification. Competitors in one industry, therefore, often expand in the same directions.

Competitor interrelationships make tangible and intangible interrelationships all the more important to recognize and exploit. A multipoint competitor may compel a firm to match an interrelationship or face a competitive disadvantage. Multipoint competitors can also have an overlapping but different set of business units linked by *different* interrelationships than the firm's, making the matching of such interrelationships difficult.

The three types of interrelationships can occur together, as has already been suggested. Tangible interrelationships involving some value activities can be supplemented by intangible interrelationships in others. Activities shared between two business units can be improved by know-how gained from similar activities in other business units Both tangible and intangible interrelationships are often present when multipoint competitors are present. Each type of interrelationship, however, leads to competitive advantage in a different way.

Synergy is not one idea, then, but three fundamentally different ideas. Thus it is no surprise that what is meant by synergy has been vague. Synergy has most often been described in terms that suggest that what was meant was intangible interrelationships – transference of skills or expertise in management from one business unit to another. This form of interrelationship is perhaps the most ephemeral, however, and its role in creating competitive advantage often is uncertain though potentially significant. Hence it is not surprising that many firms have had great difficulty realizing the fruits of synergy in practice.

I will discuss all three forms of interrelationships in this chapter. Tangible and competitive interrelationships have the most compelling link to competitive advantage, and are easier to implement. Intangible interrelationships are fraught with pitfalls and are often difficult to implement, but can still be a powerful source of competitive advantage in some industries.[3]

TANGIBLE INTERRELATIONSHIPS

The value chain provides the starting point for the analysis of tangible interrelationships. A business unit can potentially share any value activity with another business unit in the firm, including both primary and supporting activities. For example, Procter & Gamble enjoys interrelationships between its disposable diaper and paper towel businesses. Certain raw materials can be procured and handled jointly, the development of technology on products and processes is shared, a joint sales force sells both products to supermarket buyers, and both products are shipped to buyers via the same physical distribution system. The interrelationships are shown schematically in Figure 8.1. As this example illustrates, tangible interrelationships between two business units can involve one or many value activities. If most value activities are shared between two business units, however, they are not strategically distinct business units but in fact one business unit.

Sharing an activity can lead to a sustainable competitive advantage if the advantage of sharing outweighs the cost, provided the sharing is difficult for competitors to match. Sharing leads to a competitive advantage if it reduces cost or enhances differentiation. Sharing always involves some cost, however, that ranges from the cost of coordinating among the business units involved to the need to modify business unit strategies to facilitate sharing.

Sharing and competitive advantage

Sharing a value activity will lead to a significant cost advantage if it involves an activity that represents a significant fraction of operating costs or assets (I term this a *large* value activity), and sharing lowers the cost of performing the activity. Sharing will significantly enhance differentiation if it involves an activity important to differentiation in which sharing either increases the uniqueness of the activity or reduces the cost of being unique. Thus sharing leads to a competitive advantage if it affects the drivers of cost position or differentiation.

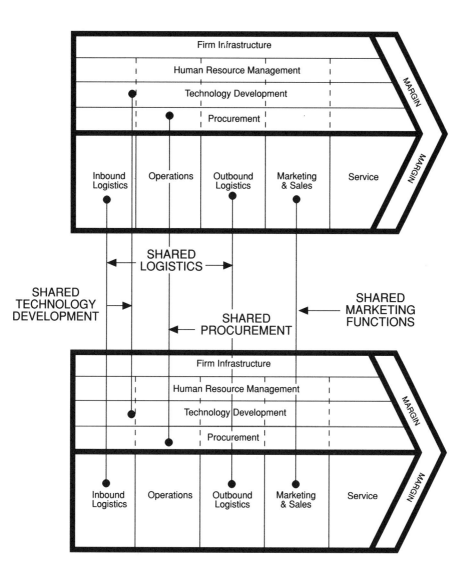

Figure 8.1 Illustrative interrelationships between value chains in paper products

Sharing and cost

Sharing will have a material impact on overall cost position only if the value activities involved are a significant proportion of operating costs or assets, or will be in the future. In the Procter & Gamble example, the shared value activities add up to more than 50 percent of revenues. Sharing does not necessarily lower cost, however, unless it favorably affects the other cost drivers of an activity. Sharing has the potential to reduce cost if the *cost of a value activity is driven by economies of scale, learning, or the pattern of capacity utilization*.[4] Sharing increases the scale of an activity and increases the rate of learning if learning is a function of cumulative volume.[5] Sharing may also improve the pattern of capacity utilization of an activity if the involved business units utilize the activity at different times. For example a sales force or logistical system that is utilized heavily during only part of the year serving one business unit may be utilized during other periods by another. All three benefits of sharing for cost position can potentially occur simultaneously.[6]

Sharing activities among business units is, then, a *potential substitute for market share* in any one business unit. A firm that can share scale or learning-sensitive activities among a number of business units may neutralize the cost advantage of a high market share firm competing with one business unit. Sharing is not exactly equivalent to increasing market share in one business unit, however, because a shared activity often involves greater *complexity* than an equivalent scale activity serving one business unit. The complexity of a shared logistical system involving ten product varieties may increase geometrically compared to one that must handle only five. The added complexity becomes a cost of sharing.

If scale, learning, or the pattern of utilization are not important cost drivers, sharing is likely to raise costs. Firms often mistakenly pursue sharing solely because of excess capacity in an activity. If sharing does not lead to scale or learning advantages or improve the long-term pattern of utilization, however, the costs of sharing will usually mean that sharing creates a disadvantage. The correct solution would have been to reduce capacity in the activity rather than share it.

Figure 8.2 illustrates how these principles can be used to highlight activities where sharing is potentially important to cost position. Interrelationships involving value activities in the upper right-hand quadrant of the diagram are of potentially greatest significance due to their large costs and sensitivity to scale, learning, or utilization. Interrelationships involving value activities in the upper left-hand quadrant are not currently important because sharing will not reduce cost, though the value activities represent a large fraction of costs or assets. However, changes in the technology for performing such activities can quickly make

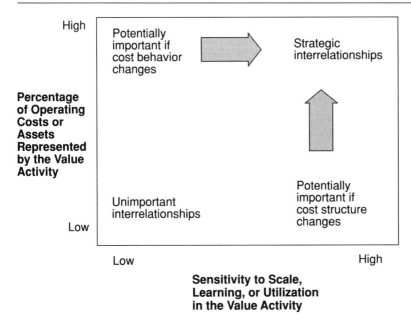

Figure 8.2 Shared value activities and cost position

interrelationships crucial if their cost becomes more sensitive to scale, learning, or utilization. The change in order processing technology from manual systems to on-line computers in many distribution industries, for example, has begun to create important advantages from sharing order processing across related product lines. Interrelationships involving value activities in the lower right-hand quadrant can become important for cost position if changes in the cost structure raise the percentage of operating costs or assets they represent. The increasing capital cost of a plant and supporting infrastructure, for example, will raise the potential advantage of sharing facilities.

Sharing and differentiation

Sharing affects differentiation in two ways. It can enhance differentiation by increasing the uniqueness of an activity, or it can lower the cost of differentiation. Sharing will be most important to differentiation if it affects value activities that are important to actual value or to signaling value. In consumer electronics, for example, sharing product development is important to differentiation because differentiation is heavily affected by product design. Sharing will also be important to differentiation where it reduces the cost of expensive forms of differentiation, such as an extensive sales and service network (e.g., IBM in office products).

Sharing can make an activity more unique both directly and through its impact on other drivers of uniqueness. Sharing enhances uniqueness directly if the shared activity is more valuable to buyers because it involves more than one business unit. Selling several products through the same sales force may increase convenience for the buyer, for example, or allow for the differentiation advantages of bundling. In telecommunications, for example, buyers want system solutions and one-vendor accountability. Similarly, joint product development may lead to greater compatibility among related products. Sharing may also increase uniqueness indirectly, through increasing scale or the rate of learning in an activity. Both scale and learning may allow an activity to be performed in a unique way.

Sharing can reduce the cost of differentiation through its impact on the cost drivers of differentiating activities. Sharing product development among business units can reduce the cost of rapid model changes if product development is subject to economies of scale, for example, while shared procurement can lower the cost of purchasing premium quality ingredients or components. The added complexity of a shared activity is a cost of sharing, however, that must be weighed against the benefits to differentiation.

The advantages of sharing and business unit position

Sharing an activity will usually not lead to an equal improvement in cost or differentiation for each of the business units involved. Differences in the scales of the business units are one important reason. A business unit that uses a large volume of a component may not gain much of a cost advantage from sharing fabrication of the component with a business unit that uses a small volume of it. However, the unit that is the smaller user may enjoy a tremendous improvement in cost position through gaining the benefits of the larger unit's scale. The advantages to the unit that is the smaller user may allow it to substantially improve its market position. Given such asymmetries, it should come as no surprise that larger business units are rarely enthusiastic about interrelationships with smaller units.[7]

Differences in the structure of the industries in which business units compete may also lead to differential benefits from sharing. A small improvement in cost position may be very important in a commodity industry, for example, but less significant in an industry where product differentiation is high and firms compete on quality and service. The significance of an interrelationship also depends on the strategies of the business units involved. An interrelationship may lead to uniqueness that is valuable for one business unit but much less valuable to another. It is rare, then, that all the business units involved in an interrelationship will perceive it as equally advantageous. This point has important implications for horizontal strategy and for the ability of senior managers to persuade business units to pursue interrelationships.

The costs of sharing

Interrelationships always involve a cost, because they require business units to modify their behavior in some way. The costs of sharing a value activity can be divided into three types:

- cost of coordination
- cost of compromise
- cost of inflexibility

The *cost of coordination* is relatively easy to understand. Business units must coordinate in such areas as scheduling, setting priorities, and resolving problems in order to share an activity. Coordination involves costs in terms of time, personnel, and perhaps money. The cost of coordination will differ widely for different types of sharing. A shared sales force requires continual coordination, for example, while joint procurement may require nothing more than periodic communication to determine the quantity of a purchased input required per period by each business unit. Different business units may also see the cost of coordination differently. The costs of coordination are often viewed as higher by smaller business units, who see a continual battle over priorities and the risk of being dictated to by larger units. Business units that do not manage a shared activity or are located at a distance from it also tend to fear that their best interests will not be protected.[8]

The cost of coordination will be influenced by the potentially greater complexity of a shared activity noted earlier. The added complexity involved in sharing will vary, depending on the specific activity. Sharing a computerized order entry system among business units will usually add little complexity, for example, in contrast to sharing a logistical system between two business units with large product lines. The added complexity of a shared activity can sometimes offset economies of scale or reduce the rate of learning compared to an activity serving one business unit. Thus sharing can both increase scale and/or learning at the same time as it alters the relationship between scale or learning and cost. This is important because changing the scale- or learning-sensitivity of an activity may benefit or hurt the firm's cost position depending on its circumstances. Computerization generally has reduced the cost of handling the complexity of sharing. That is one of the reasons why interrelationships are getting more important.

A second, often more important, cost of sharing is the *cost of compromise*. Sharing an activity requires that an activity be performed in a consistent way that may not be optimal for either of the business units involved. Sharing a sales force, for example, may mean that the salesperson gives less attention to both business units' products and is less knowledgeable about either product than a dedicated sales force would be. Similarly, sharing component fabrication may mean that the component's design cannot exactly match one business unit's needs because it must also meet another's. The cost of compromise may include costs not only in the shared value activity but also in other linked value activities. Sharing a sales force, for example, may reduce the availability of salespeople to perform minor service functions, thereby increasing the number of service technicians required. Policy choices required to facilitate sharing, then, can adversely affect the cost or differentiation of one or more of the business units involved.

That business units must in some way compromise their needs to share an activity is almost a given. The cost of compromise may be minor, or may be great enough to nullify the value of sharing. For example, attempting to share a logistical system among business units producing products of widely differing sizes, weights, delivery frequencies, and sensitivities to delivery time may well lead to a logistical system that is so inappropriate to any of the business unit's needs that the cost savings of sharing are overwhelmed. However, sharing a brand name or sharing procurement of commodities may involve little or no compromise.

The cost of compromise to share an activity will often differ for each of the affected business units. A business unit with a product that is difficult to sell may have to compromise the most in employing a shared sales force, for example. The cost of compromise may also differ because the particular value activity plays a differing role in one business unit compared to another because of its strategy. The compromise involved in joint procurement of a common grade of milk or butter may be more serious for a business unit of a food manufacturer pursuing a premium quality strategy than it is for one attempting to be the low-cost producer if the common grade is not top quality.

The cost of compromise required to achieve an interrelationship is much less if the strategies of the business units involved are consistent with respect to the role of the shared value activity. Achieving such consistency often involves little or no sacrifice to the affected business units *if their strategic directions are coordinated over time*. A particular component can be highly effective in the products of two business units if both units design their products with the component in mind, for example. If the design groups of the two business units are allowed to proceed independently, however, the chances are high that the common component will not meet either business unit's needs. Consistency among business units' strategies that facilitates sharing will rarely happen naturally. An example of both the opportunities to shape the cost of compromise and the indirect costs of compromise that must be weighed comes from General Foods' successful new Pudding Pops. Pudding Pops were designed to melt at a higher temperature than ice cream so that distribution then could be shared with General Foods' Birds Eye frozen vegetables. While frozen foods are transported at zero degrees Fahrenheit, ice cream must be transported at 20 degrees below zero or it will build up ice crystals. While the benefits in shared logistics were clear, however, sharing had some unforeseen consequences elsewhere in the value chain. Because Pudding Pops had to be ordered by supermarket frozen food managers along with vegetables, instead of with other freezer case novelty items, Pudding Pops were often forgotten. As this example illustrates, the benefits and costs of an interrelationship must be examined *throughout the value chain* and not just in the activity shared.

The cost of compromise is frequently reduced if an activity is *designed for sharing* rather than if previously separate activities are simply combined or if an activity designed to serve one business unit simply takes on another with no change in procedures or technology. Recent events in financial services have highlighted this point. Merging computer systems initially designed for separate financial products has proven difficult, though a system designed to process many products would be effective. Similarly, attempting to sell insurance and other financial products through a distribution system designed for selling stocks and bonds has not served any of the products very well and has created organizational problems. However, a new conception of a brokerage office is emerging that combines brokers, customer service personnel to handle simple problems and screen clients, and specialists to sell other financial products together with a new shared information system. The cost of compromise in sharing distribution is likely to be much less as a result.

The third cost of sharing is the *cost of inflexibility*. Inflexibility takes two forms: (1) potential difficulty in responding to competitive moves, and (2) exit barriers. Sharing can make it more difficult to respond quickly to competitors because attempting to counter a threat in one business unit may undermine or reduce the value of the interrelationship for sister business units. Sharing also can raise exit barriers. Exiting from a business unit with no competitive advantage may harm other business units sharing an activity with it.[9] Unlike other costs of sharing, the cost of inflexibility is not an ongoing cost but a potential cost should the need for flexibility arise. The cost of inflexibility will depend on the likelihood of the need to respond or exit.

Some costs of coordination, compromise, or inflexibility are involved in achieving any interrelationship. These costs, particularly any required compromise to achieve an interrelationship, will be very real concerns raised by business units when sharing is discussed. They may appear far more obvious than the advantages of the interrelationship, which may appear theoretical and speculative. Business units will also tend to view a potential interrelationship in the light of their existing strategy, rather than weigh its cost if their strategies are modified to minimize the costs of sharing. Finally, the value of interrelationships is often clouded by organizational issues involved in sharing, including those of turf and autonomy. Thus business units can sometimes oppose interrelationships that may result in a clear competitive advantage to them.

The advantages of sharing an activity must be weighed against the costs of coordination, compromise, and inflexibility to determine the *net* competitive advantage of sharing. The assessment of the competitive advantage from an interrelationship must be performed separately for each of the involved business units, and the value of an interrelationship to the firm as a whole is the sum of the net advantages to the involved business units. The net competitive advantage from sharing an activity will almost inevitably vary for each business unit involved. In some cases, the net value of an interrelationship may even be *negative* from the viewpoint of one business unit because of the required compromise, but will be more than offset by a positive net value for other affected business units. For this reason and because of the natural biases in approaching interrelationships noted above, then, business units will often not readily agree on pursuing interrelationships that will benefit a firm as a whole. Interrelationships will *only* happen under such circumstances if there is an explicit horizontal strategy.

While there are always costs of sharing, forces are at work to reduce them in many industries. The new technologies described earlier in this chapter are having the effect of reducing the cost of coordination, compromise, and, to a lesser extent, the cost of inflexibility. Easier communication and better information systems make coordination easier. Low-cost computers and information systems also introduce flexibility into value activities, or the technical capability to minimize the cost of compromise. Programmable machines and robots can adapt to the different needs of business units sharing them. Many firms are only beginning to perceive these possibilities for lowering the cost of sharing, but continue to base their assessment of interrelationships on outdated methods.

Difficulty of matching

The sustainability of the net competitive advantage of an interrelationship will depend on the difficulty competitors have in matching it. Competitors have two basic options in matching the competitive advantage of an interrelationship: (1) duplicating the interrelationship, or (2) offsetting it through other means such as gaining share in the affected business unit or exploiting a different interrelationship. The ease of duplicating an interrelationship will vary depending on whether competitors are in the same group of related industries involved. The most valuable interrelationships from a strategic point of view are those involving industries that competitors are not in and that have high barriers to entry. For example, Procter & Gamble's advantage from the interrelationships between its disposable diaper and paper towel business units is quite sustainable because its paper towel competitors are blocked from entering the diaper business by enormous entry barriers. A competitor may also face higher or lower costs of coordination and compromise than the firm in achieving an interrelationship depending on the strategies and circumstances of its business units. Other things being equal, then, a firm should pursue most aggressively those interrelationships that its competitors will find the most difficult to match because of the costs of coordination or compromise.

The ability of competitors to offset an interrelationship is a function of whether they can find some other way of improving position in the affected business unit through changes in its strategy or by pursuit of *different* interrelationships. Since nearly any value activity can potentially be shared, a competitor may be able to forge an interrelationship among a different group of business units or share different value activities among the same group of businesses. If a firm, through pursuing an interrelationship, causes a competitor to respond by pursuing different interrelationships, it faces the danger that the ultimate outcome will be an erosion in its relative position.

A final consideration in assessing the difficulty of matching an interrelationship is whether the same benefits can be achieved by a competitor through a coalition or long-term contract. Sometimes a firm can gain the benefits of sharing through a joint venture or other form of coalition with another firm, without actually entering another industry. While such coalitions may be difficult to forge, they should always be considered in assessing the value of an interrelationship and how to achieve it.

Identifying tangible interrelationships

To aid in identifying the tangible interrelationships present in a firm, a useful starting point is to catalog all the forms of sharing that occur in practice as well as the alternative ways they can create competitive advantage. Figure 8.3 divides forms of sharing into five categories: production, market, procurement, technology, and infrastructure. I have included shared human resource management as part of shared

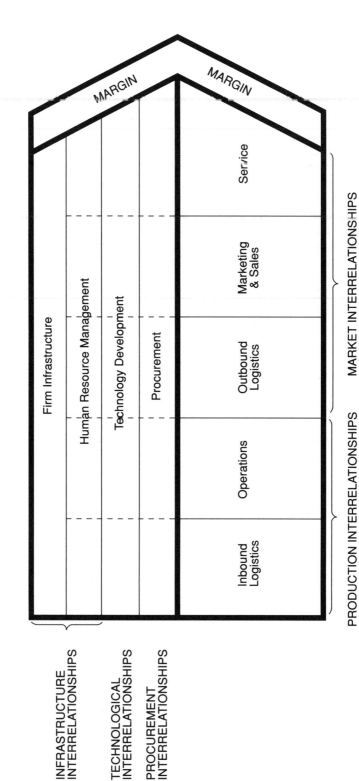

Figure 8.3 Categories of tangible interrelationships

infrastructure. It is useful to separate these categories of interrelationships because they raise different issues in sharing. Interrelationships ultimately stem from *commonalities* of various types among industries, such as common buyers, channels, or production processes. These commonalities define potential interrelationships; whether the interrelationships lead to a competitive advantage is a function of the benefits and costs described earlier. The sources of each category of interrelationship and the possible forms of sharing to capture it are shown in Table 8.1.

Market interrelationships

Market interrelationships involve the sharing of primary value activities involved in reaching and interacting with the buyer, from outbound logistics to service. When business units have only the geographic location of their buyers in common, sharing is usually restricted to physical distribution systems, order processing, and to servicing and sales if the products have similar sales and servicing needs. Richer opportunities for sharing are present when business units also have common buyers, common channels, or both. If buyers or channels are the same, sharing of physical distribution or order processing systems among business units usually involves less complexity and lower costs of sharing. In addition, common buyers or channels open up a wide variety of other possible forms of sharing shown in Table 8.1.

The subtleties in identifying potential market interrelationships stem from the tendency to view the buyer or channel too broadly. A wide variety of products and services are sold to oil companies, for example, including drilling equipment, refinery equipment, and transportation equipment such as oil tankers and tanker trucks. Thus oil companies might be identified as a common buyer by business units in many industries. The various products are sold to different parts of the oil company, however, which often have little contact with each other. Even within a product category such as drilling equipment, equipment used in exploration is frequently sold to a different organizational unit than production equipment. Even in instances when the same unit of the oil company makes the purchase, the particular individuals making the purchase decision or influencing the decision maker will often differ for different pieces of equipment. Engineers may be responsible for choosing some high-technology equipment such as blowout preventers, for example, while purchasing agents often choose more standard items such as pipe.

Another example of viewing the buyer too broadly is becoming apparent from recent experience in financial services. The traditional buyer of stocks and bonds is a different individual than the average life

Table 8.1 Possible sources of interrelationships

Procurement interrelationships		Technological interrelationships		Infrastructure interrelationships	
Source of interrelationship	*Possible forms of sharing*	*Source of interrelationship*	*Possible forms of sharing*	*Source of interrelationship*	*Possible forms of sharing*
Common purchased inputs	Joint procurement	Common product technology	Joint technology development	Common firm infrastructure needs	Shared raising of capital (financing)
		Common process technology	Joint interface design	Common capital	Shared cash utilization
		Common technology in other value activities			Shared accounting
		One product incorporated into another			Shared legal department
		Interface among products			Shared government relations
					Shared hiring and training
					Other shared infrastructure activities

Table 8.1 Continued

Production interrelationships		Market interrelationships	
Source of interrelationship	*Possible forms of sharing*	*Source of interrelationship*	*Possible forms of sharing*
Common location of raw materials	Shared inbound logistics	Common buyer	Shared brand name
Identical or similar fabrication process	Shared component fabrication	Common channel	Cross selling of products
Identical or similar assembly process	Shared assembly facilities	Common geographic market	Bundled or packaged selling
Identical or similar testing/ quality control procedures	Shared testing/quality control facilities		Cross subsidization of complementary products
Common factory support needs	Shared factory indirect activities		Shared marketing department
	Shared site infrastructure		Shared sales force
			Shared service/repair network
			Shared order processing system
			Shared physical distribution system
			Shared buyer or distributor financing organization

insurance buyer. Both are different individuals than the typical buyer of futures. These differences are nullifying simplistic efforts to achieve market interrelationships in financial services. Meaningful opportunities for exploring market interrelationships among business units are usually present only where the decision makers for the products are the same or have some contact with each other.

The same issues arise in identifying common channels. Though two products might both be sold through department stores, few actual channel interrelationships are likely to be present if one is sold through discount department stores and the other through exclusive department stores such as Lord & Taylor and Neiman-Marcus. There are also often different buying executives responsible for different classes of products in the same channel. In most supermarket chains, for example, frozen foods are typically bought by a different buyer than meats, even though some frozen foods are meat products. Even if the decision makers are different, however, opportunities for sharing logistical and order processing systems may exist with both common buyers and common channels.

Whether products sold to a common buyer are substitutes or complements can also affect the advantage of sharing market-related activities. Shared marketing can yield less of a cost advantage when products are substitutes because the buyer will purchase either one product or the other but not both. However, offering substitute products to buyers can reduce the risk of substitution because losses in one product can be compensated in the other. Joint marketing of substitutes can also enhance a firm's differentiation.

When business units sell complementary products to common buyers, the advantage of sharing is often greater than if the products are unrelated or substitutes. Complementary products usually have correlated demand that facilitates the efficient utilization of shared value activities, and other practices such as common branding, joint advertising and bundling.

The potential competitive advantages of the important forms of market interrelationships and the most likely sources of compromise cost are shown in Table 8.2. Indirect activities such as market research, sales force administration and advertising production (e.g., artwork, layout) can often be shared more easily than direct activities because they require lower compromise costs.[10] The benefits of market interrelationships can often be enhanced by changes in the strategies of the involved business units that reduce the cost of compromise. Standardizing sales force practices, repositioning brands to make their images more compatible, or standardizing delivery standards or payment terms may make sharing easier, for example.

Production interrelationships

Interrelationships in production involve the sharing of upstream value activities such as inbound logistics, component fabrication, assembly, testing, and indirect functions such as maintenance and site infrastructure. All these forms of sharing require that activities be located together. Doing so can lead to a compromise cost if the suppliers or buyers of the business units sharing the activities have greatly different geographic locations since inbound or outbound freight costs may be increased. Shared procurement is different from production interrelationships because merging facilities is not implied. Purchased inputs can be procured centrally but shipped from suppliers to dispersed facilities.

Production interrelationships can be illusory when apparently similar value activities are examined closely. For example, though the machines themselves are generically the same, a job-shop manufacturing process for one product may involve different machine tolerances than another, or lot sizes or run lengths can be quite different. As with market interrelationships, indirect value activities offer particularly attractive opportunities for sharing because the compromise costs are often low. For example, such activities as building operations, maintenance, site infrastructure, and testing laboratories can be shared despite the fact that the actual manufacturing processes are different.

Table 8.3 shows the potential competitive advantages of important forms of production interrelationships, and the likely sources of compromise cost. The balance will depend on the strategies of the involved business units. For example, two business units with differentiation strategies are more likely to have similar needs in terms of component specifications, manufacturing tolerances, and testing standards than if one business unit pursues cost leadership while another offers a premium product.

Procurement interrelationships

Procurement interrelationships involve the shared procurement of common purchased inputs. Common inputs are frequently present in diversified firms, particularly if one looks beyond major raw materials and pieces of capital equipment. Suppliers are increasingly willing to make deals based on supplying the needs of plants located around the world and negotiate prices reflecting total corporate needs. Some firms go overboard in shared procurements, however, because they fail to recognize the potential costs of compromise or they establish a rigid procurement process that does not allow for opportunism in negotiating attractive opportunities.

Table 8.2 Determinants of net competitive advantage from market interrelationships

Form of sharing	Potential competitive advantages	Most likely sources of compromise cost
Shared brand name	Lower advertising costs	Product images are inconsistent or conflicting
	Reinforcing product images/reputations	Buyer is reluctant to purchase too much from one firm
		Diluted reputation if one product is inferior
Shared advertising	Lower advertising costs	Appropriate media or messages are different
	Greater leverage in purchasing advertising space	Advertising effectiveness reduced by multiple products
Shared promotion	Lower promotion costs through shared couponing and cross couponing	Appropriate forms and timing of promotion differ
Cross selling of products to each others' buyers	Lower cost of finding new buyers	Product images are inconsistent or conflicting
	Lower cost of selling	Buyer is reluctant to purchase too much from one firm
Interrelated pricing of complementary products	See Chapter 12, Porter, *Competitive Advantage*	See Chapter 12, ibid.
Bundled selling	See Chapter 12, Porter, *Competitive Advantage*	See Chapter 12, ibid.
Shared marketing department	Lower cost of market research	Product positionings are different or inconsistent
	Lower marketing overhead	Buyer's purchasing behavior is not the same
Shared channels	Enhanced bargaining power with the channels leading to improvements in service, shelf positioning, maintenance/repair/ support, or channel margins	Channel gains too much bargaining power *vis-à-vis* the firm
	One-stop shopping for the buyer improves differentiation	Channel unwilling to allow a single firm to account for a major portion of its sales
	Lower cost of channel support infrastructure	Use of shared channel will erode support from other channels

Table 8.2   Continued

Form of sharing	Potential competitive advantages	Most likely sources of compromise cost
Shared sales force or sales offices	Lower selling costs or sales force infrastructure costs	Different buyer purchasing behavior
	Better quality salespersons	Buyer reluctance to purchase large amounts from a single salesperson
	More products to sell improves access to the buyer or enhances buyer convenience	Salesperson is not allowed adequate time with the buyer to present a number of products effectively
	Better sales force utilization if the pattern of utilization is not the same	Different type of salesperson is most effective
		Certain products get more attention than others
Shared services network	Lower servicing costs	Differences in equipment or knowledge necessary to make typical repairs
	More sophisticated or responsive servicing, due to improved technology or denser service locations	Differences in the need for timeliness in service calls
	Better capacity utilization if demand for service is inversely correlated	Differing degrees to which the buyer performs service in-house
Shared order processing	Lower order processing costs	Differences in the form and composition of typical orders
	Lower cost of employing improved technology that improves responsiveness or billing information	Differences in ordering cycles that lead to inconsistent order processing needs
	Better capacity utilization if order flows are inversely correlated	
	One-stop shopping for the buyer improves differentiation	

Table 8.3 Determinants of net competitive advantage from production interrelationships

Form of sharing	Potential competitive advantages	Most likely sources of compromise cost
Shared inbound logistical system	Lower freight and material handling costs	Input sources are located in different geographic areas
	Better technology enhances delivery reliability, reduces damage, etc.	Plants are located in differing geographic areas
	Sharing allows more frequent, smaller deliveries that reduce inventory or improve plant productivity	Varying physical characteristics of inputs imply that a logistical system which can handle all of them is suboptimal
		Needs for frequency and reliability of inbound delivery differ among business units
Shared components (identical components used in different end products)	Lower cost of component fabrication	Needs for component design and quality differ among business units
	Better technology for component manufacturing improves quality	
Shared component fabrication facilities (similar or related components are produced using the *same* equipment and facilities)	Lower component costs	High setup costs for different component varieties
	Better fabrication technology improves quality	Needs for component quality or tolerances differ among business units
	Capacity utilization is improved because demand for similar components is not perfectly correlated	Flexible manufacturing equipment has higher cost than specialized equipment
		Larger workforce in one location leads to potential hiring, unionization or productivity problems

Table 8.3   Continued

Form of sharing	Potential competitive advantages	Most likely sources of compromise cost
Shared assembly facilities (similar or related end products are assembled using the same equipment/lines)	Lower assembly costs Better assembly technology improves quality Utilization is improved because demand is not perfectly correlated A shared materials handling system can feed different assembly lines	High setup costs for different products Needs for quality or tolerances differ Flexible assembly equipment is higher cost Larger workforce in one location leads to potential hiring, unionization or productivity problems
Shared testing/ quality control	Lower testing costs Better technology increases the extensiveness of testing and improves quality control	Testing procedures and quality standards differ Flexible testing facilities and equipment are higher cost
Shared indirect activities (including maintenance, plant overhead, personnel department, cafeteria, etc.)	Lower indirect activity costs Improved quality of indirect activities	Differing needs for indirect activities among business units Larger workforce in one location leads to potential hiring, unionization or productivity problems

The potential competitive advantage of shared procurement and the likely sources of compromise cost are shown in Table 8.4.

Technological interrelationships

Technological interrelationships involve the sharing of technology development activities throughout the value chain. They are distinguished from production interrelationships because their impact is on the cost or uniqueness of technology development, while production interrelationships involve sharing activities involved in the actual production of the product on an ongoing basis. It is important to recognize, however, that interrelationships in process development often occur together with production or market interrelationships. Interrelationships in process technology typically grow out of interrelationships in the primary activities.

Table 8.4 Determinants of net competitive advantage from procurement
interrelationships

Form of sharing	Potential competitive advantage	Most likely sources of compromise cost
Joint procurement of common inputs	Lower costs of inputs	Input needs are different in terms of quality or specifications, leading to higher costs than necessary in business units requiring less quality
	Improved input quality	Technical assistance and delivery needs from suppliers vary among business units
	Improved service from vendors in terms of responsiveness, holding of inventory, etc.	Centralization can reduce the information flow from factory to purchasing, and make purchasing less responsive

As with other forms of interrelationships, apparently promising technological interrelationships can be illusory. Scientific disciplines that overlap for two business units may be of minor importance to success
compared to scientific disciplines that do not overlap. Harris Corporation, for example, thought it could reduce the development expense
involved in entering word processing through adapting software from
its text editing system sold to newspapers. Harris discovered that the
text editing system had so many features that were specific to the needs
of newspapers that development of a word processing system had to
start from scratch.

Truly significant technological interrelationships are ones involving
technologies important to the cost or differentiation of the products or
processes involved, as microelectronics technology is to both telecommunications and data processing. Many products have superficial
technological similarities, making the identification of true technological
interrelationships difficult. As with other types of interrelationship, the
net competitive advantage of a technological interrelationship will differ
depending on the industry and strategies of the business units involved.
For example, the benefits of sharing microelectronics technology will
tend to be greater for two consumer products business units than for a
defense business unit and a consumer business unit. Rockwell International learned this lesson when it put a team of engineers from its

defense business into its Admiral TV set division. The sensitivity to cost was so much greater in TV sets than in defense equipment that sharing did not succeed. The same thing occurred in business aircraft, where a design developed originally for military use (the Sabreliner) proved too expensive for the commercial market.

Table 8.5 shows the potential competitive advantages that can stem from sharing technology development as well as the most likely sources of compromise costs.

Infrastructure interrelationships

The final category of interrelationships involve firm infrastructure, including such activities as financing, legal, accounting, and human resource management. Some infrastructure activities are almost always shared in diversified firms. In most cases, the effect of sharing on competitive advantage is not great because infrastructure is not a large proportion of cost and sharing has little impact on differentiation. It is ironic, therefore, that the vast majority of literature on sharing has been on sharing infrastructure – principally finance and the utilization of capital. Interrelationships in finance, particularly, have been seen as a significant benefit the diversified firm contributes to its business units.

There are two basic sources of financial interrelationships: joint raising of capital and shared utilization of capital (primarily working capital). Economies of scale in raising capital may indeed exist, especially up to a certain quantity of capital needed. Efficient utilization of working capital is made possible by countercyclical or counterseasonal needs for funds among business units, which allows cash freed up by one business unit to be deployed in another. Financial interrelationships typically involve relatively few compromise costs that must be offset against any savings. Moreover, financial interrelationships are among the easiest to achieve if they are present, perhaps a reason why they are so frequently discussed.

The major limitation to the competitive advantage of shared financing is the *efficiency of capital markets*. Scale economies in financing appear to be moderate for most firms and lead to a relatively small difference in financing costs. Firms can also borrow to cover short-term cash needs and lend excess cash in the highly efficient markets for commercial paper and other instruments, mitigating the value of sharing working capital. Hence financial interrelationships are rarely the basis for creating a significant competitive advantage, unless the size and credit rating of competitors differ greatly. Other forms of infrastructure interrelationships can be important in particular industries. Shared infrastructure for hiring and training is important in some service industries, while shared government relations can be significant in natural resource firms.

Table 8.5 Determinants of net competitive advantage from technological interrelationships

Form of sharing	Potential competitive advantages	Most likely sources of compromise cost
Shared technology development (for separate products or where one product is incorporated into another)	Lower product or process design costs (including shorter design time)	Technologies are the same, but the tradeoffs in applying the technology are different among business units
	Larger critical mass in R&D, or the ability to attract better people improves the innovativeness of product or process designs	
	Transference of developments among product areas enhances differentiation or allows early entry into new technologies	
Shared interface design for products with a technological interface	Lower interface design costs	A nonstandard interface reduces the available market
	Differentiation through superior and proprietary interface performance	Risks of bundling
	Bundling opportunities created through a nonstandard interface	

INTANGIBLE INTERRELATIONSHIPS

Intangible interrelationships lead to competitive advantage through the transfer of skills among separate value chains. Through operating one business unit, a firm gains know-how that allows it to improve the way another generically similar business unit competes. The transference of skills can go in either direction – e.g., from existing business units to a new business unit or from a new business unit back to existing business units. The transference of generic know-how can occur anywhere in the value chain. Philip Morris transferred generic know-how in the marketing of consumer packaged goods from its cigarette business to Miller

Beer, while Emerson Electric transferred plant design and cost reduction skills when it acquired the chain saw firm Beaird-Poulan. In both cases, the transference of skills *changed* the way that the receiving business unit competed and enhanced its competitive advantage.

Intangible interrelationships lead to a competitive advantage if the improvement in cost or differentiation in the business unit receiving the know-how exceeds the costs of transferring it. Know-how residing in one business unit has already been paid for, and hence transferring it may involve little cost compared to its cost of development. The actual transference of know-how always involves some cost, however, whether it be the cost of time of skilled personnel or perhaps the greater risk that proprietary information will leak out. Using the know-how that is transferred will also typically involve some cost in adapting it to the circumstances of the receiving business unit. These costs of transferring know-how must be weighed against the potential benefits to determine whether an intangible interrelationship will create competitive advantage.

Intangible interrelationships are important to competitive advantage when the transference of know-how or skills allows the receiving business unit to lower costs or enhance differentiation. This occurs if the transference of skills leads to policy changes that lower cost or enhance differentiation, or because the transference of skills gives the receiving business unit better insight into its other drivers of cost or uniqueness. The transference of skills from Philip Morris to Miller Beer, for example, resulted in policy changes in the way beer was positioned and marketed, as well as an escalation of advertising spending that increased scale economies in the industry and worked to the advantage of large brands like Miller.

Identifying Intangible Interrelationships   Intangible interrelationships arise from a variety of generic similarities among business units:[11]

- same generic strategy
- same *type* of buyer (though not the same buyer)
- similar configuration of the value chain (e.g., many dispersed sites of mineral extraction and processing)
- similar important value activities (e.g., relations with government)

Although value activities cannot be shared, these similarities among business units mean that know-how gained in one business unit is valuable and transferable to another.[12]

Because of the myriad possible generic similarities among business units, it is not possible to be as complete in identifying the important types as it was with tangible interrelationships. However, the value chain provides a systematic way of searching for intangible interrelationships.

A firm can examine the major value activities in its business units to unearth similarities in activities or the way the chain is configured that might provide the basis for transference of know-how or highlight generic skills that might be applied to new industries.

Intangible Interrelationships and Competitive Advantage   Intangible interrelationships of one type or another are very widespread. It is always possible to point to some generic similarity in some value activity between almost any two business units. An airline is widely dispersed, has multiple sites, and relies heavily on scheduling, characteristics shared by trucking companies, international trading companies and industrial gas producers. Widespread similarities of some kind make the analysis of intangible interrelationships quite subtle.

The key tests in identifying intangible interrelationships that are important to competitive advantage are the following:

- *How similar* are the value activities in the business units?
- *How important* are the value activities involved to competition?
- *How significant* is the know-how that would be transferred to competitive advantage in the relevant activities?

These questions must be answered together. The similarity of two business units is a function of how much know-how can be usefully transferred. The importance of the transferred know-how is a function of its contribution to improving competitive advantage in the receiving business unit. The transference of just one insight can sometimes make an enormous difference to competitive advantage, so even business units that are not very similar can have important intangible interrelationships. However, truly important intangible interrelationships are much less common than an initial search for them might imply. It is frequently difficult, moreover, to predict whether the transference of know-how will prove to be valuable.

The most common pitfall in assessing intangible interrelationships is to identify generic similarities among business units that are not important to competition. Either the know-how that can be transferred does not affect value activities that are important to cost or differentiation in the receiving business unit, or it does not provide insights that competitors do not already have. Philip Morris's acquisition of the Seven Up soft drink company provides a possible example of the latter. While the beer industry had historically been populated by family firms with little marketing flair, the soft drink industry has long been characterized by sophisticated marketing by the likes of Coke, Pepsi, and Dr Pepper. Philip Morris's marketing expertise appears to have offerred much less of an advantage for Seven Up than it did for Miller.

Many firms have fallen into the trap of identifying intangible interrelationships that are illusory or do not matter for competitive advantage. Often, it seems, intangible interrelationships are forced, and represent more of an *ex poste* rationalization of diversification moves undertaken for other reasons. Intangible interrelationships were prominent in discussions of synergy. The difficulty of finding and implementing significant intangible interrelationships is one of the reasons synergy proved such a disappointment to many firms.

The effective exploitation of intangible interrelationships thus requires an acute understanding of the business units involved as well as the industries they compete in. The importance of an intangible interrelationship for competition can only be truly understood by identifying *specific* ways in which know-how can be transferred so as to make a difference. The mere hope that one business unit might learn something useful from another is frequently a hope not realized.

Even intangible interrelationships where the benefits of transferring know-how far exceed the cost of transferring it do not lead to competitive advantage unless the transference of know-how actually takes place. Know-how is transferred through interchange between managers or other personnel in the affected business units. This process does not occur without active efforts on the part of senior management. Personnel in the receiving business unit may be wary or unsure of the value of know-how from a "different" industry. They may even openly resist it. Business units with know-how may be hesitant to commit the time of important personnel and may view the know-how as highly proprietary. Finally, transference of know-how is subjective and the benefits of doing so often are hard for managers to understand when compared to tangible interrelationships. All these factors imply that even important intangible interrelationships can be very difficult to achieve. Doing so requires a sustained commitment and the existence of formal mechanisms through which the required transference of skills will take place. A conducive organizational setting can greatly reduce the cost of transferring know-how.

COMPETITOR INTERRELATIONSHIPS

Competitor interrelationships are present when a firm actually or potentially competes with diversified rivals in more than one business unit. Any action taken against multipoint competitors must consider the entire range of jointly contested businesses. In addition, a firm's competitive advantage *vis-à-vis* a multipoint competitor depends in part on the interrelationships that both have achieved. The competitive position of a multipoint competitor is often more a function of its *overall* position in a group of related industries than its market share in any one industry because of interrelationships. While multipoint competitors and interrelationships do not necessarily occur together, they often do because both tangible and intangible interrelationships lead firms to follow parallel diversification paths.[13]

Identifying existing multipoint competitors is relatively easy with a diagram such as that shown in Figure 8.4. For the firm shown in Figure 8.4, competitors A, B, C, D, and E are multipoint competitors. The other competitors are single point, but represent *potential* multipoints. Analysis of the figure suggests that business units 2 and 3 are in strongly related industries, because four competitors compete in both industries. The presence of many competitors in two industries is a relatively strong, though not perfect, indication that they are related. The relatedness of industries is also a clue to predicting which firms are the most likely potential multipoint competitors. Given the apparent relationship of the industries in which business units 2 and 3 compete, competitor H may be the most likely potential multipoint competitor.

Table 8.6 shows the multipoint competitor matrix for the consumer paper products sector in 1983, along with each firm's year of entry. It is clear that competitor interrelationships are numerous and that they have increased significantly over time, particularly during the 1960s and 1970s. We would observe a similar pattern in many other groups of industries. The pattern of competitor interrelationships in the table will be discussed further below.

Closely analogous to the analysis of multipoint competitors is the analysis of single-point competitors with *different patterns of interrelationships* from the firm's. For example, Xerox, Canon, and Matsushita all compete in convenience copiers. However, Xerox draws on interrelationships with its high-volume copiers and office automation equipment. Canon's interrelationships have historically been strongest with its calculator and camera businesses, while Matsushita draws on interrelationships involving its broad range of consumer electronic and other electronic products. Interestingly, both Canon and Matsushita are diversifying into office automation to match Xerox's interrelationships there.

Single-point competitors with different patterns of interrelationships are important because they bring differing sources of competitive advantage to an industry. These may be difficult for a firm to match and may shift the basis of competition. Moreover, as the copier example illustrates, single-point competitors with different patterns of interrelationships are sometimes prime candidates to become multipoint competitors.

Multipoint competitors in unrelated industries

Where a firm faces a multipoint competitor in industries that are not related, the strategic issues revolve around how actions in one business

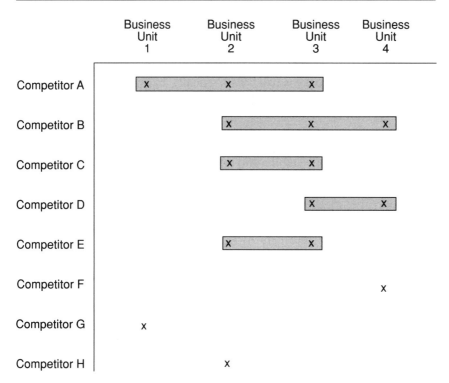

Figure 8.4 Corporate competitor matrix

unit can lead to reactions in another and how equilibrium with the competitor can be reached in several contested industries. Because a firm and a multipoint competitor meet each other in a number of industries rather than one, a greater number of variables enter into determining their relative position. This implies that firms need more information about each other to avoid mistaken interpretations of moves. It also often means that destabilizing events in one industry can spread to others. This added complexity of the game makes peaceful coexistence potentially difficult.

On the other hand, competing in a number of industries also opens up greater possibilities for signaling, making threats, establishing blocking positions, and taking reciprocal actions. For example, a firm threatened in one industry might retaliate in a different industry, sending a signal of displeasure but creating less risk of escalation than if the response were direct. The threat that a firm can retaliate in several industries (and inflict a higher cost on the competitor) may also tend to deter a competitor from making a threatening move in the first place.

Another stabilizing factor in multipoint competition is the fact that focal points, or natural equilibrium points for competition, may be more prevalent.[14] Where only one industry is contested, the number of focal points consistent with each competitor's perception of its relative strength is likely to be small. With equally balanced competitors, for example, an equal division of shares may be the only focal point. It may well be an unstable one because any temporary shift in market shares is likely to trigger a strong response to preserve the balance. With two jointly contested industries, there may be a number of additional focal points that are more stable, and one of them will tend to be found sooner.

Table 8.7 illustrates this. Here focal points 2 and 3 will tend to be more stable than focal point 1. In each industry, the high-share competitor will tend to have a clear competitive advantage, and hence a small disturbance will be less likely to cause either firm to precipitate a war. Similarly, the asymmetry of positions reduces the chances that the high-share competitor in one industry will seek an even greater share, since it remains vulnerable to retaliation in the industry in which it is weak.

Multipoint competitors must be viewed in their totality for purposes of offensive and defensive strategy. Most competitor analysis is done at the business unit level, however, and looks exclusively at competitors' positions in a single industry. Some corporate or group-level analysis of multipoint competitors is essential. Minimally, a broader perspective on multipoint competitors needs to be applied to test that business unit actions against them will not have adverse consequences in other business units. Ideally a more comprehensive analysis of existing and potential multipoint competitors should be done to uncover opportunities for a coordinated offensive or defensive strategy across business units.

Some additional considerations in developing strategy *vis-à-vis* multipoint competitors in unrelated businesses are as follows:

Forecast possible retaliation in all jointly contested industries A multipoint competitor may retaliate against a move in any or all jointly contested industries. It may well choose to respond in the industry where its response will be the most cost-effective. For example, it may respond in an industry in which it has a small share because it can inflict a large penalty on the firm at low cost. Each industry is not a separate battlefield.

Beware of a small position by a multipoint competitor in a key industry A small position held by a multipoint in an industry in which the firm has a large share (or high cash flow) can give the multipoint a lever against the firm. Such a position may be an effective blocking position.

Table 8.6 Competitor interrelationships in consumer paper products, 1983

	Disposable diapers	Bathroom tissue	Paper towels	Facial tissue	Paper napkins	Feminine napkins	Tampons	Towel wipes
Scott Paper	In and out (1966)	X (1904)	X (1931)	X (1943)	X (1958)			X (1976)
Kimberly-Clark	X (1968)	X (1924)	X (1976)	X (1924)	X (1951)	X (1924)	X (1960) Entered and exited (1974)	X (1975)
Procter & Gamble	X (1966)	X (1957)	X (1965)	X (1960)		X (1983)		
Georgia-Pacific		X (1909)	X (1909)	X (1909)	X (1909)			
Johnson & Johnson	X (1972)					X (1927)	X (1978)	X* (1980)
Weyerhaeuser	X							
Tampax						X (1981)	X (1936)	

* Towel wipes of this competitor are designed primarily for use with babies.

Table 8.7 Focal points and multipoint competitors

	Focal point 1		Focal point 2		Focal point 3	
	Share of market 1	*Share of market 2*	*Share of market 1*	*Share of market 2*	*Share of market 1*	*Share of market 2*
Competitor A	50	50	60	40	70	30
Competitor B	50	50	40	60	30	70

Look for opportunities to exploit overall corporate position vis-à-vis a multipoint
The overall corporate position *vis-à-vis* a multipoint may provide less costly and less risky means of responding to threats. Similarly, coordinated actions in a number of industries may make it difficult and very costly for a competitor to respond.

Establish blocking positions for defensive purposes   A small presence in one of a multipoint competitor's key industries can provide a way to inflict serious penalties on it at relatively low cost.

Strategy toward a multipoint competitor is affected by whether or not the competitor *perceives* the connections among industries. Perceiving the connection among jointly contested industries cannot be assumed where a multipoint competitor is managed via highly autonomous business units. In some cases, a competitor's ignorance of multi-industry linkages may allow the firm to gain in relative position. For example, an attack on one business unit may divert competitor attention and resources from defending its position in a more important business unit.

Multipoint competition in related industries

When a firm faces multipoint competitors in related industries, the strategic problem increases in complexity. The issues discussed in the previous section still apply and are often even more important because relatedness increases the likelihood that a competitor will perceive the linkages among businesses. The presence of tangible interrelationships among industries, however, complicates the assessment of relative position.

A firm's competitive advantage or disadvantage in any business unit that faces a multipoint competitor is a function of *overall position* in value activities involving interrelationships. If a firm and the competitor employ a shared sales force or logistical system, for example, the relative cost or differentiation of the sales force or logistical system as a whole is what matters. The extent to which interrelationships are *actually achieved* is what determines their effect on competitive advantage, not the potential to share. In addition, the net competitive advantage from an interrelationship for both a firm and a competitor will be influenced by their respective strategies. A competitor may potentially face higher or lower costs of coordination or compromise than the firm does, making an interrelationship more or less valuable to it.

A competitor's group of interrelated business units may not exactly overlap with the firm's. For example, Procter & Gamble competes in disposable diapers, paper towels, feminine hygiene products, and bathroom tissue, but not in paper napkins and towel wipes. Kimberly-Clark, on the other hand, is in all these businesses. When the related industries that are jointly contested do not overlap exactly, the comparison between a firm and a competitor must center on the firm's whole array of interrelationships relative to the competitor's. Each shared activity must be analyzed for the competitor as a whole, and compared to the firm's cost or differentiation in that activity. The volume provided by all five of Procter & Gamble's paper-related business units compared to that of Kimberly's eight business units will affect their relative position in shared value activities such as the logistical system, for example. Relative position in any business unit is built up by comparing all shared activities as well as value activities that are not shared.

A weak relative position in one related business unit can be partially or completely offset by superior positions in other related business units. Procter & Gamble is in fewer paper products industries than Kimberly-Clark, for example, but it is the market leader in diapers, toilet tissue, and paper towels. Diapers, particularly, is a very large industry relative to the others. Procter & Gamble's total consumer paper products volume is undoubtedly higher than Kimberly's. Analyzing a firm's relative position *vis-à-vis* multipoint competitors thus requires an examination of the complete portfolios of the two firms.

The most basic strategic implication of multipoint competition in related industries is the same as in unrelated industries – competitor analysis must encompass the competitor's entire portfolio of business units instead of examining each business unit in isolation. Competitive advantage in one business unit can be strongly affected by the extent of potential interrelationships with other business units in the competitor's portfolio and by whether they are achieved.

Balance or superiority in shared value activities relative to a multipoint competitor can potentially be achieved in many ways. Investing to gain a stronger position in industries where a firm is already strong can offset the advantages a competitor has from being in a broader array of related industries. If the competitive advantage from shared activities is significant and no compensating advantages can be found, a firm may be forced to match a competitor's portfolio of related business units. Matching can be important for defensive reasons as well as offensive ones. It may be necessary to match a competitor's diversification even if the firm has a competitive advantage in its existing business units, to prevent the competitor from gaining the advantages of interrelationships without opposition. Conversely, if a firm can discover new related industries that competitors are not in, it may be able to strengthen position in important shared value activities.

In consumer paper products, for example, there has been a great deal of offensive and defensive diversification. Table 8.6 shows the dates of entry of each competitor into the respective industries. Competitors' portfolios of businesses have broadened since the late 1950s. Procter & Gamble's actions triggered this sequence of moves. P&G began in toilet tissue and then moved into facial tissue, disposable diapers, and paper towels defensively.

Competitors with different patterns of interrelationships

Single-point and multipoint competitors may well pursue different types of interrelationships, involving different shared activities or activities shared in a different way. A good example of this situation is again the consumer paper products field (Table 8.6). Competitors have pursued interrelationships in paper products in different ways, reflecting their overall portfolios of business units and the strategies employed in them. In disposable diapers, for example, Procter & Gamble enjoys joint procurement of common raw materials, shared technology development, a shared sales force, and a shared logistical system among its paper product lines. However, Procter & Gamble has separate brand names for each paper product line. In contrast, Johnson & Johnson (J&J) competes in disposable diapers as well as a wide line of other baby care products, all sold under the Johnson & Johnson brand name. Its interrelationships include that shared brand name, plus a shared sales force and shared market research in the baby care field. J&J enjoys little sharing in production, logistics, and product or process technology development. Each competitor in Table 8.6 has a somewhat different pattern of interrelationships.

A competitor with a different pattern of interrelationships represents both an opportunity and a threat. It is a threat because the competitive advantage gained through interrelationships cannot be readily replicated, since a firm may not be in the appropriate group of industries, or have the right strategy to allow matching the interrelationships. To match J&J's shared brand name, for example, Procter & Gamble would have to change its strategy of using a different brand for each product. This would probably fail, however, because of the inappropriateness of using the diaper brand name on other paper products unrelated to babies. Thus to match this particular advantage of J&J's, Procter & Gamble would probably have to diversify further into baby care, where J&J is dominant.

A smart competitor with different interrelationships will attempt to shift the nature of competition in each industry in the direction that makes its interrelationships more strategically valuable than the firm's. An escalation in advertising spending in diapers would work to the advantage of J&J because of its shared brand, for example, holding other things constant. A competitor with different interrelationships might also attempt to reduce the ability of a firm to achieve its interrelationships. For example, a move by J&J to make diapers from textile-based materials would, if feasible, reduce P&G's ability to share value activities because of its broad presence in paper products. Similarly, a competitor might shift its strategy in a way that raised the cost of compromise for the firm to achieve its type of interrelationships, thereby forcing the firm to damage one business unit in responding to a threat to another.

Thus the essence of the competitive game between firms pursuing different forms of interrelatedness is a tug of war to see which firm can shift the basis of competition to compromise the other's interrelationships, or to enhance the value of its own. The disposable diaper industry offers a good illustration of how this game can play itself out. Procter & Gamble has retained leadership in the diaper industry, while J&J was forced to exit from the US market after costly losses. Though J&J's market interrelationships were strong, advertising is a relatively small proportion of total costs in disposable diapers. Sales force and logistical costs, where Procter & Gamble enjoyed comparable if not superior interrelationships to J&J, are each as high or higher than advertising. J&J could not match Procter & Gamble's production, procurement, and technological interrelationships, and this proved fatal since total manufacturing costs for diapers are a very large percentage of total cost and the pace of technological change in both product and process is rapid. Without a markedly superior product, therefore, J&J was unable to match the combination of Procter & Gamble's large market share and its interrelationships.

Forecasting potential competitors

Tangible interrelationships, intangible interrelationships, and competitor interrelationships can be used to forecast likely potential competitors. Likely potential entrants into an industry will be firms for which that industry is:

- a logical way to create or extend an important interrelationship
- a necessary extension to match the interrelationships of competitors

To forecast potential competitors, all possible interrelationships involving an industry are identified, including competitor interrelationships. Each potential interrelationship will typically lead to a number of other industries. The industries in which existing competitors compete besides the industry may suggest possible interrelationships of other types. By identifying related industries, a firm can locate potential competitors for whom entry into the firm's industries would be logical. Analysis must assess the probability that these potential competitors will actually choose to enter the industry rather than pursue their other investment opportunities.

NOTES

1 In a recent article, Haspeslagh (1982) found evidence that portfolio planning techniques were in use in someway by over 300 of the Fortune 1000.
2 Recent work on stock market valuation has identified a conglomerate discount, where unrelated business units in a firm are worth less than if they were stand-alone units. Without a horizontal strategy that actually exploits interrelationships, a conglomerate-discount is often justified.
3. John R. Wells (1984) has done an important study on interrelationships that provides evidence of how portfolio membership has affected business units in a sample of diversified firms.
4 Economists have begun to use the term "economies of scope" to refer to economies available to multiproduct firms (see Baumol, Panzar, and Willig, 1982). The sources of economies of scope have not been operationalized, nor have the conditions that nullify them.
5 Sharing can increase the rate of learning in an activity by increaing its throughput. Intangible interrelationships are also a form of learning, but one in which knowledge gained in one business unit is transferred to another though each business unit has separate activities.
6 Terms such as shared experience or shared resources are sometimes used to reflect the possibility that activities can be shared. Such terms are not well defined, however; nor do they grow out of a framework that specifies the potential competitive advantages of sharing and its costs.
7 The important scale differences among business units are those *in the value activity being shared*, which is not necessarily the same as the overall scale of the business unit. A small business unit may utilize logistics very intensively, for example.
8 The cost of coordination is clearly dependent on a firm's organizational practices.
9 See Porter, *Competitive Strategy*, Chapter 1, for a discussion of exit barriers.
10 See Wells (1984).
11 John R. Wells's (1984) study contains important work on intangible interrelationship that provides further insight into when and how they arise.
12 There may be a fine line in some cases between transferring know-how and sharing technology development. The basis for separating tangible and intangible interrelationships is whether an activity is shared in some way on

an ongoing basis, or whether know-how is transferred between essentially separate activities.

13 The analysis of multipoint competitors in both related and unrelated industries has strong parallels to the analysis of competitors in local or regional industries, as well as to competitive analysis in global competition. In a regional industry such as airlines, for example, firms compete with each other in a number of overlapping routes. Internationally, firms often compete in a number of country markets. The principles described here can be applied in all of these settings (see Porter 1985).

14 For a definition and discussion of focal points, see Thomas Schelling (1960) and *Competitive Strategy*, Chapter 5

REFERENCES

Baumol, William J., Panzar, John C. and Willig, Robert D. (1982) with contributions by Elizabeth E. Bailey, Dietrich Fischer and Herman C. Quirmbach, *Contestable Markets and The Theory of Industry Structure*, New York: Harcourt Brace Jovanovich.

Haspeslagh, Phillipe (1982) "Portfolio Planning: Uses and Limits," *Harvard Business Review*, (1): 58–73, January–February.

Porter, Michael E. (1980) *Competitive Strategy: Techniques for Analyzing Industries and Competitors*, New York: The Free Press.

Porter, Michael E. (ed). (1985) *Competition in Global Industries*, Cambridge, Mass.: Harvard Graduate School of Business Administration.

Schelling, Thomas C. (1960) *The Strategy of Conflict*, Cambridge, Mass.: Harvard University Press.

Wells, John R. (1984) "In Search of Synergy: Strategies for Related Diversification," Doctoral Dissertation, Harvard Graduate School of Business Administration.

Chapter 9

The core competence of the corporation

C. K. Prahalad and Gary Hamel

The most powerful way to prevail in global competition is still invisible to many companies. During the 1980s, top executives were judged on their ability to restructure, declutter and delayer their corporations. In the 1990s, they'll be judged on their ability to identify, cultivate, and exploit the core competencies that make growth possible – indeed, they'll have to rethink the concept of the corporation itself.

Consider the last ten years of GTE and NEC. In the early 1980s, GTE was well positioned to become a major player in the evolving information technology industry. It was active in telecommunications. Its operations spanned a variety of businesses including telephones, switching and transmission systems, digital PABX, semiconductors, packet switching, satellites, defense systems, and lighting products. And GTE's Entertainment Products Group, which produced Sylvania color TVs, had a position in related display technologies. In 1980, GTE's sales were $9.98 billion, and net cash flow was $1.73 billion. NEC, in contrast, was much smaller, at $3.8 billion in sales. It had a comparable technological base and computer businesses, but it had no experience as an operating telecommunications company.

Yet look at the positions of GTE and NEC in 1988. GTE's 1988 sales were $16.46 billion, and NEC's sales were considerably higher at $21.89 billion. GTE has, in effect, become a telephone operating company with a position in defense and lighting products. GTE's other businesses are small in global terms. GTE has divested Sylvania TV and Telenet, put switching, transmission, and digital PABX into joint ventures, and closed down semiconductors. As a result, the international position of GTE has eroded. Non-US revenue as a percent of total revenue dropped from 20 percent to 15 percent between 1980 and 1988.

NEC has emerged as the world leader in semiconductors and as a first-tier player in telecommunications products and computers. It has consolidated its position in mainframe computers. It has moved beyond public switching and transmission to include such lifestyle products as mobile telephones, facsimile machines, and laptop computers – bridging the gap between telecommunications and office automation. NEC is the only company in the world to be in the top five in revenue in telecommunications, semiconductors, and mainframes. Why did these two companies, starting with comparable business portfolios, perform so differently? Largely because NEC conceived of itself in terms of "core competencies," and GTE did not.

RETHINKING THE CORPORATION

Once, the diversified corporation could simply point its business units at particular end product markets and admonish them to become world leaders. But with market boundaries changing ever more quickly, targets are elusive and capture is at best temporary. A few companies have proven themselves adept at inventing new markets, quickly entering emerging markets, and dramatically shifting patterns of customer choice in established markets. These are the ones to emulate. The critical task for management is to create an organization capable of infusing products with irresistible functionality or, better yet, creating products that customers need but have not yet even imagined.

This is a deceptively difficult task. Ultimately, it requires radical change in the management of major companies. It means, first of all, that top managements of Western companies must assume responsibility for competitive decline. Everyone knows about high interest rates, Japanese protectionism, outdated antitrust laws, obstreperous unions, and impatient investors. What is harder to see, or harder to acknowledge, is how little added momentum companies actually get from political or macroeconomic "relief." Both the theory and practice of Western management have created a drag on our forward motion. It is the principles of management that are in need of reform.

NEC versus GTE, again, is instructive and only one of many such comparative cases we analyzed to understand the changing basis for global leadership. Early in the 1970s, NEC articulated a strategic intent to exploit the convergence of computing and communications, what it called "C&C."[1] Success, top management reckoned, would hinge on acquiring *competencies*, particularly in semiconductors. Management adopted an appropriate "strategic architecture," summarized by C&C, and then communicated its intent to the whole organization and the outside world during the mid-1970s.

NEC constituted a "C&C Committee" of top managers to oversee the development of core products and core competencies. NEC put in place coordination groups and committees that cut across the interests of individual businesses. Consistent with its strategic architecture, NEC shifted enormous resources to strengthen its position in components and central processors. By using collaborative arrangements to multiply internal resources, NEC was able to accumulate a broad array of core competencies.

NEC carefully identified three interrelated streams of technological and market evolution. Top management determined that computing would evolve from large mainframes to distributed processing, components from simple ICs to VLSI, and communications from mechanical cross-bar exchange to complex digital systems we now call ISDN. As things evolved further, NEC reasoned, the computing, communications, and components businesses would so overlap that it would be very hard to distinguish among them, and that there would be enormous opportunities for any company that had built the competencies needed to serve all three markets.

NEC top management determined that semiconductors would be the company's most important "core product." It entered into myriad strategic alliances – over 100 as of 1987 – aimed at building competencies rapidly and at low cost. In mainframe computers, its most noted relationship was with Honeywell and Bull. Almost all the collaborative arrangements in the semiconductor-component field were oriented toward technology access. As they entered collaborative arrangements, NEC's operating managers understood the rationale for these alliances and the goal of internalizing partner skills. NEC's director of research summed up its competence acquisition during the 1970s and 1980s this way: "From an investment standpoint, it was much quicker and cheaper to use foreign technology. There wasn't a need for us to develop new ideas."

No such clarity of strategic intent and strategic architecture appeared to exist at GTE. Although senior executives discussed the implications of the evolving information technology industry, no commonly accepted view of which competencies would be required to compete in that industry were communicated widely. While significant staff work was done to identify key technologies, senior line managers continued to act as if they were managing independent business units. Decentralization made it difficult to focus on core competencies. Instead, individual businesses became increasingly dependent on outsiders for critical skills, and collaboration became a route to staged exits. Today, with a new management team in place, GTE has repositioned itself to apply its competencies to emerging markets in telecommunications services.

THE ROOTS OF COMPETITIVE ADVANTAGE

The distinction we observed in the way NEC and GTE conceived of themselves – a portfolio of competencies versus a portfolio of businesses – was repeated across many industries. From 1980 to 1988, Canon grew by 264 percent, Honda by 200 percent. Compare that with Xerox and Chrysler. And if Western managers were once anxious about the low cost and high quality of Japanese imports, they are now overwhelmed by the pace at which Japanese rivals are inventing new markets, creating new products, and enhancing them. Canon has given us personal copiers; Honda has moved from motorcycles to four-wheel off-road buggies. Sony developed the 8mm camcorder, Yamaha, the digital piano. Komatsu developed an underwater remote-controlled bulldozer, while Casio's latest gambit is a small-screen color LCD television. Who would have anticipated the evolution of these vanguard markets?

In more established markets, the Japanese challenge has been just as disquieting. Japanese companies are generating a blizzard of features and functional enhancements that bring technological sophistication to everyday products. Japanese car producers have been pioneering four-wheel steering, four-valve-per-cylinder engines, in-car navigation systems, and sophisticated electronic engine-management systems. On the strength of its product features, Canon is now a player in facsimile transmission machines, desktop laser printers, even semiconductor manufacturing equipment.

In the short run, a company's competitiveness derives from the price/performance attributes of current products. But the survivors of the first wave of global competition, Western and Japanese alike, are all converging on similar and formidable standards for product cost and quality – minimum hurdles for continued competition, but less and less important as sources of differential advantage. In the long run, competitiveness derives from an ability to build, at lower cost and more speedily than competitors, the core competencies that spawn unanticipated products. The real sources of advantage are to be found in management's ability to consolidate corporatewide technologies and production skills into competencies that empower individual businesses to adapt quickly to changing opportunities.

Senior executives who claim that they cannot build core competencies either because they feel the autonomy of business units is sacrosanct or because their feet are held to the quarterly budget fire should think again. The problem in many Western companies is not that their senior executives are any less capable than those in Japan nor that Japanese companies possess greater technical capabilities. Instead, it is their adherence to a concept of the corporation that unnecessarily limits the ability of individual businesses to fully exploit the deep reservoir of technological capability that many American and European companies possess.

The diversified corporation is a large tree. The trunk and major limbs are core products, the smaller branches are business units; the leaves, flowers, and fruit are end products. The root system that provides nourishment, sustenance, and stability is the core competence. You can

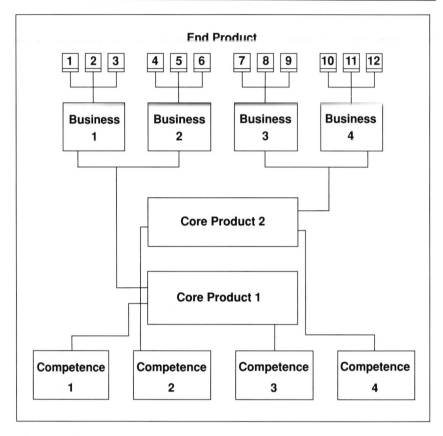

Figure 9.1 Competencies: the roots of competitiveness
The corporation, like a tree, grows from its roots. Core products are nourished by competencies and engender business units, whose fruits are end products.

miss the strength of competitors by looking only at their end products, in the same way you miss the strength of a tree if you look only at its leaves. (See Figure 9.1).

Core competencies are the collective learning in the organization, especially how to coordinate diverse production skills and integrate multiple streams of technologies. Consider Sony's capacity to miniaturize or Philips's optical-media expertise. The theoretical knowledge to put a radio on a chip does not in itself assure a company the skill to produce a miniature radio no bigger than a business card. To bring off this feat, Casio must harmonize know-how in miniaturization, microprocessor design, material science, and ultrathin precision casing – the same skills it applies in its miniature card calculators, pocket TVs, and digital watches.

If core competence is about harmonizing streams of technology, it is also about the organization of work and the delivery of value. Among Sony's competencies is miniaturization. To bring miniaturization to its products, Sony must ensure that technologists, engineers, and marketers have a shared understanding of customer needs and of technological possibilities. The force of core competence is felt as decisively in services as in manufacturing. Citicorp was ahead of others investing in an operating system that allowed it to participate in world markets twenty-four hours a day. Its competence in systems has provided the company the means to differentiate itself from many financial service institutions.

Core competence is communication, involvement, and a deep commitment to working across organizational boundaries. It involves many levels of people and all functions. World-class research in, for example, lasers or ceramics can take place in corporate laboratories without having an impact on any of the businesses of the company. The skills that together constitute core competence must coalesce around individuals whose efforts are not so narrowly focused that they cannot recognize the opportunities for blending their functional expertise with those of others in new and interesting ways.

Core competence does not diminish with use. Unlike physical assets, which do deteriorate over time, competencies are enhanced as they are applied and shared. But competencies still need to be nurtured and protected; knowledge fades if it is not used. Competencies are the glue that binds existing businesses. They are also the engine for new business development. Patterns of diversification and market entry may be guided by them, not just by the attractiveness of markets.

Consider 3M's competence with sticky tape. In dreaming up businesses as diverse as "Post-it" notes, magnetic tape, photographic film, pressure-sensitive tapes, and coated abrasives, the company has brought to bear widely shared competencies in substrates, coatings, and adhesives and devised various ways to combine them. Indeed, 3M has invested consistently in them. What seems to be an extremely diversified portfolio of businesses belies a few shared core competencies.

In contrast, there are major companies that have had the potential to build core competencies but failed to do so because top management was unable to conceive of the company as anything other than a collection of discrete businesses. GE sold much of its consumer electronics business to Thomson of France, arguing that it was becoming increasingly difficult to maintain its competitiveness in this sector. That was undoubtedly so, but it is ironic that it sold several key businesses to competitors who were already competence leaders – Black & Decker in small electrical motors, and Thomson, which was eager to build its competence in microelectronics and had learned from the Japanese that a position in consumer electronics was vital to this challenge.

Management trapped in the strategic business unit (SBU) mind-set almost inevitably finds its individual businesses dependent on external sources for critical components, such as motors or compressors. But these are not just components. They are core products that contribute to the competitiveness of a wide range of end products. They are the physical embodiments of core competencies.

HOW NOT TO THINK OF COMPETENCE

Since companies are in a race to build the competencies that determine global leadership, successful companies have stopped imagining themselves as bundles of businesses making products. Canon, Honda, Casio, or NEC may seem to preside over portfolios of businesses unrelated in terms of customers, distribution channels, and merchandising strategy. Indeed, they have portfolios that may seem idiosyncratic at times: NEC is the only global company to be among leaders in computing, telecommunications, and semiconductors *and* to have a thriving consumer electronics business.

But looks are deceiving. In NEC, digital technology, especially VLSI and systems integration skills, is fundamental. In the core competencies underlying them, disparate businesses become coherent. It is Honda's core competence in engines and power trains that gives it a distinctive advantage in car, motorcycle, lawn mower, and generator businesses. Canon's core competencies in optics, imaging, and microprocessor controls have enabled it to enter, even dominate, markets as seemingly diverse as copiers, laser printers, cameras, and image scanners. Philips worked for more than fifteen years to perfect its optical-media (laser disc) competence, as did JVC in building a leading position in video recording. Other examples of core competencies might include mechantronics (the ability to marry mechanical and electronic engineering), video displays, bioengineering, and microelectronics. In the early stages of its competence building, Philips could not have imagined all the products that would be spawned by its optical-media competence, nor could JVC have anticipated miniature camcorders when it first began exploring videotape technologies.

Unlike the battle for global brand dominance, which is visible in the world's broadcast and print media and is aimed at building global "share of mind," the battle to build world-class competencies is invisible to people who aren't deliberately looking for it. Top management often tracks the cost and quality of competitors' products, yet how many managers untangle the web of alliances their Japanese competitors have constructed to acquire competencies at low cost? In how many Western boardrooms is there an explicit, shared understanding of the competencies the company must build for world leadership? Indeed, how many senior executives discuss the crucial distinction between competitive strategy at the level of a business and competitive strategy at the level of an entire company?

Let us be clear. Cultivating core competence does *not* mean outspending rivals on research and development. In 1983, when Canon surpassed Xerox in worldwide unit market share in the copier business, its R&D budget in reprographics was but a small fraction of Xerox's. Over the past twenty years, NEC has spent less on R&D as a percentage of sales than almost all of its American and European competitors.

Nor does core competence mean shared costs, as when two or more SBUs use a common facility – a plant, service facility, or sales force – or share a common component. The gains of sharing may be substantial, but the search for shared costs is typically a *post hoc* effort to rationalize production across existing businesses, not a premeditated effort to build the competencies out of which the businesses themselves grow.

Building core competencies is more ambitious and different than integrating vertically, moreover. Managers deciding whether to make or buy will start with end products and look upstream to the efficiencies of the supply chain and downstream toward distribution and customers. They do not take inventory of skills and look forward to applying them in nontraditional ways. (Of course, decisions about competencies *do* provide a logic for vertical integration. Canon is not particularly integrated in its copier business, except in those aspects of the vertical chain that support the competencies it regards as critical.)

IDENTIFYING CORE COMPETENCIES – AND LOSING THEM

At least three tests can be applied to identify core competencies in a company. First, a core competence provides potential access to a wide variety of markets. Competence in display systems, for example, enables a company to participate in such diverse businesses as calculators, miniature TV sets, monitors for laptop computers, and automotive dashboards – which is why Casio's entry into the hand-held TV market was predictable. Second, a core competence should make a significant contribution to the perceived customer benefits of the end product. Clearly, Honda's engine expertise fills this bill.

Finally, a core competence should be difficult for competitors to imitate. And it *will* be difficult if it is a complex harmonization of individual technologies and production skills. A rival might acquire some of the technologies that comprise the core competence, but it will find it more difficult to duplicate the more or less comprehensive pattern of internal coordination and learning. JVC's decision in the early 1960s to pursue the development of a videotape competence passed the three tests outlined here. RCA's decision in the late 1970s to develop a stylus-based video turnable system did not.

Few companies are likely to build world leadership in more than five or six fundamental competencies. A company that compiles a list of 20 to 30 capabilities has probably not produced a list of core competencies. Still, it is probably a good discipline to generate a list of this sort and to see aggregate capabilities as building blocks. This tends to prompt the search for licensing deals and alliances through which the company may acquire, at low cost, the missing pieces.

Most Western companies hardly think about competitiveness in these terms at all. It is time to take a tough-minded look at the risks they are running. Companies that judge competitiveness, their own and their competitors', primarily in terms of the price/performance of end products are courting the erosion of core competencies – or making too little effort to enhance them. The embedded skills that give rise to the next generation of competitive products cannot be "rented in" by outsourcing and OEM-supply relationships. In our view, too many companies have unwittingly surrendered core competencies when they cut internal investment in what they mistakenly thought were just "cost centers" in favor of outside suppliers.

Consider Chrysler. Unlike Honda, it has tended to view engines and power trains as simply one more component. Chrysler is becoming increasingly dependent on Mitsubishi and Hyundai: between 1985 and 1987, the number of outsourced engines went from 252,000 to 382,000. It is difficult to imagine Honda yielding manufacturing responsibility, much less design, of so critical a part of a car's function to an outside company – which is why Honda has made such an enormous commitment to Formula One auto racing. Honda has been able to pool its engine-related technologies; it has parlayed these into a corporatewide competency from which it develops world-beating products, despite R&D budgets smaller than those of GM and Toyota.

Of course, it is perfectly possible for a company to have a competitive product line up but be a laggard in developing core competencies – at least for a while. If a company wanted to enter the copier business today, it would find a dozen Japanese companies more than willing to supply copiers on the basis of an OEM private label. But when fundamental technologies changed or if its supplier decided to enter the market directly and become a competitor, that company's product line, along with all of its investments in marketing and distribution, could be vulnerable. Outsourcing can provide a shortcut to a more competitive product, but it typically contributes little to building the people-embodied skills that are needed to sustain product leadership.

Nor is it possible for a company to have an intelligent alliance or sourcing strategy if it has not made a choice about where it will build competence leadership. Clearly, Japanese companies have benefited from alliances. They've used them to learn from Western partners who were not fully committed to preserving core competencies of their own. As we've argued in these pages before, learning within an alliance takes a positive commitment of resources – travel, a pool of dedicated people, test-bed facilities, time to internalize and test what has been learned.[2] A company may not make this effort if it doesn't have clear goals for competence building.

Another way of losing is foregoing opportunities to establish competencies that are evolving in existing businesses. In the 1970s and 1980s, many American and European companies – like GE, Motorola, GTE, Thorn, and GEC – chose to exit the color television business, which they regarded as mature. If by "mature" they meant that they had run out of new product ideas at precisely the moment global rivals had targeted the TV business for entry, then yes, the industry was mature. But it certainly wasn't mature in the sense that all opportunities to enhance and apply video-based competencies had been exhausted.

In ridding themselves of their television businesses, these companies failed to distinguish between divesting the business and destroying their video media-based competencies. They not only got out of the TV business but they also closed the door on a whole stream of future opportunities reliant on video-based competencies. The television industry, considered by many US companies in the 1970s to be unattractive, is today the focus of a fierce public policy debate about the inability of US corporations to benefit from the $20-billion-a-year opportunity that HDTV will represent in the mid- to late 1990s. Ironically, the US Government is being asked to fund a massive research project – in effect, to compensate US companies for their failure to preserve critical core competencies when they had the chance.

In contrast, one can see a company like Sony reducing its emphasis on VCRs (where it has not been very successful and where Korean companies now threaten), without reducing its commitment to video-related competencies. Sony's Betamax led to a débâcle. But it emerged with its videotape recording competencies intact and is currently challenging Matsushita in the 8mm camcorder market.

There are two clear lessons here. First, the costs of losing a core competence can be only partly calculated in advance. The baby may be thrown out with the bath water in divestment decisions. Second, since core competencies are built through a process of continuous improvement and enhancement that may span a decade or longer, a company that has failed to invest in core competence building will find it very difficult to enter an emerging market, unless, of course, it will be content simply to serve as a distribution channel.

American semiconductor companies like Motorola learned this painful lesson when they elected to forgo direct participation in the 256k generation of DRAM chips. Having skipped this round, Motorola, like most of its American competitors, needed a large infusion of technical help from Japanese partners to rejoin the battle in the 1-megabyte generation. When it comes to core competencies, it is difficult to get off the train, walk to the next station, and then reboard.

FROM CORE COMPETENCIES TO CORE PRODUCTS

The tangible link between identified core competencies and end products is what we call the core products – the physical embodiments of one or more core competencies. Honda's engines, for example, are core products, linchpins between design and development skills that ultimately lead to a proliferation of end products. Core products are the components or subassemblies that actually contribute to the value of the end products. Thinking in terms of core products forces a company to distinguish between the brand share it achieves in end product markets (for example, 40 percent of the US refrigerator market) and the manufacturing share it achieves in any particular core product (for example, 5 percent of the world share of compressor output).

Canon is reputed to have an 84 percent world manufacturing share in desktop laser printer "engines," even though its brand share in the laser printer business is minuscule. Similarly, Matsushita has a world manufacturing share of about 45 percent in key VCR components, far in excess of its brand share (Panasonic, JVC and others) of 20 percent. And Matsushita has a commanding core product share in compressors worldwide, estimated at 40 percent, even though its brand share in both the air-conditioning and refrigerator businesses is quite small.

It is essential to make this distinction between core competencies, core products, and end products because global competition is played out by different rules and for different stakes at each level. To build or defend leadership over the long term, a corporation will probably be a winner at each level. At the level of core competence, the goal is to build world leadership in the design and development of a particular class of product functionality – be it compact data storage and retrieval, as with Philips's optical-media competence, or compactness and ease of use, as with Sony's micromotors and microprocessor controls.

To sustain leadership in their chosen core competence areas, these companies *seek to maximize their world manufacturing share in core products.* The manufacture of core products for a wide variety of external (and internal) customers yields the revenue and market feedback that, at least partly, determines the pace at which core competencies can be enhanced and extended. This thinking was behind JVC's decision in the mid-1970s to establish VCR supply relationships with leading national consumer electronics companies in Europe and the United States. In supplying Thomson, Thorn, and Telefunken (all independent companies at that time) as well as US partners, JVC was able to gain the cash and the diversity of market experience that ultimately enabled it to outpace Philips and Sony. (Philips developed videotape competencies in parallel with JVC, but it failed to build a worldwide network of OEM relationships that would have allowed it to accelerate the refinement of its videotape competence through the sale of core products.)

JVC's success has not been lost on Korean companies like Goldstar, Sam Sung, Kia, and Daewoo, who are building core product leadership in areas as diverse as displays, semiconductors, and automotive engines through their OEM-supply contracts with Western companies. Their avowed goal is to capture investment initiative away from potential competitors, often US companies. In doing so, they accelerate their competence-building efforts while "hollowing out" their competitors. By focusing on competence and embedding it in core products, Asian competitors have built up advantages in component markets first and have then leveraged off their superior products to move downstream to build brand share. And they are not likely to remain the low-cost suppliers forever. As their reputation for brand leadership is consolidated, they may well gain price leadership. Honda has proven this with its Acura line, and other Japanese car makers are following suit.

Control over core products is critical for other reasons. A dominant position in core products allows a company to shape the evolution of applications and end markets. Such compact audio disc-related core products as data drives and lasers have enabled Sony and Philips to influence the evolution of the computer-peripheral business in optical-media storage. As a company multiplies the number of application arenas for its core products, it can consistently reduce the cost, time, and risk in new product development. In short, well-targeted core products can lead to economies of scale *and* scope.

THE TYRANNY OF THE SBU

The new terms of competitive engagement cannot be understood using analytical tools devised to manage the diversified corporation of twenty years ago, when competition was primarily domestic (GE versus Westinghouse, General Motors versus Ford) and all the key players were speaking the language of the same business schools and consultancies. Old prescriptions have potentially toxic side effects. The need for new principles is most obvious in companies organized exclusively according to the logic of SBUs. The implications of the two alternate concepts of the corporation are summarized in "Two Concepts of the Corporation: SBU or Core Competence."

	SBU	*Core Competence*
Basis for competition	Competitiveness of today's products	Interfirm competition to build competencies
Corporate structure	Portfolio of businesses related in product-market terms	Portfolio of competencies, core products, and businesses
Status of the business unit	Autonomy is sacrosanct; the SBU "owns" all resources other than cash	SBU is a potential reservoir of core competencies
Resource allocation	Discrete businesses are the unit of analysis; capital is allocated business by business	Businesses and competencies are the unit of analysis: top management allocates capital and talent
Value added of top management	Optimizing corporate returns through capital allocation trade-offs among businesses	Enunciating strategic architecture and building competencies to secure the future

Figure 9.2 Two concepts of the corporation: SBU or core competence

Obviously, diversified corporations have a portfolio of products and a portfolio of businesses. But we believe in a view of the company as a portfolio of competencies as well. US companies do not lack the technical resources to build competencies, but their top management often lacks the vision to build them and the administrative means for assembling resources spread across multiple businesses. A shift in commitment will inevitably influence patterns of diversification, skill deployment, resource allocation priorities, and approaches to alliances and out-sourcing.

We have described the three different planes on which battles for global leadership are waged: core competence, core products, and end products. A corporation has to know whether it is winning or losing on each plane. By sheer weight of investment, a company might be able to beat its rivals to blue-sky technologies yet still lose the race to build core competence leadership. If a company is winning the race to build core competencies (as opposed to building leadership in a few technologies), it will almost certainly outpace rivals in new business development. If a company is winning the race to capture world manufacturing share in core products, it will probably outpace rivals in improving product features and the price/performance ratio.

Determining whether one is winning or losing end product battles is more difficult because measures of product market share do not necessarily reflect various companies' underlying competitiveness. Indeed, companies that attempt to build market share by relying on the competitiveness of others, rather than investing in core competencies and world core-product leadership, may be treading on quicksand. In the race for global brand dominance, companies like 3M, Black & Decker, Canon, Honda, NEC, and Citicorp have built global brand umbrellas by proliferating products out of their core competencies. This has allowed their individual businesses to build image, customer loyalty, and access to distribution channels.

When you think about this reconceptualization of the corporation, the primacy of the SBU – an organizational dogma for a generation – is now clearly an anachronism. Where the SBU is an article of faith, resistance to the seductions of decentralization can seem heretical. In many companies, the SBU prism means that only one plane of the global competitive battle, the battle to put competitive products on the shelf *today*, is visible to top management. What are the costs of this distortion?

Underinvestment in Developing Core Competencies and Core Products   When the organization is conceived of as a multiplicity of SBUs, no single business may feel responsible for maintaining a viable position in core products nor be able to justify the investment required to build world leadership in some core competence. In the absence of a more comprehensive view imposed by corporate management, SBU managers will tend to underinvest. Recently, companies such as Kodak and Philips have recognized this as a potential problem and have begun searching for new organizational forms that will allow them to develop and manufacture core products for both internal and external customers.

SBU managers have traditionally conceived of competitors in the same way they've seen themselves. On the whole, they've failed to note the emphasis Asian competitors were placing on building leadership in core products or to understand the critical linkage between world manufacturing leadership and the ability to sustain development pace in core competence. They've failed to pursue OEM-supply opportunities or to look across their various product divisions in an attempt to identify opportunities for coordinated initiatives.

Imprisoned Resources   As an SBU evolves, it often develops unique competencies. Typically, the people who embody this competence are seen as the sole property of the business in which they grew up. The manager of another SBU who asks to borrow talented people is likely to get a cold rebuff. SBU managers are not only unwilling to lend their competence carriers but they may actually hide talent to prevent its redeployment in the pursuit of new opportunites. This may be compared to residents of an underdeveloped country hiding most of their cash under their mattresses. The benefits of competencies, like the benefits of the money supply, depend on the velocity of their circulation as well as on the size of the stock the company holds.

Western companies have traditionally had an advantage in the stock of skills they possess. But have they been able to reconfigure them quickly to respond to new opportunities? Canon, NEC, and Honda have had a lesser stock of the people and technologies that compose core competencies but could move them much quicker from one business unit to another. Corporate R&D spending at Canon is not fully indicative of the size of Canon's core competence stock and tells the casual observer nothing about the velocity with which Canon is able to move core competencies to exploit opportunities.

When competencies become imprisoned, the people who carry the competencies do not get assigned to the most exciting opportunities, and their skills begin to atrophy. Only by fully leveraging core competencies can small companies like Canon afford to compete with industry giants like Xerox. How strange that SBU managers, who are perfectly willing to compete for cash in the capital budgeting process, are unwilling to compete for people – the company's most precious asset. We find it ironic that top management devotes so much attention to the capital budgeting process yet typically has no comparable mechanism for allocating the human skills that embody core competencies. Top managers are seldom able to look four or five levels down into the organization, identify the people who embody critical competencies, and move them across organizational boundaries.

Bounded Innovation   If core competencies are not recognized, individual SBUs will pursue only those innovation opportunities that are close at hand – marginal product-line extensions or geographic expansions. Hybrid opportunities like fax machines, laptop computers, hand-held televisions, or portable music keyboards will emerge only when managers take off their SBU blinkers. Remember, Canon appeared to be in the camera business at the time it was preparing to become a world leader in copiers. Conceiving of the corporation in terms of core competencies widens the domain of innovation.

DEVELOPING STRATEGIC ARCHITECTURE

The fragmentation of core competencies becomes inevitable when a diversified company's information systems, patterns of communication,

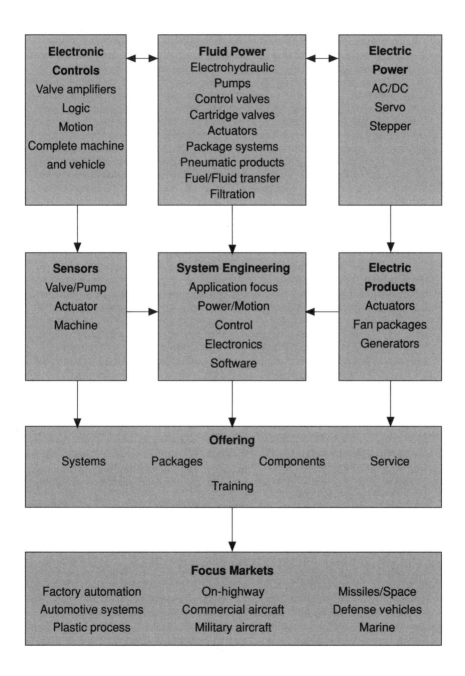

Figure 9.3 Vickers map of competencies

Vickers Learns the Value of Strategic Architecture

The idea that top management should develop a corporate strategy for acquiring and deploying core competencies is relatively new in most US companies. There are a few exceptions. An early convert was Trinova (previously Libbey Owens Ford), a Toledo-based corporation, which enjoys a worldwide position in power and motion controls and engineered plastics. One of its major divisions is Vickers, a premier supplier of hydraulics components like valves, pumps, actuators, and filtration devices to aerospace, marine, defense, automotive, earth-moving, and industrial markets.

Vickers saw the potential for a transformation of its traditional business with the application of electronics disciplines in combination with its traditional technologies. The goal was "to ensure that change in technology does not displace Vickers from its customers." This, to be sure, was initially a defensive move: Vickers recognized that unless it acquired new skills, it could not protect existing markets or capitalize on new growth opportunities. Managers at Vickers attempted to conceptualize the likely evolution of (a) technologies relevant to the power and motion control business, (b) functionalities that would satisfy emerging customer needs, and (c) new competencies needed to creatively manage the marriage of technology and customer needs.

Despite pressure for short-term earnings, top management looked to a 10- to 15-year time horizon in developing a map of emerging customer needs, changing technologies, and the core competencies that would be necessary to bridge the gap between the two. Its slogan was "Into the 21st Century." (A simplified version of the overall architecture developed is shown here.)

Vickers is currently in fluid-power components. The architecture identifies two additional competencies, electric-power components and electronic controls. A systems integration capability that would unite hardware, software, and service was also targeted for development.

The strategic architecture, as illustrated by the Vickers example, is not a forecast of specific products or specific technologies but a broad map of the evolving linkages between customer functionality requirements, potential technologies, and core competencies. It assumes that products and systems cannot be defined with certainty for the future but that preempting competitors in the development of new markets requires an early start to building core competencies. The strategic architecture developed by Vickers, while describing the future in competence terms, also provides the basis for making "here and now" decisions about product priorities, acquisitions, alliances, and recruitment.

Since 1986, Vickers has made more than ten clearly targeted acquisitions, each one focused on a specific component or technology gap identified in the overall architecture. The architecture is also the basis for internal development of new competencies. Vickers has undertaken, in parallel, a reorganization to enable the integration of electronics and electrical capabilities with mechanical-based competencies. We believe that it will take another two to three years before Vickers reaps the total benefits from developing the strategic architecture, communicating it widely to all its employees, customers, and investors, and building administrative systems consistent with the architecture.

career paths, managerial rewards, and processes of strategy development do not transcend SBU lines. We believe that senior management should spend a significant amount of its time developing a corporatewide strategic architecture that establishes objectives for competence building. A strategic architecture is a road map of the future that identifies which core competencies to build and their constituent technologies.

By providing an impetus for learning from alliances and a focus for internal development efforts, a strategic architecture like NEC's C&C can dramatically reduce the investment needed to secure future market leadership. How can a company make partnerships intelligently without a clear understanding of the core competencies it is trying to build and those it is attempting to prevent from being unintentionally transferred?

Of course, all of this begs the question of what a strategic architecture should look like. The answer will be different for every company. But it is helpful to think again of that tree, of the corporation organized around core products and, ultimately, core competencies. To sink sufficiently strong roots, a company must answer some fundamental questions: How long could we preserve our competitiveness in this business if we did not control this particular core competence? How central is this core competence to perceived customer benefits? What future opportunities would be foreclosed if we were to lose this particular competence?

The architecture provides a logic for product and market diversification, moreover. An SBU manager would be asked: Does the new market opportunity add to the overall goal of becoming the best player in the world? Does it exploit or add to the core competence? At Vickers, for example, diversification options have been judged in the context of becoming the best power and motion control company in the world (see the insert "Vickers Learns the Value of Strategic Architecture").

The strategic architecture should make resource allocation priorities transparent to the entire organization. It provides a template for allocation decisions by top management. It helps lower level managers understand the logic of allocation priorities and disciplines senior management to maintain consistency. In short, it yields a definition of the company and the markets it serves. 3M, Vickers, NEC, Canon, and Honda all qualify on this score. Honda *knew* it was exploiting what it had learned from motorcycles – how to make high-revving, smooth-running, lightweight engines – when it entered the car business. The task of creating a strategic architecture forces the organization to identify and commit to the technical and production linkages across SBUs that will provide a distinct competitive advantage.

It is consistency of resource allocation and the development of an administrative infrastructure appropriate to it that breathes life into a strategic architecture and creates a managerial culture, team-work, a capacity to change, and a willingness to share resources, to protect proprietary skills, and to think long term. That is also the reason the specific architecture cannot be copied easily or overnight by competitors. Strategic architecture is a tool for communicating with customers and other external constituents. It reveals the broad direction without giving away every step.

REDEPLOYING TO EXPLOIT COMPETENCIES

If the company's core competencies are its critical resource and if top management must ensure that competence carriers are not held hostage by some particular business, then it follows that SBUs should bid for core competencies in the same way they bid for capital. We've made this point glancingly. It is important enough to consider more deeply.

Once top management (with the help of divisional and SBU managers) has identified overarching competencies, it must ask businesses to identify the projects and people closely connected with them. Corporate officers should direct an audit of the location, number, and quality of the people who embody competence.

This sends an important signal to middle managers: core competencies are *corporate* resources and may be reallocated by corporate management. An individual business doesn't own anybody. SBUs are entitled to the services of individual employees so long as SBU management can demonstrate that the opportunity it is pursuing yields the highest possible pay-off on the investment in their skills. This message is further underlined if each year in the strategic planning or budgeting process, unit managers must justify their hold on the people who carry the company's core competencies.

Elements of Canon's core competence in optics are spread across businesses as diverse as cameras, copiers, and semiconductor lithographic equipment and are shown in "Core Competencies at Canon." When Canon identified an opportunity in digital laser printers, it gave SBU managers the right to raid other SBUs to pull together the required pool of talent. When Canon's reprographics products division undertook to develop microprocessor-controlled copiers, it turned to the photo products group, which had developed the world's first microprocessor-controlled camera.

Also, reward systems that focus only on product-line results and career paths that seldom cross SBU boundaries engender patterns of behavior among unit managers that are destructively competitive. At NEC, divisional managers come together to identify next-generation competencies. Together they decide how much investment needs to be made to build up each future competency and the contribution in capital and staff support that each division will need to make. There is also a

	Precision Mechanics	Fine Optics	Microelectronics
Basic camera	■	■	
Compact fashion camera	■	■	
Electronic camera	■	■	
EOS autofocus camera	■	■	■
Video still camera	■	■	■
Laser beam printer	■	■	■
Color video printer	■		■
Bubble jet printer	■		■
Basic fax	■		■
Laser fax	■		■
Calculator			■
Plain paper copier	■	■	■
Battery PPC	■	■	■
Color copier	■	■	■
Laser copier	■	■	■
Color laser copier	■	■	■
NAVI	■	■	■
Still video system	■	■	■
Laser imager	■	■	■
Cell analyzer	■	■	■
Mask aligners	■		■
Stepper aligners	■		■
Excimer laser aligners	■	■	■

Figure 9.4 Core competencies at Canon

sense of equitable exchange. One division may make a disproportionate contribution or may benefit less from the progress made, but such short-term inequalities will balance out over the long term.

Incidentally, the positive contribution of the SBU manager should be made visible across the company. An SBU manager is unlikely to surrender key people if only the other business (or the general manager of that business who may be a competitor for promotion) is going to benefit from the redeployment. Cooperative SBU managers should be celebrated as team players. Where priorities are clear, transfers are less likely to be seen as idiosyncratic and politically motivated.

Transfers for the sake of building core competence must be recorded and appreciated in the corporate memory. It is reasonable to expect a business that has surrendered core skills on behalf of corporate opportunities in other areas to lose, for a time, some of its competitiveness. If these losses in performance bring immediate censure, SBUs will be unlikely to assent to skills transfers next time.

Finally, there are ways to wean key employees off the idea that they belong in perpetuity to any particular business. Early in their careers, people may be exposed to a variety of businesses through a carefully planned rotation program. At Canon, critical people move regularly between the camera business and the copier business and between the copier business and the professional optical-products business. In mid-career, periodic assignments to cross-divisional project teams may be necessary, both for diffusing core competencies and for loosening the bonds that might tie an individual to one business even when brighter opportunities beckon elsewhere. Those who embody critical core competencies should know that their careers are tracked and guided by corporate human resource professionals. In the early 1980s at Canon, all engineers under thirty were invited to apply for membership on a seven-person committee that was to spend two years plotting Canon's future direction, including its strategic architecture.

Competence carriers should be regularly brought together from across the corporation to trade notes and ideas. The goal is to build a strong feeling of community among these people. To a great extent, their loyalty should be to the integrity of the core competence area they represent and not just to particular businesses. In traveling regularly, talking frequently to customers, and meeting with peers, competence carriers may be encouraged to discover new market opportunities.

Core competencies are the wellspring of new business development. They should constitute the focus for strategy at the corporate level. Managers have to win manufacturing leadership in core products and capture global share through brand-building programs aimed at exploiting economies of scope. Only if the company is conceived of as a hierarchy of core competencies, core products, and market-focused business units will it be fit to fight.

Nor can top management be just another layer of accounting consolidation, which it often is in a regime of radical decentralization. Top management must add value by enunciating the strategic architecture that guides the competence acquisition process. We believe an obsession with competence building will characterize the global winners of the 1990s. With the decade underway, the time for rethinking the concept of the corporation is already overdue.

NOTES

1 For a fuller discussion, see our article, "Strategic Intent," *Harvard Business Review* May–June 1989, p. 63.
2 "Collaborate with Your Competitors and Win," *Harvard Business Review*, January–February 1989, p. 133, with Yves L. Doz.

Chapter 10

Achieving synergies

Rosabeth Moss Kanter

EDITORS' NOTE

The following selection is taken from a chapter of When Giants Learn to Dance. *In this book, Rosabeth Moss Kanter examines the challenges confronting corporations, and the changes required to meet them. Many corporations have downsized and restructured, and Kanter argues that this makes it all the more important for firms to search for synergies, in order to exploit their remaining resources as fully as possible. In this selection, Kanter discusses both the importance of synergy, and how companies can gain synergy benefits.*

VALUE MULTIPLIED: THE PAYOFF FROM SYNERGIES

The structure that is "right" in theory, the "right" combination of parts, is still not enough to produce synergy. A business mix that is good from a strategic analysis standpoint brings benefits in practice only if the relationships and processes are established to ensure cooperation and communication – with managers of every area committed to contributing value to one another.

The only real justification for a multibusiness corporation, in my view, is the achievement of synergy – that magical mix of business activities that are stronger and more profitable together than they would be separately. The "portfolio" or "holding company" approach – in which each part stands alone and needs to be different in order to compensate for the weakness of other parts – has been increasingly discredited. For example, strategy expert Michael Porter's longitudinal data on a set of Fortune 500 companies showed that most could not digest acquisitions unrelated to their core business; over 70 percent of the firms divested such unrelated units after about five years.[1]

Sometimes companies have moved away from a portfolio strategy for defensive reasons: the costs of administering diversity or the vulnerability to takeovers engendered by the ease with which the pieces could be unbundled and sold at a premium. But more often, the quest for value multipliers comes from growth goals. There is a growing conviction that doing-more-with-less is possible when the right combination of parts, working together in the right way, can actively contribute to one another's success.

Nowhere do synergies seem more important than in global technology companies, which face brutal, fast-paced competition. PPG Industries, for example, knew this when it launched a Biomedical Products Division out of diverse worldwide acquisitions. Edward Voboril, the group executive, put "teamwork" number one on his priority list, and he convened the first management conference of the group to build the foundation for it.

From the noncommittal expressions on the faces of the audience as he opened the conference, I could see that he had a hard sell ahead of him. On paper, the fit between the parts was excellent. But he had to cajole suspicious managers from different nations and different businesses out of their territoriality. "The eggs have gotten scrambled, and we can't unscramble them," he said, to remind listeners that they had better accept the situation. "But now we've got the raw materials to succeed on a bigger scale than any of us have seen," he continued, to appeal to their ambition. And then the real pitch; "We must turn our attention to the goals we have in common. We can pool our strengths instead of dissipating them." He had a few carrots to offer them: higher R&D funding than any of the businesses separately had ever known, a world-wide marketing and sales organization to expand the sales of what had been geographically localized products. But still, the formal programs and structures would not be enough unless heads of different business units from different parts of the world agreed to cooperate.

In the global Olympics, this is indeed what differentiates winners from losers. As international management researchers Christopher Bartlett and Sumantra Ghoshal show, the best competitors in world markets know how to build cooperation at the business unit level.[2] Instead of either dictating everything from headquarters (the "centralized" strategy) or allowing every country and every business to go its own way (the ultimate "decentralized" strategy), multiproduct transnational companies like Procter and Gamble, Philips, NEC, and increasingly, Colgate have created a balanced organizational strategy. Such a balanced approach helps the separate parts see shared goals, develop common values and standards, communicate among themselves (Colgate uses, among other things, a creative video magazine), pool resources for some activities, create joint ventures and projects, build career paths flowing across their borders, and divide responsibility for innovation.

PPG Biomedical Division's goal was to be among those world-class companies. For the next three days, the assembled managers talked about their businesses, identified areas of overlap with potential for cooperation, found solutions in another corner of the world to the problems plaguing them at home, and built the foundation for continuing communication. By the end of the conference, some teams had formed to explore matters of mutual interest, and there was an agreement to divide the innovation labors – for example, one country taking the lead in development technology that many countries and many divisions could use. "The work has just begun," Voboril commented afterward. "My job will be to keep pushing those synergies, to help each division take advantage of the knowledge and the marketing inroads that their peers develop. We'll keep sliding back, and I'll keep pushing."

Cross-selling, product links, combining expertise, improved market intelligence, and leaps in efficiency are some of the outcomes of synergy. For example:

- *Cross-selling* By 1986 Prudential expected over $30 million in commissions from sales shared by stockbrokers and insurance agents, up from $4 million two years earlier.[3]
- *Product links* General Foods, after restructuring to decentralize, wanted to keep the benefits of a whole company identity. Chairman Philip Smith set up a task force of marketing executives to work on integrative programs aimed at retailers that would get more shelf space for all products. This led to a program, Team Up for Kids, tying in a number of products.[4]
- *Combining expertise* Pillsbury applied the expertise of its packaged food researchers to help revitalize its Godfather's Pizza chain, developing new food products for sale in the restaurants. (Individually packaged slices of pizza was the first such product.) Similarly, Pillsbury used the expertise and resources of the restaurant group in finding sources of, storing, and distributing fresh vegetables to open the possibility of a Green Giant line of branded fresh vegetables for supermarket sales. Similarly, coordinating research and development on a worldwide basis allowed Procter and Gamble to take advantage of the varieties of expertise found in different countries to speed new product development.
- *Market intelligence* A technology company got its multinational product divisions to alert one another to market signals, a practice that helped make product launchings in new countries more effective than ever in the company's history. Each product division served a different array of countries. Combining experience and data through communication across divisions, the company saw immediate payoffs in world market share growth.
- *Leaps in efficiency* Combining operations of several divisions allowed Shenandoah Life Insurance to increase productivity and quality

dramatically. Before: one form was routed to thirty-two people, across nine sections and three departments, taking twenty-seven days. After: the job was done by one self-managing clerical team of six people handling 13 percent more work faster, with fewer errors and 80 percent less supervision.[5]

Such benefits have led companies with a cowboylike tradition to develop new structures aimed at achieving synergies. For example, Procter and Gamble's traditional emphasis on internal competition grew out of a respected organizational innovation by Neil McElroy, later chairman, over fifty years ago: the assignment of a single marketing manager, a "brand manager," to each product. The rationale back then was that each product should receive distinctive treatment, treatment more likely to produce creative ideas, and that the company would grow faster by competing intensely against itself. In the early 1980s, in light of a changing marketplace and a proliferation of categories and brands, Procter and Gamble moved away from this cowboylike stance to a greater reliance on business teams. Now, as an observer put it, Procter and Gamble's brand managers "no longer operate like mini-czars but are assigned to teams with manufacturing, sales, and research managers, people they once outranked." CEO John Smale explained the business team to the *Harvard Business Review* as "a concept that says, 'When you're going to address a problem, get the people who have something to contribute in the way of creativity if not direct responsibility. Get them together.'" Teams are credited with turning around the sales of a losing product (Pringles potato chips), with packaging inventions, and with speeding the process of getting a new product to market.[6] A network of "organizational effectiveness consultants" trained in skills for facilitating team formation supports the search for synergies.

One especially comprehensive and successful case of a concerted effort to build value multipliers is American Express. In 1986, roughly 10 percent of American Express's net income came from cross-selling and other synergies. The one *big* success was selling life insurance, but there were also many "singles and doubles instead of home runs," as CEO James Robinson put it. Robinson made achieving synergies a priority in 1982, emphasizing that American Express was "one enterprise" united by common overall goals and asking senior executives to identify two or three promising "One Enterprise" synergy projects in their annual plans. A manager of corporate strategy watched over this, issuing a One Enterprise report among one hundred top executives, giving visibility to those engaged in collaboration. Evaluations and incentives were tied to this program: The Chairman of American Express Bank received one of two 1985 bonuses for efforts such as selling travelers checks for the card division and introducing brokerage services to its overseas clients. And by 1987 the company had sifted through about 260 ideas for collaboration between businesses, about 70 percent of which have worked. Among these ideas were sharing of office space, data processing capabilities, and marketing expertise among departments and also cross-marketing of products.[7]

American Express's search for synergies rests on an entrepreneurial foundation – a set of rather autonomous and focused business units concentrating on their own businesses, with a corporate staff of about eight hundred auditors, lawyers, and public relations experts. The One Enterprise program is an attempt to convey that American Express is "one big family" of entrepreneurial companies. Each unit or division is trying to maximize its profit, and if its leaders see that help from someone else in another unit is going to aid them, they will seek it out and try to convince the others that it is in their best interest also. This approach is based on decentralization with voluntary cooperation, not centralization with top-down commands. The synergies the company finds tend to be ways of augmenting what one unit wants to do rather than forcing all units to rely on a single method or a single corporate function. American Express never thought that one sales force could cross-sell life insurance, annuities, stocks and bonds, and credit cards, but the One Enterprise approach means that each company can find occasional marketing leads for the others.

There are nice cash bonuses and recognition for the people who work on One Enterprise projects – something they often have to do after hours and in their spare time. These were among the winning One Enterprise projects for 1987:

- A ten-person team representing all four major business units (Travel Related Services, IDS, Shearson Lehman Hutton, the American Express Bank) and a data processing unit (First Data Resources) negotiated a deal with AT&T for major price reductions. The team discussed the telecommunication needs of their respective companies, pulled the information into a coherent plan, and then worked with AT&T, saving tens of millions of dollars.
- Jim and Malcolm of TRS expanded business opportunities for the whole company by introducing other units to key TRS contacts – for example, a large airline that might be able to use SLH financing for the purchase of new planes.
- Katie, Pete, and Julie of IDS developed a new investment service for Trade Development Bank customers in Luxembourg.
- Gustavo of TRS supported SLH in developing a Financial Management Account product for Latin America, after SLH requested the help of TRS people who were familiar with the cultural differences and business expectations of the area.

- Craig and Ramesh of TRS and Jack of IDS assisted in the development of an Investment Management Account for American Express credit card holders, using IDS expertise to find ways to sell mutual funds to TRS customers.

Two forms of synergy seem most common at American Express, one externally oriented (marketing leads) and one internally oriented (efficiencies from using another company's "back-office" information-processing capacity). For example, the TRS marketing organization that places traveler's checks with banks and other institutions to sell them helps IDS market financial planning on a mass basis through those banks. Similarly, TRS or Shearson professionals who have relationships with the chief financial officer or controller or companies planning large restructurings can pave the way for IDS to offer financial counseling to employees deciding whether to take early-retirement options. "When they help IDS, they sort of expect that the favor will be returned," Harry Freeman, executive vice president, observed. "This starts a cycle of internal synergies that build on each other and create a companywide spirit of cooperation."

Back-office collaborations might take the following form: IDS may want to create a new mutual fund which will require an information processing capacity; by going to Shearson to see about using its Boston Safe subsidiary, a very efficient back office for mutual funds, IDS can save a substantial amount in setup expenses while compensating Shearson for use of the system; Shearson gets a source of additional return on its investment.

But even when synergy is a stated goal, there are many roadblocks. In other financial services companies, for example, synergies such as cross-marketing and the development of financial supermarkets seem limited by territoriality – the unwillingness of salesmen representing different products to work together. When Prudential first experimented with joint sales programs involving insurance agents and stockbrokers, the efforts were "crashing failures," according to George Ball, head of the brokerage unit. Or the attempt to achieve synergy is hurt by the unwillingness of executives to share customer lists, as with American Express's charge card people's initial reluctance to share their lists with the brokerage. Or internal cooperation and cross-marketing can threaten external relationships. Sears wondered whether to give its merchandise group access to the Discover credit card customer list because other merchants who have accepted the card could be upset.[8] All of these roadblocks were internal, having nothing to do with any unwillingness of customers to change their habits.

Similar problems are by-products of the very decentralization that also gives some companies their entrepreneurial strength. But without the ability to cooperate across areas, the units might as well be split up into independent businesses. This was the dilemma faced by the $200 million technology development company I will call "Firestar." In 1986, a new president put the issue of internal competition high on his list of things to change:

> There are natural competitive forces in a technology business. With the breadth of technology we have, it is easy to look at one area, e.g., electronics, and say that that group might do work in electronic materials, while the materials group might feel like that business is part of its scope and mission in life. Another example is the Computer Integrated Manufacturing Systems (CIMS) market. Our manufacturing technology *and* information systems groups have the technical knowledge to compete against each other for business in that market – or they could work jointly.

In his view, each of the six sectors of Firestar saw itself in competition with the others. Compensation to senior managers had been based on the performance of their sectors *vis-à-vis* the others. There was no incentive to cooperate internally, and as a result, the business sectors didn't "see the whole company" when making decisions. The groups acted independently rather than with a shared interest in the division. The president remarked that "I didn't see everyone's oar in the water at the same time." Some cooperation did exist from time to time, but it was not encouraged enough; if it happened, it happened by chance more than by design. "We don't have a bunch of Machiavellian types running around screwing their buddies," he said, "but we also are not getting enough synergies."

"Turf battles" had clearly arisen between business sectors in this company. For example, two groups separately approached the same customer, without a coordinated effort – "The left hand didn't know what the right was doing." As the president put it:

> Group A had studied the problem, decided it wasn't a good opportunity for us, and did not bid on the contract. Group A was the main line technology group for the type of problem involved here, the next best suited to evaluate the project. Unbeknownst to Group A, though, Group B looked at the same project and made a bid. The bid is still pending, but it probably won't be accepted. When Group A found out what Group B had done, they were livid, outraged. You may ask, "How could a group feel a charter to make a bid like that?" Well, Group B could see it as part of its mission.

Another example was even more vivid:

> Last year we established a new Aerospace office to be closer to an air

force base, one of our biggest customers. This new office appeared to me to be in direct competition with several business sectors here at headquarters. In fact, they could have been in competition with all of the other divisions, that is how broad their mission statement was. This has set up a "we/they" mentality. As it was, we had three other groups in competition for aerospace business: the materials and electronic groups and the business development staff. This had to be changed. The new office staff are supposed to be our point people on the scene, not to compete with us but rather to use all the company resources to solve the customers' problems.

Then there were the minor instances of rivalry – minor, but no less irritating and costly, such as two different groups investing in the same piece of equipment, each purchasing one when instead they could have shared one.

Seeing these barriers to synergy, the president made the search for value multipliers in Firestar his major priority, shaping his approach to every aspect of the business, from strategic planning to compensation.

Successful efforts to increase synergy generally have three components: a focus from the top and the development of methods and managers to find value multipliers; shifts in incentives and rewards; and a culture of communication and cooperation resting on a foundation of personal relationships.

Providing leadership and vehicles to identify opportunities

The first ingredient in the search for synergies is a familiar one: leadership from the top. American Express's Jim Robinson made identification of synergies a priority in 1982, when he asked senior executives to define two or three One Enterprise projects in their annual plans. Executives are quick to point out that One Enterprise is not *forced* on anyone; projects must be in the best interests of the business unit. But Robinson's leadership is also clear. Consider Harry Freeman's view:

Over the years we have managed to achieve a lot of useful synergies. Useful synergy does not come from directives from the top. It really comes when somebody in one of the business units thinks he can do a hell of a lot better, or make more money, or introduce a much better product, and really needs somebody or sees that some unit in another business unit can be really helpful. He then tries to convince the other guy that it is in his or her interest. What you try to do is create an environment of entrepreneurship about the whole place. One Enterprise was never meant to be the total program. The main driver of synergy does not come from directives. It comes from shared self-interest.

Jim Robinson is a great One Enterprise guy. If you go outside the company and were using someone else's system, you'd better have a very good answer ready for him. Now if your answer is good, he'll say, "Terrific," or he may call up those other guys and say, "Hey, why don't you get more reasonable?" There is a certain amount of executive pressure to cooperate. But if you do go outside and find it cheaper for the same quality, Jim Robinson is going to say, "go outside. We are in business for the profit of the shareholders."

Once top management identifies synergy goals, a "synergy czar" may then swing into action, serving as chief cheerleader and recorder of the efforts to find value multipliers. Sometimes the corporate strategy office plays this role, nudging cross-area projects into strategic plans, suggesting areas of overlap offering joint possibilities, convening task forces and councils to hammer out ways to maximize the payoffs from joint resource use, and encouraging collaborative efforts. This alone represents a striking shift of mind-set for many strategic planners, who are more accustomed to identifying the value of assets before an acquisition or divestiture than to finding ways to gain the benefits of internal collaboration.

At Pillsbury, the appointment of a synergy czar was a valiant attempt to shore up some ailing businesses by bringing the resources of various units together to create value multiplier effects. The then CEO John Stafford realized that segmentation of the food industry required giving each division great autonomy; at the same time, someone was needed at the top to pull things together in order to capitalize on new opportunities that might cut across division lines. In March 1986, Stafford assigned James Behnke to the new position of senior vice-president for Growth and Technology – or, as Behnke put it on business cards he had printed. "Senior Vice-President, Blurring."

Behnke's business development group worked with the divisions to marshal all of Pillsbury's resources, which in practice meant getting restaurant divisions to help food divisions, and vice versa. As a result of Behnke's efforts, new business opportunities opened up. For example, when Green Giant (specialists in canned vegetables) decided to develop branded fresh vegetables, they lacked three critical resources, which Burger King helped provide: year-round supply, a distribution system, and food service customers. Behnke extracted three lessons from Pillsbury's experience:

First, it must be a win/win situation. If company A wins 10 points, and company B loses 5 points, Pillsbury gains 5 points, but it will never work. Both companies A and B must gain points, even if it is only 2.5 points each.

Second, if you go too low down an organization, then it gets tougher and tougher to cross disciplines. At the lower levels, people are more provincial, more guarded, more defensive. If the effort is important enough – you should tackle only the big projects – then the negotiations need to go on between the top levels of the organization. More senior people must be involved.

What makes it work is the chemistry of the people. There can be no systems, no rules, no manuals – people hate that stuff. There can be no pressure, only suction.

Unfortunately for Pillsbury and Stafford, the search for multipliers came too late to dilute the effects of other business problems. Mounting losses led to the return of the former chairman, Stafford's resignation in 1988, and frequent mention of Pillsbury as a takeover target. The search for value multipliers is a long process that cannot guarantee the quick rescue of failing businesses.

Realizing the importance of a concerted long-term effort to build synergy, the president of Firestar, the technology development company, built a number of planning and action vehicles. First, he and his senior managers shifted their strategic planning exercise from a near-term outlook (which leads to pressures to "beat your buddy in competition") to more long-term goals. They reviewed the standard business plan questions – Where are you now? Where do you want to be? How are you going to get there? But they added a twist of their own, approaching planning on two levels. Each sector came up with its own business plan; then, working together, the groups wrote strategic plans for different market areas, such as the industrial market and the defense business.

The president also created an investment council, comprising Firestar's senior business sector leaders and the business development staff. The council was guided by the strategic direction of each sector and of Firestar as a whole. It evaluated investments in R&D, capital equipment, and human resources (hiring needs). The goal was to change the past practice of tactical investing to a more strategic, holistic approach; for example, instead of having the manufacturing sector tactically purchase a piece of equipment, that purchase would now be considered a more general investment, an item with potential utility for other sectors as well.

Both components of the strategic planning were part of an effort to struggle against the forces that make a diverse technological company's sectors compete single technology with single technology. Instead, Firestar wanted to become a more fully integrated company, gaining power from a multidisciplinary approach. The company's strength was always its broad technological offerings; to capitalize on this required cross-business-unit cooperation. As the president put it, "A good materials company is limited to only materials. We can do materials, but also do process design, environmental impact – we can provide our customers with many ancillary support services. We take a systems approach to the problem." His goal was to "foster a culture in which everyone gravitates toward working together to create synergy."

Incentives and rewards

The approaches necessary to build synergy could not be more different from the shootouts of cowboy management. Destructive competition is set up so that the losers lose as much as the winners gain. There's a single prize, which the winner takes; but in addition to missing the prize, the losers also incur costs. What drives the competition in a negative direction, then, is largely fear of losing. The destructive side of the battle stems as much from avoiding punishment as from seeking rewards. Cooperation is likely, however, when there are incentives for performing well, regardless of who comes in first. If one of the goals of competition is to develop options, then it is important to reward the generating of alternatives, not just getting the right answer. Some rewards come from playing the game well, even if the ultimate prize goes to someone else. Joint incentives, which give everyone something if anyone reaches high levels of performance, make cooperation even more likely.

The creation of an inter-business-sector development fund was one of Firestar's new president's first moves. He held a reserve of funds for use in projects that spanned the boundaries of two or more sectors. Previously, if a sector was going to work with another sector, it had to invest by itself – only one sector put up the money, though the other would also get some benefits. This situation did not encourage cooperation; why help support a competitor? The president found these new funds to be an immediate incentive for joint projects. The atmosphere at the company soon began to reflect this emphasis. As he said:

> In an environment where team play gets rewarded, we now openly discuss the pros and cons of major bidding decisions. The decision making is more holistic. If two separate groups think they should both bid on a contract, they'll put together a joint proposal. The problems in the past have arisen when one group thinks bidding is a good idea and another does not. Then I bring the two groups together for a meeting to discuss both sides of the decision. When sectors can't agree, I help them resolve the problems by making the ultimate decision.

Although some of this crossing of lines did happen before, there was no necessity or drive to do so. Now there was *incentive*, as opposed to just a hope that cooperation would happen.

A second approach is to add team incentives to senior managers' evaluation and compensation. American Express has a variety of ways to reward achievement of synergy goals, starting with special awards, bonuses, and publicity for specific One Enterprise projects, available to contributors at any organizational level. Synergy goals are also built into top management incentives. Incentive compensation awards (called portfolio awards) for senior managers in one of the businesses are determined primarily by the performance of their business unit, but a significant chunk of each award is determined by the performance of all the business units. For senior corporate managers, the portfolio award is divided into quarters, and 25 percent is determined by the performance of each of the major business units. Furthermore, a large number of employees own shares in the company, and a large number of officers have stock options. This package of incentives and rewards directs people's attention to the performance of the whole company, not just the performance of their own business.

Firestar's new president had to revise both incentive and evaluation systems. He began to ask the question, "How much business did you develop for the rest of the company, not just for yourself?" Sector leaders were asked to develop inter-sector markets and programs. In the past, managers hadn't been evaluated on the combined results of two or three sectors together. Now that was part of the evaluation. This provided an incentive for sector leaders to work together and avoid one-to-one competition; they could be rewarded for working together and across sectors. Managers were now encouraged to bring back leads for others, to market for the entire division. "Instead of dangling the carrot in front of each sector manager, I've put the carrot between organizations," the president said.

Similarly, at Bankers Trust, the heads of corporate banking and corporate finance review the proposed bonuses for each other's officers and can influence the amount if an officer has been uncooperative. If trends toward synergy incentives and rewards continue, there is also a need for new measurement systems that can permit attribution of the benefits from collaboration.[9]

Communication, relationships, and the foundation for cooperation

Communications is the third key to achieving synergies. Many opportunities for synergy come in the form of information sharing; thus, the channels need to be established to enable managers and professionals from different business units and different parts of the world to communicate. Post-entrepreneurial companies tend to be characterized by more frequent events that draw people together across areas – executive conferences, meetings of professionals assigned to different businesses, boards and councils that oversee efforts in diverse places and transmit learning from them. Training centers and educational events are a potent means for increasing communication. General Electric's facility in Crotonville, New York, is much more than a corporate college; it is in effect a synergy center than helps people identify shared interests across businesses and tackle common problems together.

Computer networks and other information systems can enhance the communication that knits a company together in pursuit of synergies. But systems – no matter how easy to use – do not necessarily guarantee cooperative communication without the knowledge of one another that people develop through face-to-face relationships. For this reason, Digital Equipment Corporation runs a helicopter service to and from major New England facilities to permit people to get together to transmit information and pursue joint projects. People develop relationships with one another this way faster than they do through electronic mail, as important as systems like that are for making communication easy and instantaneous; and those relationships make cooperation possible.

It is harder to get the benefits of cooperation and easier for rivalry to get out of hand when there is no history of past relationships to draw on to give the rivals understanding of one another, when there are no shared experiences to prevent mistrust and hostility – or worse, when past experiences have been negative. Cooperation flourishes on a foundation of shared experience. Even in encounters involving strangers, relationships make a difference. For example, players in laboratory games like "prisoners' dilemma" do better when given the chance to talk with one another beforehand.[10] Friendships help. After first encountering resistance to joint sales programs involving stockbrokers and insurance agents, Prudential made the programs work by encouraging joint efforts where there seemed to be natural affinities on the basis of friendship.[11]

Synergy is also difficult to achieve when there is a clear and apparently unbridgeable structural separation between areas. Their activities are not intertwined, they seem to need nothing from one another, and their apparent independence is reinforced by separate career paths or communication patterns or reporting relationships. Cooperation, in contrast, is engendered by structural links that make the parties interdependent. Awareness of mutual need reduces rivalries to a friendlier level. So do integrating mechanisms that remind the parties of joint interests – for example, liaisons between groups or people with a foot in each camp.

Expectations also help. The anticipation of a shared future dampens the killer instinct. Even in competition, there will be more cooperative relationships among rivals when the competition is viewed as temporary, when the composition of the opposing team is known to change regularly, when today's losers can join winners in another effort toward another goal. Robert Axelrod's computer simulations of prisoners' dilemma games found the most successful strategy to be TIT for TAT, a strategy that began by cooperating and then simply reciprocated the opponent's last move. He argued that cooperating was most likely when people or groups knew they would have to deal with one another again in the future.[12]

In short, cooperation is encouraged when people perceive a shared fate. They see that they and other rivals have a joint stake in a larger outcome – advancing their joint enterprise as a whole. This idea was behind James Robinson's One Enterprise program at American Express. Another CEO stressed "dual citizenship" to all his managers, making them members, simultaneously, of both their business unit and a corporate project team, with "citizenship responsibilities, rights, and rewards" stemming from each.

We have come full circle in the search for synergies. To get value multiplied requires removing the sources of value subtracted. Tilting the balance toward cooperation offers the possibility of tackling new business opportunities as well as eliminating the costs of in-fighting. Encouraging cooperation even among nominal rivals helps organizations gain the synergies that come with the transfer of good ideas from one unit to another. It makes it easier to focus on standards for quality performance and to concentrate organizational energy where it should be concentrated, on achieving the goal, not on eliminating rivals. And it offers flexibility; today's friends can more easily be tomorrow's collaborators.

There is so much competition already inherent in most organizations – from the "pyramid squeeze" that means that not all of the talented people can rise to top positions, to the natural pride that one department takes in doing better than another – that the task of managers is often not to fuel the fires but to dampen them.

The real danger of performance shootouts is that someone you need may die of the wounds.

THE CORPORATION'S NEW SHAPE

Striving for synergies is essential to managing the do-more-with-less imperative of the corporate Olympics. Fewer resources, intelligently combined, can work together to bring greater payoffs and to pursue new opportunities with greater speed. A stress on synergies can help companies save on fixed costs and tackle new opportunities at the same time.

Getting there, however, requires the corporation to take on a new shape. The company that achieves synergies looks and operates very differently from the swollen, lethargic "corpocracy" that many large American businesses allowed themselves to become. No longer does the typical corporate organization chart resemble the Eiffel Tower – a broad pyramid of productive activities on the bottom and a tall, narrow hierarchy of many levels of managers piled upon managers, stretching all the way to the top. The model for the post-entrepreneurial corporation is a leaner organization, one that has fewer "extraneous" staff and is thus more focused on doing only those things in which it has competence. In the post-entrepreneurial company, there are fewer and fewer people or departments that are purely "corporate" in nature; more responsibilities are delegated to the business units, and more services are provided by outside suppliers. And fewer layers of management mean that the hierarchy itself is flatter. Thus, the "vertical" dimension of the corporation is much less important. At the same time, the "horizontal" dimension – the process by which all the divisions and departments and business units communicate and cooperate – is the key to getting the benefits of collaboration.

The post-entrepreneurial corporation represents a triumph of process over structure. That is, relationships and communication and the flexibility to temporarily combine resources are more important than the "formal" channels and reporting relationships represented on an organizational chart. *In Olympic contests requiring speed and dexterity, what is important is not how responsibilities are divided but how people can pull together to pursue new opportunities.*

Management sage Peter Drucker recently used the image of a symphony orchestra to describe the new model of the leaner, flatter corporation.[13] In the orchestra, performers with different skills concentrate on perfecting their professional competence, while a single conductor coordinates the overall performance; performers with similar specialties form self-managed work teams, operating without a bureaucratic hierarchy above them. The image is useful and evocative as far as it goes. But for corporate players to make beautiful music together they must achieve a balance between concentrating on their own areas of skill and responsibility and working together with others. They need to do their own jobs well while keeping one eye on what might be useful for someone else. They need to understand enough about the company's other areas to identify possibilities for joint action and mutual enhancement. They need to simultaneously focus and collaborate. They must function in many roles: as soloist, ensemble players, and members of the orchestra.

NOTES

1 Michael Porter, "From Competitive Advantage to Corporate Strategy," *Harvard Business Review*, vol. 65, no. 3 (May–June 1987), pp. 43–59.
2 Christopher Bartlett and Sumantra Ghoshal, *Managing Across Borders: The Transnational Solution* (Boston: Harvard Business School Press, 1989).
3 Steve Swartz and Steve Weiner, "Stalled Synergy: Many Firms Back Off from Offering Arrays of Financial Services," *Wall Street Journal*, November 12, 1986.
4 Aimee L. Stern, "General Foods Tries the Old Restructure Ploy," *Business Month*, November 1987, pp. 37–9.
5 John J. Sherwood, "Creating Work Cultures with Competitive Advantage," *Organizational Dynamics*, 16 (Winter 1988), pp. 5–27.
6 Julie Solomon and Carol Hymovitz, "Team Strategy: P&G Makes Changes in the Way It Develops and Sells Its Products," *Wall Street Journal*, August 11, 1987.
7 Monci Jo Williams, "Synergy Works at American Express," *Fortune*, February 16, 1987, pp. 79–80.
8 Swartz and Weiner, op. cit.
9 Dwight B. Crane and Robert G. Eccles, "Commercial Banks: Taking Shape for Turbulent Times," *Harvard Business Review*, vol. 65, no. 6 (November–December 1987), pp. 94–100. See also Robert Eccles and Dwight Crane, *Doing Deals* (Boston: Harvard Business School Press, 1988).
10 Alfie Kohn, *No Contest* (Boston: Houghton Mifflin, 1986), p. 69.
11 Swartz and Weiner, op. cit.
12 Robert Axelrod, *The Evolution of Cooperation* (New York: Basic Books, 1984).
13 Peter F. Drucker, "The Coming of the New Organization," *Harvard Business Review*, vol 66, no. 1 (January–February 1988), pp. 45–53.

Part IV

Diversification, performance and restructuring

The earlier parts of this book have explored the economic logic of multibusiness companies from a theoretical perspective, and examined some of the practical approaches and tools available to managers to help them realize benefits from the common ownership of diverse businesses. Here, we turn to the question of how multibusiness companies actually perform. While, in theory, multibusiness companies can create value by allocating resources more efficiently than the market and by achieving synergy benefits across their businesses, the evidence on performance suggests that, in practice, multibusiness companies often fail to create value, or even destroy value.

Many academics have investigated the performance of diversified companies over the last twenty years. In 1974, Richard Rumelt published a landmark study on this issue. In *Strategy, Structure, and Economic Performance*, Rumelt proposed a methodology for categorizing different kinds of diversification. In Rumelt's schema there are four main categories of firms:

1 single business firms are focused on one main business;
2 dominant business firms have diversified to some extent, but most of their sales revenue comes from one major business;
3 related business firms have businesses which are linked by common skills and strengths;
4 unrelated firms have businesses with no common skills or resources.

In his study, Rumelt compared the performance of a sample of large US firms in different diversification categories. He found that related diversifiers outperformed both single business firms and unrelated diversifiers.[1] Rumelt's study suggested that diversification did pay off, but only if firms could exploit their skills or technologies in new areas.

Academics have continued to explore the link between diversification strategies and performance, building on Rumelt's original work, and the literature on this issue is large and complex.[2] Researchers have refined Rumelt's original diversification categories and proposed new methodologies for measuring diversity; they have explored whether Rumelt's findings hold in different countries, and in different time periods; they have explored the impact of factors such as industry profitability and risk; they have suggested different ways of measuring performance. While some studies support Rumelt's original findings, others indicate that conglomerate firms outperform related diversifiers, or suggest that there are no significant differences in the performance of firms pursuing different diversification strategies. The first reading in this part is a survey by V. Ramanujam and P. Varadarajan of this extensive literature. The authors provide both a guide to the research on this issue, and a critical appraisal of research approaches. Ramanujam and Varadarajan point out that the evidence on diversification and performance, despite numerous studies, is ambiguous and contradictory, and they conclude that this type of research is unlikely to yield new insights into whether one kind of diversification is more successful than another.

While the research discussed by Ramanujam and Varadarajan focuses on performance differences among firms pursuing different diversification strategies, other writers have examined the overall performance of diversified companies. Two pre-eminent Harvard professors, Michael Porter and Michael Jensen, wrote influential articles on corporate performance during the 1980s, aiming to explain the unprecedented wave of corporate takeovers and breakups. Both authors claim that hostile takeovers and the breakup of large companies occur because so many multibusiness companies fail to create value. In particular, Porter and Jensen argue that diversification strategies have undermined corporate performance.

Michael Porter's article, 'From Competitive Advantage to Corporate Strategy', is an analysis of the acquisition records of thirty-three large American companies since the 1950s. Porter shows that most acquisitions made by these companies were subsequently divested, and he argues that this is strong evidence of the failure of corporate-level strategies. Porter argues that there is a critical need for better corporate strategies, and he claims that most companies should focus on creating value by sharing activities or skills across their businesses. Porter's article in the previous part of this book explains how managers can use value chain analysis to identify synergy opportunities. Here, Porter highlights the need for managers to avoid the failed acquisitions of the 1970s and 1980s and to develop more successful, value creating corporate strategies.

Weak performance in multibusiness companies caused widespread restructuring during the late 1980s and early 1990s. Some firms have focused on cutting corporate-level costs, often by scaling down or dismantling corporate services and functions. Other companies have refocused their corporate portfolios on a few core businesses.[3] Constantinos

Markides has investigated the extent of diversification among large US companies during the 1980s, finding that diversification decreased among these firms. Markides suggests that one reason for this trend is because external capital markets have become increasingly sophisticated, and it is therefore more difficult for multibusiness companies to gain benefits from internal resource allocation.[4]

Changes in capital markets, and their effect on firms, is also the focus of the article by Michael Jensen. In this reading, Jensen examines corporate restructuring in the US and argues that a fundamental change is taking place. Jensen defends the takeovers and corporate breakups, the divisional sell-offs and LBOs which caused so much controversy and criticism in the 1980s. In his view, this restructuring is beneficial because it helps resolve the inherent conflict between owners and managers in public corporations. According to Jensen, corporate managers often fail to make the best use of corporate resources, choosing to diversify into uneconomic ventures rather than returning funds to shareholders who could invest them more profitably. This problem is especially severe in mature industries with low growth, where managers have few opportunities for profitable investments. In public corporations, shareholders cannot easily discipline managers who choose to retain free cash flow. LBO partnerships, such as KKR, provide one answer to the conflict of interests between shareholders and managers. Once they gain control of a firm, LBO partnerships use high debt levels and performance-related incentives to force managers to focus on value creation and to eschew unprofitable investments. Jensen argues that new ownership structures are a necessary and beneficial correction to the excessive diversification of many public corporations.[5]

While there are theoretical arguments that show how diversified, multibusiness companies can create value, and also much practical advice to help managers focus on critical issues such as resource allocation and synergy, diversification none the less often fails. As Porter shows, acquisitions are frequently disappointing and subsequently divested, and Jensen argues that many businesses would perform much better as stand-alone entities, controlled either directly by their managers or by LBO partnerships. Academic research into diversification has not provided many insights into the kinds of diversification strategies that work and those that do not. Clearly, it is not at all easy for a multibusiness company to create value, no matter what type of diversification it pursues. A key issue for managers, then, is to understand why diversification so often destroys value and leads to poor performance, and to find ways of avoiding such value destruction. These issues are the focus of the next part, 'How Corporate Parents Influence their Businesses'.

NOTES

1 Rumelt, Richard P. (1974) *Strategy, Structure, and Economic Performance*, Boston: Harvard Business School Press.
2 See Christensen, Kurt H. and Montgomery, Cynthia A. (1981) 'Corporate Economic Performance: Diversification Strategy Versus Market Structure', *Strategic Management Journal*, 2: 327–43; Rumelt, Richard P. (1982) 'Diversification Strategy and Profitability', *Strategic Management Journal*, 3: 359–69; Seth, Anju (1990) 'Value Creation in Acquisitions: A Re-examination of Performance Issues', *Strategic Management Journal*, 11: 99–115. For a summary of the findings of some of the major studies see Grant, Robert (1991) *Contemporary Strategy Analysis*, Oxford: Blackwell.
3 Bowman, Edward H. and Singh, Harbir (1990) 'Overview of Corporate Restructuring Trends and Consequences', in Milton L. Rock and Robert H. Rock (eds) *Corporate Restructuring*, New York: McGraw-Hill.
4 Markides, Constantinos C. (1991) 'Back to Basics: reversing corporate diversification', *Multinational Business*, (4):12–25.
5 See also Jensen, Michael C. (1991) 'Corporate Control and the Politics of Finance', *Journal of Applied Corporate Finance* 4(2):13–33, Summer.

ADDITIONAL READING

Bowman, Edward H. and Singh, Harbir (1990) "Overview of Corporate Restructuring Trends and Consequences", in Milton L. Rock and Robert H. Rock eds *Corporate Restructuring*, New York: McGraw-Hill.
The authors examine the phenomenon of the merger wave of the 1980s and compare it to earlier merger waves, and provide an overview of portfolio and financial restructuring.
Christensen, Kurt H. and Montgomery, Cynthia A. (1981) "Corporate Economic Performance: Diversification Strategy Versus Market Structure, *Strategic Management Journal*, 2: 327–43.
A re-examination of Rumelt's original findings on diversification and performance, controlling for industry effects. In the sample of firms studied, related diversifiers were in higher performing industries compared with unrelated diversifiers, and this difference helps explain performance differences between the two categories.
Jensen, Michael C. (1991) "Corporate Control and the Politics of Finance", *Journal of Applied Corporate Finance* 4(2): 13–33, Summer.
An examination of changes in the market for corporate control and why new forms of control, such as LBOs, have developed.
Markides, Constantinos C. (1991) 'Back to basics: reversing corporate diversification', *Multinational Business*, (4): 12–25.
Provides data on recent trends in diversification, showing a decrease in the extent of diversification in the 1980s. Markides argues that changes in product and financial markets have reduced the optimal level of diversification for most firms, i.e., the costs of diversification have increased and benefits of diversification have decreased.
Rumelt, Richard P. (1974) *Strategy, Structure, and Economic Performance*, Boston: Harvard Business School Press.
Study of diversification trends and performance differences among various categories of firms pursuing different diversification strategies.
——, (1982) 'Diversification Strategy and Profitability', *Strategic Management Journal*, 3: 359–69.

A follow-up study on the link between diversification strategies and performance, examining the impact of industry effects on the original findings and developing the concept of relatedness among businesses.

Seth, Anju (1990) 'Value Creation in Acquisitions: A Re-examination of Performance Issues', *Strategic Management Journal*, 11: 99–115.

A study of different types of acquisitions and their performance. Seth provides a survey of both the theoretical literature and of empirical studies on the performance of firms pursuing related and unrelated acquisitions. He argues that there are different types of value created by related and unrelated acquisitions.

Chapter 11

Research on diversification

Vasudevan Ramanujam and P. Rajan Varadarajan

EDITORS' NOTE

This reading is taken from V. Ramanujam and P. Varadarajan's comprehensive survey of the research on corporate diversification. In their original study, the authors provide a framework for the extensive literature on diversification and discuss the major research finding of various research streams. This selection focuses on one of these research streams – the relationship between diversification and performance. The authors summarize the major studies on this issue, and provide a critique of research methodologies.

For the purpose of this paper, *diversification* is defined as the entry of a firm or business unit into new lines of activity, either by processes of internal business development or acquisition, which entail changes in its administrative structure, systems, and other management processes. From this perspective, simple product line extensions that are not accompanied by changes in administrative linkage mechanisms do not fall under the conceptualization of diversification adopted by us. Further, following Pitts and Hopkins (1982), we use the term *diversity* to describe the extent to which firms are simultaneously active in many distinct businesses.

The motivation behind defining diversification in terms of both 'what it is' and 'what it does' is consistent with the objective of developing an overarching research framework to classify extant research. It should be realized, however, that narrower definitions are both necessary and unavoidable when conducting empirical research.

A FRAMEWORK FOR CLASSIFYING RESEARCH ON CORPORATE DIVERSIFICATION

The schematic framework of Figure 11.1 is proposed as a convenient means of classifying the literature on diversification. It was arrived at after a process of trial and error in selecting appropriate concepts that might help perform the integration of the diverse body of literature that

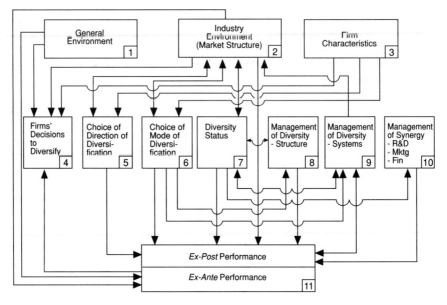

Figure 11.1 Research on diversification: themes and linkages

was assembled. Basically, Figure 11.1 consists of 11 boxes that represent central themes or concepts in the literature of diversification. Boxes 1 through 3 and 11 represent 'generic' strategic management concepts – namely, the general environment, the industry environment, firm characteristics (an omnibus term which includes a wide assortment of firm characteristics), and corporate performance.[1] We will not offer an extended discussion of these concepts in this paper. In contrast, boxes 4 through 10 in the middle level of the framework include themes specific to the topic of diversification.

EDITORS' NOTE

In Table 11.1, the authors list examples of studies exploring the links between diversification and performance; in the framework given, these are the studies focusing on the links between boxes 5, 6 and 7 and box 11.

A CRITIQUE OF RESEARCH ON CORPORATE DIVERSIFICATION

It is obvious from a glance at Figure 11.1 and Table 11.1 that empirical research on diversification has explored several of the simple and complex relationships discernible in Figure 11.1. Undoubtedly some linkages have been the subject of more extensive attention than others. One of

Table 11.1 Conceptual and empirical studies exploring the relationships between diversification and performance

Study	Link(s)	Key ideas/findings
Berry (1971)	5–11	Four-digit inter-industry activity within two-digit industry groups (narrow spectrum diversification) is more conducive to corporate growth than four-digit inter-industry activity among two-digit industry groups (broad spectrum diversification)
Jacquemin and Berry (1979)	5–11	Both diversification *into new* two-digit categories and diversification *within present* two-digit categories are positively related to the asset growth of the firms
Lubatkin (1987)	5–11	Test of the stock market's valuation of conglomerate acquisitions revealed that conglomerate acquisitions typically outperform related acquisitions
Halpern (1973) Dodd (1980) Asquith (1983) Jensen and Ruback (1983) Weston and Chung (1983)	6–11	The emerging consensus on the effects of mergers on stockholder's wealth is that (a) the acquired firm's shareholders receive significant positive abnormal returns and (b) the acquiring firm's shareholders receive positive but non-significant abnormal returns
Backaitis, Balakrishnan and Harrigan (1984)	7–3–11	As a result of the sales dispersion effect, diversified firms with market power perform better than diversified firms that are not market leaders
Weston and Mansinghka (1971)	7–11	Performance, measured by ratio of net income to net worth, is somewhat higher for conglomerate firms, but the difference is not statistically significant
Weston and Mansinghka (continued)	7–2–11	Defensive diversification (i.e., diversification away from low-profitability industries) often enables firms to increase their profitability from inferior to average levels
Rumelt (1974)	7–11	Evaluated in terms of capital productivity measures, related–constrained firms outperform related–linked firms which in turn outperform unrelated–diversified firms
Salter and Weinhold (1979)	7–11	Conglomerates show poorer performance relative to industry averages, particularly with respect to capital productivity measures
Bettis (1981)	7–11	Related–diversified firms outperform unrelated–diversified firms
Bettis and Hall (1982)	7–11	Performance differences between related and unrelated firms in Rumelt's (1974) study were largely due to the overrepresentation in the related–constrained category of firms from one industry noted for high levels of profitability (pharmaceuticals). Differences noted by Rumelt (1974) disappeared after correcting for this bias in the sample

Table 11.1 Continued

Study	Link(s)	Key ideas/findings
Michel and Shaked (1984)	7–11	Firms diversifying into unrelated areas are able to generate statistically superior performance over those with businesses that are predominantly related
Montgomery and Singh (1984)	7–11	The systematic risk (beta values) for unrelated diversifiers is significantly higher than for other diversification categories
Palepu (1985)	7–3–11	The debt position and lower market power of unrelated diversifiers contribute to their lower betas.
	7–11	Firms pursuing a predominantly related diversification strategy outperform firms pursuing a predominantly unrelated diversification strategy
Varadarajan (1986)	7–11	Firms pursuing a strategy of low broad-spectrum diversification (BSD)–high mean narrow-spectrum diversification (MNSD) financially outperform those pursuing a strategy of high BSD–low MNSD
Varadarajan and Ramanujam (1987)		
Jose, Nichols and Stevens (1986)	7–11	Diversification has a statistically significant and positive influence on the value of the firm
	7–10–11	Firms' R&D intensity and promotional intensity also influence the value of the firm
	7–10–11	Differences exist between related and unrelated diversified firms with respect to advertising expenditures, R&D expenditures, and capital intensity
		Firms pursuing related–constrained diversification strategies are more tightly knit (i.e., depend on fewer business units for the bulk of their revenues) than firms pursuing either related-linked or unrelated diversification strategies
Christensen and Montgomery (1981)	7–2–11	Market structure variables have a moderating effect on the diversification–performance link
Rumelt (1982)	7–2–11	Even after adjusting for industry effects, a declining profitability premium is associated with increasing diversity
Galbraith, Samuelson, Stiles and Merrill (1986)	7–2–11	Unrelated diversification represents a hedging strategy against the technological surprises that occur in R&D-intensive industries
Wernerfelt and Montgomery (1986)	7–2–11	Industry growth rate and average industry profitability have different implications for efficient (i.e., firms with a low Herfindahl diversification index) versus inefficient diversifiers
Bettis and Mahajan (1985)	7–2, 3–11	Related diversification is a necessary but not sufficient condition to achieve a favorable risk/return performance. Firms in efficient clusters (relatively high performance at a medium risk level) tend to be in higher growth industries and have relatively lower level of debt financing
Montgomery (1985)	7–2, 3–11	After controlling for a firm's weighted market share (market power in individual markets) and market structure variables (industry profitability and concentration), there is no statistical support for the generalized market power view of diversification, which sees firms' profitability as a function of their extent of diversification

Table 11.1 Continued

Study	Link(s)	Key ideas/findings
Hoskisson (1987)	7–8–11	The implementation of the M-form structure increases the rate of return of firms that diversify through an unrelated business strategy, but decreases the rate of return of firms that adopt vertically integrated and related business approaches to diversification. Risk or variability of firm rate of return generally decreases after the M-form restructuring regardless of the diversification strategy a firm has implemented
Hill and Hoskisson (1987)	7–8, 9–11	Different control arrangements within the basic M-form framework are necessary to realize the economic benefits associated with different diversification strategies
Nathanson and Cassano (1982)	7–8, 9–11	Performance differences between diversification categories are related to organizational differences in how diversity is managed: (a) the presence, size, and reporting relationship of group staff; (b) the presence, size, and reporting relationship of corporate staff; (c) the extent of divisional self-containment; (d) family ownership and domination; (e) top-down planning; and (f) strength of coordinating devices
Dundas and Richardson (1982)	7–8, 9–11	A number of administrative contingencies are critical for successful implementation of the unrelated diversification strategy. These concern policies regarding acquisition, divestment, portfolio structure, management and organization
The vast literature on portfolio matrices (e.g., Day, 1977; Hedley, 1977; Haspeslagh, 1982)	9–2, 11–7	The firm's relative competitive position (e.g., relative market share in the BCG matrix: link 11–9) and industry attractiveness (e.g., market growth rate in the matrix link 2–9) are relevant considerations for making decisions as to which business units to retain and which ones to delete from a firm's portfolio. Divestitures based on such analysis lead to a change in the diversity status of a firm (link 9–7)
Montgomery, Thomas, and Kamath (1984)	9–7–11	The diversity status of a firm is affected not only by its actions in the realm of acquisitions and internal development, but also by its divestitures. The stock market's valuation of a firm's divestiture decisions (link 9–11) has been investigated by a number of researchers. The deliberations of a firm that culminate in its decision to divest one or more of its lines of business is represented by link 9–7
Grant, Jammine, and Thomas (1986)	11–7	Among large British manufacturing firms profitability is positively related to both product diversification and multinational diversification. The principal direction of causation runs from profitability to diversification. No significant differences exist between related and unrelated diversification strategies

the most pervasive themes in the empirically based literature is the interrelationships among diversity status, market structure, and performance.

Diversity status, market structure, and performance

These concepts come together in studies exploring links originating in box 7 and terminating in box 2 or 11. Most prominent of all these studies is the work of Rumelt (1974), which established differences in financial performance across diversification categories (link 7–11) and has been extended and replicated in numerous ways. Some studies argue that, far from being a causal influence on performance, diversity is really a result of poor or superior performance in core businesses, suggesting the link 11–7. For instance, Peters and Waterman (1982) suggest that excellent (i.e., superior-performing) companies generally 'stick to the knitting'. Along similar lines, Burgelman (1983) asserts that initiatives toward the creation of new ventures are often stimulated by deteriorating performance in existing businesses.

Most early industrial organization economics studies have been concerned with the effects of diversification on market structure (e.g., Berry 1974; Rhoades 1973, 1974) rather than performance, and provide the basis for link 7–2. The diversified firm was, and perhaps still is, widely believed to be able to exercise market power through such mechanisms as cross-subsidization, predatory pricing, reciprocity in buying and selling, and creating or raising barriers to entry (Palepu 1985). Literature focusing on multipoint competition (the phenomenon of groups of diversified firms whose activities span to a significant extent the same markets) also provides support for the importance of examining link 7–2 (Heggestad and Rhoades 1978; Karnani and Wernerfelt 1985; Porter 1985; Scott 1982).

The converse idea that market structure determines diversity suggests the reverse link 2–7, and follows from the work of Williamson (1975). Specifically, the argument goes that different diversity profiles arise due to different forms of market failure (Dundas and Richardson 1980; Lecraw 1984). Note, therefore, the bidirectional arrow connecting boxes 2 and 7 in Figure 11.1. Furthermore, in an influential dissertation, Montgomery (1979) proposed that performance differences attributed by Rumelt (1974) to diversification categories may, in fact, be due to systematic market structure differences across the diversification categories. In other words, the relative strengths of links 2–11 and 7–11 are at issue. The studies of Bettis and Mahajan (1985), Lecraw (1984) and Montgomery (1985) also attest to the importance of links 7–2, 7–11, and 7–2–11. For these reasons, market structure must be considered a central variable in the literature on diversification and performance.

Although market structure has been most often examined as a mediator of the relationship between diversity and performance, on rare
occasion it has also been posited to influence other aspects of diversification, e.g., choice of diversification mode (see Yip 1982, who examines
link 2–6 focusing on barriers to entry, a market structure variable).
The central location of box 2 in Figure 11.1 is, therefore, not just
accidental.

The collective evidence from this stream of work seems to be that
diversity status is a powerful predictor of performance but market
structure does exert an influence on performance of diversified firms
that is independent of the effect of diversity *per se*.

OVERALL EVALUATION

We will concentrate on what is perhaps the most extensively researched
stream, namely the relationship between diversity status and performance. This work has primarily been cross-sectional in nature, which is
disconcerting given that diversification efforts typically take a very long
time to reach reasonable levels of effectiveness (Biggadike 1979). Much
of the work also happens to be bivariate in nature, although recently
many studies have adopted contingency perspectives to examine more
complex interrelationships.

Aside from its cross-sectional and predominantly bivariate nature,
the research stream also raises several conceptual and methodological
issues. We will focus our discussion on the following five issues: (a)
the theoretical bases for the diversification–performance nexus, (b)
the measurement of diversity and performance, (c) temporal stability
issues, (d) possible spuriousness of observed results, and (e) implementation of diversification strategies. Each of these issues will be discussed
next.

Theoretical bases for the diversification–performance nexus

While many arguments rooted in economic theory exist as to why
diversification is pursued by managers (Reid 1968; Sutton 1973) or
why the diversified form of business organization arises (Dundas and
Richardson, 1980; Williamson, 1975), in most empirical tests of the
diversification–performance nexus these theoretical bases are largely
implicit.

Beattie (1980) provides an overview of various theories of conglomerate diversification. First, there are different variants of profit-maximizing
behavior; namely, the pursuit of monopoly power, the exploitation of
cost opportunities due to synergy, and the reduction of risk. Second,
some theories of diversification posit managerial growth-maximizing

behavior as the wellspring of diversification decisions. Finally, financial models assume "financial gamesmanship" on the part of corporate managers as a result of capital market imperfections. These models concentrate on the accounting effects of diversification activities *per se*, more in order to verify the efficiency of financial markets than to assess the effectiveness of diversification pursued as a growth strategy. Indeed, their central proposition is that under perfect capital markets, diversification should provide no benefits to investors since they can diversify their portfolios themselves at a lesser cost.

Most empirical studies proceed on the assumption that only one of these models is operating, and accordingly posit unitary motives for diversification. This is implicit in their restricted choice of indicators for the assessment of performance, an issue we will discuss in greater detail later. Economic studies have generally emphasized the market power effects of diversification, finance studies have focused on the market efficiency argument, and strategy studies have explored the extent to which the benefits of synergy have been or can be translated into profitability (Lubatkin, 1983).

Speaking of strategy studies, most have ignored the risk aspects entirely until recently, with the notable exception of Amit and Livnat (1988b), Barton (1988), Bettis and Mahajan (1985), Hoskisson (1987), and Montgomery and Singh (1984). Thus, the possibility that, under efficient capital markets, the rationale for expecting differences in performance (risk-adjusted) between diversified and undiversified firms may be unfounded is seldom admitted explicitly.

Strategic management research on diversification appears to be just as negligent in regard to examining the managerial goals argument, which has been, paradoxically enough, more thoroughly studied by industrial organization economics scholars (e.g., Amihud and Lev, 1981). This criticism has been well expressed recently by Reed and Luffman (1986).

To sum up, each stream of research examining the relationship between diversity status and performance has been guided by a set of critical paradigmatic assumptions regarding managerial motives for diversification with a consequent restriction of the research to narrow performance measures. Their explanatory power has been limited because of their neglect of other equally potent motives. An integrative perspective will hopefully impel future efforts to examine more closely the underlying rationale for diversification before proceeding with assessments of the strength of empirical relationships. By integrative approach is meant the use of multiple conceptual lenses to examine a phenomenon at hand, *à la* Allison (1971). Such a perspective should help accommodate the complex web of reasons that induce a firm to diversify.

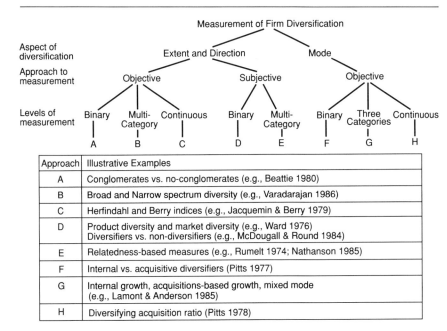

Figure 11.2 Approaches to the measurement of firm diversification

Measurement of diversity and performance

Diversity

In contrast to the inadequate attention given to direct examinations of the motives underlying the diversification decision, the extent of energy devoted to developing measures of diversity is impressive. Figure 11.2 is intended to give an overview of the variety of approaches used. A survey of the literature reveals stark differences across disciplines, as well as within them, in the definitions and operationalizations adopted.

Basically, studies of diversification have focused on the extent (i.e., less or more), direction (i.e., relatedness or unrelatedness) and mode (i.e., internal versus acquisition-based) of diversification. Studies rooted in the industrial organization economics paradigm have generally been concerned mainly with the extent of diversification, and have used objective measures based on SIC counts to capture this aspect of diversification. Despite the apparent objectivity, concerns about the quality of data from different sources and their level of aggregation (i.e., plant versus firm) have led to empirical assessments of the likely impact of alternate operational measures of diversity (e.g., Amit and Livnat 1988a,b; Gorecki 1980).

Many of the early studies in both the finance and industrial organization economics areas focused almost exclusively on the so-called 'conglomerate' form, giving rise to a large body of work on the performance of conglomerate firms (Beattie 1980, Conn 1973; Holzmann, Copeland and Hayya 1975; Levy and Sarnat 1970; Lynch 1971; Markham 1973; Mason and Goudzwaard 1976; Melicher and Rush 1973, 1974; Smith and Schreiner 1969; Westerfield 1970). Interestingly, the term 'conglomerate' is not consistently applied, and is used in reference to both the firm as an entity and to certain types of merger activity resulting in a firm's entry into unrelated lines of business (e.g., Boyle 1970; Reid 1971). However, in our framework the term conglomerate has been used to describe a firm's diversity status, and not its preferred mode of diversification.

In many studies diversification is treated as a continuous variable, while in others, particularly within the strategic management discipline, categories are developed using somewhat arbitrary cut-off points. While in some studies only two categories are employed (e.g., conglomerates and non-conglomerates, as in Beattie 1980), other studies group firms into multiple categories. For instance, Daniels, Pitts and Tretter (1984) categorized firms as low, medium, or high in diversity according to the number of distinct lines of business in which they were active. Some researchers have used multiple continuous measures in an attempt to capture both the extent and direction of diversification. Such an approach is best exemplified by Jacquemin and Berry's (1979) entropy measures. Yet other studies start with multiple continuous measures but subsequently transform them into categorical measures in order to develop a parsimonious set of diversification categories, typically using the median or a point of discontinuity along their continuous measures as cut-off points. Studies by Palepu (1985) and Varadarajan (1986) illustrate these recent approaches.

Strategic management studies of diversification have generally followed Wrigley's (1970) and Rumelt's (1974) lead and employed subjective categories. In many studies, Rumelt's (1974) classification is adopted after a subjective reclassification by the researcher to confirm the appropriateness or current validity of Rumelt's original classification. Bettis (1981), Bettis and Hall (1982), Bettis and Mahajan (1985), Bettis, Hall and Prahalad (1978), and Montgomery (1979) basically relied on Rumelt's (1974) sample and categories. Montgomery (1982) showed that Rumelt's categories are generally robust and accord well with the conventional and more objective SIC count measures. Nathanson (1985), however, casts some doubts on the managerial relevance of Rumelt's approach and goes on to propose a classification scheme of his own.

Other variations of the subjective approach to measuring diversity are also evident in studies of diversification. McDougall and Round (1984) created a binary scheme to classify firms as 'diversifiers' and 'non-diversifiers' using managers' perceptions. Ward (1976) also relied on managerial perceptions, but used the notion of 'difficulty of entry' and distinguished between 'product diversity' and 'market diversity'. Bane and Neubauer (1981) constructed multidimensional diversity classes using subjective *a priori* dimensions and clustering procedures. Their basic proposition was that the failure of foreign subsidiaries of continental European companies could be explained by their diversity. They found that their results were sensitive to the method used to measure diversity.

Since the development of the body of literature on diversification within the strategic management field has essentially involved successive refinements in the measurement of the concept of diversification, it is appropriate to comment at this point on the cumulative findings of this research. The use of alternative approaches for measuring diversity has not led to greater insights into the impact of diversification on performance. The results of most studies have merely extended or marginally modified Rumelt's (1974) original findings. Christensen and Montgomery (1981) and Montgomery (1979, 1982) raised a controversy about the relative influence of key market structure variables and diversity status as alternative explanators of firm performance, but Rumelt (1982) used a rigorous theoretical framework to defend the role of diversification strategy as a key influence on performance even after controlling for market structure influences.

Montgomery's (1985) study attempted to assess the relative importance of the collusive or general market power that is believed to result from increasing levels of diversification versus the specific market power that stems from a firm's relative competitive position in particular market settings. She found that, after controlling for a firm's weighted market share and selected market structure variables (industry profitability and industry concentration), the effect of diversification on performance was small and non-significant. Whether the use of an alternative measure of diversity in her study would have led to a different pattern of results is speculative, but our point is that despite various refinements in the approach to measuring diversity, the findings of studies attempting to demonstrate the effects of diversification on performance remain inconclusive. In a recent study, Wernerfelt and Montgomery (1986) add yet another dimension to the debate by making a distinction between efficient diversifiers and inefficient diversifiers, which are defined as firms with low or high Herfindahl diversification indices, respectively. Market structure variables (industry growth and industry profitability) were found to have differential implications for the two categories of diversifiers.

In summary, the concept of diversification does not lend itself to easy conceptualization and measurement. A variety of measures have been developed, but as Pitts and Hopkins (1982) stress, the choice of measure must be guided by the research question at hand. In addition, it would be desirable for researchers to employ multiple measures in order to establish the robustness of their findings to the choice of measure, as was done in a recent study by Amit and Livnat (1988b).

Performance

Regarding the measurement of performance, there are clear differences again within the three disciplinary streams. Early studies in industrial organization economics were concerned with the possible anti-competitive effects of diversification, and focused their attention on market structure variables. Using a public policy perspective, studies have examined the effect of diversification on such variables as concentration, industry growth, innovation, etc. The effect of diversification on the firm's rate of growth and vice-versa has also been of significant interest (Berry 1971; Hassid 1977).

The finance literature has been concerned with testing the extent of portfolio risk reduction achieved by diversification from an investor's, as opposed to a managerial, point of view. Their dependent variables have been various market measures of return and risk, although some studies have also used accounting-based measures of risk as well as return.

A review of the literature reveals that accounting-based measures have been the primary focus of much of the strategic management research on diversification. However, there is at present a lively interest within the strategic management field in adopting market-based performance measures (Amit and Livnat 1988a, b; Dubofsky and Varadarajan 1987; Galbraith, Samuelson, Stiles and Merrill 1986; Hitt and Ireland 1987; Montgomery, Thomas and Kamath 1984; Woo 1984). We welcome this trend given the general weaknesses attributed to accounting-based measures of performance, but it is interesting to note that several years ago, Holzmann, Copeland and Hayya (1975) deplored the exclusive focus on market-based measures of performance in studies of diversification in the finance area. They argued that decisions regarding diversification are made by managers using profitability data derived from financial statements and, hence, it would be more appropriate to use accounting-based measures to assess the efficacy of diversification efforts. Thus, it appears that tradition dictates the use of a particular performance focus, and there are occasional rumbles of dissatisfaction with the dominant focus within each discipline.

In summary, the same conclusions that we presented in regard to the measurement of diversity pertain here also. The availability of alternative measures argues strongly for the use of an integrative view and reliance on multiple measures of effectiveness so that the cumulation of knowledge across disciplines can proceed smoothly.

Temporal stability issues

Most explorations of the diversity–performance relationship are cross-sectional in nature. Whether the relationship observed in a particular study is generalizable over time remains an interesting but relatively less researched issue. Some studies that specifically tested for the temporal stability of the diversity–performance relationship over the business cycle have found that the relationship does vary over the cycle. Hill (1983) studied the performance of single and closely related businesses, concentric diversifiers, and conglomerates over the period 1970–6. He characterized this time period as encompassing boom conditions from 1970 to 1973, slump conditions thereafter, followed by a recovery beginning in 1976. He reported that the performance of conglomerates improved significantly more than that of non-conglomerates during the upturn, but deteriorated more rapidly during the downturn, than that of the two non-conglomerate categories.

A study by Ciscel and Evans (1984) found that returns to diversification are sensitive to the business cycle but their results do not strictly correspond to those of Hill (1983). Using a business count approach, Ciscel and Evans (1984) examined the diversity–performance relationship over two recessionary periods (1969–70 and 1974–5) and two expansionary periods (1971–3 and 1976–8). They found that moderate levels of diversification show improved relative performance in the expansionary periods, while high levels of diversification generally hurt performance in recessionary periods. Yet another attempt at capturing business cycle effects was reported by Amit and Livnat (1988a). Unlike Hill (1983) and Ciscel and Evans (1984), however, they did not assess the relationship at different points in time, but constructed an elaborate diversification measure that took into account the business cycle characteristics of the sectors into which a firm had diversified. Based on data for the 1977–83 time-frame, they concluded that the cash flows and earnings of firms that diversified into industries with different economic attributes were more stable than those of undiversified firms.

But for these exceptions, most strategy studies have spanned the 1970s and have made no allowance for business cycle effects. Michel and Shaked's (1984) study is among the few that allude to this issue. The authors characterize the time-frame of Rumelt's (1974) study (the 1949–69 period) as a stable, low inflation and low interest rate environment. In contrast, the time-frame of their own study (1975–81) is stated to be one of considerable uncertainty largely precipitated by the oil crisis of the early 1970s. Not surprisingly, the two studies reach different conclusions regarding the performance consequences of unrelated diversification.

The implication of the above studies is that the diversity–performance relationship is not time-invariant. Obvious as this may seem, broad generalizations regarding the value of diversification are by no means uncommon (e.g., Porter 1987). For the researcher interested in pursuing this topic further, the importance of periodic replications does not require belaboring. An examination of such a reassessment of the diversification–performance connection using a new conceptualization of diversity and current data is the work of Varadarajan and Ramanujam (1987).

In addition to the apparent temporal instability of the diversity–performance connection, another troubling issue is the frequent practice in strategic management research of using 4- or 5-year averages of performance, on the one hand, while examining diversity at only one point in time, on the other. While some researchers (e.g., Rumelt 1974) took particular care to ensure that the diversity profiles of the firms in their sample remained unchanged throughout the time-frame over which the performance variable was averaged, many studies provide no evidence of having performed this crucial control check. Unlike structural features of industries, which tend to change little or only slowly, firm diversification profiles are likely to change quite abruptly due to acquisitions and divestitures.

Acquisition and mergers have not only become more and more prevalent, but there has also been a progressive increase in their size (Bradley and Korn 1982; Davidson 1985; *Fortune* 1982, 1983, 1984, 1985, 1986, 1987). The increasing incidence of divestitures (Adkins 1981; Brooks 1984; Duhaime 1981; Duhaime and Grant 1984; Hearth and Zaima 1984; Landro 1984; Montgomery, Thomas and Kamath 1984; Nees 1981) and other forms of restructuring (*Business Week* 1981, 1985b) are also equally well documented. Under these circumstances it is extremely difficult to untangle the effects of diversity on performance over 3–5-year time-frames, since diversity profiles may change over those periods. Also, in the case of a large merger it is probably unreasonable to expect the acquiring firm to achieve performance improvements within the time windows usually monitored in diversity–performance studies. Internal growth may take even longer to yield returns, as shown by Biggadike's (1979) research. All these factors further reinforce the criticism that the issue of stability of diversification categories, as well as the stability of the diversity–performance relationship, are pressing issues that warrant as much attention as the measurement of diversity itself. Given these facts, the findings of studies using 5-year time spans to examine cross-sectional differences across diversity categories seem to be of questionable validity.[2]

Another timing-related criticism of the diversification–performance research is the fact that most of the results may be dated and of limited managerial significance today. As Davis (1985) notes, the environment of today is marked by numerous structural changes. Results of studies using 1970s' data may not have much practical relevance anymore.

In summary, researchers need to (a) be cautious in specifying the time-frames of their study (for instance, whether recessionary or expansionary); (b) qualify their findings to reflect the possibility of temporal effects; (c) avoid excessive reliance on the data bases of earlier studies; and (d) perform periodic replications.

Possible spuriousness of observed relationships

It has been frequently suggested that the diversity–performance relationship may be a spurious one, or that it may be an artifact of sampling problems. For instance, Abell (1980) critiqued the stream of research focusing on the relationship between *corporate* diversity and performance by pointing out that these studies fail to address the question of how the *product-market* or business unit strategies of the individual businesses within the corporation relate to overall organizational performance. Along similar lines, Porter (1987) notes that diversified firms do not compete, but their business units do. He adds that corporate diversification strategy must grow out of and reinforce competitive (business unit) strategy.

Christensen and Montgomery's (1981) study was based on the idea that market structure exerts a stronger impact on performance and that Rumelt's (1974) findings may simply be a reflection of systematic market structure differences across the diversification categories. In another challenge to the robustness of Rumelt's (1974) conclusions, Bettis and Hall (1981a, 1982) pointed out the predominance of one particular industry (pharmaceuticals) in Rumelt's (1974) related–constrained category, and thereby suggested that his findings may be distorted by sampling bias.

Rumelt's (1974) use of a highly heterogeneous sample that included firms from diverse economic sectors also raises concerns regarding the appropriateness of using pooled data in cross-sectional analysis of the diversity–performance relationship. Bass, Cattin and Wittink (1978) warn against such pooling unless tests of sample homogeneity yield positive results. While a few studies restricted their samples to a single industry category or homogeneous groups of industries, sample heterogeneity is more the rule than the exception in large sample cross-sectional diversification studies. Exceptions include Palepu (1985) who confined his sample to food-processing firms, and Porter (1974, 1976) who compared samples of convenience and non-convenience goods industries. If the possibility can be admitted that the relationship between diversity and performance can be industry- or environment-specific, then pooling of data is a vital issue that needs to be addressed.

More recently, Bettis and Mahajan (1985) found support for the hypothesis that *on a risk-adjusted basis* diversification categories should be performance neutral. Many low performers were found to be related diversifiers and different diversification strategies were associated with similar risk/return performance. However, since different industries conceivably present different levels of risk, adjusting for risk may be tantamount to adjusting for industry effects. The point is that in examining the diversity–performance relationship, it is very important to control for industry and/or risk effects. The possibility of other variables moderating the relationship must also be considered.

It should be noted, however, that none of the studies has been able to show conclusively that performance differences across diversification categories could be explained away on the basis of variables other than diversification category membership. This may have been due, in one way or other, to their authors' reliance on Rumelt's own original data base. In a recent study using current data Varadarajan and Ramanujam (1987) found that the basic robustness of Rumelt's findings is still intact, although it is necessary to temper his assertion of an absolute performance advantage for related diversification and of the performance penalty associated with unrelated diversification. This suggests that the management of diversity, rather than the type and mode of diversification, may be a more important factor determining performance. Fortunately, this issue has been receiving increasing attention recently.

In summary, the prospect for gaining new empirical insights by examining cross-sectional relationships between alternative measures of diversity and performance seems to be slim. This stream of research is at a point of diminishing returns. We need to begin to address the process and contextual issues in diversification, since the link between diversity and performance is likely to be moderated by a host of other factors. Difficult as they are to design and execute, longitudinal studies of diversification are a vital but unmet need in this stream of research, and must be attempted.

NOTES

1 We are indebted to one of the referees for explicitly emphasizing the distinction between *ex-ante* and *ex-post* performance, and for suggesting the linkages between these two distinct notions of performance and other concepts in our framework.

2 An important issue here is that looking at the performance consequences of decisions pertaining to direction or mode of diversification represents an examination of a disequilibrium situation, while examining the relationship

between diversity status and performance entails an equilibrium assumption, given a large enough sample. Metering the performance consequences of a diversifying move, whether it entails changes in direction or mode, is extremely problematic. In a large sample study there is no assurance that all the firms in the sample of diversifying firms will register a performance effect in say, 3, 4, or 5 years. The use of event studies and associated market measures may get around this problem, but any information asymmetries between a firm and the capital market will lead to erroneous valuation of the future benefits of the move. Thus, the tradition of using cross-sectional research designs focusing on diversity status may well prove to be a 'second-best' if not an ideal alternative. We are thankful to one of the referees for raising this issue and offering the above insights. A recent study that looks at the performance implications of both diversity status and changes in diversity over time (termed 'diversification') is the work of Grant, Jammine and Thomas (1988).

REFERENCES

Abell, D. F. *Defining the Business: The Starting Point of Strategic Planning*. Prentice-Hall, Englewood Cliffs, NJ, 1980.

Adkins, L. 'Divestitures: a new business rage', *Dun's Review*, March 1981, pp. 111–14.

Allison, G. T. *Essence of Decision: Explaining the Cuban Missile Crisis*. Little, Brown and Co., Boston, MA, 1971.

Amihud, Y. and B. Lev. 'Risk reduction as a managerial motive for conglomerate mergers', *Bell Journal of Economics*, 1981, pp. 605–17.

Amit, R. and J. Livnat. 'Diversification strategies, business cycles and economic performance', *Strategic Management Journal*, **9**, 1988a, pp. 99–110.

——, Livnat. 'Diversification and the risk-return trade-off', *Academy of Management Journal*, **31**, 1988b, pp. 154–66.

Ansoff, H. I. *Corporate Strategy*. McGraw-Hill, New York, 1965.

Asquith, P. 'Merger bids, uncertainty, and stockholder returns', *Journal of Financial Economics*, **11**, April 1983, pp. 51–83.

Backaitis, N. T., R. Balakrishnan and K. R. Harrigan. 'The dimensions of diversification posture, market power, and performance: the continuing debate'. Working Paper, Columbia University, 1984.

Bane, W. T. and F. F. Neubauer. 'Diversification and the failure of new foreign activities', *Strategic Management Journal*, **2**, 1981, pp. 219–33.

Barton, S. L. 'Diversification strategy and systematic risk: another look', *Academy of Management Journal*, **31**, 1988, pp. 166–75.

Bass, F. M., P. J. Cattin and D. R. Wittink. 'Firm effects and industry effects in the analysis of market structure and profitability', *Journal of Marketing Research*, **15**, 1978, pp. 3–10.

Beattie, D. L. 'Conglomerate diversification and performance: a survey and time series analysis', *Applied Economics*, 1980, pp. 251–73.

Berry, C. H. 'Corporate growth and diversification', *Journal of Law and Economics*, **14**(2), 1971, pp. 371–83.

——, 'Corporate diversification and market structure', *Bell Journal of Economics and Management Science*, **5**(1), 1974, pp. 196–204.

Bettis, R. A. 'Performance differences in related and unrelated diversified firms', *Strategic Management Journal*, **2**, 1981, pp. 379–93.

Bettis, R. A. and W. K. Hall. 'Risk and industry effects in large diversified firms', *Academy of Management Proceedings*, 1981a, pp. 17–20.

——, 'Strategic portfolio management in the multi-business firm', *California Management Review*, **14**(1), 1981b, pp. 23–38.

——, 'Diversification strategy, accounting determined risk, and accounting determined return', *Academy of Management Journal*, **25**, 1982, pp. 254–64.

Bettis, R. A. and V. Mahajan. 'Risk/return performance of diversified firms', *Management Science*, **31**, 1985, pp. 785–99.

Bettis, R. A., W. K. Hall and C. K. Prahalad. 'Diversity and performance in the multibusiness firm', *AIDS Proceedings*, 1978, pp. 210–12.

Biggadike, R. 'The risky business of diversification', *Harvard Business Review*, **57**(3), 1979, pp. 103–11.

Boyle, S. E. 'Pre-merger growth and profit characteristics of large conglomerate mergers in the United States 1948–1968', *St John's Law Review*, **44**, Spring 1970, pp. 152–70.

Bradley, J. W. and D. H. Korn. 'The changing role of acquisitions', *Journal of Business Strategy*, **2**(4), 1982, pp. 30–42.

Brooks, G. 'Some concerns find that the push to diversify was a costly mistake', *Wall Street Journal*, 2 October 1984, p. 33.

Burgelman, R. A. 'Corporate entrepreneurship and strategic management: insights from a process study', *Management Science*, **29**, 1983, pp. 1349–64.

Business Week. 'Asset redeployment: everything is for sale now', 24 August 1981, pp. 68–74.

——, 'Splitting up: the other side of merger mania', 1 July 1985b, pp. 50–5.

Carter, J. 'In search of synergy: a structure–performance test', *Review of Economics and Statistics*, **59**, 1977, pp. 279–89.

Chatterjee, S. 'Types of synergy and economic value: the impact of acquisitions on merging and rival firms', *Strategic Management Journal*, **7**(2), 1986, pp. 119–39.

Christensen, H. K. and C. A. Montgomery. 'Corporate economic performance: diversification strategy vs. market structure', *Strategic Management Journal*, **2**, 1981, pp. 327–43.

Ciscel, D. H. and D. Evans. 'Returns to corporate diversification in the 1970s', *Managerial and Decision Economics*, **5**(2), 1984, pp. 67–71.

Conn, R. L. 'Performance of conglomerate firms: comment', *Journal of Finance*, **28**, 1973, pp. 754–9.

Daniels, J. D., R. A. Pitts and M. J. Tretter. 'Strategy and structure of U.S. multinationals: an exploratory study', *Academy of Management Journal*, **27**, 1984, pp. 292–307.

Davidson, K. M. *Megamergers: Corporate America's Billion-Dollar Takeovers*. Ballinger, Cambridge, MA, 1985.

Davis, M. S. 'Two plus two doesn't equal five', *Fortune*, 9 December 1985, pp. 171–9.

Day, G. S. 'Diagnosing the product portfolio', *Journal of Marketing*, **41**(2), 1977, pp. 29–38.

Dodd, P. 'Merger proposals, management discretion, and stockholder wealth', *Journal of Financial Economics*, **8**, June 1980, pp. 105–37.

Dubofsky, P. and P. Varadarajan. 'Diversification and measures of performance: additional empirical evidence', *Academy of Management Journal*, **30**, 1987, pp. 597–608.

Duhaime, I. M. 'Influences on the divestment decisions of large diversified companies'. Doctoral dissertation, University of Pittsburg, 1981.

Duhaime, I. M. and J. H. Grant. 'Factors influencing divestment decision making: evidence from a field study', *Strategic Management Journal*, **5**, 1984, pp. 301–18.

Dundas, K. M. and P. R. Richardson. 'Corporate strategy and the concept of market failure', *Strategic Management Journal*, **1**, 1980, pp. 177–88.

——, 'Implementing the unrelated product strategy', *Strategic Management Journal*, **3**, 1982, pp. 287–301.

Fortune. 'Deals of the year', 25 January 1982, pp. 36–9.

——, 'Deals of the year', 24 January 1983, pp. 48–52.

——, 'Deals of the year', 23 January 1984, pp. 54–8.

——, 'Deals of the year', 21 January 1985, pp. 126–30.

——, 'Deals of the year', 20 January 1986, pp. 26–30.

——, 'Deals of the year', 2 February 1987, pp. 68–74.

Galbraith, C., B. Samuelson, C. Stiles and G. Merrill. 'Diversification, industry research and development and performance', *Academy of Management Proceedings*, 1986, pp. 17–20.

Gorecki, P. K. 'An inter-industry analysis of diversification in the U.K. manufacturing sector', *Journal of Industrial Economics*, **24**, 1975, pp. 131–46.

Grant, R., A. Jammine and H. Thomas. 'The impact of diversification strategy upon the profitability of British manufacturing firms', *Academy of Management Proceedings*, 1986, pp. 26–30.

——, 'Diversity, diversification, and profitability among British manufacturing companies, 1972–1984', *Academy of Management Journal*, **31**, 1988, pp. 771–801.

Halpern, P. 'Empirical estimates of the amount and distribution of gains to companies in mergers', *Journal of Business*, **46**, 1973, pp. 554–75.

Haspeslagh, P. 'Portfolio planning: uses and limits', *Harvard Business Review*, **60**(1), 1982, pp. 58–73.

Hassid, J. 'Recent evidence on conglomerate diversification in U.K. manufacturing industry', *Manchester School of Economic Social Studies*, **43**, 1975, pp. 372–95.

Hearth, D. and J. K. Zaima. 'Voluntary corporate divestitures and value', *Financial Management*, **13**(1), 1984, pp. 10–16.

Hedley, B. 'Strategy and the business portfolio', *Long Range Planning*, **10**(1), 1977, pp. 9–15.

Heggestad, A. A. and S. A. Rhoades. 'Multi-market interdependence and local market competition in banking', *Review of Economics and Statistics*, **60**, 1978, pp. 523–32.

Hill, C. W. L. 'Conglomerate performance over the economic cycle', *Journal of Industrial Economics*, **32**(12), 1983, pp. 197–211.

Hill, C. W. L. and R. E. Hoskisson. 'Strategy and structure in the multiproduct firm', *Academy of Management Review*, **12**, 1987, pp. 331–41.

Hitt, M. A. and R. D. Ireland. 'Peters and Waterman revisited: the unended quest for excellence', *Academy of Management Executive*, **1**(2), 1987, pp. 91–7.

Holzmann, O. J., R. M. Copeland and J. Hayya. 'Income measures of conglomerate performance', *Quarterly Review of Economics and Business*, **15**(3), 1975, pp. 67–78.

Hoskisson, R. E. 'Multidivisional structure and performance: The contingency of diversification strategy', *Academy of Management Journal*, **30**, 1987, pp. 625–44.

Jacquemin, A. P. and C. H. Berry. 'Entropy measure of diversification and corporate growth', *Journal of Industrial Economics*, **27**, 1979, pp. 359–69.

Jensen, M. C. and R. S. Ruback. 'The market for corporate control: the scientific evidence', *Journal of Financial Economics*, **11**, April 1983, pp. 5–50.

Jose, M. L., L. M. Nichols and J. L. Stevens. 'Contributions of diversification, promotion, and R&D to the value of multiproduct firms: a Tobin's *q* approach', *Financial Management*, Winter 1986, pp. 33–81.

Karnani, A. and B. Wernerfelt. 'Multiple point competition', *Strategic Management Journal*, **6**, 1985, pp. 87–96.

Landro, L. 'G&W chief nears completion of strategy to reshape firm, selling units, portfolio', *Wall Street Journal*, 21 August 1984, p. 13.

Levitt, T. 'Dinosaurs among the bears and bulls', *Harvard Business Review* **53**(1), 1975, pp. 41–53.

Levy, H. and M. Sarnat. 'Diversification, portfolio analysis and the uneasy case for conglomerate mergers', *Journal of Finance*, **25**, 1970, pp. 795–802.

Lubatkin, M. 'Mergers and the performance of the acquiring firm', *Academy of Management Review*, **8**, 1983, pp. 218–25.

——, 'Merger strategies and stockholder value', *Strategic Management Journal*, **8**, 1987, pp. 39–53.

Lynch, H. H. *Financial Performance of Conglomerates*. Harvard Business School, Boston, MA, 1971.

Markham, J. W. *Conglomerate Enterprise and Economic Performance*. Harvard University Press, Cambridge, MA, 1973.

McDougall, F. M. and D. K. Round. 'A comparison of diversifying and nondiversifying Australian industrial firms', *Academy of Management Journal*, **27**, 1984, pp. 384–98.

Mason, R. H. and M. B. Goudzwaard. 'Performance of conglomerate firms: a portfolio approach', *Journal of Finance*, **31**, 1976, pp. 39–48.

Melicher, R. W. and D. F. Rush. 'The performance of conglomerate firms: recent risk and return experience', *Journal of Finance*, **28**, 1973, pp. 381–8.

——, 'Evidence on the acquisition-related performance of conglomerate firms', *Journal of Finance*, **29**, 1974, pp. 141–9.

Michel, A. and I. Shaked. 'Does business diversification affect performance?', *Financial Management*, **13**(4), 1984, pp. 18–25.

Montgomery, C. A. 'Diversification, Market Structure, and Firm Performance: An Extension of Rumelt's Work'. Doctoral dissertation, Purdue University, 1979.

——, 'The measurement of firm diversification: some new empirical evidence', *Academy of Management Journal*, **25**, 1982, pp. 299–307.

——, 'Product-market diversification and market power', *Academy of Management Journal*, **28**, 1985, pp. 789–98.

Montgomery, C. A. and H. Singh. 'Diversification strategy and systematic risk', *Strategic Management Journal*, **5**, 1984, pp. 181–91.

Montgomery, C. A., A. R. Thomas and R. Kamath. 'Divestiture, market valuation, and strategy', *Academy of Management Journal*, **27**, 1984, pp. 830–40.

Nathanson, D. A. 'The strategic diversity classification system: a framework for decision making'. In Guth, W. D. (ed.), *Handbook of Business Strategy*. Warren, Gorham, and Lamont, New York, 1985.

Nathanson, D. A. and J. Cassano. 'Organization, diversity, and performance', *Wharton Magazine*, Summer 1982, pp. 19–26.

Nees, D. 'Increase your divestment effectiveness', *Strategic Management Journal*, **2**, 1981, pp. 119–30.

Palepu, K. 'Diversification strategy, profit performance, and the entropy measure', *Strategic Management Journal*, **6**, 1985, pp. 239–55.

Peters, T. J. and R. H. Waterman. *In Search of Excellence: Lessons from America's Best-Run Companies*. Harper & Row, New York, 1982.

Pitts, R. A. and H. D. Hopkins. 'Firm diversity: conceptualization and measurement', *Academy of Management Review*, **7**, 1982, pp. 620–9.

Porter, M. E. 'Consumer behavior, retailer power, and market performance in consumer goods industries', *Review of Economics and Statistics*, **56** 1974, pp. 419–36.

——, *Interbrand Choice, Strategy, and Bilateral Market Power*. Harvard University Press, Cambridge, MA, 1976.

——, *Competitive Advantage: Creating and Sustaining Superior Performance*. Free Press, New York, 1985.

——, 'From competitive advantage to corporate strategy', *Harvard Business Review*, **65**(3), 1987, pp. 43–59.

Reed, R. and G. A. Luffman. 'Diversification: the growing confusion', *Strategic Management Journal*, **7**, 1986, pp. 29–35.

Reid, S. R. *Mergers, Managers, and the Economy*. McGraw-Hill, New York, 1968.

——, 'A reply to the Weston/Mansinghka criticisms dealing with conglomerate mergers', *Journal of Finance*, **26**, 1971, pp. 937–46.

Rhoades, S. A. 'The effect of diversification on industry profit performance in 241 manufacturing industries: 1963', *Review of Economics and Statistics*, **55**(2), 1973, pp. 146–55.

——, 'A further evaluation of the effect of diversification on industry profit performance', *Review of Economics and Statistics*, **56**, 1974, pp. 557–9.

Rumelt, R. P. *Strategy, Structure, and Economic Performance*. Harvard University Press, Cambridge, MA, 1974.

——, 'Diversification strategy and profitability', *Strategic Management Journal*, **3**, 1982, pp. 359–69.

Salter, M. S. and W. S. Weinhold. *Diversification Through Acquisition*. Free Press, New York, 1979.

Scott, J. T. 'Multi-market contact and economic performance', *Review of Economics and Statistics*, **64**, 1982, pp. 368–75.

Smith, K. V. and J. C. Schreiner. 'A portfolio analysis of conglomerate diversification', *Journal of Finance*, **24**, 1969, pp. 413–27.

Sutton, C. J. 'Management behavior and a theory of diversification', *Scottish Journal of Political Economy*, **20**(1), 1973, pp. 27–41.

Varadarajan, P. 'Product diversity and firm performance: an empirical investigation', *Journal of Marketing*, **50**(3), 1986, pp. 43–57.

Varadarajan, P. and V. Ramanujam. 'Diversification and performance: a reexamination using a new two-dimensional conceptualization of diversity in firms', *Academy of Management Journal*, **30**, 1987, pp. 380–97.

Ward, J. L. 'The opportunity to measure strategic variables: an attempt to quantify product-market diversity', *Journal of Economics and Business*, **28**(3), 1976, pp. 219–26.

Wernerfelt, B. and C. A. Montgomery. 'What is an attractive industry?', *Management Science*, **32**, 1986, pp. 1223–30.

Westerfield, R. 'A note on the measurement of conglomerate diversification', *Journal of Finance*, **25**, 1970, pp. 909–14.

Weston, J. F. and K. S. Chung. 'Some aspects of merger theory', *Journal of Midwest Finance Association*, **12**, October 1983, pp. 1–33.

Weston, J. F. and S. K. Mansinghka. 'Tests of the efficiency performance of conglomerate firms', *Journal of Finance*, **26**, 1971, pp. 919–36.

Williamson, O. E. *Markets and Hierarchies: Analysis and Anti-Trust Implications*. Free Press, New York, 1975.

Woo, C. Y. Y. 'An empirical test of value-based planning models and implications', *Management Science*, **30**, 1984, pp. 1031–50.

Wrigley, L. 'Divisional autonomy and diversification'. Doctoral dissertation, Harvard Business School, 1970.

Yip, G. S. 'Diversification entry: internal development versus acquisition', *Strategic Management Journal*, **3**, 1982, pp. 331–45.

Chapter 12

From competitive advantage to corporate strategy

Michael E. Porter

Corporate strategy, the overall plan for a diversified company, is both the darling and the stepchild of contemporary management practice – the darling because CEOs have been obsessed with diversification since the early 1960s, the stepchild because almost no consensus exists about what corporate strategy is, much less about how a company should formulate it.

A diversified company has two levels of strategy: business unit (or competitive) strategy and corporate (or companywide) strategy. Competitive strategy concerns how to create competitive advantage in each of the businesses in which a company competes. Corporate strategy concerns two different questions: what businesses the corporation should be in and how the corporate office should manage the array of business units.

Corporate strategy is what makes the corporate whole add up to more than the sum of its business unit parts.

The track record of corporate strategies has been dismal. I studied the diversification records of thirty-three large, prestigious US companies over the 1950–86 period and found that most of them had divested many more acquisitions than they had kept. The corporate strategies of most companies have dissipated instead of created shareholder value.

The need to rethink corporate strategy could hardly be more urgent. By taking over companies and breaking them up corporate raiders thrive on failed corporate strategy. Fueled by junk bond financing and growing acceptability, raiders can expose any company to takeover, no matter how large or blue chip.

Recognizing past diversification mistakes, some companies have initiated large-scale restructuring programs. Others have done nothing at all. Whatever the response, the strategic questions persist. Those who have restructured must decide what to do next to avoid repeating the past; those who have done nothing must awake to their vulnerability. To survive, companies must understand what good corporate strategy is.

A SOBER PICTURE

While there is disquiet about the success of corporate strategies, none of the available evidence satisfactorily indicates the success or failure of corporate strategy. Most studies have approached the question by measuring the stock market valuation of mergers, captured in the movement of the stock prices of acquiring companies immediately before and after mergers are announced.

These studies show that the market values mergers as neutral or slightly negative, hardly cause for serious concern.[1] Yet the short-term market reaction is a highly imperfect measure of the long-term success of diversification, and no self-respecting executive would judge a corporate strategy this way.

Studying the diversification programs of a company over a long period of time is a much more telling way to determine whether a corporate strategy has succeeded or failed. My study of 33 companies, many of which have reputations for good management, is a unique look at the track record of major corporations. Each company entered an average of 80 new industries and 27 new fields. Just over 70 percent of the new entries were acquisitions, 22 percent were start-ups, and 8 percent were joint ventures. IBM, Exxon, Du Pont, and 3M, for example, focused on start-ups, while ALCO Standard, Beatrice, and Sara Lee diversified almost solely through acquisitions (Table 12.1 has a complete rundown).

My data paint a sobering picture of the success ratio of these moves (see Table 12.2). I found that on average corporations divested more than half their acquisitions in new industries and more than 60 percent of their acquisitions in entirely new fields. Fourteen companies left more than 70 percent of all the acquisitions they had made in new fields. The track record in unrelated acquisitions is even worse – the average divestment rate is a startling 74 percent (see Table 12.3). Even a highly respected company like General Electric divested a very high percentage of its acquisitions, particularly those in new fields. Companies near the top of the list in Table 12.2 achieved a remarkably low rate of divestment. Some bear witness to the success of well-thought-out corporate strategies. Others, however, enjoy a lower rate simply because they have not faced up to their problem units and divested them.

I calculated total shareholder returns (stock price appreciation plus dividends) over the period of the study for each company so that I could compare them with its divestment rate. While companies near the top of the list have above-average shareholder returns, returns are not a reliable measure of diversification success. Shareholder return often depends heavily on the inherent attractiveness of companies' base industries. Companies like CBS and General Mills had extremely profitable base businesses that subsidized poor diversification track records.

I would like to make one comment on the use of shareholder value to judge performance. Linking shareholder value quantitatively to diversification performance only works if you compare the shareholder value that is with the shareholder value that might have been without diversification. Because such a comparison is virtually impossible to make, my own measure of diversification success – the number of units retained by the company – seems to be as good an indicator as any of the contribution of diversification to corporate performance.

My data give a stark indication of the failure of corporate strategies.[2] Of the 33 companies, 6 had been taken over as my study was being completed (see the note on Table 12.2). Only the lawyers, investment bankers and original sellers have prosperd in most of these acquisitions, not the shareholders.

PREMISES OF CORPORATE STRATEGY

Any successful corporate strategy builds on a number of premises. These are facts of life about diversification. They cannot be altered, and when ignored, they explain in part why so many corporate strategies fail.

Competition occurs at the business unit level   Diversified companies do not compete; only their business units do. Unless a corporate strategy places primary attention on nurturing the success of each unit, the strategy will fail, no matter how elegantly constructed. Successful corporate strategy must grow out of and reinforce competitive strategy.

Diversification inevitably adds costs and constraints to business units   Obvious costs such as the corporate overhead allocated to a unit may not be as important or subtle as the hidden costs and constraints. A business unit must explain its decisions to top management, spend time complying with planning and other corporate systems, live with parent company guidelines and personnel policies, and forgo the opportunity to motivate employees with direct equity ownership. These costs and constraints can be reduced but not entirely eliminated.

Shareholders can readily diversify themselves   Shareholders can diversify their own portfolios of stocks by selecting those that best match their preferences and risk profiles.[3] Shareholders can often diversify more cheaply than a corporation because they can buy shares at the market price and avoid hefty acquisition premiums.

These premises mean that corporate strategy cannot succeed unless it truly adds value – to business units by providing tangible benefits that offset the inherent costs of lost independence and to shareholders by diversifying in a way they could not replicate.

Table 12.1 Diversification profiles of 33 leading US companies

Company	Number total entries	All entries into new industries	Percent acqui- sitions	Percent joint ventures
ALCO Standard	221	165	99%	0%
Allied Corp.	77	49	67	10
Beatrice	382	204	97	1
Borden	170	96	77	4
CBS	148	81	67	16
Continental Group	75	47	77	6
Cummins Engine	30	24	54	17
Du Pont	80	39	33	16
Exxon	79	56	34	5
General Electric	160	108	47	20
General Foods	92	53	91	4
General Mills	110	102	84	7
W.R. Grace	275	202	83	7
Gulf & Western	178	140	91	4
IBM	46	38	18	18
IC Industries	67	41	85	3
ITT	246	178	89	2
Johnson & Johnson	88	77	77	0
Mobil	41	32	53	16
Procter & Gamble	28	23	61	0
Raytheon	70	58	86	9
RCA	53	46	35	15
Rockwell	101	75	73	24
Sara Lee	197	141	96	1
Scovill	52	36	97	0
Signal	53	45	67	4
Tenneco	85	62	81	6
3M	144	125	54	2
TRW	119	82	77	10
United Technologies	62	49	57	18
Westinghouse	129	73	63	11
Wickes	71	47	83	0
Xerox	59	50	66	6
Total	3,788	2,644		
Average	114.8	80.1	70.3%	7.9%

Note: Beatrice, Continental Group, General Foods, RCA, Scovill, and Signal were taken over as the study was being completed. Their data cover the period up through takeover but not subsequent divestments.

Table 12.1 Continued

Percent start-ups	Entries into new industries that represented entirely new fields	Percent acquisitions	Percent joint ventures	Percent start-ups
1%	56	100%	0%	0%
22	17	65	6	29
2	61	97	0	3
19	32	75	3	22
17	28	65	21	14
17	19	79	11	11
29	13	46	23	31
51	19	37	0	63
61	17	29	6	65
33	29	48	14	38
6	22	86	5	9
9	27	74	7	19
10	66	74	5	21
6	48	88	2	10
63	16	19	0	81
12	17	88	6	6
9	50	92	0	8
23	18	56	0	44
31	15	60	7	33
39	14	79	0	21
5	16	81	19	6
50	19	37	21	42
3	27	74	22	4
4	41	95	2	2
3	12	92	0	8
29	20	75	0	25
13	26	73	8	19
45	34	71	3	56
13	28	64	11	25
24	17	23	17	39
26	36	61	3	36
17	22	68	0	32
28	18	50	11	39
	906			
21.8%	27.4	67.9%	7.0%	25.9%

Note: The percentage averages may not add up to 100 percent because of rounding off.

Table 12.2 Acquisition track records of leading US diversifiers ranked by percent divested

Company	All acquisitions in new industries	Percent made by 1980 and then divested	Percent made by 1975 and then divested	Acquisitions in new industries that represented entirely new fields	Percent made by 1980 and then divested	Percent made by 1975 and then divested
Johnson & Johnson	59	17%	12%	10	33%	14%
Procter & Gamble	14	17	17	11	17	17
Raytheon	50	17	26	13	25	33
United Technologies	28	25	13	10	17	0
3M	67	26	27	24	42	45
TRW	63	27	31	18	40	38
IBM	7	33	0*	3	33	0*
Du Pont	13	38	43	7	60	75
Mobil	17	38	57	9	50	50
Borden	74	39	40	24	45	50
IC Industries	35	42	50	15	46	44
Tenneco	50	43	47	19	27	33
Beatrice	198	46	45	59	52	51
ITT	159	52	52	46	61	61
Rockwell	55	56	57	20	71	71
Allied Corp.	33	57	45	11	40	80
Exxon	19	62	20*	5	80	50*
Sara Lee	135	62	65	39	80	76

General Foods	48	63	62	19	93	93
Scovill	35	64	77	11	64	70
Signal	30	65	63	15	70	67
ALCO Standard	164	65	70	56	72	76
W.R. Grace	167	65	70	49	71	70
General Electric	51	67	78	14	100	100
Wickes	38	68	72	15	73	70
Westinghouse	46	71	69	22	61	59
Xerox	33	71	79	9	100	100
Continental Group	36	75	72	15	60	60
General Mills	86	79	73	20	65	60
Gulf & Western	127	80	78	42	75	72
Cummins Engine	13	80	80	6	83	83
RCA	16	80	92	7	86	100
CBS	54	87	89	18	88	88
Total	2,021			661		
Average per company†	61.2	53.4%	56.5%	20.0	60.0%	61.5%

Note: Beatrice, Continental Group, General Foods, RCA, Scovill, and Signal were taken over as the study was being completed. Their data cover the period up through takeover but not subsequent divestments.

* Companies with three or fewer acquisitions by the cut off year.

† Companies with three or fewer acquisitions by the cut off year are excluded from the average to minimize statistical distortions.

Table 12.3 Diversification performance in joint ventures, start-ups, and unrelated acquisitions

Company	Joint ventures as a percent of new entries	Percent made by 1980 and then divested	Percent made by 1975 and then divested	Start-ups as a percent of new entries
Johnson & Johnson	0%	†	†	23%
Procter & Gamble	0	†	†	39
Raytheon	9	60%	60%	5
United Technologies	18	50	50	24
3M	2	100*	100*	45
TRW	10	20	25	13
IBM	18	100*	†	63
Du Pont	16	100*	†	51
Mobil	16	33	33	31
Borden	4	33	33	19
IC Industries	3	100*	100*	13
Tenneco	6	67	67	13
Beatrice	1	†	†	2
ITT	2	0*	†	8
Rockwell	24	38	42	3
Allied Corp.	10	100	75	22
Exxon	5	0	0	61
Sara Lee	1	†	†	4
General Foods	4	†	†	6
Scovill	0	†	†	3
Signal	4	†	†	29
ALCO Standard	0	†	†	1
W.R. Grace	7	33	38	10
General Electric	20	20	33	33
Wickes	0	†	†	17
Westinghouse	11	0*	0*	26
Xerox	6	100*	100*	28
Continental Group	6	67	67	17
General Mills	7	71	71	9
Gulf & Western	4	75	50	6
Cummins Engine	17	50	50	29
RCA	15	67	67	50
CBS	16	71	71	17
Average per company‡	7.9%	50.3%	48.9%	21.8%

Note: Beatrice, Continental Group, General Foods, RCA, Scovill, and Signal were taken over as the study was being completed. Their data cover the period up through takeover but not subsequent divestments.
* Companies with two or fewer entries.   † No entries in this category.
‡ Average excludes companies with two or fewer entries to minimize statistical distortions.

Table 12.3 Continued

Percent made by 1980 and then divested	Percent made by 1975 and then divested	Acquisitions in unrelated new fields as a percent of total acquisitions in new fields	Percent made by 1980 and then divested	Percent made by 1975 and then divested
14%	20%	0%	†	†
0	0	9	†	†
50	50	46	40%	40%
11	20	40	0*	0*
2	3	33	75	86
63	71	39	71	71
20	22	33	100*	100*
61	61	43	0*	0*
50	56	67	60	100
17	13	21	80	80
80	30	33	50	50
67	80	42	33	40
0	0	63	59	53
38	57	61	67	64
0	0	35	100	100
38	29	45	50	0
27	19	100	80	50*
75	100*	41	73	73
67	50	42	86	83
100	100*	45	80	100
20	11	67	50	50
†	†	63	79	81
71	71	39	65	65
33	44	36	100	100
63	57	60	80	75
44	44	36	57	67
50	56	22	100	100
14	0	40	83	100
89	80	65	77	67
100	100	74	77	74
0	0	67	100	100
99	55	36	100	100
86	80	39	100	100
44.0%	40.9%	46.1%	74.0%	74.4%

WHERE THE DATA COME FROM

We studied the 1950–1986 diversification histories of 33 large diversified US companies. They were chosen at random from many broad sectors of the economy.

To eliminate distortions caused by World War II, we chose 1950 as the base year and then identified each business the company was in. We tracked every acquisition, joint venture, and start-up made over this period – 3,788 in all. We classified each as an entry into an entirely new sector or field (financial services, for example), a new industry within a field the company was already in (insurance, for example), or a geographic extension of an existing product or service. We also classified each new field as related or unrelated to existing units. Then we tracked whether and when each entry was divested or shut down and the number of years each remained part of the corporation.

Our sources included annual reports, 10K forms, the F&S Index, and Moody's, supplemented by our judgment and general knowledge of the industries involved. In a few cases, we asked the companies specific questions. It is difficult to determine the success of an entry without knowing the full purchase or start-up price, the profit history, the amount and timing of ongoing investments made in the unit, whether any write-offs or write-downs were taken, and the selling price and terms of sale. Instead, we employed a relatively simple way to gauge success: *whether the entry was divested or shut down.* The underlying assumption is that a company will generally not divest or close down a successful business except in a comparatively few special cases. Companies divested many of the entries in our sample within five years, a reflection of disappointment with performance. Of the comparatively few divestments where the company disclosed a loss or a gain, the divestment resulted in a reported loss in more than half the cases.

The data in Table 12.1 cover the entire 1950–1986 period. However, the divestment ratios in Table 12.2 and Table 12.3 do not compare entries and divestments over the entire period because doing so would overstate the success of diversification. Companies usually do not shut down or divest new entries immediately but hold them for some time to give them an opportunity to succeed. Our data show that the average holding period is five to slightly more than ten years, though many divestments occur within five years. To accurately gauge the success of diversification, we calculated the percentage of entries made by 1975 and by 1980 that were divested or closed down as of January 1987. If we had included more recent entries, we would have biased upward our assessment of how successful these entries had been.

As compiled, these data probably understate the rate of failure. Companies tend to announce acquisitions and other forms of new entry with a flourish but divestments and shutdowns with a whimper, if at all. We have done our best to root out every such transaction, but we have undoubtedly missed some. There may also be new entries that we did not uncover, but our best impression is that the number is not large.

PASSING THE ESSENTIAL TESTS

To understand how to formulate corporate strategy, it is necessary to specify the conditions under which diversification will truly create shareholder value. These conditions can be summarized in three essential tests:

1 *The attractiveness test.* The industries chosen for diversification must be structurally attractive or capable of being made attractive.
2 *The cost-of-entry test.* The cost of entry must not capitalize all the future profits.
3 *The better-off test.* Either the new unit must gain competitive advantage from its link with the corporation or vice versa.

Of course, most companies will make certain that their proposed strategies pass some of these tests. But my study clearly shows that when companies ignored one or two of them, the strategic results were disastrous.

HOW ATTRACTIVE IS THE INDUSTRY?

In the long run, the rate of return available from competing in an industry is a function of its underlying structure, which I have described in another *Harvard Business Review* article.[4] An attractive industry with a high average return on investment will be difficult to enter because entry barriers are high, suppliers and buyers have only modest bargaining power, substitute products or services are few, and the rivalry among competitors is stable. An unattractive industry like steel will have structural flaws, including a plethora of substitute materials, powerful and price-sensitive buyers, and excessive rivalry caused by high fixed costs and a large group of competitors, many of whom are state supported.

Diversification cannot create shareholder value unless new industries have favorable structures that support returns exceeding the cost of capital. If the industry doesn't have such returns, the company must be able to restructure the industry or gain a sustainable competitive advantage that leads to returns well above the industry average. An industry need not be attractive before diversification. In fact, a company might benefit from entering before the industry shows its full potential. The diversification can then transform the industry's structure.

In my research, I often found companies had suspended the attractiveness test because they had a vague belief that the industry "fit" very closely with their own businesses. In the hope that the corporate "comfort" they felt would lead to a happy outcome, the companies ignored fundamentally poor industry structures. Unless the close fit allows substantial competitive advantage, however, such comfort will turn into pain when diversification results in poor returns. Royal Dutch Shell and other leading oil companies have had this unhappy experience in a number of chemicals businesses, where poor industry structures overcame the benefits of vertical integration and skills in process technology.

Another common reason for ignoring the attractiveness test is a low entry cost. Sometimes the buyer has an inside track or the owner is anxious to sell. Even if the price is actually low, however, a one-shot gain will not offset a perpetually poor business. Almost always, the company finds it must reinvest in the newly acquired unit, if only to replace fixed assets and fund working capital.

Diversifying companies are also prone to use rapid growth or other simple indicators as a proxy for a target industry's attractiveness. Many that rushed into fast-growing industries (personal computers, video games, and robotics, for example) were burned because they mistook early growth for long-term profit potential. Industries are profitable not because they are sexy or high tech; they are profitable only if their structures are attractive.

WHAT IS THE COST OF ENTRY?

Diversification cannot build shareholder value if the cost of entry into a new business eats up its expected returns. Strong market forces, however, are working to do just that. A company can enter new industries by acquisition or start-up. Acquisitions expose it to an increasingly efficient merger market. An acquirer beats the market if it pays a price not fully reflecting the prospects of the new unit. Yet multiple bidders are commonplace, information flows rapidly, and investment bankers and other intermediaries work aggressively to make the market as efficient as possible. In recent years, new financial instruments such as junk bonds have brought new buyers into the market and made even large companies vulnerable to takeover. Acquisition premiums are high and reflect the acquired company's future prospects – sometimes too well. Philip Morris paid more than four times book value for Seven-Up Company, for example. Simple arithmetic meant that profits had to more than quadruple to sustain the preacquisition ROI. Since there proved to be little Philip Morris could add in marketing prowess to the sophisticated marketing wars in the soft-drink industry, the result was the unsatisfactory financial performance of Seven-Up and ultimately the decision to divest.

In a start-up, the company must overcome entry barriers. It's a real catch-22 situation, however, since attractive industries are attractive because their entry barriers are high. Bearing the full cost of the entry barriers might well dissipate any potential profits. Otherwise, other entrants to the industry would have already eroded its profitability.

In the excitement of finding an appealing new business, companies sometimes forget to apply the cost-of-entry test. The more attractive a new industry, the more expensive it is to get into.

WILL THE BUSINESS BE BETTER OFF?

A corporation must bring some significant competitive advantage to the new unit, or the new unit must offer potential for significant advantage to the corporation. Sometimes, the benefits to the new unit accrue only once, near the time of entry, when the parent instigates a major overhaul of its strategy or installs a first-rate management team. Other diversification yields ongoing competitive advantage if the new unit can market its product, through the well-developed distribution system of its sister units, for instance. This is one of the important underpinnings of the merger of Baxter Travenol and American Hospital Supply.

When the benefit to the new unit comes only once, the parent company has no rationale for holding the new unit in its portfolio over the long term. Once the results of the one-time improvement are clear, the diversified company no longer adds value to offset the inevitable costs imposed on the unit. It is best to sell the unit and free up corporate resources.

The better-off test does not imply that diversifying corporate risk creates shareholders value in and of itself. Doing something for shareholders that they can do themselves is not a basis for corporate strategy. (Only in the case of a privately held company, in which the company's and the shareholder's risk are the same, is diversification to reduce risk valuable for its own sake.) Diversification of risk should only be a by-product of corporate strategy, not a prime motivator.

Executives ignore the better-off test most of all or deal with it through arm waving or trumped-up logic rather than hard strategic analysis. One reason is that they confuse company size with shareholder value. In the drive to run a bigger company, they lose sight of their real job. They may justify the suspension of the better-off test by pointing to the way they manage diversity. By cutting corporate staff to the bone and giving business units nearly complete autonomy, they believe they avoid the pitfalls. Such thinking misses the whole point of diversification, which is to create shareholder value rather than to avoid destroying it.

CONCEPTS OF CORPORATE STRATEGY

The three tests for successful diversification set the standards that any corporate strategy must meet; meeting them is so difficult that most diversification fails. Many companies lack a clear concept of corporate strategy to guide their diversification or pursue a concept that does not address the tests. Others fail because they implement a strategy poorly.

My study has helped me identify four concepts of corporate strategy that have been put into practice – portfolio management, restructuring, transferring skills, and sharing activities. While the concepts are not always mutually exclusive, each rests on a different mechanism by which the corporation creates shareholder value and each requires the diversified company to manage and organize itself in a different way. The first two require no connections among business units; the second two depend on them (see Table 12.4). While all four concepts of strategy have succeeded under the right circumstances, today some make more sense than others. Ignoring any of the concepts is perhaps the quickest road to failure.

Portfolio management

The concept of corporate strategy most in use is portfolio management, which is based primarily on diversification through acquisition. The corporation acquires sound, attractive companies with competent managers who agree to stay on. While acquired units do not have to be in the same industries as existing units, the best portfolio managers generally limit their range of businesses in some way, in part to limit the specific expertise needed by top management.

The acquired units are autonomous, and the teams that run them are compensated according to unit results. The corporation supplies capital and works with each to infuse it with professional management techniques. At the same time, top management provides objective and dispassionate review of business unit results. Portfolio managers categorize units by potential and regularly transfer resources from units that generate cash to those with high potential and cash needs.

In a portfolio strategy, the corporation seeks to create shareholder value in a number of ways. It uses its expertise and analytical resources to spot attractive acquisition candidates that the individual shareholder could not. The company provides capital on favorable terms that reflect corporatewide fund-raising ability. It introduces professional management skills and discipline. Finally, it provides high-quality review and coaching, unencumbered by conventional wisdom or emotional attachments to the business.

The logic of the portfolio management concept rests on a number of vital assumptions. If a company's diversification plan is to meet the attractiveness and cost-of-entry tests, it must find good but undervalued companies. Acquired companies must be truly undervalued because the parent does little for the new unit once it is acquired. To meet the better-off test, the benefits the corporation provides must yield a significant competitive advantage to acquired units. The style of operating through highly autonomous business units must both develop sound business strategies and motivate managers.

In most countries, the days when portfolio management was a valid concept of corporate strategy are past. In the face of increasingly well-developed capital markets, attractive companies with good managements show up on everyone's computer screen and attract top dollar in terms of acquisition premium. Simply contributing capital isn't contributing much. A sound strategy can easily be funded; small to medium-size companies don't need a munificent parent.

Other benefits have also eroded. Large companies no longer corner the market for professional management skills; in fact, more and more observers believe managers cannot necessarily run anything in the absence of industry-specific knowledge and experience. Another supposed advantage of the portfolio management concept – dispassionate review – rests on similarly shaky ground since the added value of review alone is questionable in a portfolio of sound companies.

The benefit of giving business units complete autonomy is also questionable. Increasingly, a company's business units are interrelated, drawn together by new technology, broadening distribution channels and changing regulations. Setting strategies of units independently may well undermine unit performance. The companies in my sample that have succeeded in diversification have recognized the value of inter-relationships and understood that a strong sense of corporate identity is as important as slavish adherence to parochial business unit financial results.

But it is the sheer complexity of the management task that has ultimately defeated even the best portfolio managers. As the size of the company grows, portfolio managers need to find more and more deals just to maintain growth. Supervising dozens or even hundreds of disparate units and under chain-letter pressures to add more, management begins to make mistakes. At the same time, the inevitable costs of being part of a diversified company take their toll and unit performance slides while the whole company's ROI turns downward. Eventually, a new management team is installed that initiates wholesale divestments and pares down the company to its core businesses. The experiences of Gulf & Western, Consolidated Foods (now Sara Lee), and ITT are just a few comparatively recent examples. Reflecting these realities, the US capital markets today reward companies that follow the portfolio management model with a "conglomerate discount"; they value the whole less than the sum of the parts.

In developing countries, where large companies are few, capital markets are undeveloped, and professional management is scarce,

Table 12.4 Concepts of corporate strategy

	Portfolio management	Restructuring	Transferring skills	Sharing activities
Strategic prerequisites	Superior insight into identifying and acquiring undervalued companies	Superior insight into identifying restructuring opportunities	Proprietary skills in activities important to competitive advantage in target industries	Activities in existing units that can be shared with new business units to gain competitive advantage
	Willingness to sell off losers quickly or to opportunistically divest good performers when buyers are willing to pay large premiums	Willingness and capability to intervene to transform acquired units	Ability to accomplish the transfer of skills among units on an ongoing basis	Benefits of sharing that outweight the costs
	Broad guidelines for and constraints on the types of units in the portfolio so that senior management can play the review role effectively	Broad similarities among the units in the portfolio	Acquisitions of beachhead positions in new industries as a base	Both start-ups and acquisitions as entry vehicles
	A private company or undeveloped capital markets	Willingness to cut losses by selling off units where restructuring proves unfeasible		Ability to overcome organizational resistance to business unit collaboration
	Ability to shift away from portfolio management as the capital markets get more efficient or the company gets unwieldy	Willingness to sell units when restructuring is complete, the results are clear, and market conditions are favorable		

Table 12.4 Continued

	Portfolio management	Restructuring	Transferring skills	Sharing activities
Organizational prerequisites	Autonomous business units A very small, low-cost, corporate staff Incentives based largely on business unit results	Autonomous business units A corporate organization with the talent and resources to oversee the turnarounds and strategic repositionings of acquired units Incentives based largely on acquired units' results	Largely autonomous but collaborative business units High-level corporate staff members who see their role primarily as integrators Cross-business-unit committees, task forces, and other forums to serve as focal points for capturing and transferring skills Objectives of line managers that include skills transfer Incentives based in part on corporate results	Strategic business units that are encouraged to share activities An active strategic planning role at group, sector, and corporate levels High-level corporate staff members who see their roles primarily as integrators Incentives based heavily on group and corporate results
Common pitfalls	Pursuing portfolio management in countries with efficient capital marketing and a developed pool of professional management talent Ignoring the fact that industry structure is not attractive	Mistaking rapid growth or a "hot" industry as sufficient evidence of a restructuring opportunity Lacking the resolve or resources to take on troubled situations and to intervene in management Ignoring the fact that industry structure is not attractive Paying lip service to restructuring but actually practicing passive portfolio management	Mistaking similarity or comfort with new businesses as sufficient basis for diversification Providing no practical ways for skills transfer to occur Ignoring the fact that industry structure is not attractive	Sharing for its own sake rather than because it leads to competitive advantage Assuming sharing will occur naturally without senior management playing an active role Ignoring the fact that industry structure is not attractive

portfolio management still works. But it is no longer a valid model for corporate strategy in advanced economies. Nevertheless, the technique is in the limelight today in the United Kingdom, where it is supported so far by a newly energized stock market eager for excitement. But this enthusiasm will wane – as well it should. Portfolio management is no way to conduct corporate strategy.

Restructuring

Unlike its passive role as a portfolio manager, when it serves as banker and reviewer, a company that bases its strategy on restructuring becomes an active restructurer of business units. The new businesses are not necessarily related to existing units. All that is necessary is unrealized potential.

The restructuring strategy seeks out undeveloped, sick, or threatened organizations or industries on the threshold of significant change. The parent intervenes, frequently changing the unit management team, shifting strategy, or infusing the company with new technology. Then it may make follow-up acquisitions to build a critical mass and sell off unneeded or unconnected parts and thereby reduce the effective acquisition cost. The result is a strengthened company or a transformed industry. As a coda, the parent sells off the stronger unit once results are clear because the parent is no longer adding value and top management decides that its attention should be directed elsewhere.

When well implemented, the restructuring concept is sound, for it passes the three tests of successful diversification. The restructurer meets the cost-of-entry test through the types of company it acquires. It limits acquisition premiums by buying companies with problems and lackluster images or by buying into industries with as yet unforeseen potential. Intervention by the corporation clearly meets the better-off test. Provided that the target industries are structurally attractive, the restructuring model can create enormous shareholder value. Some restructuring companies are Loew's, BTR, and General Cinema. Ironically, many of today's restructurers are profiting from yesterday's portfolio management strategies.

To work, the restructuring strategy requires a corporate management team with the insight to spot undervalued companies or positions in industries ripe for transformation. The same insight is necessary to actually turn the units around even though they are in new and unfamiliar businesses.

These requirements expose the restructurer to considerable risk and usually limit the time in which the company can succeed at the strategy. The most skillful proponents understand this problem, recognize their mistakes, and move decisively to dispose of them. The best companies realize they are not just acquiring companies but restructuring an industry. Unless they can integrate the acquisitions to create a whole new strategic position, they are just portfolio managers in disguise. Another important difficulty surfaces if so many other companies join the action that they deplete the pool of suitable candidates and bid their prices up.

Perhaps the greatest pitfall, however, is that companies find it very hard to dispose of business units once they are restructured and performing well. Human nature fights economic rationale. Size supplants shareholder value as the corporate goal. The company does not sell a unit even though the company no longer adds value to the unit. While the transformed units would be better off in another company that had related businesses, the restructuring company instead retains them. Gradually, it becomes a portfolio manager. The parent company's ROI declines as the need for reinvestment in the units and normal business risks eventually offset restructuring's one-shot gain. The perceived need to keep growing intensifies the pace of acquisition; errors result and standards fall. The restructuring company turns into a conglomerate with returns that only equal the average of all industries at best.

Transferring skills

The purpose of the first two concepts of corporate strategy is to create value through a company's relationship with each autonomous unit. The corporation's role is to be a selector, a banker, and an intervenor.

The last two concepts exploit the interrelationships between businesses. In articulating them, however, one comes face-to-face with the often ill-defined concept of synergy. If you believe the text of the countless corporate annual reports, just about anything is related to just about anything else! But imagined synergy is much more common than real synergy. GM's purchase of Hughes Aircraft simply because cars were going electronic and Hughes was an electronics concern demonstrates the folly of paper synergy. Such corporate relatedness is an *ex post facto* rationalization of a diversification undertaken for other reasons.

Even synergy that is clearly defined often fails to materialize. Instead of cooperating, business units often compete. A company that can define the synergies it is pursuing still faces significant organizational impediments in achieving them.

But the need to capture the benefits of relationships between businesses has never been more important. Technological and competitive developments already link many businesses and are creating new possibilities for competitive advantage. In such sectors as financial services, computing, office equipment, entertainment, and health care, interrelationships among previously distinct businesses are perhaps the central concern of strategy.

To understand the role of relatedness in corporate strategy, we must give new meaning to this often ill-defined idea. I have identified a good way to start – the value chain.[5] Every business unit is a collection of discrete activities ranging from sales to accounting that allow it to compete. I call them value activities. It is at this level, not in the company as a whole, that the unit achieves competitive advantage.

I group these activities in nine categories. *Primary* activities create the product or service, deliver and market it, and provide aftersale support. The categories of primary activities are inbound logistics, operations, outbound logistics, marketing and sales, and service. *Support* activities provide the input and infrastructure that allow the primary activities to take place. The categories are company infrastructure, human resource management, technology development, and procurement.

The value chain defines the two types of interrelationships that may create synergy. The first is a company's ability to transfer skills or expertise among similar value chains. The second is the ability to share activities. Two business units, for example, can share the same sales force or logistics network.

The value chain helps expose the last two (and most important) concepts of corporate strategy. The transfer of skills among business units in the diversified company is the basis for one concept. While each business unit has a separate value chain, knowledge about how to perform activities is transferred among the units. For example, a toiletries business unit, expert in the marketing of convenience products, transmits ideas on new positioning concepts, promotional techniques, and packaging possibilities to a newly acquired unit that sells cough syrup. Newly entered industries can benefit from the expertise of existing units and vice versa.

These opportunities arise when business units have similar buyers or channels, similar value activities like government relations or procurement, similarities in the broad configuration of the value chain (for example, managing a multisite service organization), or the same strategic concept (for example, low cost). Even though the units operate separately, such similarities allow the sharing of knowledge.

Of course, some similarities are common; one can imagine them at some level between almost any pair of businesses. Countless companies have fallen into the trap of diversifying too readily because of similarities; mere similarity is not enough.

Transferring skills leads to competitive advantage only if the similarities among businesses meet three conditions:

1 The activities involved in the businesses are similar enough that sharing expertise is meaningful. Broad similarities (marketing intensiveness, for example, or a common core process technology such as bending metal) are not a sufficient basis for diversification. The

resulting ability to transfer skills is likely to have little impact on competitive advantage.

2 The transfer of skills involves activities important to competitive advantage. Transferring skills in peripheral activities such as government relations or real estate in consumer goods units may be beneficial but is not a basis for diversification.

3 The skills transferred represent a significant source of competitive advantage for the receiving unit. The expertise or skills to be transferred are both advanced and proprietary enough to be beyond the capabilities of competitors.

The transfer of skills is an active process that significantly changes the strategy or operations of the receiving unit. The prospect for change must be specific and identifiable. Almost guaranteeing that no shareholder value will be created, too many companies are satisfied with vague prospects or faint hopes that skills will transfer. The transfer of skills does not happen by accident or by osmosis. The company will have to reassign critical personnel, even on a permanent basis, and the participation and support of high-level management in skills transfer is essential. Many companies have been defeated at skills transfer because they have not provided their business units with any incentives to participate.

Transferring skills meets the tests of diversification if the company truly mobilizes proprietary expertise across units. This makes certain the company can offset the acquisition premium or lower the cost of overcoming entry barriers.

The industries the company chooses for diversification must pass the attractiveness test. Even a close fit that reflects opportunities to transfer skills may not overcome poor industry structure. Opportunities to transfer skills, however, may help the company transform the structures of newly entered industries and send them in favorable directions.

The transfer of skills can be one-time or ongoing. If the company exhausts opportunities to infuse new expertise into a unit after the initial postacquisition period, the unit should ultimately be sold. The corporation is no longer creating shareholder value. Few companies have grasped this point, however, and many gradually suffer mediocre returns. Yet a company diversified into well-chosen businesses can transfer skills eventually in many directions. If corporate management conceives of its role in this way and creates appropriate organizational mechanisms to facilitate cross-unit interchange, the opportunities to share expertise will be meaningful.

By using both acquisitions and internal development, companies can build a transfer-of-skills strategy. The presence of a strong base of skills sometimes creates the possibility for internal entry instead of the acquisition of a going concern. Successful diversifiers that employ the concept of skills transfer may, however, often acquire a company in the target industry as a beachhead and then build on it with their internal expertise. By doing so, they can reduce some of the risks of internal entry and speed up the process. Two companies that have diversified using the transfer-of-skills concept are 3M and Pepsico.

An uncanny British restructurer

Hanson Trust, on its way to becoming Britain's largest company, is one of several skillful followers of the restructuring concept. A conglomerate with units in many industries, Hanson might seem on the surface a portfolio manager. In fact, Hanson and one or two other conglomerates have a much more effective corporate strategy. Hanson has acquired companies such as London Brick, Ever Ready Batteries, and SCM, which the city of London rather disdainfully calls 'low tech'.

Although a mature company suffering from low growth, the typical Hanson target is not just in any industry; it has an attractive structure. Its customer and supplier power is low and rivalry with competitors moderate. The target is a market leader, rich in assets but formerly poor in management. Hanson pays little of the present value of future cash flow out in an acquisition premium and reduces purchase price even further by aggressively selling off businesses that it cannot improve. In this way, it recoups just over a third of the cost of a typical acquisition during the first six months of ownership. Imperial Group's plush properties in London lasted barely two months under Hanson ownership, while Hanson's recent sale of Courage Breweries to Elders recouped £1.4 billion of the original £2.1 billion acquisition price of Imperial Group.

Like the best restructures, Hanson approaches each unit with a modus operandi that it has perfected through repetition.

Hanson emphasizes low costs and tight financial controls. It has cut an average of 25 percent of labor costs out of acquired companies, slashed fixed overheads, and tightened capital expenditures. To reinforce its strategy of keeping costs low, Hanson carves out detailed one-year financial budgets with divisional managers and (through generous use of performance-related bonuses and share option schemes) gives them incentive to deliver the goods.

It's too early to tell whether Hanson will adhere to the last tenet of restructuring – selling turned-around units once the results are clear. If it succumbs to the allure of bigness, Hanson may take the course of the failed US conglomerates.

Sharing activities

The fourth concept of corporate strategy is based on sharing activities in the value chains among business units. Procter & Gamble, for example,

---

Adding value with hospitality

Marriott began in the restaurant business in Washington, DC. Because its customers often ordered takeouts on the way to the national airport, Marriott eventually entered airline catering. From there, it jumped into food service management for institutions. Marriott then began broadening its base of family restaurants and entered the hotel industry. More recently, it has moved into restaurants, snack bars, and merchandise shops in airport terminals and into gourmet restaurants. In addition, Marriott has branched out from its hotel business into cruise ships, theme parks, wholesale travel agencies, budget motels and retirement centers.

Marriott's diversification has exploited well-developed skills in food service and hospitality. Marriott's kitchens prepare food according to more than 6,000 standardized recipe cards; hotel procedures are also standardized and painstakingly documented in elaborate manuals. Marriott shares a number of important activities across units. A shared procurement and distribution system for food serves all Marriott units through nine regional procurement centers. As a result, Marriott earns 50 percent higher margins on food service than any other hotel company. Marriott also has a fully integrated real estate unit that brings corporatewide power to bear on site acquisitions as well as on the designing and building of all Marriott locations.

Marriott's diversification strategy balances acquisitions and start-ups. Start-ups or small acquisitions are used for initial entry, depending on how close the opportunities for sharing are. To expand its geographic base, Marriott acquires companies and then disposes of the parts that do not fit.

Apart from this success, it is important to note that Marriott has divested 36 percent of both its acquisitions and its start-ups. While this is an above-average record, Marriott's mistakes are quite illuminating. Marriott has largely failed in diversifying into gourmet restaurants, theme parks, cruise ships, and wholesale travel agencies. In the first three businesses, Marriott discovered it could not transfer skills despite apparent similarities. Standardized menus did not work well in gourmet restaurants. Running cruise ships and theme parks was based more on entertainment and pizzazz than the carefully disciplined management of hotels and mid-priced restaurants. The wholesale travel agencies were ill fated from the start because Marriott had to compete with an important customer for its hotels and had no proprietary skills or opportunities to share with which to add value.

employs a common physical distribution system and sales force in both paper towels and disposable diapers. McKesson, a leading distribution company, will handle such diverse lines as pharmaceuticals and liquor through superwarehouses.

The ability to share activities is a potent basis for corporate strategy because sharing often enhances competitive advantage by lowering cost or raising differentiation. But not all sharing leads to competitive advantage, and companies can encounter deep organizational resistance to even beneficial sharing possibilities. These hard truths have led many companies to reject synergy prematurely and retreat to the false simplicity of portfolio management.

A cost-benefit analysis of prospective sharing opportunities can determine whether synergy is possible. Sharing can lower costs if it achieves economies of scale, boosts the efficiency of utilization, or helps a company move more rapidly down the learning curve.

The cost of General Electric's advertising, sales, and after-sales service activities in major appliances are low because they are spread over a wide range of appliance products. Sharing can also enhance the potential for differentiation. A shared order-processing system, for instance, may allow new features and services that a buyer will value. Sharing can also reduce the cost of differentiation. A shared service network, for example, may make more advanced, remote servicing technology economically feasible. Often, sharing will allow an activity to be wholly reconfigured in ways that can dramatically raise competitive advantage.

Sharing must involve activities that are significant to competitive advantage, not just any activity. P&G's distribution system is such an instance in the diaper and paper towel business, where products are bulky and costly to ship. Conversely, diversification based on the opportunities to share only corporate overhead is rarely, if ever, appropriate.

Sharing activities inevitably involves costs that the benefits must outweigh. One cost is the greater coordination required to manage a shared activity. More important is the need to compromise the design or performance of an activity so that it can be shared. A salesperson handling the products of two business units, for example, must operate in a way that is usually not what either unit would choose were it independent. And if compromise greatly erodes the unit's effectiveness, then sharing may reduce rather than enhance competitive advantage.

Many companies have only superficially identified their potential for sharing. Companies also merge activities without consideration of whether they are sensitive to economies of scale. When they are not, the coordination costs kill the benefits. Companies compound such errors by not identifying costs of sharing in advance, when steps can be taken to minimize them. Costs of compromise can frequently be mitigated by redesigning the activity for sharing. The shared salesperson, for example, can be provided with a remote computer terminal to boost productivity and provide more customer information. Jamming business units together without such thinking exacerbates the costs of sharing.

Despite such pitfalls, opportunities to gain advantage from sharing activities have proliferated because of momentous developments in technology, deregulation, and competition. The infusion of electronics and information systems into many industries creates new opportunities to link businesses. The corporate strategy of sharing can involve both acquisition and internal development. Internal development is often possible because the corporation can bring to bear clear resources in launching a new unit. Start-ups are less difficult to integrate than acquisitions. Companies using the shared-activities concept can also make acquisitions as beachhead landings into a new industry and then integrate the units through sharing with other units. Prime examples of companies that have diversified via using shared activities include P&G, Du Pont, and IBM. The fields into which each has diversified are a cluster of tightly related units. Marriott illustrates both successes and failures in sharing activities over time.

Following the shared-activities model requires an organizational context in which business unit collaboration is encouraged and reinforced. Highly autonomous business units are inimical to such collaboration. The company must put into place a variety of what I call horizontal mechanisms – a strong sense of corporate identity, a clear corporate mission statement that emphasizes the importance of integrating business unit strategies, an incentive system that rewards more than just business unit results, cross-business-unit task forces, and other methods of integrating.

A corporate strategy based on shared activities clearly meets the better-off test because business units gain ongoing tangible advantages from others within the corporation. It also meets the cost-of-entry test by reducing the expense of surmounting the barriers to internal entry. Other bids for acquisitions that do not share opportunities will have lower reservation prices. Even widespread opportunities for sharing activities do not allow a company to suspend the attractiveness test, however. Many diversifiers have made the critical mistake of equating the close fit of a target industry with attractive diversification. Target industries must pass the strict requirement test of having an attractive structure as well as a close fit in opportunities if diversification is to ultimately succeed.

CHOOSING A CORPORATE STRATEGY

Each concept of corporate strategy allows the diversified company to create shareholder value in a different way. Companies can succeed with any of the concepts if they clearly define the corporation's role and objectives, have the skills necessary for meeting the concept's prerequisites, organize themselves to manage diversity in a way that fits the strategy, and find themselves in an appropriate capital market environment. The caveat is that portfolio management is only sensible in limited circumstances.

A company's choice of corporate strategy is partly a legacy of its past. If its business units are in unattractive industries, the company must start from scratch. If the company has few truly proprietary skills or activities it can share in related diversification, then its initial diversification must rely on other concepts. Yet corporate strategy should not be a once-and-for-all choice but a vision that can evolve. A company should choose its long-term preferred concept and then proceed pragmatically toward it from its initial starting point.

Both the strategic logic and the experience of the companies I studied over the last decade suggest that a company will create shareholder value through diversification to a greater and greater extent as its strategy moves from portfolio management toward sharing activities. Because they do not rely on superior insight or other questionable assumptions about the company's capabilities, sharing activities and transferring skills offer the best avenues for value creation.

Each concept of corporate strategy is not mutually exclusive of those that come before, a potent advantage of the third and fourth concepts. A company can employ a restructuring strategy at the same time it transfers skills or shares activities. A strategy based on shared activities becomes more powerful if business units can also exchange skills. A company can often pursue the two strategies together and even incorporate some of the principles of restructuring with them. When it chooses industries in which to transfer skills or share activities, the company can also investigate the possibility of transforming the industry structure. When a company bases its strategy on interrelationships, it has a broader basis on which to create shareholder value than if it rests its entire strategy on transforming companies in unfamiliar industries.

My study supports the soundness of basing a corporate strategy on the transfer of skills or shared activities. The data on the sample companies' diversification programs illustrate some important characteristics of successful diversifiers. They have made a disproportionately low percentage of unrelated acquisitions, *unrelated* being defined as having no clear opportunity to transfer skills or share important activities (see Table 12.3). Even successful diversifiers such as 3M, IBM, and TRW have terrible records when they have strayed into unrelated acquisitions. Successful acquirers diversify into fields, each of which is related to many others. Procter & Gamble and IBM, for example, operate in 18 and 19 interrelated fields, respectively, and so enjoy numerous opportunities to transfer skills and share activities.

Companies with the best acquisition records tend to make heavier-than-average use of start-ups and joint ventures. Most companies shy away from modes of entry besides acquisition. My results cast doubt on the conventional wisdom regarding start-ups. Table 12.3 demonstrates that while joint ventures are about as risky as acquisitions, start-ups are not. Moreover, successful companies often have very good records with start-up units, as 3M, P&G, Johnson & Johnson, IBM, and United Technologies illustrate. When a company has the internal strength to start up a unit, it can be safer and less costly to launch a company than to rely solely on an acquisition and then have to deal with the problem of integration. Japanese diversification histories support the soundness of start-up as an entry alternative.

My data also illustrate that none of the concepts of corporate strategy works when industry structure is poor or implementation is bad, no matter how related the industries are. Xerox acquired companies in related industries, but the businesses had poor structures and its skills were insufficient to provide enough competitive advantage to offset implementation problems.

An action program

To translate the principles of corporate strategy into successful diversification, a company must first take an objective look at its existing businesses and the value added by the corporation. Only through such an assessment can an understanding of good corporate strategy grow. That understanding should guide future diversification as well as the development of skills and activities with which to select further new businesses. The following action program provides a concrete approach to conducting such a review. A company can choose a corporate strategy by:

Identifying the interrelationships among already existing business units.

A company should begin to develop a corporate strategy by identifying all the opportunities it has to share activities or transfer skills in its existing portfolio of business units. The company will not only find ways to enhance the competitive advantage of existing units but also come upon several possible diversification avenues. The lack of meaningful interrelationships in the portfolio is an equally important finding, suggesting the need to justify the value added by the corporation or, alternately, a fundamental restructuring.

Selecting the core businesses that will be the foundation of the corporate strategy.

Successful diversification starts with an understanding of the core businesses that will serve as the basis for corporate strategy. Core businesses are those that are in an attractive industry, have the potential to achieve sustainable competitive advantage, have important interrelationships with other business units, and provide skills or activities that represent a base from which to diversify.

The company must first make certain its core businesses are on sound footing by upgrading management, internationalizing strategy or improving technology. My study shows that geographic extensions of existing units, whether by acquisition, joint venture or start-up, had a substantially lower divestment rate than diversification.

The company must then patiently dispose of the units that are not core businesses. Selling them will free resources that could be better deployed elsewhere. In some cases disposal implies immediate liquidation, while in others the company should dress up the units and wait for a propitious market or a particularly eager buyer.

Creating horizontal organizational mechanisms to facilitate interrelationships among the core businesses and lay the groundwork for future related diversification.

Top management can facilitate interrelationships by emphasizing cross-unit collaboration, grouping units organizationally and modifying incentives, and taking steps to build a strong sense of corporate identity.

Pursuing diversification opportunities that allow shared activities.

This concept of corporate strategy is the most compelling, provided a company's strategy passes all three tests. A company should inventory activities in existing business units that represent the strongest foundation for sharing, such as strong distribution channels or world-class technical facilities. These will in turn lead to potential new business areas. A company can use acquisitions as a beachhead or employ start-ups to exploit internal capabilities and minimize integrating problems.

Pursuing diversification through the transfer of skills if opportunities for sharing activities are limited or exhausted.

Companies can pursue this strategy through acquisition, although they may be able to use start-ups if their existing units have important skills they can readily transfer.

Such diversification is often riskier because of the tough conditions necessary for it to work. Given the uncertainties, a company should avoid diversifying on the basis of skills transfer alone. Rather it should also be viewed as a stepping-stone to subsequent diversification using shared activities. New industries should be chosen that will lead naturally to other businesses. The goal is to build a cluster of related and mutually reinforcing business units. The strategy's logic implies that the company should not set the rate of return standards for the initial foray into a new sector too high.

Pursuing a strategy of restructuring if this fits the skills of management or no good opportunities exist for forging corporate interrelationships.

When a company uncovers undermanaged companies and can deploy adequate management talent and resources to the acquired units, then it can use a restructuring strategy. The more developed the capital markets and the more active the market for companies, the more restructuring will require a patient search for that special opportunity rather than a headlong race to acquire as many bad apples as possible. Restructuring can be a permanent strategy, as it is with Loew's, or a way to build a group of businesses that supports a shift to another corporate strategy.

Paying dividends so that the shareholders can be the portfolio managers.

Paying dividends is better than destroying shareholder value through diversification based on shaky underpinnings. Tax considerations, which some companies cite to avoid dividends, are hardly legitimate reason to diversify if a company cannot demonstrate the capacity to do it profitably.

Creating a corporate theme

Defining a corporate theme is a good way to ensure that the corporation will create shareholder value. Having the right theme helps unite the efforts of business units and reinforces the ways they interrelate as well as guides the choice of new businesses to enter, NEC Corporation, with its "C&C" theme, provides a good example. NEC integrates its computer, semiconductor, telecommunications, and consumer electronics businesses by merging computers and communication.

It is all too easy to create a shallow corporate theme. CBS wanted to be an "entertainment company," for example, and built a group of businesses related to leisure time. It entered such industries as toys, crafts, musical instruments, sports teams, and hi-fi retailing. While this corporate theme sounded good, close listening revealed its hollow ring. None of these businesses had any significant opportunity to share activities or transfer skills among themselves or with CBS's traditional broadcasting and record businesses. They were all sold, often at significant losses, except for a few of CBS's publishing-related units. Saddled with the worst acquisition record in my study, CBS has eroded the shareholder value created through its strong performance in broadcasting and records.

Moving from competitive strategy to corporate strategy is the business equivalent of passing through the Bermuda Triangle. The failure of corporate strategy reflects the fact that most diversified companies have failed to think in terms of how they really add value. A corporate strategy that truly enhances the competitive advantage of each business unit is the best defense against the corporate raider. With a sharper focus on the tests of diversification and the explicit choice of a clear concept of corporate strategy, companies' diversification track records from now on can look a lot different.

NOTES AND REFERENCES

1 The studies also show that sellers of companies capture a large fraction of the gains from merger. See Michael C. Jensen and Richard S. Ruback, "The Market for Corporate Control: The Scientific Evidence," *Journal of Financial Economics* (April 1983), p. 5, and Michael C. Jensen, "Takeovers: Folklore and Science," *Harvard Business Review* (November–December 1984), p. 109.
2 Some recent evidence also supports the conclusion that acquired companies often suffer eroding performance after acquisition. See Frederick M. Scherer, "Mergers, Sell-Offs and Managerial Behavior," in *The Economics of Strategic Planning*, Lacy Glenn Thomas (ed.) (Lexington, Mass.: Lexington Books, 1986), p. 143, and David A. Ravenscraft and Frederick M. Scherer, "Mergers and Managerial Performance," paper presented at the Conference on Takeovers and Contests for Corporate Control, Columbia Law School (1985).
3 This observation has been made by a number of authors. See, for example, Malcolm S. Salter and Wolf A. Weinhold, *Diversification Through Acquisition* (New York: Free Press, 1979).
4 See Michael E. Porter, "How Competitive Forces Shape Strategy," *Harvard Business Review* (March–April 1979), p. 86.
5 Michael E. Porter, *Competitive Advantage* (New York: Free Press, 1985).

Chapter 13

Eclipse of the public corporation

Michael C. Jensen

The publicly held corporation, the main engine of economic progress in the United States for a century, has outlived its usefulness in many sectors of the economy and is being eclipsed. New organizations are emerging in its place – organizations that are corporate in form but have no public shareholders and are not listed or traded on organized exchanges. These organizations use public and private debt, rather than public equity, as their major source of capital. Their primary owners are not households but large institutions and entrepreneurs that designate agents to manage and monitor on their behalf and bind those agents with large equity interests and contracts governing the use and distribution of cash.

Takeovers, corporate breakups, divisional spinoffs, leveraged buyouts and going-private transactions are the most visible manifestations of a massive organizational change in the economy. These transactions have inspired criticism, even outrage, among many business leaders and government officials, who have called for regulatory and legislative restrictions. The backlash is understandable. Change is threatening; in this case, the threat is aimed at the senior executives of many of our largest companies.

Despite the protests, this organizational innovation should be encouraged. By resolving the central weakness of the public corporation – the conflict between owners and managers over the control and use of corporate resources – these new organizations are making remarkable gains in operating efficiency, employee productivity, and shareholder value. Over the long term, they will enhance US economic performance relative to our most formidable international competitor, Japan, whose companies are moving in the opposite direction. The governance and financial structures of Japan's public companies increasingly resemble US companies of the mid-1960s and early 1970s – an era of gross corporate waste and mismanagement that triggered the organizational transformation now under way in the United States.

Consider these developments in the 1980s:

The capital markets are in transition. The total market value of equity in publicly held companies has tripled over the past decade – from $1 trillion in 1979 to more than $3 trillion in 1989. But newly acquired capital comes increasingly from private placements, which have expanded more than ten times since 1980, to a rate of $200 billion in 1988. Private placements of debt and equity now account for more than 40 percent of annual corporate financings. Meanwhile, in every year since 1983, at least 5 percent of the outstanding value of corporate equity has disappeared through stock repurchases, takeovers, and going-private transactions. Finally, households are sharply reducing their stock holdings.[1]

The most widespread going-private transaction, the leveraged buyout, is becoming larger and more frequent. In 1988, the total value of the 214 public-company and divisional buyouts exceeded $77 billion – nearly one-third of the value of all mergers and acquisitions. The total value of the 75 buyouts in 1979 was only $1.3 billion (in constant 1988 dollars), while the 175 buyouts completed in 1983 had a total value of $16.6 billion. This process is just getting started; the $77 billion of LBOs in 1988 represented only 2.5 percent of outstanding public-company equity (see Table 13.1).

Entire industries are being reshaped. Just five years ago, the leading US truck and automobile tire manufacturers were independent and diversified public companies. Today each is a vastly different enterprise. Uniroyal went private in 1985 and later merged its tire-making operations with those of B. F. Goodrich to form a new private company called Uniroyal Goodrich. In late 1986, Goodyear borrowed $2.6 billion and repurchased nearly half its outstanding shares to fend off a hostile tender offer by Sir James Goldsmith. It retained its core tire and rubber business while moving to divest an array of unrelated operations, including its Celeron oil and gas subsidiary, California-to-Texas oil pipeline, aerospace operation, and Arizona resort hotel. In 1987, GenCorp issued $1.75 billion of debt to repurchase more than half its outstanding shares. It divested several operations, including its General Tire subsidiary, to pay down the debt and focus on aerospace and defense. Last year, Firestone was sold to Bridgestone, Japan's largest tiremaker, for $2.6 billion, a transaction that created shareholder gains of $1.6 billion.

Developments as striking as the restructuring of our financial markets and major industries reflect underlying economic forces more fundamental and powerful than financial manipulation, management greed, reckless speculation, and the other colorful epithets used by defenders of the corporate *status quo*. The forces behind the decline of the public corporation differ from industry to industry. But its decline is real, enduring,

The privatization of equity

The last share of publicly traded common stock owned by an individual will be sold in the year 2003 if current trends persist. This forecast may be fanciful (short-term trends never persist), but the basic direction is clear. By the turn of the century, the primacy of public stock ownership in the United States may have all but disappeared.

Households have been liquidating their direct holdings and indirect positions (through channels like mutual funds) at an unprecedented rate. Over the last five years, they have been net sellers of more than $500 billion of common stock, 38 percent of their holdings at the beginning of 1984.

Why have stock prices risen sharply despite this massive sell-off? Because there has been one huge buyer—corporations themselves. LBOs, MBOs, share repurchases, leveraged mergers and acquisitions, and takeovers have been contracting the supply of publicly held equity. In 1988, 5 percent of the market value of public equity (more than $130 billion) disappeared through these kinds of transactions, even after adding back all of the new issues brought to market during the year.

Of course, the risks and returns from the underlying corporate assets have not disappeared. To some extent they now reside in quasi-equity debt instruments like high-yield bonds, whose total market value exceeds $200 billion. But many of the risks and returns still exist as equity; they just take the form of large positions of privately held equity. The 'privatization of equity' is now a central feature of corporate ownership in the United States.

Historically, public stock markets dominated by individual investors developed to a greater extent in the United States than in any other country. Broad public ownership offered managers a reasonably priced source of more or less permanent equity capital that could buffer the company against adversity in a way debt could not. Share ownership allowed individual investors to participate in equity returns and get the benefits of liquidity (because they could sell their shares and diversification (because they could hold a small number of shares from many corporations).

The virtues of broad public ownership are not what they used to be, for managers or investors. One important factor is the emergence of an active market for corporate control. A capital structure consisting mostly of equity still offers managers protection against the risks of economic downturn. But it also carries substantial risks of inviting a hostile takeover or other threats to management control.

The role of the public market has also changed because investors themselves have changed. For decades, stock ownership has been migrating from direct holdings by millions of individuals to indirect beneficial ownership through large pools of capital–in particular, the huge corporate and governmental pension funds whose total value exceeded $1.5 trillion in 1988. These institutional funds, which now comprise more than 40 percent of total stock ownership, used to behave like large public investors. They kept diversified by retaining many different investment managers, each of whom traded an array of highly liquid public securities. But their investment philosophy has been evolving in recent years to include participation in a select number of private illiquid investments and private pools of equity capital.

This new investment philosophy makes broad public markets less essential for institutions.

Large pools of capital such as pension funds and endowments don't really need the liquidity the public market offers. Liquidity serves two basic purposes. It allows investors to meet unexpected cash needs and to trade their stocks. Unlike individuals, the large funds can project their cash needs well into the future based on predictable factors such as employee demographics, life expectancies, and health trends. So they can take a long-term view of investment returns and keep their holdings in illiquid assets.

Fund managers are also realizing that trading is a tough discipline in which they hold little comparative advantage. Trading is a zero-sum game played in a fairly efficient market against equally talented rivals. Worse still, large funds face diseconomies of scale when executing trades. The larger a fund, the more difficult it is to trade quickly, based on transient information advantages. The very act of trading moves markets.

Still, these managers remain charged with generating returns in excess of passive benchmarks. Enter the market for private assets such as real estate, venture capital, and, more recently, the market for corporate control and restructurings. Instead of trading a large number of small, liquid positions, the funds can buy and own smaller numbers of large, illiquid positions in a form where they (or, more likely, their agents) participate more actively with management in the control of the assets.

This alternative can be a positive-sum game; real changes in corporate policies can be a route to enhanced value. The very large funds also have a competitive advantage here. The larger their positions, the more actively they can participate in the ownership and management of the underlying assets. In the extreme, as with LBO funds, these changes can be dramatic. The LBO fund itself becomes the managing owner in partnership with company managers. In short, large institutional funds can behave more like owners and less like traders.

The same basic changes are at work in a wide variety of corporate recapitalizations where outside (or related) parties acquire large, relatively nontraded equity positions. Large pools of capital can participate in these private equity positions yet remain diversified by virtue of their own enormous size. Smaller funds and households cannot.

In the short run, this new investment philosophy has been, in the aggregate, a great success. Without the sobering influence of an economic contraction, the returns from these private investments have been very attractive. In the long run, the institutions' new philosophy is ushering in a system of equity ownership dominated by 'private positions' that resembles ownership systems in Germany and Japan. Individual investors in this system will increasingly be free riders on the coattails of a small number of very large private investors rather than the central feature of the financial markets.

Jay O. Light is the George Fisher Baker, Jr. Professor of Business Administration at the Harvard Business School.

and highly productive. It is not merely a function of the tax deductibility of interest. Nor does it reflect a transitory LBO phase through which companies pass before investment bankers and managers cash out by making them public again. Nor, finally, is it premised on a systematic fleecing of shareholders and bondholders by managers and other insiders with superior information about the true value of corporate assets.

The current trends do not imply that the public corporation has no future. The conventional twentieth-century model of corporate governance – dispersed public ownership, professional managers without substantial equity holdings, a board of directors dominated by management-appointed outsiders – remains a viable option in some areas of the economy, particularly for growth companies whose profitable investment opportunities exceed the cash they generate internally. Such companies can be found in industries like computers and electronics, biotechnology, pharmaceuticals, and financial services. Companies choosing among a surplus of profitable projects are unlikely to invest systematically in unprofitable ones, especially when they must regularly turn to the capital markets to raise investment funds.

The public corporation is not suitable in industries where long-term growth is slow, where internally generated funds outstrip the opportunities to invest them profitably, or where downsizing is the most productive long-term strategy. In the tire industry, the shift to radials, which last three times longer than bias-ply tires, meant that manufacturers needed less capacity to meet world demand. Overcapacity inevitably forced a restructuring. The tenfold increase in oil prices from 1973 to 1981, which triggered worldwide conservation measures, forced oil producers into a similar retrenchment.[2]

Industries under similar pressure today include steel, chemicals, brewing, tobacco, television and radio broadcasting, wood and paper products. In these and other cash-rich, low-growth or declining sectors, the pressures on management to waste cash flow through organizational slack or investments in unsound projects is often irresistible. It is in precisely these sectors that the publicly held corporation has declined most rapidly. Barring regulatory interference, the public corporation is also likely to decline in industries such as aerospace, automobiles and auto parts, banking, electric power generation, food processing, industrial and farm implements and transportation equipment.

The public corporation is a social invention of vast historical importance. Its genius is rooted in its capacity to spread financial risk over the diversified portfolios of millions of individuals and institutions and to allow investors to customize risk to their unique circumstances and predilections. By diversifying risks that would otherwise be borne by owner-entrepreneurs and by facilitating the creation of a liquid market for exchanging risk, the public corporation lowered the cost of capital.

Table 13.1 Rise of the LBO

| Year | Public-company buyouts | | Divisional Buyouts | | |
	Number	Average Value (in millions of 1988 dollars)	Number	Average value (in millions of 1988 dollars)	Total Value of Buyouts (in billions of 1988 dollars)
1979	16	$64.9	59	$5.4	$1.4
1980	13	106.0	47	34.5	3.0
1981	17	179.1	83	21.0	4.8
1982	31	112.2	115	40.7	8.2
1983	36	235.8	139	58.2	16.6
1984	57	473.6	122	104.0	39.7
1985	76	349.4	132	110.1	41.0
1986	76	303.3	144	180.7	49.0
1987	47	488.7	90	144.2	36.0
1988	125	487.4	89	181.3	77.0

Source: George P. Baker, "Management Compensation and Divisional Leveraged Buyouts," unpublished dissertation, Harvard Business School, 1986. Updates from W. T. Grimm, *Mergerstat Review 1988.* Transactions with no public data are valued at the average price of public transactions.

These tradable claims on corporate ownership (common stock) also allowed risk to be borne by investors best able to bear it, without requiring them to manage the corporations they owned.

From the beginning, though, these risk-bearing benefits came at a cost. Tradable ownership claims create fundamental conflicts of interest between those who bear risk (the shareholders) and those who manage risk (the executives). The genius of the new organizations is that they eliminate much of the loss created by conflicts between owners and managers, without eliminating the vital functions of risk diversification and liquidity once performed exclusively by the public equity markets.

In theory, these new organizations should not be necessary. Three major forces are said to control management in the public corporation: the product markets, internal control systems led by the board of directors, and the capital markets. But product markets often have not played a disciplining role. For most of the past sixty years, a large and vibrant domestic market created for US companies economies of scale and significant cost advantages over foreign rivals. Recent reversals at the hands of the Japanese and others have not been severe enough to sap most companies of their financial independence. The idea that outside directors with little or no equity stake in the company could effectively monitor and discipline the managers who selected them has proven hollow at best. In practice, only the capital markets have played much of a control function – and for a long time they were hampered by legal constraints.

Indeed, the fact that takeover and LBO premiums average 50 percent above market price illustrates how much value public-company managers can destroy before they face a serious threat of disturbance. Takeovers and buyouts both create new value and unlock value destroyed by management through misguided policies. I estimate that transactions associated with the market for corporate control unlocked shareholder gains (in target companies alone) of more than $500 billion between 1977 and 1988 – more than 50 percent of the cash dividends paid by the entire corporate sector over this same period.

The widespread waste and inefficiency of the public corporation and its inability to adapt to changing economic circumstances have generated a wave of organizational innovation over the past fifteen years – innovation driven by the rebirth of "active investors." By active investors I mean investors who hold large equity or debt positions, sit on boards of directors, monitor and sometimes dismiss management, are involved with the long-term strategic direction of the companies they invest in, and sometimes manage the companies themselves.

Active investors are creating a new model of general management. These investors include LBO partnerships such as Kohlberg Kravis Roberts and Clayton & Dubilier; entrepreneurs such as Carl Icahn, Ronald Perelman, Laurence Tisch, Robert Bass, William Simon, Irwin Jacobs, and Warren Buffett; the merchant banking arms of Wall Street houses such as Morgan Stanley, Lazard Frères, and Merrill Lynch; and family funds such as those controlled by the Pritzkers and the Bronfmans. Their model is built around highly leveraged financial structures, pay-for-performance compensation systems, substantial equity ownership by managers and directors, and contracts with owners and creditors that limit both cross-subsidization among business units and the waste of free cash flow. Consistent with modern finance theory, these organizations are not managed to maximize earnings per share but rather to maximize *value*, with a strong emphasis on cash flow.

More than any other factor, these organizations' resolution of the owner-manager conflict explains how they can motivate the same people, managing the same resources, to perform so much more effectively under private ownership than in the publicly held corporate form.

In effect, LBO partnerships and the merchant banks are rediscovering the role played by active investors prior to 1940, when Wall Street banks such as J.P. Morgan & Company were directly involved in the strategy and governance of the public companies they helped create. At the height of his prominence, Morgan and his small group of partners served on the boards of US Steel, International Harvester, First National Bank of New York, and a host of railroads, and were a powerful management force in these and other companies.

Morgan's model of investor activism disappeared largely as a result of populist laws and regulations approved in the wake of the Great Depression. These laws and regulations – including the Glass-Steagall Banking Act of 1933, the Securities Act of 1933, the Securities Exchange Act of 1934, the Chandler Bankruptcy Revision Act of 1938, and the Investment Company Act of 1940 – may have once had their place. But they also created an intricate web of restrictions on company "insiders" (corporate officers, directors, or investors with more than a 10 percent ownership interest), restrictions on bank involvement in corporate reorganizations, court precedents, and business practices that raised the cost of being an active investor. Their long-term effect has been to insulate management from effective monitoring and to set the stage for the eclipse of the public corporation.

Indeed, the high cost of being an active investor has left financial institutions and money management firms, which control more than 40 percent of all corporate equity in the United States, almost completely uninvolved in the major decisions and long-term strategies of the companies their clients own. They are almost never represented on corporate boards. They use the proxy mechanism rarely and usually ineffectively, notwithstanding recent efforts by the Council of Institutional Investors and other shareholder activists to gain a larger voice in corporate affairs.

All told, institutional investors are remarkably powerless; they have few options to express dissatisfaction with management other than to sell their shares and vote with their feet. Corporate managers criticize institutional selloffs as examples of portfolio churning and short-term investor horizons. One guesses these same managers much prefer churning to a system in which large investors on the boards of their companies have direct power to monitor and correct mistakes. Managers really want passive investors who can't sell their shares.

The absence of effective monitoring led to such large inefficiencies that the new generation of active investors arose to recapture the lost value. These investors overcome the costs of the outmoded legal constraints by purchasing entire companies – and using debt and high equity ownership to force effective self-monitoring.

A central weakness and source of waste in the public corporation is the conflict between shareholders and managers over the payout of free cash flow – that is, cash flow in excess of that required to fund all investment projects with positive net present values discounted at the relevant cost of capital. For a company to operate efficiently and maximize value, free cash flow must be distributed to shareholders rather than retained. But this happens infrequently; senior management has few incentives to distribute the funds, and there exist few mechanisms to compel distribution.

A vivid example is the senior management of Ford Motor Company, which sits on nearly $15-billion in cash and marketable securities in an industry with excess capacity. Ford's management has been deliberating about acquiring financial services companies, aerospace companies, or making some other multibillion-dollar diversification move – rather than deliberating about effectively distributing Ford's excess cash to its owners so they can decide how to reinvest it.

Ford is not alone. Corporate managers generally don't disgorge cash unless they are forced to do so. In 1988, the 1,000 largest public companies (by sales) generated total funds of $1.6 trillion. Yet they distributed only $108 billion as dividends and another $51 billion through share repurchases.[3]

Managers have incentives to retain cash in part because cash reserves increase their autonomy *vis-à-vis* the capital markets. Large cash balances (and independence from the capital markets) can serve a competitive purpose, but they often lead to waste and inefficiency. Consider a hypothetical world in which companies distribute excess cash to shareholders and then must convince the capital markets to supply funds as sound economic projects arise. Shareholders are at a great advantage in this world, where management's plans are subject to enhanced monitoring by the capital markets. Wall Street's analytical, due diligence, and pricing disciplines give shareholders more power to quash wasteful projects.

Managers also resist distributing cash to shareholders because retaining cash increases the size of the companies they run – and managers have many incentives to expand company size beyond that which maximizes shareholder wealth. Compensation is one of the most important incentives. Many studies document that increases in executive pay are strongly related to increases in corporate size rather than value.[4]

The tendency of companies to reward middle managers through promotions rather than annual performance bonuses also creates a cultural bias toward growth. Organizations must grow in order to generate new positions to feed their promotion-based reward systems.

Finally, corporate growth enhances the social prominence, public prestige, and political power of senior executives. Rare is the CEO who wants to be remembered as presiding over an enterprise that makes fewer products in fewer plants in fewer countries than when he or she took office – even when such a course increases productivity and adds hundreds of millions of dollars of shareholder value. The perquisites of the executive suite can be substantial, and they usually increase with company size.

The struggle over free cash flow is at the heart of the role of debt in the decline of the public corporation. Bank loans, mezzanine securities, and high-yield bonds have fueled the wave of takeovers, restructurings, and going-private transactions. The combined borrowings of all nonfinancial corporations in the United States approached $2 trillion in 1988, up from $835 billion in 1979. The interest charges on these borrowings represent more than 20 percent of corporate cash flows, high by historical standards.[5]

This perceived "leveraging of corporate America" is perhaps the central source of anxiety among defenders of the public corporation and critics of the new organizational forms. But most critics miss three important points. First, the trebling of the market value of public-company equity over the last decade means that corporate borrowing had to increase to avoid a major deleveraging.

Second, debt creation *without retention of the proceeds of the issue* helps limit the waste of free cash flow by compelling managers to pay out funds they would otherwise retain. Debt is in effect a substitute for dividends – a mechanism to force managers to disgorge cash rather than spend it on empire-building projects with low or negative returns, bloated staffs, indulgent perquisites, and organizational inefficiencies.

By issuing debt in exchange for stock, companies bond their managers' promise to pay out future cash flows in a way that simple dividend increases do not. "Permanent" dividend increases or multiyear share repurchase programs (two ways public companies can distribute excess cash to shareholders) involve no contractual commitments by managers to owners. It's easy for managers to cut dividends or scale back share repurchases.

Take the case of General Motors. On March 3, 1987, several months after the departure of GM's only active investor, H. Ross Perot, the company announced a program to repurchase up to 20 percent of its common stock by the end of 1990. As of mid-1989, GM had purchased only 5 percent of its outstanding common shares, even though its $6.8 billion cash balance was more than enough to complete the program. Given management's poor performance over the past decade, shareholders would be better off making their own investment decisions with the cash GM is retaining. From 1977 to 1987, the company made capital expenditures of $77.5 billion while its US market share declined by 10 points.

Borrowing allows for no such managerial discretion. Companies whose managers fail to make promised interest and principal payments can be declared insolvent and possibly hauled into bankruptcy court. In the imagery of G. Bennett Stewart and David M. Glassman, "Equity is soft, debt hard. Equity is forgiving, debt insistent. Equity is a pillow, debt a sword."[6] Some may find it curious that a company's creditors wield far more power over managers than its public shareholders, but it is also undeniable.

Third, debt is a powerful agent for change. For all the deeply felt anxiety about excessive borrowing, "overleveraging" can be desirable and effective when it makes economic sense to break up a company, sell off parts of the business, and refocus its energies on a few core operations. Companies that assume so much debt they cannot meet the debt service payments out of operating cash flow force themselves to rethink their entire strategy and structure. Overleveraging creates the crisis atmosphere managers require to slash unsound investment programs, shrink overhead, and dispose of assets that are more valuable outside the company. The proceeds generated by these overdue restructurings can then be used to reduce debt to more sustainable levels, creating a leaner, more efficient and competitive organization.

In other circumstances, the violation of debt covenants creates a board-level crisis that brings new actors onto the scene, motivates a fresh review of top management and strategy, and accelerates response. The case of Revco D.S., Inc., one of the handful of leveraged buyouts to reach formal bankruptcy, makes the point well.

Critics cite Revco's bankruptcy petition, filed in July 1988, as an example of the financial perils associated with LBO debt. I take a different view. The $1.25 billion buyout, announced in December 1986, did dramatically increase Revco's annual interest charges. But several other factors contributed to its troubles, including management's decision to overhaul pricing, stocking, and merchandise layout in the company's drugstore chain. This mistaken strategic redirection left customers confused and dissatisfied, and Revco's performance suffered. Before the buyout, and without the burden of interest payments, management could have pursued these policies for a long period of time, destroying much of the company's value in the process. Within six months, however, debt served as a brake on management's mistakes, motivating the board and creditors to reorganize the company before even more value was lost.[7]

Developments at Goodyear also illustrate how debt can force managers to adopt value-creating policies they would otherwise resist. Soon after his company warded off Sir James Goldsmith's tender offer, Goodyear chairman Robert Mercer offered his version of the raiders' creed: "Give me your undervalued assets, your plants, your expenditures for technology, research and development, the hopes and aspirations of your people, your stake with your customers, your pension funds, and I will enhance myself and the dealmakers."[8]

What Mr. Mercer failed to note is that Goodyear's forced restructuring dramatically increased the company's value to shareholders by compelling him to disgorge cash and shed unproductive assets. Two years after this bitter complaint, Tom Barrett, who succeeded Mercer as Goodyear's CEO, was asked whether the company's restructuring had hurt the quality of its tires or the efficiency of its plants. "No," he replied. "We've been able to invest and continue to invest and do the things we've needed to do to be competitive."[9]

Robert Mercer's harsh words are characteristic of the business establishment's response to the eclipse of the public corporation. What explains such vehement opposition to a trend that clearly benefits shareholders and the economy? One important factor, as my Harvard Business School colleague Amar Bhide suggests, is that Wall Street now competes directly with senior management as a steward of shareholder wealth. With its vast increases in data, talent, and technology, Wall Street can allocate capital among competing businesses and monitor and discipline management more effectively than the CEO and headquarters staff of the typical diversified company. KKR's New York offices and Irwin Jacobs' Minneapolis base are direct substitutes for corporate headquarters in Akron or Peoria. CEOs worry that they and their staffs will lose lucrative jobs in favor of competing organizations. Many are right to worry; the performance of active investors versus the public corporation leaves little doubt as to which is superior.

Active investors are creating new models of general management, the most widespread of which I call the LBO Association. A typical LBO Association consists of three main constituencies: an LBO partnership that sponsors going-private transactions and counsels and monitors management in an ongoing cooperative relationship; company managers who hold substantial equity stakes in an LBO division and stay on after the buyout; and institutional investors (insurance companies, pension funds, and money management firms) that fund the limited partnerships that purchase equity and lend money (along with banks) to finance the transactions.

Much like a traditional conglomerate, LBO Associations have many divisions or business units, companies they have taken private at different points in time. KKR, for example, controls a diverse collection of nineteen businesses including all or part of Beatrice, Duracell, Motel 6, Owens-Illinois, RJR Nabisco, and Safeway. But LBO Associations differ from publicly held conglomerates in at least four important respects (see Figure 13.1).

Management incentives are built around a strong relationship between pay and performance

Compensation systems in LBO Associations usually have higher upper bounds than do public companies (or no upper bounds at all), tie bonuses much more closely to cash flow and debt retirement than to

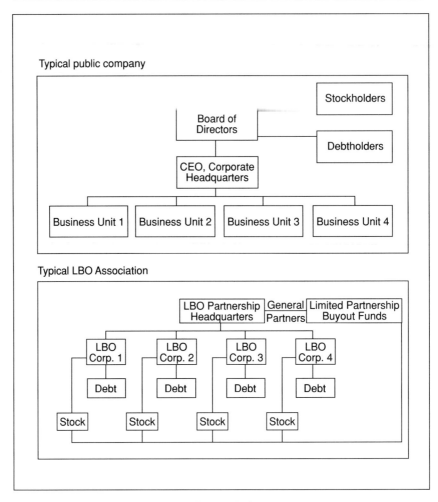

Figure 13.1 Public company vs. LBO Association

accounting earnings, and otherwise closely link management pay to divisional performance. Unfortunately, because these companies are private, little data are available on salaries and bonuses.

Public data are available on stock ownership, however, and equity holdings are a vital part of the reward system in LBO Associations. The University of Chicago's Steven Kaplan studied all public-company buyouts from 1979 through 1985 with a purchase price of at least $50 million.[10] Business unit chiefs hold a median equity position of 6.4 percent in their unit. Even without considering bonus and incentive plans, a $1,000 increase in shareholder value triggers a $64 increase in the personal wealth of business unit chiefs. The median public-company

CEO holds only 0.25 percent of the company's equity. Counting all sources of compensation – including salary, bonus, deferred compensation, stock options, and dismissal penalties – the personal wealth of the median public-company CEO increases by only $3.25 for a $1,000 increase in shareholder value.[11]

Thus the salary of the typical LBO business-unit manager is almost twenty times more sensitive to performance than that of the typical public-company manager. This comparison understates the true differences in compensation. The personal wealth of managing partners in an LBO partnership (in effect, the CEOs of the LBO Associations) is tied almost exclusively to the performance of the companies they control. The general partners in an LBO Association typically receive (through overrides and direct equity holdings) 20 percent or more of the gains in the value of the divisions they help manage. This implies a pay-for-performance sensitivity of $200 for every $1,000 in added shareholder value. It's not hard to understand why an executive who receives $200 for every $1,000 increase in shareholder value will unlock more value than an executive who receives $3.25.

LBO Associations are more decentralized than publicly held conglomerates

The LBO Association substitutes compensation incentives and ownership for direct monitoring by headquarters. The headquarters of KKR, the world's largest LBO partnership, has only 16 professionals and 44 additional employees. In contrast, the Atlanta headquarters of RJR Nabisco employed 470 people when KKR took it private last year in a $25 billion transaction. At the time of the Goldsmith tender offer for Goodyear, the company's Akron headquarters had more than 5,000 people on its salaried payroll.

It is physically impossible for KKR and other LBO partnerships to become intimately involved in the day-to-day decisions of their operating units. They rely instead on stock ownership, incentive pay that rewards cash flow, and other compensation techniques to motivate managers to maximize value without bureaucratic oversight. My survey of 7 LBO partnerships found an average headquarters staff of 13 professionals and 19 nonprofessionals that oversees almost 24 business units with total annual sales of more than $11 billion (see Table 13.2)

LBO Associations rely heavily on leverage

The average debt ratio (long-term debt as a percentage of debt plus equity) for public companies prior to a buyout is about 20 percent. The

Table 13.2 LBO partnerships keep staff lean

LBO Partnership	Year Started	Number of Professionals	Number of Nonprofessionals	Number of Business Units	Combined Annual Revenues (in billions of dollars)
Berkshire Partners	1986	14	6	15	$1
Butler Capital	1979	8	14	33	2.3
Clayton & Dubilier	1976	10	11	8	4.8
Gibbons Green van Amerongen	1969	6	7	12	5.3
Kohlberg Kravis Roberts	1976	16	44	19	58.7
Thomas H. Lee Co.	1974	15	12	25	8
Odyssey Partners	1950	19	39	53	NA

Kaplan study shows the average debt ratio for an LBO is 85 percent on completion of the buyout.

Intensive use of debt dramatically shrinks the amount of equity in a company. This allows the LBO general partners and divisional managers to control a large fraction of the total ownership without requiring huge investments they would be unable to make or large grants of free equity. For example, in a company with $1 billion in assets and a debt ratio of 20 percent management would have to raise $80 million to buy 10 percent of the equity. If that same company had a debt ratio of 90 percent, management would have to raise only $10 million to control a 10 percent stake. By concentrating equity holdings among managers and LBO partners, debt intensifies the ownership incentives that are so important to efficiency.

High debt also allows LBO Associations and other private organizations to tap the benefits of risk diversification once provided only by the public equity market. Intensive use of debt means much of it must be in the form of public, high-yield, noninvestment-grade securities, better known as junk bonds. This debt, which was pioneered by Drexel Burnham Lambert, reflects more of the risk borne by shareholders in the typical public company. Placing this public debt in the well-diversified portfolios of large financial institutions spreads equitylike risk among millions of investors, who are the ultimate beneficiaries of mutual funds and pension funds—without requiring those risks to be held as equity. Indeed, high-yield debt is probably the most important and productive capital market innovation in the last forty years.

LBO Associations have well-defined obligations to their creditors and residual claimants

Most buyout funds are organized as limited partnerships in which the partners of the sponsoring LBO firm serve as general partners. The buyout fund purchases most of the equity and sometimes provides debt financing. The limited partnership agreement denies the general partner the right to transfer cash or other resources from one LBO division to another. That is, all returns from a business must be distributed to the limited partners and other equity holders of that business. Such binding agreements reduce the risk of unproductive reinvestment by prohibiting cross-subsidization among LBO units. In effect, the LBO sponsor must ask its institutional investors for permission to reinvest funds, a striking difference from the power of public-company managers to freely shift resources among business units.

The management, compensation, and financial structures of the LBO Association square neatly with the rebirth of active investors. Institutional investors delegate the job of being active monitors to agents best qualified to play the role. The LBO partnerships bond their performance by investing their own resources and reputations in the transaction and taking the bulk of their compensation as a share in the companies' increased value.

To be sure, this delegation is not without its tensions. The fact that LBO partnerships and divisional managers control the LBO Association's small equity base but hold little of the debt creates incentives for them to take high-risk management gambles. If their gambles succeed, they reap large rewards by increasing their equity value; if their gambles fail, creditors bear much of the cost. But the reputational consequences of such reckless behavior can be large. As long as creditors behave rationally, an LBO partnership that tries to profit at the expense of its creditors or walks away from a deal gone sour will not be able to raise funds for future investments.

To date, the performance of LBO Associations has been remarkable. Indeed it is difficult to find any systematic losers in these transactions, and almost all of the gains appear to come from real increases in productivity. The best studies of LBO performance reach the following conclusions:

LBOs create large gains for shareholders Studies estimate that the average total premium to public shareholders ranges from 40 percent to 56 percent.[12] Kaplan finds that in buyouts that go public again or are otherwise sold (which occurs on average 2.7 years after the original transaction), total shareholder value increases by an average of 235 percent, or nearly 100 percent above market-adjusted returns over the same period.[13] These returns are distributed about equally between prebuyout shareholders and the suppliers of debt and equity to the transaction. Prebuyout shareholders earn average market-adjusted premiums of 38 percent, while the total return to capital (debt plus equity) for buyout investors is 42 percent. This return to buyout investors is measured on the total purchase price of the LBO, not the buyout equity. Because equity returns are almost a pure risk premium, and therefore independent of the amount invested, they are very high. The median market-adjusted return on buyout equity is 785 percent, or 125 percent per year.

Value gains do not come at the expense of other financial constituencies Some critics argue that buyout investors, especially managers, earn excessive returns by using inside information to exploit public shareholders. Managers do face severe conflicts of interest in these transactions; they cannot simultaneously act as buyer and agent for the seller. But equity-owning managers who are not part of postbuyout management teams systematically sell their shares into LBOs. This would be foolish if the buyout were significantly underpriced in light of inside information, assuming that these nonparticipating insiders have the same inside information as the continuing management team. Moreover, LBO auctions are becoming common; underpriced buyout proposals (including those initiated by management) quickly generate competing bids.

No doubt some bondholders have lost value through going-private transactions. By my estimate, RJR Nabisco's prebuyout bondholders lost almost $300 million through the downgrading of their claims on the newly leveraged company. This is a small sum in comparison to the $12 billion in total gains the transaction produced. As yet, there is no evidence that bondholders lose on average from LBOs. Evidence on LBOs completed through 1986 does show that holders of convertible bonds and preferred stock gain a statistically significant amount and that straight bondholders suffer no significant gains or losses.[14]

New data may document losses for bondholders in recent transactions. But the expropriation of wealth from bondholders should not be a continuing problem. The financial community is perfecting many techniques, including poison pills and repurchase provisions, to protect bondholders in the event of substantial restructurings. In fact, versions of these loss-prevention techniques have been available for some time. In the past, bondholders such as Metropolitan Life, which sued RJR Nabisco over the declining value of the company's bonds, chose not to pay the premium for protection.

LBOs increase operating efficiency without massive layoffs or big cuts in research and development   Kaplan finds that average operating earnings increase by 42 percent from the year prior to the buyout to the third year after the buyout. Cash flows increase by 96 percent over this same period. Other studies document significant improvements in profit margins, sales per employee, working capital, inventories and receivables.[15] Those who doubt these findings might take a moment to scan the business press, which has chronicled the impressive postbuyout performance of companies such as Levi Strauss, A. O. Scott. Safeway, and Weirton Steel.

Importantly, employment does not fall systematically after buyouts, although it does not grow as quickly as in comparable companies. Median employment for all companies in the Kaplan study, including those engaged in substantial divestitures, increased by nearly 1 percent. Companies without significant divestitures increased employment by 5 percent.

Moreover, the great concern about the effect of buyouts on R&D and capital investment is unwarranted. The low-growth companies that make the best candidates for LBOs don't invest heavily in R&D to begin with. Of the 76 companies in the Kaplan study, only 7 spent more than 1 percent of sales on R&D before the buyout. Another recent study shows that R&D as a fraction of sales grows at the same rate in LBOs as in comparable public companies.[16] According to Kaplan's study, capital expenditures are 20 percent lower in LBOs than in comparable non-LBO companies. Because these cuts are taking place in low-growth or declining industries and are accompanied by a doubling of market-adjusted value, they appear to be coming from reductions in low-return projects rather than productive investments.

Taxpayers do not subsidize going-private transactions　Much has been made of the charge that large increases in debt virtually eliminate the tax obligations of an LBO. This argument overlooks five sources of additional tax revenues generated by buyouts: capital gains taxes paid by prebuyout shareholders; capital gains taxes paid on postbuyout asset sales; tax payments on the large increases in operating earnings generated by efficiency gains; tax payments by creditors who receive interest payments on the LBO debt; and taxes generated by more efficient use of the company's total capital.

Overall, the US Treasury collects an estimated 230 percent more revenues in the year after a buyout than it would have otherwise and 61 percent more in long-term present value. The $12 billion gain associated with the RJR Nabisco buyout will generate net tax revenues of $3.3 billion in the first year of the buyout; the company paid $370 million in federal taxes in the year before the buyout. In the long term, the transaction will generate total taxes with an estimated present value of $3.8 billion.[17]

LBO sponsors do not have to take their companies public for them to succeed　Most LBO transactions are completed with a goal of returning the reconfigured company to the public market within three to five years. But recent evidence indicates that LBO sponsors are keeping their companies under private ownership. Huge efficiency gains and high-return asset sales produce enough cash to pay down debt and allow LBOs to generate handsome returns as going concerns. The very proliferation of these transactions has helped create a more efficient infrastructure and liquid market for buying and selling divisions and companies. Thus LBO investors can "cash out" in a secondary LBO or private sale without recourse to a public offering. One recent study finds that only 5 percent of the more than 1,300 LBOs between 1981 and 1986 have gone public again.[18]

Public companies can learn from LBO Associations and emulate many of their characteristics. But this requires major changes in corporate structure, philosophy, and focus. They can reduce the waste of free cash flow by borrowing to repurchase stock or pay large dividends. They can alter their charters to encourage large investors or experiment with alliances with active investors such as Lazard Frères' Corporate Partners fund. They can increase equity ownership by directors, managers, and employees. They can enhance incentives through pay-for-performance systems based on cash flow and value rather than accounting earnings. They can decentralize management by rethinking the role of corporate headquarters and shrinking their staffs.

Some corporations are experimenting with such changes – FMC, Holiday, and Owens-Corning – and the results have been impressive. But only a coordinated attack on the *status quo* will halt the eclipse of the public company. It is unlikely such an attack will proceed fast enough or go far enough.

Who can argue with a new model of enterprise that aligns the interests of owners and managers, improves efficiency and productivity, and unlocks hundreds of billions of dollars of shareholder value? Many people, it seems, mainly because these organizations rely so heavily on debt. As I've discussed, debt is crucial to management discipline and resolving the conflict over free cash flow. But critics, even some who concede the control function of debt, argue that the costs of leverage outweigh the benefits.

Wall Street economist Henry Kaufman, a prominent critic of the going-private trend, issued a typical warning earlier this year:

> Any severe shock – a sharp increase in interest rates in response to Federal Reserve credit restraint, or an outright recession that makes the whole stock market vulnerable, or some breakdown in the ability of foreign firms to bid for pieces of U.S. companies – will drive debt-burdened companies to the government's doorstep to plead for special assistance.[19]

The relationship between debt and insolvency is perhaps the least understood aspect of this entire organizational evolution. New hedging techniques mean the risk associated with a given level of corporate debt is lower today than it was five years ago. Much of the bank debt associated with LBOs (which typically represents about half of the total debt) is done through floating-rate instruments. But few LBOs accept unlimited exposure to interest rate fluctuations. They purchase caps to set a ceiling on interest charges or use swaps to convert floating-rate debt into fixed-rate debt. In fact, most banks require such risk management techniques as a condition of lending.

Critics of leverage also fail to appreciate that insolvency in and of itself is not always something to avoid – and that the costs of becoming insolvent are likely to be much smaller in the new world of high leverage than in the old world of equity-dominated balance sheets. The proliferation of takeovers, LBOs, and other going-private transactions has inspired innovations in the reorganization and workout process. I refer to these innovations as "the privatization of bankruptcy." LBOs *do* get in financial trouble more frequently than public companies do. But few LBOs ever enter formal bankruptcy. They are reorganized quickly (a few months is common), often under new management, and at much lower costs than under a court-supervised process.

How can insolvency be less costly in a world of high leverage? Consider an oversimplified example. Companies A and B are identical in every respect except for their financial structures. Each has a going-concern value of $100 million (the discounted value of its expected future cash flows) and a liquidation or salvage value of $10 million. Company A has an equity-dominated balance sheet with a debt ratio of 20 percent, common for large public companies. Highly leveraged Company B has a debt ratio of 85 percent, common for LBOs (see Figure 13.2).

Now both companies experience business reversals. What happens? Company B will get in trouble with its creditors much sooner than Company A. After all, Company B's going-concern value doesn't have to shrink very much for it to be unable to meet its payments on $85 million of debt. But when it does run into trouble, its going-concern value will be nowhere near its liquidation value. If the going-concern value shrinks to $80 million, there remains $70 million of value to preserve by avoiding liquidation. So Company B's creditors have strong incentives to preserve the remaining value by quickly and efficiently reorganizing their claims outside the courtroom.

No such incentives operate on Company A. Its going-concern value can fall dramatically before creditors worry about their $20 million of debt. By the time creditors do intervene, Company A's going-concern value will have plummeted. And if Company A's value falls to under $20 million, it is much more likely than Company B to be worth less than its $10 million salvage value. Liquidation in this situation is the likely and rational outcome, with all its attendant conflicts, dislocations, and costs.

The evolving US system of corporate governance and finance exhibits many characteristics of the postwar Japanese system. LBO partnerships act much like the main banks (the real power center) in Japan's keiretsu business groupings. The keiretsu make extensive use of leverage and intercorporate holdings of debt and equity. Banks commonly hold substantial equity in their client companies and have their own executives help them out of difficulty. (For years, Nissan has been run by an alumnus of the Industrial Bank of Japan, who became CEO as part of the bank's effort to keep the company out of bankruptcy.) Other personnel, including CFOs, move frequently between banks and companies as part of an ongoing relationship that involves training, consulting, and monitoring. Japanese banks allow companies to enter formal bankruptcy only when liquidation makes economic sense – that is, when a

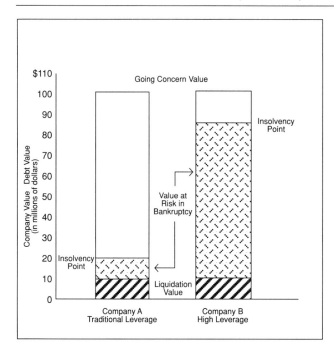

Figure 13.2 The privatization of bankruptcy

company is worth more dead than alive. Japanese corporate boards are composed almost exclusively of insiders.

Ironically, even as more US companies come to resemble Japanese companies, Japan's public companies are becoming more like US companies of fifteen years ago. Japanese shareholders have seldom had any power. The banks' chief disciplinary tool, their power to withhold capital from high-growth, cash-starved companies, has been vastly reduced as a result of several factors. Japan's victories in world product markets have left its companies awash in profits. The development of domestic and international capital markets has created ready alternatives to bank loans, while deregulation has liberalized corporate access to these funds. Finally, new legal constraints prevent banks from holding more than 5 percent of the equity of any company, which reduces their incentive to engage in active monitoring.

Many of Japan's public companies are flooded with free cash flow far in excess of their opportunities to invest in profitable internal growth. In 1987, more than 40 percent of Japan's large public companies had no net bank borrowings – that is, cash balances larger than their short- and long-term borrowings. Toyota, with a cash hoard of $10.4 billion, more than 25 percent of its total assets, is commonly referred to as the Toyota Bank.[20]

In short, Japanese managers are increasingly unconstrained and un-monitored. They face no effective internal controls, little control from the product markets their companies already dominate, and fewer controls from the banking system because of self-financing, direct access to capital markets, and lower debt ratios. Unless shareholders and creditors discover ways to prohibit their managers from behaving like US managers, Japanese companies will make uneconomic acquisitions and diversification moves, generate internal waste, and engage in other value-destroying activities. The long-term result will be the growth of bureaucracy and inefficiency and the demise of product quality and organizational responsiveness – until the waste becomes so severe it triggers a market for corporate control to remedy the excesses.

The Japanese remedy will reflect that country's unique legal system and cultural practices. But just as hostile takeovers, LBOs, and other control transactions went from unacceptable behavior in the United States to a driving force in corporate restructuring, so too will they take hold in Japan – once the potential returns outweigh the costs and risks of challenging the corporate *status quo*.

Meanwhile, in the United States, the organizational changes revitalizing the corporate sector will create more nimble enterprises and help reverse our losses in world product markets. As this profound innovation continues, however, people will make mistakes. To learn, we have to push new policies to the margin. It will be natural to see more failed deals.

There are already some worrisome structural issues. I look with discomfort on the dangerous tendency of LBO partnerships, bolstered by their success, to take more of their compensation in front-end fees rather than in back-end profits earned through increased equity value. As management fees and the fees for completing deals get larger, the incentives to do deals, rather than good deals, also increases. Institutional investors (and the economy as a whole) are best served when the LBO partnership is the last member of the LBO Association to get paid and when the LBO partnership gets paid as a fraction of the back-end value of the deals, including losses.

Moreover, we have yet to fully understand the limitations on the size of this new organizational form. LBO partnerships are understandably tempted to increase the reach of their talented monitors by reconfiguring divisions as acquisition vehicles. This will be difficult to accomplish successfully. It is likely to require bigger staffs, greater centralization of decision rights, and dilution of the high pay-for-performance sensitivity that is so crucial to success. As LBO Associations expand, they run the risk of recreating the bureaucratic waste of the diversified public corporation.

These and other problems should not cloud the remarkable benefits associated with the eclipse of the large public corporation. What surprises me is how few mistakes have occurred thus far in an organizational change as profound as any since World War II.

NOTES AND REFERENCES

1 Equity values based on trends in the Wilshire Index. Private-placement data from IDD Information Services as published in Sarah Bartlett, "Private Market's Growing Edge," *New York Times*, June 20, 1989.
2 For more analysis of the oil industry, see my article, "The Takeover Controversy: Analysis and Evidence," in *Corporate Restructuring and Executive Compensation* (Cambridge, Mass.: Ballinger, 1989).
3 Calculated from Standard & Poor's Compusat file.
4 Kevin J. Murphy, "Corporate and Managerial Remuneration," *Journal of Accounting and Economics* (1985), vol. 7, no. 1–3.
5 Federal Reserve Board, Balance Sheets of US, Economy.
6 G. Bennett Stewart III and David M. Glassman. "The Motives and Methods of Corporate Restructuring: Part II," *Journal of Applied Corporate Finance* (Summer 1988).
7 Stephen Phillips, "Revco: Anatomy of an LBO That Failed," *Business Week*, October 3, 1988.
8 "A Hollow Victory for Bob Mercer," *Industry Week*, February 23, 1987.
9 Jonathan P. Hicks, "The Importance of Being Biggest," *New York Times*, June 20, 1989.
10 Steven Kaplan, "The Effects of Management Buyouts on Operating Performance and Value," *Journal of Financial Economics* (1989), vol. 24, no. 2.
11 Michael C. Jensen and Kevin J. Murphy, "Performance Pay and Top Management Incentives," *Journal of Political Economy* (1990), vol. 98, no. 2.
12 Yakov Amihud, "Leveraged Management Buyouts and Shareholders' Wealth," in *Leveraged Management Buyouts: Causes and Consequences* (Homewood, III.: Dow Jones-Irwin, 1989).
13 That is, returns net of the returns that would normally be earned on these securities, given their level of systematic risk (beta) and general market returns.
14 L. Marais, K. Schipper and A. Smith, "Wealth Effects of Going Private for Senior Securities," *Journal of Financial Economics* (1989), vol. 23, no. 1.
15 In addition to Kaplan, see Abbie Smith, "Corporate Ownership Structure and Performance," unpublished paper, University of Chicago, 1989. See also Frank R. Lichtenberg and Donald Siegel, "The Effects of Leveraged Buyouts on Productivity and Related Aspects of Firm Behavior," *National Bureau of Economic Research*, 1989.
16 Lichtenberg and Siegel, NBER, 1989.
17 Michael C. Jensen, Steven Kaplan, and Laura Stiglin, "Effects of LBOs on Tax Revenues of the U.S. Treasury," *Tax Notes*, February 6, 1989.
18 Chris Muscarella and Michael Vetsuypens, "Efficiency and Organizational Structure: A Study of Reverse LBOs," unpublished paper, Southern Methodist University, April 1989.
19 Henry Kaufman, "Bush's First Priority: Stopping the Buyout Mania," *Washington Post*, January 1, 1989.
20 Average (book value) debt ratios fell from 77 percent in 1976 to 68 percent in 1987. Given the 390 percent increase in stock prices over this period,

market value debt ratios fell even more dramatically. Figures caculated from the NEEDS Nikkei Financials file for all companies on the First Section of the Tokyo Stock Exchange.

Part V

How corporate parents influence their businesses

Authors in the previous part presented some strong criticisms of the performance of diversified companies; Michael Porter charged that the corporate strategies of many large companies have failed, and Michael Jensen advocated new ownership structures to prevent managers from pursuing unprofitable diversification. It is difficult to square these views with those in earlier sections, where notable economists such as Oliver Williamson and David Teece argued that multibusiness companies can be economically efficient, and other authorities provided advice on how diversified companies can create value through resource allocation, portfolio building and synergy management. It is paradoxical that while economic theory and managerial advice focus on how multibusiness companies can create value, much of the evidence on performance suggests that such companies frequently destroy value in their businesses. Evidently, the influence that corporate parents actually exert on their businesses often undermines the benefits that are at least ideally possible in multibusiness companies. The readings in this part therefore examine the nature of the influence that corporate parents in fact have, and the circumstances in which this influence is likely to be positive or negative.

There has been relatively little empirical research on the sort of influence that corporate managers exercise on their businesses. Alfred Chandler's seminal book, *Strategy and Structure*, about the historical development of multidivision, multibusiness companies is a notable exception, as is Alfred Sloan's personal account of his experiences as chief executive of General Motors.[1] Norman Berg has also investigated the workings of Textron, a classic diversified conglomerate of the 1960s.[2] None of these writings, however, casts much light on why corporate managements so often fail to create value.

During the 1980s, contingency theory helped to provide new understandings about the potential for good or ill of corporate management. In simple terms, contingency theory asserts that different businesses need different sorts of corporate management, and that the extent to which corporate managements will add or detract value depends on the degree to which their particular influence fits the businesses in their portfolio. Thus, researchers studying the impact of portfolio planning observed that, while many companies identified different strategic missions for their businesses, they none the less stuck to a common administrative approach to those differing businesses, thereby undermining performance. Authorities such as Philippe Haspeslagh and Richard Hamermesh therefore urged corporate managers to think harder about the requirements of businesses with differing strategic missions, and to tailor their administrative approaches to the needs of their businesses.[3] Michael Goold and Andrew Campbell also developed a contingency approach, classifying multibusiness companies into one of three basic management styles and arguing that the style needed to match with the needs of the businesses.[4]

In the first chapter in this part, 'The functions of headquarters in the multibusiness firm', Alfred Chandler develops and refines this line of argument. Chandler reviews the historical development of multibusiness companies, distinguishing between the 'entrepreneurial' functions of top management (i.e., devising strategies to create value by exploiting corporate resources) and the 'administrative' functions (i.e., monitoring the use of resources and the performance of the different businesses or divisions in the company). Chandler claims that in industries that involve high R & D expenditures, costly investments and specialized marketing, the corporate headquarters needs to concentrate on its entrepreneurial functions and be closely involved in strategic planning for its businesses. In more mature, stable industries, however, the emphasis needs to be on the administrative functions, with more reliance on financial control processes. Chandler's basic message is, therefore, that corporate headquarters will only add value to their businesses if they adopt a role that is suitable for them; otherwise they are liable to damage performance.

Chandler draws on empirical research into companies both in the US and the UK. Similar conclusions are reached, however, by Charles Hill, whose work is more strictly theoretical.[5] Hill argues that multibusiness firms can pursue different types of economic benefits; related diversifiers seek economies of scale and scope, while unrelated firms or conglomerates aim to achieve more efficient resource allocation and control than external capital markets. The appropriate role and organization of headquarters therefore depend on a firm's economic rationale. Conglomerate firms that have businesses across a range of industries should have small corporate headquarters with competence in acquiring underperforming businesses whose performance can be improved through appropriate controls, while the headquarters units of firms with closely related businesses should be larger, much more closely involved in co-ordination, and knowledgeable about the strategic issues facing their businesses. Hill, therefore, also proposes a contingency approach to the role of corporate headquarters, arguing that it should depend on the needs of the businesses in the portfolio.

In the chapter, 'The value of the parent company', Andrew Campbell, Michael Goold and Marcus Alexander, co-directors of the Ashridge Strategic Management Centre, draw on research into a cross section of multibusiness companies. They argue that the fit between the corporate centre and the businesses in the portfolio must go beyond the overall role or function of the corporate centre. These authors examine the specific ways in which a corporate parent exerts its influence: through influence on the stand-alone performance of businesses – for example, decisions about resource allocation and the setting of objectives and performance targets; through facilitating linkages across businesses; through corporate development activities such as acquisitions and new ventures; and through corporate functions and services. But in each of these areas, the potential for destroying value is much greater than most managers recognize. Even when the corporate level does succeed in adding value in one area, this is often offset by value destruction in other areas. The authors argue that only under certain conditions is a corporate parent likely to create value: there must be scope for improvement in the businesses, the corporate parent must possess specific capabilities or resources that fit the needs of the businesses and therefore enable it to correct under-performance, and the parent must understand the businesses well enough to avoid influencing them in inappropriate ways.

C. K. Prahalad and Richard Bettis provide a further insight into the ways in which top managers in multibusiness firms influence their businesses in their chapter, 'The dominant logic: a new linkage between diversity and performance', which won the prize for the best *Strategic Management Journal* article in the decade from 1980 to 1989. Prahalad and Bettis develop the concept of 'dominant logic'. The dominant logic of a corporate management group is the approaches, systems and mind-sets that are typically used to address critical issues in the businesses. Prahalad and Bettis argue that a group of businesses is best managed when the dominant logic of top managers matches the strategic characteristics and requirements of the businesses. If a multibusiness company includes many businesses with different strategic characteristics, the task of top executives becomes much more difficult, because a single dominant logic would not fit all of the businesses. Even businesses which utilize a common technology or resource may none the less have very different strategic requirements. These authors suggest that dominant logic helps us understand the limits to successful diversification. It is not simply the number of different businesses which makes managing diversified companies a complex task, but the strategic differences across those businesses.

Thus, when the businesses in the portfolio have different strategic logics, it is likely that top managers, with their single dominant logic, will have a negative impact on some of the businesses. The authors included in this Part V help us to understand why some multibusiness companies succeed in enhancing the performance of their businesses while many others are much less successful. They emphasize the importance of the fit between the corporate parent and the needs of the businesses. Such fit is essential because of the powerful influence corporate parents exercise over their businesses. When the characteristics of the parent do not match the needs of the business, the parent can easily undermine business performance and destroy value.

NOTES

1 Chandler, Alfred D. (1962) *Strategy and Structure*, Cambridge, Mass: The MIT Press. Mass.; Sloan, Alfred P. (1963) *My Years With General Motors*, New York: Doubleday.
2 Berg, Norman A. (1969) 'What's different about conglomerate management?' *Harvard Business Review*, pp. 112–20, November–December.
3 Haspeslagh, Philippe (1982) 'Portfolio Planning: uses and limits', *Harvard Business Review*, pp. 58–73, January–February; Hamermesh, Richard G. and White, Roderick E. (1984) 'Manage beyond portfolio Analysis', *Harvard Business Review*, pp. 103–9, January–February.
4 Goold, Michael and Campbell Andrew (1987) *Strategies and Styles*, Oxford: Basil Blackwell.
5 Hill, Charles W. L. (1994) 'Diversification and Economic Performance: Bringing Structure and Corporate Management Back into the Picture', in Rumelt, Richard P., Schendel, Dan and Teece, David J. (eds) *Fundamental Issues in Strategy Research: A Research Agenda*, Boston, Mass.: Harvard Business School Press.

ADDITIONAL READING

Berg, Norman A. (1969) 'What's different about conglomerate management?' *Harvard Business Review*, pp. 112–20, November–December.
A study of the new conglomerates of the 1960s and their management techniques.
Chandler, Alfred D. (1962) *Strategy and Structure*, Cambridge, Mass.: The MIT Press.
The definitive study of the development of multidivisional companies in the US.
Goold, Michael and Campbell, Andrew (1987) *Strategies and Styles*, Oxford: Basil Blackwell.
Study of how the corporate centre adds value in large diversified companies. The authors identify distinct management styles, explore the strengths and weaknesses of each style and discuss the types of businesses likely to benefit from each management style.
Grant, Robert M. (1988) 'On "Dominant Logic", Relatedness and the Link between Diversity and Performance', *Strategic Management Journal* 9(6): 639–42, November–December.

An elaboration of Prahalad and Bettis's argument on dominant logic. Grant argues that the key contribution of the concept is looking for relatedness at the strategic, rather than operational, level.

Hill, Charles W. L. (1994) 'Diversification and Economic Performance: Bringing Structure and Corporate Management Back into the Picture', in Rumelt, Richard P., Schendel, Dan and Teece, David J. (eds) *Fundamental Issues in Strategy Research: A Research Agenda*, Boston, Mass.: Harvard Business School Press.

A survey of the economic and management literature on multibusiness firms and a framework for understanding the appropriate functions of Headquarters in different types of multibusiness companies which have different economic rationales.

Sloan, Alfred P. (1963) *My Years With General Motors*, New York: Doubleday.

A classic account of the development of the modern corporation and the functions of the head office.

Chapter 14

The functions of headquarters in the multibusiness firm

Alfred D. Chandler, Jr

The functions of the headquarter (HQ) unit in the multibusiness firm is indeed a basic question for the understanding of the operations of modern business enterprise. The decisions made by the senior executives at their headquarters have been absolutely critical to the performance of such multinational and multiproduct companies. For those corporate executives not only monitor the current performance of their several businesses but also determine and implement investment in facilities and personnel required for future production and distribution in the different product and geographical markets they serve. On such decisions depend the competitive success or failure of their enterprises and the national industries in which they operate.

I begin this analysis of the functions of the HQ unit by reviewing the evolution of the multibusiness firm and the administrative structures created to operate it. I then examine how corporate headquarters carry out its functions, focusing largely on its entrepreneurial and administrative activities. Throughout this analysis I stress that industries have different characteristics, reflecting different technologies of production and different market demands. So I conclude by examining how in implementing these functions senior executives at HQ units came to understand the limits to growth and the boundaries of the firm and how, in turn, the functions and boundaries were shaped by the different characteristics of the industries in which the firms operated.

THE HISTORICAL EVOLUTION OF THE MULTIBUSINESS FIRM

The modern business enterprise with its hierarchy of lower, middle and top management appeared in the United States and Europe suddenly in the 1850s to operate the new forms of transportation and communication. By the 1880s railroad and telegraph companies had created organizational structures and internal control systems (including the adoption of the M-Form [multidivisional form] for multiregional systems) as complex as those created a half century later in industry and commerce. At the same time the unprecedented volume, speed, and above all, regularity of the flow of goods and messages through the economy made possible by the railroad and the telegraph, revolutionized the processes of production and distribution. In distribution the modern mass retailer appeared – the department store, the mail-order house and the chain store. In production, the technological potential created by the new flows precipitated a wave of technological innovations that swept across Western Europe and the United States – a phenomenon that historians have properly termed the Second Industrial Revolution.

The new technologies transformed the processing of tobacco, grains, whiskey, beer, sugar, vegetable oil and other foods. They revolutionized the refining of oil and the making of metals and materials – steel, nonferrous metals, particularly copper and aluminum, glass, abrasives and other materials. They created brand new chemical industries that produced man-made dyes, fibers, fertilizers and medicines. They brought into being a wide range of machinery – light machines for sewing, agriculture and office uses; heavier standardized machinery such as elevators, refrigerating equipment, and greatly improved printing presses, pumps and boilers. Most revolutionary of all were the new machines to mass produce and distribute electric power. That new energy source not only transformed the mechanical process of production within factories and created new forms of urban transportation, but it revolutionized the processing of many metals and chemicals.

These industries that began to drive economic growth and transformation late in the nineteenth century had two basic characteristics that differentiated them from existing labor-intensive industries such as textiles, apparel, furniture, paper, lumber, leather, shipbuilding, and mining. So did the transforming industries of later decades – those based on the internal combustion engine before World War II and those based on electronics, particularly the computer, after that war. First, all the processes of production were far more capital-intensive than in the older industries. That is, the ratio of capital to labor per unit of output was much higher. Secondly in these industries large plants had significant cost advantages over smaller ones in producing a single line of products. Up to a minimum efficient size (based on the nature of technology and the size of the market) the cost per unit dropped more quickly as the volume of output increased than was the case in the labor-intensive industries. Besides such economies of scale large works often utilized economies of scope – those resulting from making different products in a set of facilities using the same raw and semi-finished materials and the same intermediate processes of production.

In all these capital-intensive industries, however, the new large plants were able to maintain the cost advantages of scale and scope only if the entrepreneurs who built them made two other sets of investments. They had to create a national and then international marketing and distributing organization. And they had to recruit lower and middle managers to coordinate the flow of products through the processes of production and distribution, and top managers to coordinate and monitor current operations and to plan and allocate resources for future activities. The small number of 'first movers', those that made the three-pronged set of investments in manufacturing, marketing and management essential to exploit fully the economies of scale and scope, quickly dominated their industries and usually continued to do so for decades. Challengers did appear, but they were only a few.

The three-pronged investment by the first movers created the modern industrial enterprise administered through functional departments whose heads, with the president, formed the corporate headquarters. (That is, new firms became administered through the U-Form [unitary form] of organization.) That investment also transformed the structure of industries. The new capital-intensive industries were quickly dominated by a small number of large managerial enterprises which competed for market share and profit in a new oligopolistic manner. Price remained a significant competitive weapon. But these firms competed more forcefully through functional and strategic efficiency; that is, by performing more effectively the different processes of production, distribution, marketing, product development and the like, and by moving more quickly into expanding markets and out of declining ones. The test of such competition was changing market share. In the new oligopolistic industries market share and profits changed constantly.

Such oligopolistic competition sharpened the product-specific capabilities of workers and managers. Such capabilities, plus retained earnings obtained from the new and profitable capital-intensive technologies became the basis for the continuing growth of these managerial enterprises. Firms did grow by combining with competitors (horizontal combination) or by moving backward to control materials and forward to control outlets (vertical integration), but they did so usually in response to specific situations that varied with time and place. For most firms in these capital-intensive industries the continuing long-term strategy of growth was expansion into new markets – either into new geographical areas, or into related product markets. The move into geographically distant markets was normally based on competitive advantage of organizational capabilities developed from exploiting economies of scale. Moves into related industries rested more on those advantages developed from the exploitation of the economies of scope. Such organizational capabilities honed by oligopolistic competition provided the dynamic for the continuing growth of such firms, of the industries which they dominated, and of the national economies in which they operated.

The extent of this growth into new geographical and related product markets by the 200 largest industrial enterprises in the United States, Britain and Germany from the 1880s to the 1940s is described and documented in my book, *Scale and Scope*. An appendix in that book gives the product lines of these companies (by three digit SIC categories of the US Census) for 1930 and 1948. A follow-up list for 1973 is given in Chandler and Tedlow (1985). Scott (1973) summarized several studies on the continuing diversification into new markets of the largest 100 firms in the United States, Britain, France and Italy between 1950 and 1970. By the 1960s the multibusiness enterprise had become the norm in modern capital-intensive, technologically complex industries.

In the interwar years in the United States, but rarely before 1950 in Europe, senior executives rationalized the management of this multimarket growth through the adoption of some variations of the M-Form with its corporate headquarters and integrated product or geographical divisions. (In this paper the terms corporate headquarters, corporate office and HQ unit are synonymous.) The M-Form came into being when senior managers operating through existing central-ized, functionally departmentalized U-Form structures realized that they had neither the time nor the necessary information to coordinate and monitor day-to-day operations, or to devise and implement long-term plans for the several product lines. The administrative overload had become simply too great. At Du Pont, the innovator in 1921 and then in other new multibusiness enterprises, the solution was to establish divisions to administer the production and distribution of their major product lines or geographical regions and a general or corporate headquarters to administer the enterprise as a whole. The divisional offices coordinated production and distribution (and often product development) using the U-Form structure. From the start the functions of the new corporate headquarters of these new multimarket business enterprises became and remained that of maintaining the long-term health (usually defined as continued profitability) and growth of their firms.

To implement this role the executives at the new headquarters carried out two closely related functions.[1] One was entrepreneurial or value-creating, that is, to determine strategies to maintain and then to utilize for the long-term the firm's organizational skills, facilities and capital and to allocate resources – capital and product-specific technical and managerial skills – to pursue these strategies. The second was more administrative or loss-preventive. It was to monitor the performance of the operating divisions; to check on the use of the resources allocated; and, when necessary, redefine the product lines of the divisions so as to continue to use effectively the firm's organizational capabilities.

The administrative tasks of monitoring were, of course, intimately related to the entrepreneurial task of strategic planning and resource allocation. For monitoring provided the essential information about changing technology and markets, and the nature and pace of competition in the different businesses. And it permitted a continuing evaluation of the performance of divisional operating managers. Indeed, management development has long been a critical function of the corporate headquarters. For of all the enterprise's resources, the product-specific and firm-specific managerial skills are the most essential to maintain the capabilities of its existing businesses and to take the enterprise into new geographical and product markets where such capabilities gave it a competitive advantage.

Facilitated by adoption of the M-form, the size and numbers of multibusiness firms – both multinational and multi-industrial – increased rapidly, particularly after World War II. So too did the variety of markets they entered; and, therefore, the number of divisions they operated. Such growth intensified competition. Until the 1960s, however, world events – the two global wars and the massive global depression of the 1930s – held back the full impact of international and inter-industry competition. In the 1960s the European and Japanese enterprises began to compete with American firms in the United States and abroad, and many more American firms moved overseas. In these same years US, enterprises, which had begun to enter into closely related markets during the interwar years, began to expand in this manner more aggressively. For example, by the 1960s, agricultural, mining, industrial, and construction machinery and truck and auto companies had moved into each other's markets, and glass, rubber, and food firms expanded their activities in chemicals. Rapidly growing R&D expenditures intensified such inter-industry competition.

Continued growth into new markets encouraged structural change, for like the initial diversification, it resulted in a decision-making overload at both the corporate office and division levels. Senior executives at Du Pont reviewing the company's organizational structure 'saw striking parallels between the company's problems in the 1920s and those of the late 1960s' (Hounshell and Smith 1988: 586). The solution at Du Pont and many other companies was to form integrated business units within the divisions that coordinated and controlled a single product or very closely related product lines. In others it was to place the divisions under larger 'group' offices.

But, whatever the names used, by the 1970s most large multibusiness enterprises had three (not just two) levels of autonomous planning and administrative offices. They are referred to in this paper as the business unit, the division and the corporate HQ or office. The first normally operated through functional U-Form structure, while the divisions, like the corporate office, operated through a version of the M-Form structure with its own staff and senior executives responsible for profit, market share, and other measures of performance.[2]

The corporate office continued to define growth paths and goals for the corporation as a whole and to monitor the performance of the subordinate operating units. In these same years the headquarter's role as a mediator with government agencies and other public bodies increased sharply with new regulatory legislation. By the 1980s, according to the study of corporate office executives of twelve large American manufacturing companies by Gordon Donaldson and Jay Lorsch, several chief executive officers (CEOs) said that they spent 30–40 percent of their time in carrying out such matters (Donaldson and Lorsch 1983: 13).

Intensified competition resulting from new players from abroad and from related industries gave many US companies the greatest competitive challenge they had faced since their founding decades earlier. Many US managers responded by reinvesting to improve their competitive capabilities in their own and closely related industries. But others began to grow by moving into industries in which their organizational competencies provided little or no competitive advantage. Because many had had little competition from abroad since World War II – and because they were being told by some academics that management was a generalist skill – many of these executives had come to believe that, if they were successful in their own industry, they could be just as successful in others. For many, as Donaldson and Lorsch (1983) have documented, the goal of this broad based diversification was for many managers long-term growth. Others simply enjoyed empire building. Moreover, their companies were cash-laden precisely because the postwar years of American hegemony had been so prosperous.

So these managers sought to invest their retained earnings in industries that appeared to show a greater profit potential than their own. And they did so even though those industries were only distantly and sometimes unrelated to their companies' core capabilities. They lacked the knowledge of their target industries' operations and they lacked, too, the necessary capabilities to build plants and develop personnel through direct internal investment as they had in the past. So these diversifiers grew by acquisition or, occasionally, merger.

In these same years a new form of multibusiness enterprise appeared, the conglomerate. The conglomerate can be defined as a firm that grew almost wholly by making acquisitions in unrelated industries. Such firms were of two types. One was firms in older sectors of the economy whose capabilities failed to give them a base for growth comparable to those of the large industrial diversifiers. They were utilities and transportation firms such as ITT, Tenneco, Illinois Central Industries, Northwest Industries, Ogden and Greyhound and industrials such as Textron, US Industries, Walter Kidde, Dart Industries and Colt Industries. These included 11 of the 15 conglomerates listed among the top 200 in 1973. A few years later similar firms appeared in Britain including BTR and Hanson Trust. As they diversified, most sold off their original business. The other type was enterprises in 1973 that entrepreneurs created from scratch. Four of the top fifteen US conglomerates were such entrepreneurial start-ups – LTV, Litton, Gulf + Western, and Teledyne. Some of these enterprises profited by improving the management and hence the profits of the companies acquired. But others increased the value of their shares through creative, but legal, accounting that recorded on the balance sheets an inflated picture of their assets, revenues, and earnings.

Table 14.1 compiled by Norman Berg documents the differences in the size and personnel of corporate HQ of conglomerates and those of diversified majors. The differences reflect the differences in the strategies of diversification. For each the number of general executives was about the same. The difference lay in the size and activities of the corporate staff. Since their unrelated activities offered no synergies, the conglomerates had no need for manufacturing, marketing, purchasing, traffic and research staff. Even in finance and control they employed smaller numbers than did the major diversifiers. Only in public, including government, relations were the numbers much the same.

IMPLEMENTING THE ENTREPRENEURIAL AND ADMINISTRATIVE FUNCTIONS

I have presented this historical review to explain why the multibusiness firm became such a pervasive and powerful institution in modern economies, why the corporate office appeared and how its functions developed. A more precise understanding of these functions and of the mechanisms used to implement them calls for a more detailed analysis based on information from specific enterprises. I rely on Michael Goold and Andrew Campbell's, *Strategies and Styles: The Role of the Centre in Managing Diversified Corporations* (1987) for information on sixteen carefully selected British diversified and conglomerate firms. For the US conglomerates I examine the historical experience of International Telephone and Telegraph (ITT) with brief references to other conglomerates. For the US multibusiness firms I review the history of two diversified majors, General Electric (GE) and Du Pont with a brief

Table 14.1 Differences in size and personnel of the offices of diversified majors and conglomerates
Statistical data on companies

| Statistical data | 1969 | | | | | | | 1959 | |
Companies	Sales (million $)	Fortune rank	Assets (million $)	Employees (thousands)	Number of divisions	4-Digit SIC #	Approx. # acquis. 1959–69	Sales (million $)	Fortune rank
Diversified majors:									
Bendix:	1,468	72	980	63.5	53	30	16	684	62
Borg-Warner	1,087	108	949	41.6	35	25	3	650	68
Ingersoll-Rand	711	160	690	33.7	27	31	11	162	269
Company 'X'	About 500	—	—	—	—	About 35	n/a	—	—
Average	About 1,000	—	—	—	—	About 30	—	—	—
Company 'Y'						About 50	n/a	—	—
Conglomerates:									
Gulf & Western	1,564	64	2,172	85.0	37	89	45	—	—
Kidde (W. J.)	786	143	775	35.7	55	n/a	74 (64–69)	41	—
Lear-Siegler	587	186	319	26.6	56	40	50	87	431
Litton	2,177	39	1,580	116.0	70	64	80	126	322
Textron	1,682	57	895	70.0	32	85	55	308	146
Average	1,359	98	1,148	66.6	50	70	61	—	—

Table 14.1 Continued
Organizational data on companies

Companies	Diversified majors							Conglomerates						
	Company				Four cos:			Company					Five cos:	
Functions	A	B	C	X	Total	Avg.	'Y'	F	G	H	I	J	Total	Avg.
General executives	5	5	4	2	16	4	23	4	1	4	3	14	26	5
Finance	28	61	101	144	334	84	582	8	22	29	91	106	256	51
(of which Control)	(10)	(36)	(78)	(107)	(231)	(58)	(424)	(6)	(12)	(8)	(38)	(49)	(113)	(23)
Legal-secretarial	4	10	22	42	78	20	92	1	7	5	6	66	85	17
Personnel adm.	11	6	20	25	62	16	90	1	2	3	10	20	36	7
Research and dev.	54	130	139	232	555	139	1,012	0	0	0	0	0	0	0
Marketing	5	0	34	0	39	10	101	0	0	0	0	0	0	0
Manufacturing	5	1	0	5	11	3	190	0	0	0	0	0	0	0
Public relations	1	6	9	16	32	8	45	5	3	5	6	9	28	6
Purchasing and traffic	10	1	33	4	48	12	30	5	0	0	2	0	2	0
Corporate planning	3	3	2	6	14	5	8	5	4	1	7	9	26	5
Totals	126	223	364	476	1,189	301	2,173	24	39	47	125	224	459	91

Source: Norman Berg, 'Corporate Role in Diversified Companies', Harvard Business School Working Paper 71-2BP2, reprinted in Alfred D. Chandler, Jr. and Richard S. Tedlow, The Coming of Managerial Capitalism: A Casebook on the History of American Economic Institutions, (Homewood, IL: Richard D. Irwin 1985), pp. 758–9.

reference to International Business Machines (IBM). As these data come almost wholly from manufacturing enterprises, the analysis here is essentially the functions of corporate HQ in industrial multibusiness enterprises.

Because the data are rich and the functions carefully categorized in the Goold and Campbell study, I begin with the British companies. In *Strategies and Styles* the two authors describe three major types of management styles used by senior managers at corporate headquarters: Strategic Planning, Strategic Control, and Financial Control. 'The three main styles,' they write, 'lead to different strategies and different results' (Goold and Campbell, 1987: 87). I would argue that these three styles, like the internal organization of the headquarters, result from different paths of growth and, therefore, from different patterns of investment and from different sets of organizational capabilities. These capabilities, in turn, reflect the different characteristics of the businesses in which the firms operate. Finally, the success of HQ units in adapting those styles to their industries' characteristics determines the effective size and boundaries of their enterprises.

Table 14.2 suggests the different paths to growth by diversification followed by the firms in each of these styles. The companies in the Strategic Planning category are by and large the least diversified, operate the smallest number of businesses, have the highest linkages between divisions and the highest overlap between business units within divisions. The Strategic Control companies operate more businesses, have fewer overlaps between the divisions and on the whole have less synergy between the business units. Three of the five Financial Control companies are the most diversified in the sample. Of the other two, Ferranti is small in terms of sales and assets and Tarmac is the only construction company on the list. All five have the lowest linkages between divisions and the lowest overlap between units within divisions.

IMPLEMENTING FUNCTIONS IN FINANCIAL CONTROL COMPANIES

The basic differences in size, personnel, and, therefore, the activities of the corporate office in Financial Control companies and those in the two Strategic categories are much the same as the differences between the American conglomerate and major diversifiers indicated in Table 14.1. The Financial Control companies in Britain grew almost wholly by acquisition, not by direct internal investment. Hanson Trust, BTR and the smaller Tarmac were true conglomerates. They followed the pattern of most US conglomerates by moving out of their original business after acquiring firms in unrelated industries. General Electric Company (GEC, no relation to the American GE) was a government sponsored merger

Table 14.2 Three types of management styles and their organization structures

The 16 participant companies

Company	Main activity	Sales 1985 (£m)	Rank in Times 1000
BP	Oil	47,156	1
ICI	Chemicals	10,725	4
GEC	Electricals	5,222	14
Imperial	Tobacco, food, drinks	4,919	15
BTR	Diversified	3,881	18
Hanson Trust	Diversified	2,675	33
Courtaulds	Textiles and chemicals	2,173	45
STC	Electronics	1,997	48
BOC	Gases and healthcare	1,901	54
Cadbury Schweppes	Confectionery, soft drinks	1,874	56
UB	Foods	1,806	60
Tarmac	Construction	1,536	72
Plessey	Electronics	1,461	76
Lex	Distribution	1,041	110
Vickers	Engineering	611	159
Ferranti	Electronics	568	169

Strategic planning companies' organization structures (1985)

	Number of divisions	Overlaps beween divisions	Number of businesses	Overlaps between businesses within divisions
BOC	4	Low–medium	37	High
BP	11	Medium	11 (S)	High
Cadbury Schweppes	4	Low–medium	45 (H)	High
Lex	3	Low	9 (H)	Medium–high
STC	4	Medium–high	20–25	High
UB	3	Medium	13	Medium

Strategic Control companies: organization structure

	Number of divisions	Overlaps between divisions	Number of businesses	Overlaps between businesses within divisions
Courtaulds	8	Low–medium	30–40	Medium
ICI	20	Generally low	50–60	High
Imperial	3	Low	20–25	Medium
Plessey	3	Medium	20–25	High
Vickers	10	Low	25–30	Medium

Financial Control companies: organization structure

	Number of divisions	Overlaps between divisions	Number of businesses	Overlaps between businesses within divisions
BTR	27	Low	150	Low
Ferranti	5	Low	3	Medium
GEC	12	Low	170	Medium
Hanson Trust	9	Low	70	Low
Tarmac	6	Low	6	—

Source: Michael Goold and Andrew Campbell, *Strategies and Styles: The Role of the Centre in Diversified Corporations*, (Oxford: Basil Blackwell, 1987), pp. 7, 48, 87, 112. Reproduced by permission of Blackwell Publishers.

of Britain's three leading electrical equipment companies which, after a modicum of rationalization, continued to operate quite autonomously with relatively little supervision from the corporate office. GEC grew largely through acquisition. Ferranti, too, is a product of British government policy. The government restored it from bankruptcy in 1974 in order to permit it to regain its position in data handling systems, instrumentation and other electronic businesses for which the military was its largest customer.

In all five the corporate office has remained small. Like those of the US conglomerates these offices include a few general line officers and almost no functional staff executives except in finance and public relations. The division managers are considered part of the corporate headquarters. The division managers 'play a linking and surveillance role between the units and the centre' (Goold and Campbell 1987: 115). So while the corporate executives may suggest strategic moves, the business units within the divisions are responsible for defining their strategies.

In these Financial Control companies the budget is the basic means of control. It thus becomes almost by default the primary instrument of planning. Budgets are prepared by the business units and reviewed and approved by the corporate office with relatively little discussion between executives in the center and the operating units. In approving capital expenditures the corporate office looks for a quick (2–3-year) payback. Each budget (and each project) is treated on its own merits and not in relation to a larger overall strategic plan. Nor do the budgets of one unit relate their activities to those of another.

The budget is taken very seriously. It is considered a contract between the corporate office and business unit. The center monitors the performance by comparing monthly and quarterly reports of actual results against the budget. (Goold and Campbell 1987: 129). Current financial performance is the critical measure of achievement. Failure to meet financial targets often means a change in the management of the unit. In drawing up budgets the goal is short-term profit rather than reinvestment for long-term earnings based on a unit's organizational capabilities. Of the sixteen companies studied by Goold and Campbell the Financial Control companies had the best profit performance and the largest growth, but growth was almost wholly through the buying of new operating units and not through direct internal investment within existing operating units (ibid.: 309–11).

The basic function of the corporate HQ in these Financial Control companies was then administrative or loss preventive. It was to review the financial performances of the businesses controlled and to adjust the enterprises' portfolio accordingly. Weak performers were sold off and new ones that met the logic of this type of control were purchased. In their acquisitions the British conglomerates avoided the buying of enterprises in technologically complex, capital-intensive industries where product and process innovations required long-term investment and associated risks. Lord Hanson and the senior executives of BTR have expressed themselves strongly about this strategy (Goold and Campbell 1987: 135, 252; Feder, 1989). Neither of the two Financial Control companies that remain in high technology industries – GEC and Ferranti – have prospered. GEC has moved out of consumer electronics and control systems, and has purchased a shipyard and a weighing machine company. Recently Ferranti sold off its basic data system division which had accounted for 37 per cent of its business. If they are to succeed, Goold and Campbell predict, 'a change to Strategic Control may occur' (1987: 144).

The history of the US conglomerates has been more complex than those in the UK, possibly because the British firms have been more successful in defining their portfolios. The experience has been one of expansive growth through unrelated acquisitions in the 1960s and into the 1970s, then drastic pullbacks in the 1980s.

A brief review of the history of ITT, the pioneering, and for a long time, the largest of the US conglomerates is revealing. Until the 1960s, ITT was a giant global telecommunication enterprise. (Formed in 1920, it acquired in 1925 all the foreign operations of Western Electric, the manufacturing arm of AT&T.) In the 1960s under Harold Geneen it began to diversify. As losses of its operating telephone companies in Eastern Europe immediately after World War II and then in Latin America reduced its operations and slowed its growth, the new CEO developed a well considered strategy of growth at home rather than abroad. This plan meant growth by acquisition in unrelated industries, for in the United States AT&T and its Western Electric dominated telecommunications. By the mid-1970s ITT had acquired some 300 companies.

Geneen, an accountant by training, required a detailed set of monthly financial reports from every operating unit. These were analyzed at monthly staff meetings attended by Geneen and all operating managers. The CEO also called for annual business plans and detailed 5-year plans. In the 1970s Geneen was heralded as a pioneer in a new form of business administration-management by the numbers. It did not work. The overload became staggering. One participant, the president of Avis, estimated that comparing and analyzing the annual business plans represented thirteen months work for the corporate staff (Dinerstein 1980).

After Geneen reluctantly retired in 1979, his successor R. V. Araskog pulled back and attempted 'to transform ITT from a loosely based conglomerate into a rational, broadly based, international electronics corporation with major stress on telecommunications,' that is to return to its core business (Sobel, 1982: 70). But it was much too late. ITT never recovered its markets abroad from its powerful competitors, Siemens and Ericsson. By 1988 it had withdrawn from telecommunications and electronics. By then Araskog had sold off over 100 companies and consolidated the remaining seven businesses: four in services – hotels, insurance, financial lending, and information services. These are today its major source of revenue. The other three were industrial businesses: auto parts, pumps and valves, and electric components and systems largely for the US military. By the late 1980s the senior executives at ITT had learned that growth was limited by the corporate HQ's ability to manage profitably its unrelated operating units.

By that time executives in corporate headquarters of other conglomerates had learned much the same lesson. Northwest Industries had been dismembered. LTV and Greyhound were then in bankruptcy proceedings. Gulf + Western had spun off over 100 of its operations to become a movie company – Paramount Communications. Kidde and US Industries had been swallowed up by the Hanson Trust. Those that remained among the US 200 largest industrials had followed ITT's pattern of selling off a major share of their operations and concentrating on industries whose production processes, final products and markets remained relatively stable. If they stayed with more technologically advanced products, they normally sold them to the Department of Defense. Thus, Tenneco focused on shipbuilding for the US Navy, agricultural equipment, and packaging materials as well as its original natural gas pipeline business. Litton had narrowed its business to four product lines – marine engines, industrial automation, oil and gas exploration and defense electronics. By 1989 well over half its business came from defense contracts. Teledyne did much the same with 35 percent of its revenues coming from the federal government. In 1985 Textron spun off twenty-two divisions and acquired Avco, a long time producer of aircraft parts and equipment which complemented its Bell aircraft unit purchased in 1960. By 1989 airspace/defense business accounted for 46 percent of sales, financial services and insurance 29 percent, and consumer products 25 percent.

As the corporate officers of the conglomerates came to realize, the small headquarters as depicted in Table 14.3 had only facilities for financial control. That is, the functions of the corporate HQ were primarily administrative or loss preventive. Such controls were effective in service industries and in industries involving relatively inexpensive production facilities and small R&D expenditures. If the conglomerates remained in more technologically complex, capital-intensive industries, they had little choice but to pull back and to concentrate their portfolios in a small number of groups of related product lines about which the

Table 14.3 Planning and control systems for multidivisional firms

	Financial control	Strategic control	Strategic planning
Size of HQ	small	large	large
Mechanisms of control:			
(a) budgets	strong	moderate	weak
(b) strategic plans and reports	none	moderate	strong
Responsibility for strategic definition	business units	divisions	corporate HQ
Inter-business unit interdependencies within divisions	low	moderate	high
Examples	ITT, Hanson Trust	Du Pont to 1980 GE in 1980s	IBM to 1980 Du Pont in 1980s

senior executives had more than just financial knowledge and experience and close contacts with buyers, particularly government officials. And they have been challenged to develop strategic and planning capabilities within those industry groups. These firms, like British GEC, appear to be shifting to a style of strategic control.

IMPLEMENTING FUNCTIONS IN STRATEGIC PLANNING AND STRATEGIC CONTROL COMPANIES

The most successful of the conglomerates, a new phenomenon of the 1960s, were those that acquired and managed companies in industries where financial control alone was sufficient to maintain profitability. On the other hand, nearly all major diversifiers in both Britain and the United States were long established enterprises whose headquarters from their beginnings carried out both the entrepreneurial, value-creation function as well as the administrative, loss-prevention one. That is, their relatively large headquarters (Table 14.3) had been involved in strategy planning and control. All but one of the companies in Goold and Campbell's sample of strategically oriented companies were long lived. That exception, Lex, began as a distributor for Volvo and then continued to operate as a distributing and leasing firm. Except for three leaders in food, drink and tobacco – Cadbury Schweppes, United Biscuits and Imperial Tobacco (Hanson acquired the last in 1986) – these British firms were in industries with relatively technologically complex processes and products. All but the food companies had large research and

development departments. All grew much more by direct internal investment than by acquisition. This was also true of the American firms
studied – IBM, GE and Du Pont. Each of the three US companies have
been for decades the leading firm in each of three significant transforming
industries of the past century. Their experience, particularly the growth
and pullback of the second two, helps to indicate the ways the ability of
the corporate office to carry out their basic functions sets limits to
growth.

The planning and control functions and the mechanisms developed by
the British companies to implement them in the two strategic styles
identified by Goold and Campbell – Strategic Planning and Strategic
Control – had many similarities. In both, the strategic definition began in
the first instance in the business units. In both, division headquarters
played a significant role in the review process. In both, the officers at
the three levels – business unit, division, and corporate office – had
extensive staffs. Both types of companies had annual planning cycles
with annual reviews of 'business plans,' and 'operating plans.' These
resulted in budgets that, unlike those in the Financial Control companies,
were linked to long-term strategic plans. In three companies such plans
were formally developed on an annual basis, and in one every two years.
For the others long-term strategic planning was less formalized. The aim
of the business plans and operating reviews was 'to raise the quality of
business thinking, to allow multiple perspectives to be expressed, and to
permit corporate views to influence strategy' (Goold and Campbell
1987: 70).

The difference between Strategic Planning and Strategic Control
companies was that in the first the corporate office played a more
decisive role. The different attributes of these two planning and control
systems and also those of financial control are summarized in Table 14.3.
Corporate executives in Strategic Planning companies reviewed strategic
themes, relating them to their portfolio mix, and examined the particular
thrusts or suggestions of the individual business units. In planning they
focused attention on interbusiness and interdivisional opportunities and
dependencies. The proposals for new projects requiring large-scale capital
allocation and entries into new businesses came from both the business
and the corporate offices; but corporate sponsorship was essential for
any major new initiative. Long- and short-term goals (both strategic and
financial) and budgets emerged from the agreed-upon plans. Such plans
did not exist at the Financial Control companies. Monitoring was carried
out through detailed, regularly scheduled reports from the business units
giving actual results. But, unlike at the Financial Control companies,
financial targets and budgets were not sacrosanct in terms of incentives
(bonuses) or sanctions (management removal). Instead, they were the
basis for discussions between the business units and centers concerning

progress made toward achieving long-term strategic and financial goals. As a result, in the Strategic Planning companies, administrative controls were employed much more flexibly than in those companies using the Financial Control style or even in those firms relying more on strategic controls.

The Strategic Control companies differed from the Strategic Planning ones in that much of the planning devolved upon the divisional headquarters. This difference reflected a greater number of business units within the firms and a wider variety of businesses served by the firms. The divisions often had as large functional staffs, including those for research and development, as had the corporate office. (Where divisions were placed in groups, the group executives had very little staff and were considered members of the corporate office.) The divisions, responsible for coordinating the activities of the business units under their command, integrated the planning process. Corporate executives rarely made or suggested strategic themes or thrusts to guide the strategic planning process. They made little attempt to coordinate synergies or review interdependencies between divisions. Capital projects and proposals for new business entries came from the divisions, not the corporate office, with the corporate office taking the initiative only on closures and divestitures.

The corporate office did make the final allocation of resources to support the agreed upon strategies and priorities. It set more precisely than did those in Strategic Planning companies' long- and short-term goals and strategic and financial targets. As in firms in the other categories, business units reported regularly and in detail to corporate management. But, unlike the Strategic Planning companies, budgets and financial goals were taken seriously. They were not the basis for discussions. They were targets to be met in terms of both incentives and sanctions.

In these companies the corporate office became a headquarters of headquarters. That is, the divisional headquarters carried out most of the functions of the corporate HQs in the Strategic Planning companies, but under the guidance of the corporate office. The arrangement had weaknesses. Often in defining and, particularly, in implementing strategy, long-term gains were sacrificed for short-term ones. Opportunities that might have been explored if closer attention had been paid to planning were lost. Such weaknesses suggest how the capabilities of the corporate HQ can limit the effective size of firms in capital-intensive, technologically complex industries. Does a corporate HQ supervising subcorporate HQs really add value? A brief review of the American leaders in each of the three most transforming industries of the past century – computers, electrical equipment and chemicals – raises the same question.

AMERICAN EXAMPLES: IBM, GE AND DU PONT

Although there are no studies comparable to that of Goold and Campbell on the American experience, an examination of the functions of the corporate headquarters at IBM, GE, and Du Pont – supplement the British story. In addition the data available on these companies provide a much longer time-span than the single decade of the 1980s – the time-frame for the British cases. The GE and Du Pont stories, in particular, tell of shifts in planning and control procedures.

In each of the three companies the relationships of the corporate office to the operating units differed widely. The IBM story is one of a highly focused business machinery company that through impressive strategic planning became one of the most powerful first movers in a modern industry. That of GE is one of a relatively unstructured, centralized industrial empire that underwent drastic and dramatic decentralization in the 1950s. In the 1960s and 1970s it probed the boundaries of strategic planning and then in the 1980s moved toward strategic control. The Du Pont experience is more one of a coming up against the limits of strategic control in the 1960s and 1970s and then in the 1980s moving closer to strategic planning.

IBM

IBM, a producer since 1911 of a variety of business machines became the first mover in the computer industry with the introduction in 1965 of its mainframe System 360, the result of five years of intense research and development. As entrepreneurs developed new computer architectures for different markets, IBM quickly moved into these markets, becoming the leading producer at home and abroad of minicomputers in the 1970s and of microcomputers in the 1980s. As it advanced in computers, it shed its typewriter and other business machine products. Even so, no other computer company operated in more different markets.

Since the 1960s senior management has been committed to a heavy investment in research and development and to the strategic planning and management development necessary to help assure long-term pay-back on that investment. Although it occasionally made forays outside of computers, it quickly pulled back. Concentrating on its core products, the corporate office continues to play a major role in planning – a process in which large staffs at both the corporate headquarters and the operating divisions participate. As one executive stressed: 'We want to integrate as much as possible and maintain control through centralized planning and tracking, but we also want to decentralize implementation and operating decisions. There are no major strategic decisions that are delegated' (Goold and Campbell, 1987: 261).

By the 1980s the planning process of IBM had become elaborate. It had three parts which were closely integrated with the control mechanisms. 'Program plans' that usually came from the operating units were meshed with a division (group) plan. The division staff working with the corporate staff then hammered out an 'operating plan' which is a 2-year rolling budget. As one executive explained: 'The operating plan is the major management vehicle at IBM. It is the point at which all resources are approved – where you get your capital, your headcount, your expense dollars, your parts committed to you from other divisions' (Goold and Campbell, 1987: 165). The 5-year Strategic Plan has been an extension of the operating plan. The literature available does not indicate how tight the financial and strategic targets are set. But given the continuing interaction between the corporate office and the operating divisions, one can assume that they have been flexible, as the reasons for differences between actual performance and targets set would have been discussed constantly as forecasted conditions changed. In these ways, then, at IBM the entrepreneurial (strategic) and the administrative (monitoring) functions have been closely intertwined and have reinforced one another. In a fast moving high technology industry, where new products are constantly coming on stream' IBM strategic planning systems have aided the corporate office to maintain dominance for forty years in competition with well established firms at home and abroad, and with entrepreneurial start-ups at home.

GE

If IBM was the first mover in the most important transforming and growth industries of the second half of the twentieth century, GE and Du Pont were leaders in the two most important of such industries at the end of the nineteenth century. Both pioneered in modern research and development. Both were among the very first to become multibusiness enterprises on the basis of such R&D.

GE, like the other first-movers in the electrical equipment sector – Westinghouse, and two German companies, Siemens and AEG – quickly expanded beyond its original line of electric power generating and transmission equipment, urban traction and industrial motors. By World War I its work on wire insulation had already taken it into varnishes, adhesives, and plastics, and its improvement of the light bulb into metal alloys and vacuum tubes. Then came the development of radio and also X-ray equipment, and other medical equipment. In the 1920s, too, GE began to produce a wide variety of electrical appliances, electric locomotives and in the 1930s diesel locomotives. The number of its product lines (lines for which operating results were accounted for separately) rose from 10 in 1900, to 30 in 1910, 85 in 1920, 193 in 1930, and 281 in 1940 (Chandler 1990: 221).

These diversified lines were administered through a hodge-podge of operating units – functional departments, integrated product divisions, subsidiaries and special ventures. Strategic planning and monitoring was carried out by the corporate office in centralized fashion, that is, on paper at least. By the late 1930s the need to rationalize these lines and to create a structure to manage them was obvious. But World War II delayed reorganization.

Then in 1946 Ralph Cordiner began to restructure. That restructuring became even more sweeping after he became president in 1950. In line with the management thinking of the time, Cordiner fashioned a highly decentralized structure. He set up seventy autonomous product departments each with its own production, marketing and engineering units. These were placed into divisions which, in turn, were administered by one of five groups (Chandler 1962: 369). If one department grew large, Cordiner divided it into smaller parts. Thus, there were several departments producing much the same consumer appliances. By 1960 the number of departments had reached 106.

By the 1960s GE's corporate office was losing control. Existing departments grew, often by developing new lines. Diversification had moved the company into more distantly related areas – commercial jet engines, nuclear power, and computers to name a few. In the late 1960s the company had 190 departments (business units in the terminology of this paper), 46 divisions and 10 groups. By then the overload on the corporate office was becoming intolerable. Profits were down, capital appropriations were made without priorities, and new ventures were doing poorly (Aguilar and Hamermesh 1985: 777–9, 783). The limits of growth appeared to have been reached.

Frederick Borsch who succeeded Cordiner in 1963 began to restructure. First, he tightened administrative controls over the departments. He did so by strengthening the divisional staffs and by improving the divisional reporting and accounting controls. Next in 1968 he strengthened the corporate office's planning procedures. He set up two boards: the Corporate Operations Board, responsible for administration; and the Corporate Policy Board, responsible for strategy formulation.

A planning structure was then laid over the existing operational structure. Strategic Business Units (SBUs) were formed to carry out the planning process. They were aligned as much as possible to discrete businesses. Close to half of the divisions (21) also became SBUs. Sixteen SBUs were departments, four were placed in groups. Each of the operating departments sent its strategic plans to one of forty-three such SBUs. After coordinating these plans each SBU forwarded it to the Corporate Policy Board. Each SBU had a manager in charge supported by a full-time planner. Thus, by 1980 there were approximately 200 senior planners at GE (Aguilar and Hamermesh 1985: 779–86; Goold and Campbell 1987: 272).

A new CEO, Reginald Jones, who took office in 1972 put the new planning process into effect. It worked well. The company product lines were pruned. Many of the less profitable spun off. A total of seventy-six lines existed during Jones' term. The profit and loss sheets improved after the hemorrhaging computer division was sold off. Similar sales helped to clean up the 'venture messes.' The corporate office was also impressed by the way the new system improved its ability to carry out the critical task of selection and development of managers.

Nevertheless, the planning overload at the top continued. To reduce that pressure Jones created another planning level – the Sector. It represented a macro-business or industry area. In the words of one senior planning officer:

> Conceptually the SBUs are expected to develop new business opportunities by extending into contiguous product-market areas. Sectors are expected to develop new SBUs by diversifying within their macro-industry scopes. And corporate is expected to develop new sectors by diversifying into unserved macroindustries.
>
> (Aguilar and Hamermesh 1985: 788)

The senior sector executive acted as the GE spokesperson for his macroindustry, had oversight for the SBUs in that Sector, and was responsible for integrating the SBUs' strategies into a Sector strategic plan.

To stimulate further the planning process the corporate office now began that process by sending 'strategic challenges' to the Sectors and SBUs. The SBUs then worked out plans with their Sector Office. Once approved these plans were converted into budgets for each of the departments. Their department general managers were expected to meet the budgeted net income and return-on-investment figures. These targets were taken seriously, but with the recognition that short-term considerations should not threaten long-term positions (Goold and Campbell 1987: 272). In these ways, then, Reginald Jones attempted to carry out both the strategic and administrative functions of the corporate office. But given the size of GE and the diversity of its product lines, planning and capital appropriations procedures became bureaucratized. The company was responsible for simply too many units for the corporate office to play an influential role in shaping their strategies. The limits of HQ planning thus determined the limits to growth of the enterprise.

Under John Welch, who took Jones' place in 1981, the company began to shift away from a Strategic Planning style toward one of Strategic Control. Welch sized down GE's product lines and shifted the company's product mix even more than Jones had done in the early

1970s. The new CEO kept the SBUs but greatly reduced their staff, as he did those at other levels. He preferred to by-pass the planning process and to have executives in corporate headquarters talk directly with one or two SBU chiefs at a time. By 1985 Welch had eliminated the sectors and groups. As he reduced the administrative and planning organization, Welch intensified the role of the corporate office in management development. GE, like IBM, had long paid close attention to the training, positioning, and evaluation of its managers.

Earlier in his tenure, Welch grouped GE business units into three categories: core, high technology, and service. The managers of the 'core' divisions – the long-established, mature, stable businesses – received relatively little planning or direction from the corporate office. Instead, it controlled through tight budgets and carefully defined strategic targets. Managers' bonuses, options and future prospects in the company were closely related to their success in meeting these targets. The same style appears to have been used for the GE services category. On the other hand, in new high technology endeavors, Welch and the corporate headquarters continued to play a large role in strategic planning.

By the end of the 1980s, the corporate office at GE had more sharply defined its corporate strategy and structure. The strategy was that, as Welch wrote in the 1989 Annual Report (page 3): 'Each business was to be number one or number two in its particular market. For those that were not, we had a very specific prescription – they were to be fixed, sold or closed.'

By then GE's many lines were integrated into thirteen different businesses whose heads report directly to Welch, the Chairman, and two Vice Chairmen. Of these businesses, three remain in high technology areas where new product development is critical to continuing competitive success – Aerospace, Aircraft Engines, and Medical Equipment. The others include Electrical Distribution and Control, Industrial Power Systems, Lighting, Motors, Transportation Systems, Plastics, Appliances, and Communication and Services. Except for the last of these, the others are all businesses in which GE has successfully operated for at least seventy years. In addition, there are Financial Services and NBC, the latter coming out of the merger with RCA.

Clearly, the new strategy has meant concentration on those products for which production, distribution and continuing improvement GE has developed impressive organizational capabilities over the decades. With the dismantling of much of Jones' planning apparatus, the management style has moved towards one of Strategic Control. At GE, strategy became based primarily on the utilization of organizational capabilities that had been honed over the decades. In managing these businesses in technologically complex, capital-intensive industries where competitive advantage lies more in constantly improving product and process rather than in developing new products and processes, Strategic Control was the most suitable style to carry out both the entrepreneurial and administrative functions of the corporate office. That is, strategic planning devolved on the businesses (on the divisions in this paper's terms) with the corporate office maintaining overall strategic control.

Du Pont

At Du Pont underlying changes in the planning and control functions of the corporate office came more slowly than they did at GE. Recently, these more evolutionary developments have turned the company from relying on a weak strategic control style to a stronger Strategic Planning one. So at Du Pont the story is the reverse of that of GE. In both, the changes in the activities of the HQ unit reflected differences in the characteristics of the industries in which they came to operate.

Du Pont, whose research organization was as old as that of General Electric, was a pioneer in creating the multidivisional form as an answer to management overload resulting from a strategy of product diversification. Indeed, its structure became a model for the growing number of multibusiness enterprises that appeared in the United States in the 1920s and 1930s. (Chandler 1962: Ch. 2). After the reorganization in 1921 the senior executives of the corporate office carried out both planning and monitoring by maintaining constant and close contact with the heads of the product divisions. (At Du Pont such divisions were termed departments.) In the 1921 reorganization the division heads were given full authority and responsibility for carrying out all activities in their product line, including the improvement of product and process and the planning for future production and distribution. Although each of the five to seven members of the Executive Committee of the board were assigned product divisions to oversee, they were explicitly denied direct line authority over division managers. They could advise but not order. And until the very end of the 1970s this distinction remained sacrosanct.

The Executive Committee met every Monday in the chart room with the senior managers of one division (in the 1920s and 1930s the divisions numbered between 7 and 10). There, with charts that incorporated nearly every aspect of past and present performance, they reviewed operations and performance and did so by relating them to earlier plans and targets. They then discussed future operations. On the basis of these meetings and the information provided by both corporate and division staffs, the corporate financial office developed budgets and capital appropriation plans that in turn were discussed and approved by the Executive Committee. In this way the corporate office influenced the direction and pace of growth and took control over the performance of the operating divisions.

From the late 1920s on, the corporate department for research began to play a major part in defining the direction of the growth of the enterprise, particularly into markets not yet reached by the divisions. It did so by investing in fundamental research in untapped fields of chemistry. In 1927 the department began such research on polymer chemistry that led to the development of man-made fibers (including Nylon, Dacron, Orlon and Lycra), and neoprene and other man-made materials. Central Research (initially called Central Chemical Department) was responsible for basic research and for the far more costly initial development of new processes and products. Once commercialized, these were turned over to the product divisions for production and distribution and for further refinement. This structure permitted Du Pont to continue its highly profitable strategy of growth through closely related diversification (Hounshell and Smith 1988: Chs. 5, 12).

After World War II the company continued to grow by expanding existing lines and developing new ones. Soon, divisions such as textile fibers became as large as the Du Pont Company itself had been in the 1920s. Because of the successful exploitation of fundamental research by Central Research, the Executive Committee now allocated extensive sums to the divisions for comparable research. At the same time other chemical firms both in the United States and Europe were making much larger investments in research and development than they had before World War II. So product lines proliferated and competition intensified.

Yet, the basic planning and administrative structure of the company remained unchanged. The Executive Committee no longer had the time nor information to influence divisional plans effectively. The divisions, in turn, became increasingly powerful large multibusiness enterprises in their own right. Close working contact between members of the Executive Committee at headquarters and the senior division managers disintegrated. The Committee now did little more than approve of divisional plans and review actual performance by relating it to the plans. As at General Electric, profits went down, product development in both divisional and corporate research became much more costly, and payback on product development was smaller and required more time. Nor were product developments and other interdependencies coordinated effectively within the company. As at GE, the limits to growth appeared to have been reached.

As these difficulties began to press upon the Executive Committee, it entered into an extended debate over what should be done. The outcome was a decision to expand the Development Department which since 1903 had carried on planning activities at the corporate office. An energetic young manager, Edwin A. Gee, took charge. Gee's mandate was to appraise each of the division's 'diversifying activities in order to detect any inadequacies in technology, markets and organization' (Hounshell and Smith 1988: Ch. 22; Fast 1977: Ch. 5). His department was also to seek out new business opportunities in areas not covered by the divisions. For antitrust reasons Gee and the Executive Committee decided not to grow through acquisition of even small firms and to stay out of defense oriented industries. Instead, Gee's department was to concentrate on developing new ventures that used some of Du Pont's specific organizational capabilities. Some of the new products developed did pay off. But by the mid-1960s the Committee and Gee agreed that the 'New Venture Program' was not a success. The heavy investment in R&D was not paying off. Too often the company's specific functional capabilities were not enough to achieve a strong competitive advantage in the new product markets. And the necessary complementary facilities and skills were too costly and time consuming to create.

This outcome and the continuing low rate of return on investment led the Executive Committee for the first time since 1920 to appraise, seriously, itself and the basic strategy and structure of the company. One Committee member, Lester Sinness, attributed the deteriorating earnings to low research productivity and the failure of the Executive Committee to play a guiding and coordinating role. He considered,

> the research output of the company as a whole to be disgraceful and inexcusably low in proportion to the caliber of the men we employ, the facilities we give them, and the amount of money we allow them to spend.
>
> (Hounshell and Smith 1988: 531)

But essentially, he insisted, the Executive Committee had only itself to blame. In the earlier self-examination, proposed changes were:

> submerged in a welter of conflicting opinions within the Executive Committee . . . Through a distorted preoccupation with the concept of the departmental autonomy . . . the Executive Committee loses sight of its own responsibilities. [It] appears to sit only as a judicial body reviewing the past performances of the Departments [divisions] and weighing whatever projects and proposals on policy and procedures may emanate from the Industrial or Staff departments. The Executive Committee seldom discusses or initiates anything of and by itself.

Through its 'ritual schedule of charts and reports' Sinness continued, 'the Committee no longer had the time needed to examine and discuss periodically the future of the company or determine whether the company policies, organizations and procedures needed altering.'

Another member urged the Committee 'to take a more critical role in originating and implementing programs to insure the future health of the company.' By the mid-1960s Du Pont suffered from ineffective planning mechanisms for the enterprise as a whole and weak controls over the operations and performance of the operating units.

Even so, change came slowly. The president, Charles B. McCoy, and other members of the Committee were cautious. In 1967 came the organizational restructuring mentioned earlier that created the autonomous business units (termed profit centers) whose managers were responsible for production, distribution, R&D and profit and loss in the product business they headed. The departmental (divisional) headquarters monitored and helped to plan the activities of the business units under their supervision. They decided, for example, how funds for research would be allocated to their different business units.

The next move came seven years later when the Committee created a small twelve person Corporate Plans Department. It was to have 'broad responsibility' for coordinating all strategic business planning activities in the company, specifically by analyzing Du Pont's portfolio of businesses (Hounshell and Smith 1988: 585). The Development Department was folded into Central Research. At the urging of the new planning department the Executive Committee reduced the research budgets in the operating divisions, particularly funds for fundamental research, and put tighter controls on the initiating of research programs not closely related to existing product lines or technologies. The company's long-term, more fundamental research became concentrated in the enlarged corporate research department. The Committee agreed that Corporate Plans working with Central Research should play a critical role in defining the company's broader strategic moves into new lines. To assure that it carried out this function the Committee in 1979 gave its member designated as research advisor, Edward G. Jefferson, line authority over Central Research. This was the first time since the 1921 reorganization that an Executive Committee member was given such authority. Jefferson's initial strategic move was a commitment to the company's long-term development of the new biogenetic field and other life sciences, particularly in pharmaceuticals and agricultural chemicals (Hounshell and Smith 1988: 505–7).

After Jefferson became CEO in May 1981 he continued to strengthen the role of the corporate office in both its planning and resource allocation and monitoring functions (Hounshell and Smith 1988: 591). Members of the Executive Committee began to have authority and responsibility for the performance of the divisions under their supervision. During the 1980s, as the company began to move into specialty chemicals, electronics, medical and other high technology products and to spin off some of its commodity chemicals, they became more deeply involved in strategic planning. But the lines of authority and responsibility were becoming unclear. Moreover, in the making of strategic and administrative decisions, Executive Committee members tended to see issues in terms of the businesses they knew best and those for which they were becoming increasingly responsible. In addition, the top managers of Conoco, the oil company, unexpectedly acquired in 1983, had not yet been integrated into the corporate office. The resulting pressures led to a careful analysis of the company's organization. In the Fall of 1991 came the announcement of the most far reaching internal restructuring that the company had undergone in seventy years.

The new organizational structure abolished the Executive Committee and existing Departments (divisions in the terminology used here). An Office of the Chairman and an Operating Group were created. The first consisted of the Chairman (the CEO), a vice chairman (whose special area was science and technology), and Executive Vice President for Conoco. Attached to that office were two Senior Vice Presidents – one for Human Resources and Corporate Planning and the other for Finance. The Operations Group included these five, plus fourteen Du Pont executives and five Conoco executives. Four of the latter were responsible for the different functional activities in the oil business, and one was in charge of Consolidation Coal, a major enterprise, that came with the Conoco acquisition. The Operating Group has oversight of all the company's products, functions and geographical regions.

As part of the reorganization, the Du Pont product lines in its reshaped portfolio of businesses were consolidated in seven 'industrial segments.' Within the segments closely related product lines were grouped for administrative purposes as profit centers. Four of these segments – Polymers, Agricultural Products, Electronics, and Imaging and Medical Products, are in industries where new product development remains essential for competitive success. Three – Fibers, Chemicals (petro-chemicals and pigments) and Automotive Products – are in more mature stable industries where competition is based more on improving product and process. The remaining six senior vice presidents that make up the corporate office are responsible for the functional activities of the corporation as a whole – Research & Development, Engineering, Information Systems, Logistics (purchasing), External Affairs and Legal. By this reorganization the executives in the corporate office now have far more direct operating and planning responsibilities than they had during the previous seventy years.

The stated objectives of the reshaping of the corporate office was to break down barriers between operating divisions and to have top management develop a corporate rather than a product or functional perspective. To encourage the latter, most Senior Vice Presidents that make up the Operating Group handle more than one activity. For example, a Senior Vice President for Chemicals also has responsibility for manufacturing for the company as a whole and that for Electronics oversees the Asia/Pacific region. In this way the corporate headquarters is expected to develop a global view, to enhance human capabilities at all levels and to speed up high level decision-making. At Du Pont, where the portfolio includes a number of new and technologically advanced products, the functions of the corporate headquarters have been strengthened, while at GE, where the strategy has concentrated on obtaining dominant positions in more mature and stable industries, the role and size of the corporate office has been reduced.

The effectiveness of the more focused long-term strategy of Du Pont and GE and the resulting structures will be determined in the 1990s. (I see the purchase of Conoco, like GE's acquisition of RCA, not as part of long-term strategy but rather responses to the more immediate and most complex business situations.) In carrying out and modifying the new strategies and in implementing and tuning of the new structures, the executives in the corporate office at Du Pont and GE should keep in mind the lessons learned during the 1970s and 1980s about the paths to growth and the limits to the size of the firm.

One lesson of those years was that moves into new businesses based on existing capabilities required the development of a set of complementary ones to supplement existing skills and facilities. If the production facilities provided competitive advantage in the new market, in most cases complementary marketing capabilities needed to be developed. Another lesson was that, not only were the size and boundaries of enterprises shaped by existing capabilities and success in the developing of complementary ones, but they were also determined by the ability of the corporate headquarters to carry out both its basic functions – entrepreneurial and administrative.

Most significant of all, they learned that the HQ functions varied with the characteristics of the industries in which they operated. Therefore, the production and distribution of different types of products or services required different types of planning and control systems. In industries in which new product development is a critical component of interfirm competition, where R&D expenditures are high, state-of-the-art facilities costly, and marketing required specialized skills, the corporate office needs to concentrate on the entrepreneurial (value-creating) function. Here it needs to play a strong role in the strategic planning process if it is to utilize fully their company's existing competitive strengths in technologically advanced businesses and to determine paths for new product and process development. In more mature industries where the nature of the final product remains stable, where R&D expenditures continue to be essential, but are primarily for improving product and in such industries the corporate office can more easily delegate strategic planning to the operating divisions, and maintain strategic control by setting targets and establishing long-term goals for the corporation as a whole. Finally, as the experience of the conglomerates reinforce, in the service industries and mature manufacturing industries in which the products remain much the same, where the technology of production is not complex, where facilities are less costly and where competition rests more in distribution and marketing, particularly advertising, than in production or R&D, financial controls alone have been usually enough to prevent losses and maintain profits in multi-business enterprises.

CONCLUSION

The story told here of Du Pont, GE and the US conglomerates is representative of much of American industry. The 1980s were for US industrial firms a decade of reshaping corporate strategies and rebuilding organizational structures. As firms focused on a smaller number of product lines, they often used funds received from the spin-offs to acquire other enterprises needed to fill out their portfolio of related lines. Most of these rearrangements were carried out through friendly transactions, but at times firms were acquired by hostile takeovers. As Bhadgat, Shleifer, and Vishny (1990) report, even hostile takeovers by raiders ended in the hands of other firms in their sectors with the raiders profiting (handsomely) as temporary brokers. On the whole, however, the capital markets in the form of raiders, and of LBOs and other privatization forms have played only a limited constructive role in the recent restructuring of American industrial enterprises.

The part played by the capital markets in this corporate restructuring reflects, in much the same way as the changes made by senior corporate managers in their strategy and structure, the characteristics of the industries in which the enterprise operates. For example, one major innovation – the privatization of enterprises through LBOs and other techniques has been insignificant in capital-intensive industries where competitive strength depends on continuing long-term investment in R&D and costly capital facilities; that is in industries where strategic planning and control has been essential to remain competitive. The great majority of the firms privatized have been in industries where financial controls were sufficient to maintain the competitive capabilities of the operating unit of a multibusiness enterprise.

As Bronwyn Hall's studies of 2000 manufacturing companies' (1990, 1992) documents, between 1977 and 1987 – the period of the LBO boom – 224 of the 1980 public companies had become privatized. (Of these only 76 were LBOs.) The 224 accounted for 5.7 percent of the total employment of the companies studied but only 1.4 percent of total

R&D expenditures. Of these 224, 150 were smaller firms in what Hall defines as low tech industries (food, textiles, including apparel, paper and wood products) and stable short-term horizon industries (fabricated metals; stone, glass and clay; rubber and plastics; soap and toiletries). Where these industries accounted for 36 percent of total manufacturing employment in her over-all sample, they accounted for 83 percent of employment of the firms that had gone private. Where for the US manufacturing sector as a whole R&D investment averaged $2,000 per employee, for the firms that went private the average was $500 per employee. Hall's information shows that after a decade of well publicized privatization, privatized firms are finding a place in low technology and other industries where R&D is minimal. It also emphasizes that the widely-held public company overwhelmingly dominates in the capital-intensive, technologically complex industries on which so much of the nation's industrial growth and competitive success depends – industries that include chemicals, pharmaceuticals, aircraft and aerospace, computers and semiconductors, electrical and electronic equipment, oil, metals, and a wide variety of agricultural, construction, mining, and industrial equipment, engines, motor vehicles and other transportation equipment.

Hall's data also emphasize that financial entrepreneurs and intermediaries have become aware, as have corporate managers, of differences in industry characteristics. Money managers learned that, if firms in the more capital-intensive, technologically complex industries were to remain competitive, they would have to make long-term investments in highly product-specific skills. Such long-term investments demanded value-creating strategic planning and control by experienced managers as well as a continuing reinvestment of earnings (particularly from established lines) into new and improved products and processes. So in assisting and even promoting LBOs and other privatization transactions, financiers concentrated on firms and industries where capital costs are relatively low, specific skills not complex, synergies from R&D, production and distribution are limited and where cash flows are relatively steady, and long-term strategic planning relatively unnecessary. In such industries multibusiness firms have few competitive advantages over single business ones. Firms in such industries, whether operated through the office of a conglomerate or an LBO association, can be administered through financial control alone. But such industries are not the major sources of economic growth and transformation, or of national competitive strengths. In the industries that require long-term investment in R&D and capital facilities the public corporation will continue into the twenty-first century to be, as it was throughout the twentieth century, the engine of industrial strength and transformation.

In the 1980s business and financial managers learned the importance of understanding the differences in industry characteristics in the management of their business and the making of their investments. The time has come for academics to learn to make comparable distinctions in their analyses of business enterprises and their management.

NOTES

1 The executives at the corporate headquarters carried out an additional and most essential function, that of handling relations of the enterprise as a whole with legislatures and other governmental bodies concerning taxes, tariffs and regulation. In this paper I concentrate on the two basic functions because they focus on managerial issues arising in matters internal to the firm.
2 In some companies there were five levels – profit centers, business units, divisions, groups and the corporate offices. But in nearly all, profit centers were within business units and were usually related to functional activities, and the group usually remained part of the corporate HQ. In this paper then, I use the term business unit for the lowest level multifunctional office, and division for the highest level office where senior line executives had profit responsibility.

REFERENCES

Aguilar, F. J. and R. Hamermesh. 'General Electric, strategic position – 1981', (Harvard Business School case 381–174). In A. D. Chandler, Jr. and R. S. Tedlow, *The Coming of Managerial Capitalism*, Richard Irwin, Homewood, IL, 1985.

Araskog, R. V. *The ITT Wars*, Henry Holt, New York, 1989.

Bhadgat, S., A. Shleifer and R. Vishny. 'Hostile takeovers in the 1980s: A return to corporate specialization', *Brookings Papers on Economic Activity*, Washington, DC, 1990.

Chandler, A. D. *Strategy and Structure: Chapters in the History of the Industrial Enterprise*, MIT Press, Cambridge, MA, 1962.

——, *Scale and Scope: The Dynamics of Industrial Capitalism*, Belknap/Harvard Press, Cambridge, MA, 1990.

Chandler, A. D. and R. S. Tedlow. *The Coming of Managerial Capitalism: A Casebook on the History of American Economic Institutions*, Richard D. Irwin, Homewood, IL, 1985.

Dinerstein, F. 'ITT: Adaptation to change in a conglomerate corporation', unpublished, Columbia University, 12 February, 1980.

Donaldson. G. and J. Lorsch. *Decision Making at the Top: Shaping of Strategic Direction*, Basic Books, New York, 1983.

Fast, N. D. *The Rise and Fall of Corporate New Venture Divisions*, UMI Research Press, Ann Arbor, MI, 1977, Ch. 5.

Feder, B. F. 'Hanson's meteoric rise', *New York Times*, 5 March 1989, Section 3, 1. F38.

Goold. M. and A. Campbell. *Strategies and Styles: The Role of the Centre in Diversified Corporations*, Basil Blackwell, Oxford, 1987.

Hall, B. W. 'The impact of corporate restructuring on industrial research and development', *Brookings Papers on Economic Activity*. Washington. DC, 1990.

Hall, B. W. 'Corporate restructuring and investment horizons'. In M. Porter (ed.), *Time Horizons in American Industry*, Harvard Business School Press, Boston, MA, 1992.

Hounshell, D. A. and J. K. Smith. *Science and Corporate Strategy: Du Pont R&D, 1902–1980*, Cambridge University Press, New York, 1988.

Mercer, D. *The Global IBM: Leadership in Multinational Management* Dodd, Meade, New York, 1988.

Scott, B. R. 'The industrial state: Old myths and new realities', *Harvard Business Review*, March–April 1973, pp. 133–45.

Sobel, R. *I.T.T.: The Management of Opportunity*, Times Books, New York, 1982.

Note: Information on individual companies not cited in the above publications are from annual reports, *Moody's Manual*, M. Moskowitz, Michael Katz, and Robert Levering, *Everybody's Business: An Almanac*, Harper & Row, San Francisco, 1980, and *Everybody's Business*, Doubleday, New York, 1990 and D. C. Stafford and R. H. A. Purkis, *Directory of Multinationals*, Stockton Press, New York, 1989. I am indebted to Gordon Smyth for information on the recent Du Pont reorganization.

Chapter 15

The value of the parent company

Andrew Campbell, Michael Goold and *Marcus Alexander*

Many, if not most, corporate parent companies destroy value. The businesses in the corporate portfolio would be better off as independent companies or as part of other corporate portfolios. This disturbing conclusion has been reached after nearly ten years of research and consulting on the subject of corporate-level strategy and the role of the corporate centre.

The evidence for this conclusion lies in the hundreds of stories and situations we have come across where the corporate parent's influence over a business unit has caused the managers in the unit to make the wrong decisions, or at least to make poorer decisions than they would have made without the parent's influence. This body of anecdotal evidence is reinforced by the groundswell of complaint and resentment that business unit managers express when talking about their corporate centres. It is also supported by the economic evidence that many large companies have a market value lower than their break-up value, and by the continuing success of management buy-outs, where business units blossom when freed from the grasp of some large corporation.[1]

On the other hand, some companies do exist, although comparatively few in number, where the parent is clearly creating value, where the business unit managers have high respect for the corporate centre and the influence it has over their businesses, and where the company's market value is greater than the sum of its parts. The stories, the atmosphere and the results in these successful corporate parents are completely different, underlining both the shortcomings in the majority of large companies and the opportunities for those who get their strategies right.[2]

FOUR WAYS TO DESTROY VALUE

Parent companies affect value in four ways – through stand-alone influence, through linkage influence, through central functions and services, and through corporate development activities.[3] In each of these areas, it is possible for parent companies to create value. It is more common, however, for these areas of influence to result in value destruction.

Stand-alone influence

After the 1970s oil crisis, many of the oil majors decided to diversify into new businesses, which would provide more growth and opportunity than their core oil businesses. A popular new area was minerals, which was seen as drawing on skills in natural resource exploration and extraction that were related to their base businesses. In the event, almost all the oil companies have found that they destroyed shareholder value through their minerals diversifications. The root cause of the problem was that parent company managers from the oil industry did not understand the subtle differences between the oil businesses and the minerals businesses, and ended up by influencing the strategies of their minerals businesses in ways that caused them to perform worse, not better. For example, we were told by a manager who had been part of British Petroleum's (BP's) minerals business:

> The problem was that the BP managing directors couldn't really get to grips with the minerals business or feel that they understood it. There was always that vestige of suspicion about the business, that in turn led to a temptation to say 'no' to proposals from the business, or, alternatively, if they said yes, to say yes for the wrong reasons.

This is an example of what we call stand-alone influence. Stand-alone influence is about the parent's influence on the strategies and performance of each business in the parent's ownership, viewed as a stand-alone profit centre. All parents exert considerable stand-alone influence on their businesses. At a minimum, they are involved in agreeing and monitoring performance targets, in approving major capital expenditures, and in selecting and replacing the business unit chief executives. These activities, in themselves, are powerful influences on the businesses. Many parents, however, go further, exercising influence on a wider range of issues, such as product-market strategies, pricing decisions and human resource development.

While corporate parents can create value through stand-alone influence, they more often destroy value instead. By pressing for inappropriate targets, by starving businesses of resources for worthwhile projects, by encouraging wasteful investment, and by appointing the wrong managers, the parent can have a serious adverse effect on its businesses. The potential for value creation must therefore always be balanced against the risk of value destruction.

Linkage influence

Linkage influence can be just as destructive. Through linkage influence, the corporate parent seeks to create value by fostering cooperation and synergy between its businesses. But the search for linkages and synergies so often leads to problems that Guy Jillings, Head of Strategic Planning of Shell International Petroleum, has coined the term 'anergy'. He believes that avoiding anergy is often a more essential goal than pursuing synergy.[4]

The problem of anergy is illustrated by a global consulting company which had made acquisitions in two new areas of consulting services to add to its traditional core. Senior managers believed that synergy could be created in a number of ways. First, economies of scale could be achieved by sharing back-office systems such as client billing and data processing. Second, a more powerful identity could be established by sharing a brand name. Third, more business could be generated by appointing client managers for the company as a whole who could deepen client relationships, coordinate approaches and cross-sell a broad range of consulting services.

In reality, the pressure for linkages nearly destroyed one of the acquisitions, and hampered the efforts of all the other businesses. The shared billing system was complicated by the different needs of each business; after several million dollars of development cost, a compromise solution was reached which most units felt was inferior to their original systems, and which was no cheaper to run. Attempts at joint branding were abandoned because the individual brands were each strong and associated with particular services, whereas the amalgam brand was hard for clients to relate to, and was rejected by staff who felt loyal to the brand values of the specific organization they had joined. Cross-selling was not increased by the new layer of client managers, who were insufficiently familiar with the full range of services available. Worse still, clients resented the imposition of a gate-keeper between them and the specialist service providers they were used to dealing with, and few valued the supposed advantages of one-stop shopping. Eventually the company was forced to drop many of the proposed linkages and to reaffirm clearly distinct lines of business.

In many companies, the pervasiveness of problems from encouraging inappropriate linkages has led to a situation in which business managers have become so cynical about the efforts of their parent that they deliberately conceal or avoid linkage opportunities. To avoid the risk of parental intervention, most managers prefer to do business with outsiders rather than with insiders.

Central functions and services

Parents also destroy value through establishing central functions and services which undermine, rather than support, business effectiveness. This is not simply a matter of excessive overhead costs. It is also about delayed decisions and sub-standard or unresponsive support. ABB's chief executive, Percy Barnevik, has acquired many companies where these problems had been rife. His dramatic response in cutting headquarters' staff has led to an ABB rule of thumb: by taking out 90 percent of the centre, you can usually improve business performance as well as saving cost. This rule has been applied to Brown Boveri's headquarters, and to acquisitions such as Combustion Engineering in the US and Strömberg in Finland. Typically, Barnevik removes 30 percent of the central functions and staff on the grounds that they are adding little except cost. A further 30 percent are set up as service units that must compete directly with outside suppliers. If they are cost effective, their services are purchased. Otherwise, they rapidly shrink or are disbanded. Thirty percent of the central staff are put under the direct control of the individual businesses. If they fulfil a valid role in the business, they stay. If not, they are replaced or fired.

This approach addresses one of the main problems of central functions and services: that their privileged status protects them from the rigours of the market. By treating the divisions as clients whose business must be won, service levels are sharpened and improved. Unless this sort of relationship exists, the hoped-for economies of scale in central functions often prove illusory, and the influence of central functions is severely damaging.

Corporate development

The final way in which parents destroy value is through corporate development activities – acquisitions, divestments, alliances, business redefinitions and new ventures. Many corporate parents believe that they create substantial value in their corporate development activities, for example, by spotting opportunities to buy businesses cheaply, by creating new ventures that provide profitable future growth opportunities, or by redefining businesses in ways that lead them to be more competitive in their market places. We have found, however, that such initiatives frequently misfire. Parents overpay for acquisitions, support losing ventures and redefine businesses in the wrong way. The weight of research evidence indicates that the majority of corporately sponsored acquisitions, alliances, new ventures and business redefinitions fail to create value.[5] In particular, corporate histories are littered with stories of acquired businesses which turned out to be worth much less than expected, and so were sold subsequently for a fraction of the purchase price.

An extreme case concerns Ferranti, a medium-sized electronics company. During the 1980s, Ferranti performed well, developing a variety of sound businesses in defence electronics and other areas. However, in 1987, Ferranti paid $670 million to acquire the US International Signal and Communication (ISC) Group, with a view to becoming a major player in international defence markets. In 1989, it was discovered that ISC had entered into various fraudulent contracts, which led to losses of around $500m for Ferranti. As a result, Ferranti was severely weakened and eventually forced into receivership after GEC had offered to buy the company for only one penny a share. A single acquisition brought Ferranti to its knees and wiped out all of the value created during the previous decades.

WHY VALUE DESTRUCTION IS SO COMMON

While corporate managers recognize that mistakes can be made at the headquarters in the same way as they can be made at other levels of management, few would accept our proposition that most corporate centres are systematically destroying value. They point to economies of scale in financial reporting, fund raising, liaising with the shareholders, tax and other areas. They identify the lower cost of debt that large companies can provide. They talk about the value of providing an informed challenge and second opinion to the narrow perspective of business unit managers. They refer to the task of allocating resources across the portfolio. Clearly, they argue, the corporate centre has a valid role and can contribute to performance.

We agree. There are economies of scale. The cost of debt can be lowered. And informed second opinion and a wise allocation of capital can add value. However, for reasons we will explain, the net influence of the parent in most companies is still negative. Inappropriate interference on linkage issues outweighs the economies of scale in financial reporting. Wise resource allocation decisions are fewer than foolish ones. Damage from over-ambitious or under-ambitious performance targets is more significant than the benefits of lower interest on debt. Value destroying influences are greater than value creating ones. Why is this so?

The basic reason why value destruction occurs is that it is hard for parent organizations to influence their businesses in ways that improve on the decisions of the managers running the businesses. As we shall see from examining each of the four ways parent organizations affect value, it is quite reasonable to expect that the parent's influence will make decisions worse, not better. In fact it is only under particular conditions that we can expect the parent's influence to be positive.

With stand-alone influence, the assumption is that parent managers know better what is right for a business than its own managers. But this is normally an improbable assumption. Indeed, the likelihood is that most parents will destroy value through their stand-alone influence. In a multi-business organization, managers in the parent can devote only a small percentage of their attention to the affairs of each business, while the managers in the businesses are fully engaged in their own units. Why should the parent managers, in 10 percent of their time, be able to improve on the decisions being made by competent managers who are giving 100 percent of their efforts to the business? The very idea that part-time managers at one remove (or more) will be able to enhance the performance of the business's own dedicated management is, in some sense, paradoxical. We refer to this as the "10 percent versus 100 percent" paradox.

The 10 percent vs. 100 percent paradox is compounded by principal/ agent problems arising from placing a parent organization between the business managers and the providers of capital.[6] In a hierarchy, the business level managers are not motivated primarily by the objective of maximizing the performance of their businesses. They are motivated primarily by the objective of gaining favour, rewards and career opportunities from their parent bosses. Unless the parent can mimic the influence of the providers of capital, the ownership relationship will result in different motivations and different objectives. Altering the motivations and objectives of business-level managers is one of the ways the parent can add value, but it often results in value destruction as the business managers play a game of cat and mouse, hiding information and disguising outcomes, to persuade parent managers that they are high quality individuals. As a result, it is possible in many companies to raise performance by a significant amount just by passing factual information that has not been filtered or disguised from the business level to the parent managers.

With linkage influence, the assumption is that the parent managers can identify benefits of linkages between businesses that would not be perceived or implemented by the businesses' own managers. But, given the business managers' much greater knowledge of their businesses, it is likely that they will have more knowledge about linkage opportunities and how to realize them than parent managers do. The difficulty of value creation from linkage influence therefore stems from another paradox. Why should the parent managers be able to perceive linkage opportunities, if they have not already been perceived as a result of mutual self-interest on the part of energetic business unit managers? It is hardly surprising that corporately inspired synergy initiatives so often prove unsatisfactory, since, by definition, they have not engaged the spontaneous interest of the business managers involved. We call this the "enlightened self-interest" paradox.

With central functions and services influence, the assumption is that central staffs can provide better functional guidance, or better value-for-money services, than are available from businesses' own staff or, in particular, from outside suppliers. But the trend in many large companies is now to decentralize or outsource central functions and services. This trend brings out another paradox. A specialist, external supplier stands or falls by its ability to provide the most responsive and cost-effective expertise in its chosen field, whether it be market research, manufacturing advice or strategic planning. Why should an in-house staff department be able to create more value than specialist competitors who undertake similar tasks and services on a third-party basis? It is this "beating the specialists" paradox that has led many companies to disband large parts of their corporate functions and services.

Finally, with corporate development activities, the assumption is that the parent can buy businesses for less than they are worth, sell businesses for more than they are worth, and launch new ventures or redefined businesses that will be worth more than they cost to set up. The odds are against any of these occurring. Given that the market for buying and selling businesses is sophisticated, and the competition to develop businesses in new areas is usually fierce, why should the parent expect to be able to create value through corporate development? We refer to this as the "beating the odds" paradox. It is seldom that a parent can expect to be able to beat the odds and create value from corporate development activities.

These four paradoxes – 10 percent vs. 100 percent, enlightened self-interest, beating the specialists, and beating the odds – explain why it is so hard to create value from the corporate centre. As a result of the paradoxes, most parent managers inevitably end up by destroying value. It is only under a limited set of conditions that value is created.

The first condition is that the businesses in the company's portfolio must have some reason for under-performing that can be corrected by the parent company. If the businesses are performing at their optimum, there is no need for a parent. In other words, the businesses must offer some "parenting opportunity".

Second, the parent must possess some special capabilities or resources that will enable it to correct the under-performance and exploit the parenting opportunity. These parenting characteristics are the engine of value creation.

Third, the parent must have a sufficient understanding of the critical success factors in each business to make sure that it does not influence the businesses in inappropriate ways. Managers refer to this understanding as having a "feel for the business". We have observed that it can take a parent manager a number of years, often including experience of a business over a complete economic cycle, before a sufficient feel develops.

SUCCESSFUL PARENT COMPANIES

Successful parent companies not only meet these basic conditions for value to be created, they are particularly good at creating value. The best parents have unusual insights about certain kinds of parenting opportunities and focus their influence and activities on creating value from these insights. They have what we call 'value creation insights'. The best parents also have special skills and resources that fit particularly well with their value creation insights. These skills and resources are normally superior to those of other similar parents. They have what we call "distinctive parenting characteristics". Finally, the best parents limit their portfolios to businesses where their parenting will create a substantial amount of value. They are more effective at doing this because they have clear criteria defining which businesses fit well with the parent and which do not. They have what we call 'heartland' criteria.

ABB, Canon and Emerson are good illustrations of these concepts. They represent a cross-section of the successful diversified companies in our research sample. All three are recognized as world leaders and exemplars of their particular management styles. All three also have excellent performance records (Table 15.1). We will, therefore, illustrate our concepts by explaining the value creation insights these companies have, the distinctive parenting characteristics that support their insights, and the heartland criteria these companies use to limit their portfolios.

One value creation insight at ABB involves linking nationally focused businesses into a global network: rationalizing production across countries, cross-selling products, sharing technical developments and transferring best practice. ABB focuses much of its parental influence on getting previously isolated national managers to work together across borders.

A second value creation insight at ABB concerns raising the commercial skills and orientation of managers. In large, engineering-dominated companies, managers can become more interested in their engineering prowess and in being involved in prestigious projects than they are in profit. Such companies often do not calculate profit except at high levels of aggregation. Most units are cost centres. The ABB parent has discovered that commercial performance can be transformed if the profit ethic can be driven into the hearts of the managers and engineers in the local businesses. Many of ABB's parenting activities are, therefore, focused on achieving this value creating objective.

A third value creation insight at ABB concerns overheads. Proud, previously rich, and nationally prominent companies have a tendency to

Table 15.1 Successful parent companies

	ABB	Canon	Emerson
Corporate HQ	Switzerland	Japan	USA
Origins	Merger of ASEA (Sweden) and Brown Boveri (Switzerland) (1988)	Research laboratory focusing on precision optics (1933)	Electrical manufacturing (1980)
Industries	Power plants, power transmission, power distribution, transportation, general industrial	Business machines, cameras, other optical equipment	Electrical-electronic products and systems such as motors, process control instruments, appliance components, etc.
Size			
sales ($bn)	30	15	8
employees (000)	210	67	69
Performance (10 yrs)			
sales growth	NA*	250%	200%
earnings growth	200% **	150%	200%
share price growth	300% **	150%	300%

*   ASEA and Brown Boveri merged in 1988
** Based on ASEA (ASEA owns 50 percent of ABB)

build large central overheads that can cost as much as 20 percent or more of profit. Much of ABB's parent activity, in the first year or two following an acquisition, is designed to reduce these overheads and release the value they have trapped. In later years the parent maintains the pressure on overheads ensuring that excessive costs do not build up again.

In Canon, one value creation insight is about developing new products. Technologists and product developers normally see themselves within the confines of a particular technology or product type. This puts bounds on their thinking defined by the accepted wisdom of the areas they are working in. Canon managers, however, discovered that it is possible to develop more creative products by blending and mixing technologies in, for example, fine optics and precision mechanics, and by challenging product development teams to produce customer solutions well beyond the scope of existing products.

Canon's second value creation insight is based on another parenting opportunity resulting from the bounded thinking of managers. In companies with traditional business unit structures, managers are influenced by the competitors and critical success factors of the industry they see themselves competing in. They are influenced by the accepted industry logic and, therefore, play into the hands of the industry leaders. Canon managers discovered that it is possible to break out of the accepted logic and develop winning strategies by avoiding traditional business unit structures and challenging managers to find new ways of competing.

Emerson's value creation insights are based on sharpening the strategic thinking of sound and profitable businesses. Emerson has found that, in certain electrical and electronic businesses, it can often push profit margins up from 5–10 percent to in excess of 15 percent at the same time as gaining market share. These improvements stem from reassessments of competitive positions and growth opportunities, detailed analysis of the components of cost and revenue in the businesses, and Emerson's special focus on manufacturing cost reductions. Emerson drives these improvements through business strategy reviews, which have been gradually refined to focus on the issues of greatest potential. Emerson is by no means unusual in conducting strategy reviews with its businesses: what is unusual is the way in which the process zeroes in on opportunities to improve performance, rather than simply being a routine re-examination of the businesses' plans.

ABB, Canon and Emerson have value creation insights that provide a focus for the parent's activities. All three companies have a specific understanding of how the parent can create value. This understanding is built on insights they have gained both about opportunities to build or improve businesses and also about how the parent can contribute. The insights affect the focus of parenting activities, the design of the parent organization and the type of businesses in the company's portfolio. Moreover, successful companies frequently have insights that are unique, giving them an advantage over other parent companies. (See insert on value creation insights.)

The second feature of successful diversified companies is their distinctive parenting. Emerson's distinctive parenting characteristics start with its planning process. At the heart of the process is the 'planning conference', an annual meeting between parent managers and businesses that is unusually combative and challenging. The degree of preparation done by both sides is unusual; the forty required charts and analyses are unusual; and the expertise of Chuck Knight, Emerson's CEO, based on twenty years' experience with running these meetings and monitoring Emerson's kind of businesses, is unusual. It is through the planning conference that Knight tests the thinking and the goals of the businesses,

VALUE CREATION INSIGHTS

Value creation insights are at the root of all successful corporate level strategies. They typically involve understandings by parent managers about how to improve the performance of businesses. Insights are based on unique knowledge or experience of:

- reasons why certain kinds of businesses have performance problems or fail to maximize their potential;
- ways in which a parent organization can influence the businesses so as to raise performance.

Value creation insights are extraordinarily diverse. Each of the successful companies we researched had its own, different value creation insights.

Value creation insights are about major areas of improvement: raising performance by 50 percent or 100 percent, not just 10 percent; doubling the value of a business, not just making marginal differences. Value creation insights are not, therefore, about providing a wise second opinion, gaining economies of scale in managing shareholder relationships or raising debt 10 percent cheaper. Value creation insights are about taking return on sales from below 10 percent to above 15 percent (Emerson and BTR), doubling sales volumes through linkages into an international network (Unilever and ABB), creating new businesses out of leveraging technologies (Canon and 3M), doubling shareholder value by buying mixed portfolios and unbundling them (Hanson and KKR).

Value creation insights are linked to specific sorts of businesses that have under-performance opportunities and critical success factors which the parent managers understand. They are, therefore, expressed in terms such as: 'In businesses that make higher added value, safety critical engineering components and systems, a parent can create value by putting together international businesses out of previously separate national entities'; or 'In long-term, technically complex natural resource businesses, a parent can create value by transferring technical and functional expertise around the world'. Thus the general form of a value creation insight is: 'In certain sorts of businesses, a parent can create value by . . .'. The value creation insight identifies both the businesses in which the parent can create value, and the means by which it does so.

Value creation insights are not always explicit. Sometimes they are embedded in the parent organization's culture and way of working. What is important is that they describe how the parent's corporate strategy leads to major value creation.

The final point about value creation insights is that they often take years of experience to develop and refine. Sometimes they appear to have sprung newly formed from the mind of a visionary chief executive or from a strategic planning process. However, more normally, they emerge from a long process of learning and experience.

pressing for improvements and helping to identify ways of achieving them. By design, the atmosphere is confrontational. 'Emerson is a contact sport,' commented one manager. 'Knight invites people to punch back. He takes positions to provoke a response and expects one.' The debates are often heated, but the parent managers have the skills to make them open and constructive. Canon has many distinctive parenting characteristics. Probably most important is Canon's uncompromising corporate commitment to developing its core technologies that goes back to its roots as a research laboratory. Professor Yamanouchi, previously a Canon employee, explained:

> R&D drives Canon's strategic thinking and is central to Canon's behaviour. As an example, the medium range plan of each product group is drawn up by the development centre of the product group. Canon's R&D staff, therefore, believe that their work is essential for the growth of Canon.[7]

This commitment is linked to Canon's very large corporate staff which includes over 1,000 central research staff. It is also revealed in Canon frequently being among the top three companies registering new US patents.

Another distinctive parenting characteristic is Canon's ability to reduce rigidity in organizational boundaries by encouraging networking and cross-company linkages. The organization operates as a 'hub and spoke' system, with matrix lines that bind the spokes together. At the centre there is a twenty-two man corporate executive committee which meets weekly, bringing together the central managers, the heads of product divisions, the heads of sales organizations and the heads of functions. This level of contact is unusual and greatly helps the effective management of the matrix. Canon also has many other mechanisms, such as heavyweight task forces, product development teams and career management processes, designed to bring people together and move them across functional and organizational boundaries.

ABB, our third example, also has distinctive parenting characteristics. Percy Barnevik, ABB's chief executive, developed his parenting approach by turning round ASEA in the late 1970s and early 1980s. ABB's 'lean matrix' of business areas and country managers topped by a corporate centre with around 100 staff has been written about frequently.[8] It is designed to break previously monolithic, national companies into small, focused business units linked to similar units in other countries, but still benefiting from a strong national presence. Business area managers are part of the parent organization. They make decisions about rationalizing production across countries and spend their lives visiting business units to persuade unit managers to share technical developments, cross-sell products and pick up on best practice.

Supporting this highly decentralized structure is a central monitoring and control system, Abacus, that provides profit statements and balance sheet information for every business unit and profit centre (5,000 in total). Units can compare themselves, and senior managers can rapidly identify anomalies or problem areas. This profit focused information system combined with the small size of most business units, often less than 200 people and sometimes as few as 50, helps drive a commercial, profit focused attitude into the culture of the lowest level engineer or manager. ABB's parenting systems and structures are distinctive and are linked to the value creation insights that provide a focus for all of ABB's parenting activities.

Successful parent companies, therefore, have a clear focus, based on value creation insights, for their parenting activities. They also have distinctive parenting characteristics that enable them to create the value they focus on. In addition, successful companies have a portfolio of businesses that fit with their parenting. They are clear about the criteria that define what we call their 'heartland businesses', the businesses that will benefit most from the centre's parenting influence, and they focus their portfolios on such businesses. In these businesses, they are able to create high value and to avoid value destruction.

An analogy can be drawn here with medicine. Successful parent companies are like specialist doctors. They know that there is an opportunity to improve the health of people with certain kinds of symptoms (value creation insights). They develop skills and equipment that enable them to improve the health of people with these particular symptoms (distinctive parenting characteristics), and they restrict their practice to working with patients that have these symptoms (heartland businesses).

Emerson's heartland is businesses that manufacture electrical, electro-mechanical or electronic products of medium technology and capital intensity where there is potential to raise performance. Emerson avoids consumer markets: 'Our ability to strategise in consumer products is less good. We like a slower rhythm. We don't like advertising and short product cycles.' Canon's heartland includes businesses where precision mechanics, fine optics and micro-electronics are important technologies, where technical innovation and creative market positioning are important sources of advantage, and where there is a sufficiently large market to justify intensive technical development. ABB's heartland includes engineering intensive, electro-technical businesses where there is potential to create linkages across national borders and which involve selling complex systems to large industrial companies or to governments.

DEVELOPING SUCCESSFUL CORPORATE STRATEGIES

ABB, Canon and Emerson are successful parent companies with value creating corporate strategies. They have value creation insights and distinctive parenting characteristics, and by focusing on a clearly defined heartland they avoid the value destroying pitfalls that afflict so many companies. But how can other companies that are currently less successful develop similarly powerful corporate strategies? We will end this article by proposing a criterion, parenting advantage, that should guide companies, and a framework that can be used to structure their search for successful corporate strategies.

We have argued that success is dependent on the value created or destroyed by the parent organization. By doing so we are identifying the parent as an organization that is separate from the business units, and that stands between the business units and the shareholders and investors. This separate organization needs to justify its existence as an intermediary. Moreover, the parent organization is in competition with other parent organizations and other intermediaries for the ownership of businesses. To succeed, a parent organization needs to create value and it needs to be better at creating value than rivals – it needs to have what we call 'parenting advantage'.

Parenting advantage is a criterion for guiding corporate strategy development, in the same way that competitive advantage is a criterion for guiding business strategy development. In business strategy, the key objective is to outperform competitors, and the concept of competitive advantage has proved immensely useful in assessing and developing business strategies. In corporate strategy, the key objective is to outperform rivals and other intermediaries and the concept of parenting advantage has similar power to help assess and develop corporate strategies.

In the increasingly active market for corporate control that exists in Anglo-Saxon economies, parenting advantage is the only robust logic for a parent company to own a business. Without parenting advantage, a company is potentially exposed to the hostile attentions of other, superior rivals, and can often enhance shareholder value simply by selling businesses to other owners. Parenting advantage is the goal and criterion that should guide both the selection of businesses to include in the portfolio and the design of the parent organization.

As companies search for parenting advantage, they need to analyse and assess a number of inputs. They need to understand the strengths and weaknesses of the existing parent organization: what are the current characteristics of the parent? They need to understand the nature of the businesses currently owned by the parent: what are the parenting opportu-

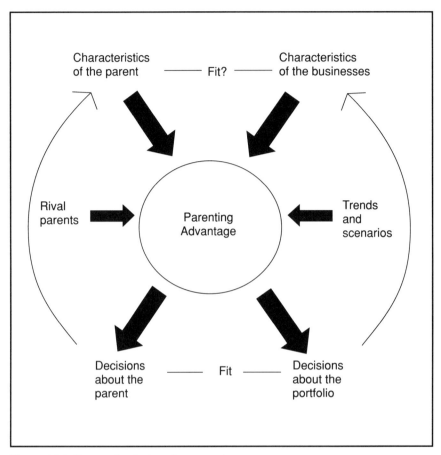

Figure 15.1 Corporate strategy framework

nities in these businesses? They need to know enough about rival parents to be able to assess which parents might be better owners of any of the current businesses. Finally, they need to understand the trends and possible scenarios for the future that might affect the other three inputs. Developing corporate strategy, therefore, involves four inputs (Figure 15.1).

These inputs do not provide answers. Rather they provide understandings that are useful in the search for value creation insights. This search is an essentially creative process guided by the objective of parenting advantage: the strategist is searching for a strategy that will give the company parenting advantage. The outputs of this strategy development process are decisions about which businesses to include in the portfolio and decisions about how the parent organization should be designed.

A useful first step in developing a new corporate strategy is to identify

---

TYPICAL REASONS FOR PARENTING OPPORTUNITIES

1   *Wrongly defined business.* The managers in the business have a wrong conception of what the business should be and, therefore, have too narrow or too broad a product market scope, and too much or too little vertical integration. The trend to outsourcing and alliances is changing the definitions of many businesses, creating new parenting opportunities.

2   *Size and Age.* Old, large, successful businesses often build up bureaucracies and overheads that are hard to eliminate from the inside. Small, young businesses may have insufficient functional skills, managerial succession problems and lack of financial resources to ride a recession. In both cases parenting opportunities exist.

3   *Temptations.* Some businesses tempt their managers to make mistakes. Mature businesses often lead managers into over-diversifying. Businesses with long product cycles cause managers to rely too much on old products. Cyclical businesses cause managers to over-invest in the upswing. In all cases there are opportunities for a parent to provide corrective influence.

4   *Linkages.* Where businesses can create value through linking with other businesses, blockages often exist preventing this from happening between independent companies. Parent organizations can remove these blockages.

5   *Major changes.* Industries undergoing change, for example, from local to international or from single product to system, require managers with real expertise at making these changes. A parent organization that develops this expertise can provide important assistance to businesses it owns.

6   *Special expertise.* Special expertise can be created by exposing managers to a number of businesses either facing similar strategic issues, such as declining sales or the need to professionalize management, or involved in similar products and markets, but in different countries. A parent organization owning these similar businesses can build the expertise.

---

areas where the parent is currently destroying value. By divesting businesses or changing the parent's behaviour these situations can be avoided. For many companies this first step greatly enhances shareholder value.

The second step is to start searching for 'parenting opportunities'. These are opportunities to improve performance through the involvement of a parent company. For example, a business may have low levels of manufacturing skills because it is dominated by marketing managers. A parent company with a manufacturing capability can, therefore, help redress the balance. Or a business may be too small, causing its costs to be too high. By combining it with another business, a parent company can cure the scale problem. The boxed list shown here describes some of the common reasons why businesses under-perform in ways that provide parenting opportunities.

The third step is to assess whether and how the company can grasp the parenting opportunities. This involves creating groupings of businesses with similar parenting opportunities. Each grouping is then assessed for its fit with the parent organization. Could the capabilities and resources in the parent fit with the parenting opportunities in the group of businesses? If fit does not currently exist, the question is what changes would be necessary in the parent organization to create a fit. Achieving a good fit may take a number of years of searching for parenting opportunities and developing capabilities and resources to match.

Once a concept of parenting advantage has been developed and the basis for a corporate strategy agreed, we have found it useful to capture this in a parenting advantage statement (see boxed statement for ABB). This statement identifies the value creation insights and distinctive parenting characteristics on which the strategy will be built, and the heartland businesses within which parenting advantage will be sought. The parenting advantage statement captures the essence of a value creating corporate strategy, and provides a succinct view of how and why parenting advantage will be achieved.

The chosen strategy can then be converted into an action plan, involving decisions about the parent organization and decisions about the portfolio of businesses. The implementation of these decisions will, in turn, feed back into changes in the parenting characteristics and the business characteristics. The ongoing corporate strategy development process thus requires continuous adjustment of the parent company and the portfolio of businesses to bring about a closer fit, and to adjust to unplanned changes in any of the important factors.

For companies whose corporate-level plan has traditionally been little more than an aggregation of the plans of the businesses, together with a page or two describing the company's overall ambitions and objectives, the corporate strategy development process we are suggesting is radically different. It puts the role of the parent in creating, and destroying, value at centre stage; it insists that decisions that impact the capabilities and resources of the parent are just as essential components of corporate strategy as portfolio choices; and it derives choices about the corporate strategy from assessment of their likely impact on net value creation and parenting advantage. As such, it forces companies to face up to the fact that they are likely to be destroying value in many of their businesses, and to search for ways in which they can become better parents for all of their businesses.

The parenting advantage framework can also lead to very different conclusions from other, more conventional theories of corporate strategy. For example, objectives such as portfolio balance, spread of risk, and growth take second place to parenting advantage. Decisions that improve balance, or increase spread of risk, or raise the rate of corporate

---

ABB PARENTING ADVANTAGE STATEMENT

Value Creation Insights:	• Most companies make direct trade-offs between centralization and decentralization, or scale and focus. There are opportunities for a parent that can combine the various benefits in new ways.
	• Many European engineering businesses have been relatively fragmented in global terms. Consolidation can reduce costs while increasing coverage and global muscle.
	• Many engineering businesses do not have a strong commercial focus, and are prone to increase sales volume and product range at the expense of margin. A parent can help redress the balance.
Distinctive Parenting Characteristics:	• Ability to combine decentralized small business units into a global network through the ABB matrix structure.
	• Systems and corporate initiatives that focus on profitability, customer needs, and simplification of operations.
	• Ability to integrate acquisitions and improve their performance rapidly.
	• Ruthless approach to cutting of overhead costs.
Heartland Businesses:	• Engineering-intensive, electro-technical businesses, usually involving complex integration into systems. Customers are large industrial or governmental institutions.

---

growth cannot, in our view, be justified if they at the same time damage parenting advantage. Many of the large chemical companies that diversified away from bulk chemicals into specialty chemicals, in search of faster growth, more spread and greater balance, have subsequently regretted their decisions. They have found that they were not able to parent the specialty businesses well, and that their results have therefore been disappointing. A focus on parenting advantage in corporate strategy development would have prevented many of these decisions. Parenting advantage thinking has more in common with core competences thinking.[9] But there are important differences. The parenting advantage framework puts the emphasis on the capabilities and resources of the *parent* (parenting competences), and the impact of these on the businesses.

The core competences logic does not distinguish so clearly between parent competences and business competences, and simply encourages companies to base their corporate strategies on competences that are or could become common across the portfolio. As a result, the development of core competences can sometimes conflict with the pursuit of parenting advantage. Texas Instruments, for example, attempted to exploit technical competences it had developed in its semi-conductor businesses in areas such as calculators, watches and home computers. It failed in these new areas not because it did not possess the requisite technical skills, but because senior managers in the parent company lacked experience and skills in parenting such consumer oriented businesses. Similarly, Minebea, the Japanese leader in miniature ball bearings, attempted to move into semi-conductors, on the basis of its skills in precision manufacturing of miniature components. It has found, however, that this undoubted competence has not proved sufficient to allow it to become successful in the semi-conductor business, and in 1991 it reported a loss of ¥5 billion from its semi-conductor subsidiary. In both cases, although the diversifications drew on common technical competences, they were not successful because the corporate centre lacked the appropriate parenting competences to avoid the mistakes that were made.

Conversely, corporate strategies that build on powerful capabilities and resources in the parent company, but do not involve the sharing of operating competences between the businesses, can be less easy to understand from a core competences perspective. BTR, the highly successful British-based industrial manufacturing company, voted best managed company in Britain in 1993, has a corporate strategy based on clear sources of parenting advantage, but it does not go in for sharing marketing, technical or engineering skills across its businesses. BTR's success with a portfolio of more than 1,000 business units in more than fifty countries is not based on core competences. Like Emerson, it is based on the influence the parent organization exerts to raise stand-alone performance in its businesses.

The parenting advantage framework that we propose therefore represents a new approach to the familiar issues of corporate strategy. Our conviction is that its use will help many corporate parents avoid destroying value through their corporate strategies, and move them towards the objective of becoming the best parent for the businesses they own.

NOTES AND REFERENCES

1 See, for example, Sebastian Green and Dean F. Berry, *Cultural, Structural and Strategic Change in Management Buyouts*, Macmillan, London, 1991; Michael Jensen, "Corporate Control and The Politics of Finance", *Journal of Applied*

Corporate Finance, Summer 1991, Vol. 4, No. 2, pp. 13–33; and David Young and Brigid Sutcliffe, "Value Gaps – Who is Right? – The Raiders, the Market or the Managers?", *Long Range Planning*, Vol. 23, No. 4, pp. 20–34, 1990.

2 See Michael Goold, Andrew Campbell and Marcus Alexander, *Corporate-Level Strategy: Creating Value in the Multi-Business Company*, John Wiley, New York, September 1994, for a fuller description of our conclusions and the research on which they are based.

3 This categorization of the ways in which parents affect value is collectively exhaustive but not mutually exclusive: particular actions can fall into one or more categories. The categorization has, however, proved practically useful. It is similar to categorizations developed by David Collis, "Managing the Multi-Business Company", teaching note, Harvard Business School; McKinsey & Co., "Corporate Centre Design", *McKinsey Quarterly*, 1991, No. 3; Bain & Co., "Internal Corporate Strategy Practice Document on The Role of the Centre".

4 Most authors on the topic of synergy have commented that it frequently fails to occur in practice. For example, Michael Porter, *Competitive Advantage: Creating and Sustaining Superior Performance*, Free Press, New York 1985; Rosabeth Moss Kanter, *When Giants Learn to Dance*, Simon and Schuster, London, 1989 and Routledge, London, 1990; John Wells, *In Search of Synergy*, doctoral dissertation, Harvard University, No. 8502578, 1984.

5 There is a large literature on the poor record of acquisitions, alliances and new ventures, see for example, Michael Porter, "From Competitive Advantage to Corporate Strategy", *Harvard Business Review*, May–June 1987; or Julian Franks and Robert Harris, "Wealth Effects of Takeovers in the UK", *Journal of Financial Economics*, August 1989.

6 See M. C. Jensen and W. H. Mekling, "Theory of the Firm: Management Behaviour, Agency Costs and Ownership Structure", *Journal of Financial Economics*, Vol. 3, 1976; S. Baiman, "Agency Research in Managerial Accountancy: A Survey", *Journal of Accounting Literature*, Vol. 1, 1982.

7 See Teruo Yamanouchi, "Breakthrough: The Development of the Canon Personal Copier", *Long Range Planning*, Vol. 22, No. 5, pp. 11–21, 1989.

8 See William Taylor, "The Logic of Global Business: An Interview with ABB's Percy Barnevik", *Harvard Business Review*, March–April 1991, pp. 90–105. See also Carol Kennedy, "ABB: Model Manager for the New Europe", *Long Range Planning*, Vol. 24, No. 15, pp. 10–17, 1992.

9 C. K. Prahalad and Gary Hamel, "The Core Competence of the Corporation", *Harvard Business Review*, No. 3, pp. 79–93, May–June 1990. See also the resource based theories of corporate strategy, for example J. Barney, "Firm Resources and Sustainable Competitive Advantage", *Journal of Management*, 1991; and Teece, Pisano and Shuen, "Firm Capabilities, Resources and the Concept of Strategy", Working Paper No. 90–8, University of California at Berkeley, 1990.

RESEARCH APPROACH

This article is based on nearly ten years of work as academics and consultants focused on the problems of multi-business companies. More specifically, however, we have spent the last three years looking at a sample of fifteen successful diversified companies – ABB, Banc One, BTR, Canon, Cooper, Dover, Emerson Electric, GE, GrandMet, Hanson, 3M, RTZ, Shell, TI, Unilever. These companies were selected because each had some claim to success in major parts of its corporate strategy. We were able, then, to contrast these companies with the many examples we knew of less successful organizations.

In the research sample, we conducted interviews with management both in the parent and in the businesses. We supplemented our interviews with published material – books, articles and case studies on the companies. We thus developed an impression of each company's parenting approach and its corporate strategy. We assessed the impact of these corporate strategies, both by analysing overall corporate results and by following through the parent's influence on specific decisions and situations.

The full report of this research is available in *Corporate-Level Strategy: Creating Value in the Multi-Business Company*, Michael Goold, Andrew Campbell and Marcus Alexander, John Wiley & Son New York: September 1994.

Chapter 16

Dominant logic

C. K. Prahalad and Richard A. Bettis

For the past 35 years product-market diversification of large firms has continued at a rapid pace. Today, over two-thirds of the firms in the USA, *Fortune* 500 are highly diversified and similar patterns of diversification exist in Western Europe and Japan (Rumelt 1974; Pavan 1972; Thanheiser 1972; Pooley 1972; Channon 1973; Suzuki 1980). As a consequence, interest in the relationship between corporate diversification and financial performance has grown among practitioners, academics, and public policy-makers.

Accompanying this interest has been a spate of research on the patterns of diversification and the determinants of performance in diversified firms by the academic community. Concurrently, consulting firms have been actively promoting a variety of approaches for managing diversified firms. The results of these efforts have been mixed at best. There is, as yet, no overall theory that links diversification with performance and the linkage, if any, remains elusive.

The purpose of this paper is to propose a crucial linkage, which has largely been ignored in the literature on the relationship between diversification and performance; and to show how this approach can add significantly to our managerial understanding of performance in the diversified firm.

This linkage is referred to as the 'dominant general management logic' (or dominant logic) and consists of the mental maps developed through experience in the core business and sometimes applied inappropriately in other businesses.

A BRIEF REVIEW OF RESEARCH ON DIVERSITY AND PERFORMANCE

The purpose of this section is to review briefly the major academic research streams and consulting framework relevant to the relationships between diversity and performance. These represent alternative approaches to research in this area. While significant literature exists in support of each of the streams of research outlined below, we will only reference and discuss the seminal works in each area.

The strategy of diversification

Pioneering work by Chandler (1962) and Ansoff (1965) established the motivations for diversification and the general nature of the diversified firm. Wrigley (1970) refined and extended Chandler's study by investigating the various options open to a diversifying firm. Building on the work of Chandler, Wrigley, and others, Rumelt (1974, 1977) investigated the relationships among diversification strategy, organizational structure, and economic performance. Rumelt used four major and nine minor categories to characterize the diversification strategy of firms. The major categories were single business, dominant business, related business and unrelated business. These categories provide a spectrum of diversification strategies – from firms that remained essentially undiversified to firms that diversified significantly into unrelated areas. Using statistical methods, Rumelt was able to relate diversification strategy to performance. The related diversification strategies – related–constrained and related–linked (e.g., General Foods and General Electric) were found to outperform the other diversification strategies on the average (relatedness was defined in terms of products, markets and technology). The related–constrained was found to be the highest performing on the average. (In related–constrained firms most component businesses are related to each other, whereas in related–linked firms only one-to-one relationships are required.) By contrast, the unrelated conglomerate strategy was found to be one of the lowest performing on the average.

Recently Nathanson and Cassano (1982) conducted a statistical study of diversity and performance using a sample of 206 firms over the years 1973–8. They developed a two-dimensional typology (market diversity and product diversity) for capturing diversification strategy that refines Rumelt's categories. They found that returns (on the average) declined as product diversity increased, while returns remained relatively steady as market diversity increased. However, they also found that size plays an important moderating role on the relationships. For both the market and product diversity, smaller firms did well relative to larger firms in categories marked by no diversification and in categories of extremely high diversification. Larger firms did significantly better than smaller firms in the in-between categories – those characterized by intermediate levels of diversification.

In both these studies linking diversification and performance (Rumelt and Nathanson/Cassano) the key point to note is that *choosing the generic strategy of diversification (how much and what kind of relatedness)* is the key to achieving performance.

Economic characteristics of individual businesses

Porter (1980), among others, established that the characteristics of the various industries in which a firm participates, and the position of the firm's businesses in these industries, impacts overall firm performance.

Two studies have in fact empirically validated these influences for diversified firms. The widely discussed PIMS program of the Marketing Science Institute (see Schoeffler, Buzzell and Heany, 1974, for an introduction) has shown that variables such as market share and relative product quality directly influence the profitability of constituent businesses in large diversified firms. More recently, Montgomery (1979) has examined the performance differences in diversified firms using the market structure variables of industrial organization economics. Montgomery found that diversified firms with higher levels of performance tended to have well-positioned businesses in industries with "favorable" market structures.

In summary, for both studies (PIMS and Montgomery) *the structure of the industries in which the firm competes and the competitive position of the firm's businesses within these industries are the key determinants of performance.*

Portfolio concepts

What are here called 'portfolio concepts' go by various names such as portfolio grids, SBU concepts, and SBU matrices. Although there are numerous slight variations among the approaches used by various consultant groups and firms, they all rely on a matrix or grid with two axes. The matrix classifies businesses by product-market attractiveness, or some variant of it, along one axis and by competitive position or some variant of it along the other axis. Typically these matrices are divided into either four or nine boxes. (For a thorough discussion see Hofer and Schendel 1978.) The position (box) that each business occupies represents its strategic position and determines the role that the business should play in the corporate portfolio. This role involves varying degrees of cash generation or cash usage. Studies by Bettis (1979), and Haspeslagh (1982) suggest that managers use these concepts to varying degrees – as a tool or as dogma – in managing a diversified portfolio of businesses.

For each variant of the portfolio concept the key points are: (1) *the strategic position of each business determines its cash flow characteristics; and* (2) *it is the 'balance' of these cash flow characteristics of the collection of businesses that determines the overall performance of the diversified firm.*

Et cetera

In addition to the streams of research discussed above, a number of studies focusing on performance in large firms, by researchers concerned with organizational theory and human motivation, have appeared recently. Representative of this line of research are Peters and Waterman (1982), Deal and Kennedy (1982), Pascale and Athos (1981), and Ouchi (1981). While these studies do not consider the problems of managing diversity explicitly, they often do make some implicit recommendations on the issue, but the nature of the recommendations varies widely. (For example, Peters and Waterman suggest that 'excellent firms' confine their operations to businesses they know or 'they stick to the knitting'.)

The three streams of research lead to somewhat different conclusions. To summarize, the linkage between diversity and performance would appear to be a function of:

1 the generic diversification strategy (how much and what kind of relatedness), or
2 the profit potential of the industries in which the individual businesses are positioned and the actual competitive position of the businesses in each industry, or
3 the cash flow characteristics of the various businesses and the internal cash flow balance for the total firm.

Undoubtedly all three perspectives *provide partial answers* to the question. Just how partial these answers are becomes more obvious when you consider that Rumelt (1974) was only able to explain less than 20 percent of the variance in performance, while Montogomery (1979) could only explain about 38 percent of the variance in performance. These results suggest that further conceptual development could enhance our understanding of diversity and performance.

The importance of 'quality of management'

Bettis, Hall and Prahalad (1978) have argued that, if we move away from the traditional research preoccupation with central tendencies, but focus on outliers – the very high and very poor performers – we may learn more about the elusive linkage between diversity and performance. By studying just twelve firms, six of which were high performers and six low performers, across the three generic categories of dominant, related, and unrelated diversifiers (with a sample of four firms each, two in high- and two in low-performance categories), they concluded that the quality of management was as critical in explaining performance as any other factor. (It should be noted that their definition of quality was somewhat ambiguous.) The study was not based on a large sample (and it could not be by design, as their concern was with outliers), and the conclusions were tentative. (In a much larger study, Bettis and Mahajan (1985) were able to show that the high-performance attributes usually attributed to related diversification were *not* recognized in the overwhelming majority of related diversifiers.) The real departure in the academic perspective on diversity and performance indicated by the study was the concern with very good and very poor performances in the same generic diversification category – or a desire to study outliers – and the inclusion of the concept of the '*quality of management*' as a major variable linking diversity and performance.

Top management in a diversified firm: a distinct skill?

Two in-depth clinical studies suggest that the skills that constitute the 'quality of management' in a single-business firm are distinct from a diversified firm; and that as firms diversify, top managers have to acquire those skills. Rajan Das (1981) studied one firm's attempt to diversify out of the core business (tobacco) and how it had to learn the process of general management in the new businesses into which it ventured. The conclusion was that it was not the quality of the business – its competitive structure – or the pattern of diversification *per se* that determined early failures and successes later, but the evolution of the top management and its ability to acquire new skills and recognize that its approach to managing a diversified firm must be different from the way it had managed the single-business firm. The study by Miles (1982) of tobacco companies in the US and their attempts to diversify away from tobacco, also leads to a similar conclusion. The firms *had to learn as much about general management in the diversified firm, as a distinct process and skill,* as about the characteristics of the new businesses. Both these studies indicate that the work of top management in diversified firms is a distinct skill and can contribute to the success or failure of any one of the businesses within the firm or the firm as a whole.

The management of a diversified firm

Studies of the work of top management and the process by which they manage a diversified firm are not numerous. Bower (1972a) demonstrated that top managers influence the strategic choices made by unit-level managers by orchestrating the organizational context – the formal structure and systems. In other words, the tools of top management were administrative in character. He labeled the term 'metamanagement' (Bower 1972b) to describe the job of top managers in diversified firms. Hamermesh (1977) outlined the process by which top managers intervene in a divisional profit crisis. Prahalad and Doz (1981) outlined, in detail, how top managers can use administrative tools to shift the strategic direction of a business. This line of research established both the broad scope of the work of top management, but more importantly how that influences the strategic choices made by lower-level managers at the business-unit level, thereby impacting on the overall performance. There exists a logical, though only partially empirically, verified link between the quality of management – or the quality of the processes by which top managers influence the business-level managers in their work – and the performance of the firm.

The two questions that we posed ourselves based on the literature were:

1 If top managers in single-business firms had to learn the process of managing a diversified portfolio, *should top managers in diversified firms go through a similar learning process when they add new businesses?* Is the task of top management in the diversified firm dependent on, or at least partially *influenced by, the underlying strategic characteristics* of the businesses?

2 If the tools available to top managers in diversified firms to influence the strategic direction of businesses are essentially administrative as regards the organizational context, does it follow that the substance of businesses is irrelevant? In other words, can the same conceptual organizational context management capabilities suffice if the mix of businesses changes?

THE ELUSIVE LINKAGE

It is important before proceeding to differentiate at least two distinct levels of general management in a diversified firm – that at the SBU or business level and the corporate management team. Often, in diversified firms, there tends to be an intermediate level of general management, called group or sector executives, between business level and corporate management. Our focus will be on the *corporate management team*, and its relationships with business- and group-level managers, as it pertains to managing the totality of the firm.

Given this focus on corporate management the conceptual framework linking diversity and performance, proposed in this paper, is based on the following premises:

1 Top management of a (diversified) firm should not be viewed 'as a faceless abstraction', but as a 'collection of key individuals' (i.e., a dominant coalition) who have significant influence on the way the firm is managed. This collection of individuals, to a large extent, influence the style and process of management, and as a result the key resource allocation choices (Donaldson and Lorsch 1983).

Few organizational events are approached by these managers (or any managers, as being totally unique and requiring systematic study. Instead, they are processed through pre-existing knowledge systems. Known as schemas (see Norman 1976, for a discussion of schemas), these systems represent beliefs, theories and propositions that have developed over time based on the manager's personal experiences. At a broader unit of analysis, Huff (1982) implied the possibility that organizations' actions can be characterized as schemas. An organizational schema is primarily a product of managers' interpretations of experiences while operating within certain firms and industries.

Schemas permit managers to categorize an event, assess its consequences, and consider appropriate actions (including doing nothing), and to do so rapidly and often efficiently. Without schemas a manager, and ultimately the organizations with which he/she is associated, would become paralyzed by the need to analyze 'scientifically' an enormous number of ambiguous and uncertain situations. In other words, managers must be able to scan environments selectively so that timely decisions can be made (Hambrick 1982). The selection of environmental elements to be scanned is likely affected by a manager's schema.

Unfortunately, schemas are not infallible guides to the organization and its environments. In fact, some are relatively inaccurate representations of the world, particularly as conditions change. Furthermore, events often are not labeled accurately, and sometimes are processed through inaccurate and/or incomplete knowledge structures.

For the purposes of this research it is important to understand what managers' schemas actually represent. Kiesler and Sproul (1982) offer the following concise description: 'Managers operate on mental representations of the world and those representations are likely to be of historical environments rather than of current ones' (p. 557). (Furthermore, as Weick (1979) discusses, it is the schema concept that provides the vehicle for his concept of the social construction (or enactment) of a firm's environment.)

For the present purposes the schema concept is introduced as a general mental structure that can store a shared dominant general management logic. (The specific nature and content of this 'logic' is discussed below.)

2 The strategic characteristics of businesses in a diversified firm, determined by the underlying competitive structure, technologies, and customers of specific businesses, vary. The differences in strategic characteristics of the businesses in the portfolio of the firm, a measure of *strategic variety*, impact the ability of a top management group to manage. This premise implies that complexity of the top management process *is a function of the strategic variety, not just the number of distinct businesses or the size of those businesses*. For example, the management of a very large, primarily one-industry firm (e.g., General Motors), or the management of a diversified firm in strategically similar businesses (e.g., Procter & Gamble), is a lot simpler than managing a diversified firm in strategically dissimilar industries (e.g., General Electric).

3 Strategically similar businesses can be managed using a single *dominant general management logic*. A dominant general management logic is defined as the way in which managers conceptualize the business and make critical resource allocation decisions – be it in technologies, product development, distribution, advertising, or in human resource management. These tasks are performed by managing the infrastructure of administrative tools like choice of key individuals, processes of planning, budgeting, control, compensation, career management and organization structure. If the businesses in a diversified firm are strategically similar, one dominant general management logic would suffice. However, diversified firms with strategic variety, impose the need for multiple dominant logics.

The dominant logic is stored via schemas and hence can be thought of as a structure. However, some of what is stored is process knowledge (e.g., what kind of process should be used in a particular kind of resource allocation decision or how new technologies should be evaluated). Hence, more broadly the dominant logic can be considered as both a knowledge structure and a set of elicited management processes. (The actual content of this knowledge structure and how this context is established is discussed below.)

4 The ability of a top management group (a group of key individuals), to manage a diversified firm is limited by the dominant general management logic(s) that they are used to. In other words, the repertoire of tools that top managers use to identify, define, and make strategic decisions, and their view of the world (mind sets), is determined by their experiences. Typically, the dominant top management logic in a diversified firm tends to be influenced by the largest business or the 'core business' which was the historical basis for the firm's growth (e.g., semiconductors at Texas Instruments, public switching and telephones at GTE). The characteristics of the core business, often the source of top managers in diversified firms, tend to cause managers to define problems in certain ways and develop familiarity with, and facility in the use of, those administrative tools that are particularly useful in accomplishing the critical tasks of the core business (Figure 16.1).

The sources of dominant logic

Dominant logic, as we have defined it here, is a mind set or a world view or conceptualization of the business and the administrative tools to accomplish goals and make decisions in that business. It is stored as a shared cognitive map (or set of schemas) among the dominant coalition. It is expressed as a learned, problem-solving behavior. As such, in order to understand the difficulties faced by a top management group in

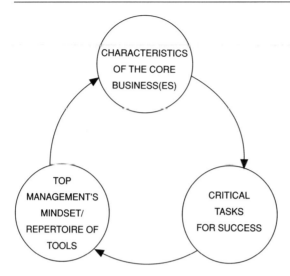

Figure 16.1 Dominant general management logic evolves due to . . .

changing the dominant logic, we need to first examine the research streams that deal with the development of cognitive maps and the associated problem-solving behavior. We identified four streams of research – operant conditioning, paradigms, cognitive biases, and artificial intelligence – to highlight the process by which a dominant logic evolves (i.e., how the cognitive map originates and changes) and the difficulties in changing it or adding new logics to one's repertoire. The relationships of these four streams to problem-solving behavior are shown in Figure 16.2.

Operant conditioning

Skinner (1953), in his seminal work on operant conditioning, argued that behavior was a function of its consequences. Behavior could be understood by considering the contingencies that were administered by the environment in response to certain behaviors. Behavior that was *reinforced* was emitted more frequently in the future. By contrast, behavior that was ignored or punished (negative reinforcement) was likely to diminish over time. A dominant logic can be seen as resulting from the reinforcement that results from doing the 'right things' with respect to a set of businesses. In other words, when top managers effectively perform the tasks that are critical for success in the core business they are positively reinforced by economic success. This reinforcement results in their focusing effort on the behaviors that led to success. Hence they develop a particular mind set and repertoire of tools and preferred

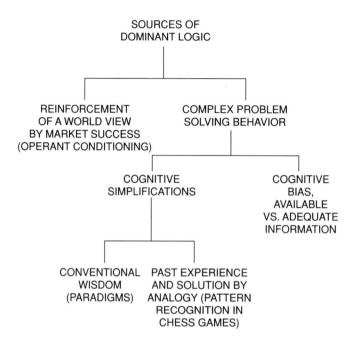

Figure 16.2 Conceptual foundations of dominant logic

processes. This in turn determines the approaches that they are likely to use in resource allocation, control over operations, and the approach to intervention in a crisis. If the firm acquires or develops a business for which the critical tasks for success are substantially different from those in the core business, because of operant conditioning the behaviors of top managers and the approaches they use to manage the new business are likely to remain those that were appropriate for the core business even though they may be inappropriate in the new business. In other words it is difficult for a top management group to be effective in managing a new business by learning and using a new dominant logic in a short time. The problems faced by American Can (e.g., Pickwick International), and Exxon (e.g., office systems), in managing acquisitions of businesses totally different from their core businesses, in the early stages, are an illustration of the power of operant conditioning on the dominant logics used by top management.

The power of paradigms

The concept of dominant logic also derives direct support from Kuhn's (1970) work on scientific paradigms and Allison's (1971) work on the importance of alternate paradigms in the context of analyzing government actions during the Cuban missile crisis.

Kuhn, a historian of science, argued that a particular science at any point in time can be characterized by a set of 'shared beliefs' or 'conventional wisdom' about the world that constitutes what he called the 'dominant paradigm'. What Kuhn calls 'normal science' is carried out efficiently under this set of shared beliefs. In a sense, Kuhn's 'paradigm' is simply a way of *defining and managing the world and a basis for action in that world.* Kuhn points out how difficult it is to shift dominant paradigms, and illustrates this with several examples such as the shift from the Ptolemaic view of the universe (earth-centered) to the Copernican view of the universe (sun-centered) in astronomy. The analogy from science to a business firm is simple and direct. The dominant paradigm and the dominant logic are conceptually similar but employed in different fields.

Allison used paradigmatic analysis to show how the adoption of a particular paradigm powerfully affects our evaluation of events. He characterized a paradigm as 'a systematic statement of the basic assumptions, concepts and propositions employed by a school of analysis'. Different paradigms resulted in dramatically different analyses of his chosen example: the Cuban missile crisis. The parallel between Allison's use of the word paradigm and our use of dominant logic is obvious.

The pattern-recognition process

As part of the development of 'intelligent' computer programs there have been numerous efforts to develop chess-playing programs (see Newell and Simon 1972, for a review). Inevitably such research has required intense studies of how chess experts make decisions in a chess game. In particular, the decision-making and problem-solving process used by grandmasters and masters has been compared to that of lesser players (de Groot 1965). These studies have shown that the better players could remember more 'patterns' of previous games than the lesser players. Simon (1979) estimated that class A players could remember about 1,300 familiar patterns while masters or grandmasters remember about 50,000. This 'vocabulary' of previous games lets players make effective decisions by comparison with earlier games. In other words, chess players decide on the basis of experience or 'what worked before', not on the basis of some best strategy or optimizing procedure. Now consider a situation where the design of the gameboard or rules of chess are changed. The stored 'vocabulary' of games is no longer as useful in this new game. Similarly, when the economic gameboard or rules are changed either by structural changes in existing businesses or by a diversification move, the vocabulary of economic moves stored through experience in the core business may no longer be as useful. In other words, solutions based on 'past experience' or solution by 'analogy' may be inappropriate.

Cognitive biases

A final area from which research results are suggestive of the concept of a dominant top management logic is cognitive psychology. The psychology of cognitive biases is the study of how people in making decisions sometimes make systematic (and often severe) errors (see Tversky and Kahneman, 1974, for an introduction and survey). When dealing with uncertain and complex tasks people often rely on a limited number of heuristic principles which greatly simplify the decision process. In general these heuristics are useful, but on some occasions they can result in significant errors.

For present purposes the most interesting of these heuristic principles is what is called the availability heuristic (see Tversky and Kahneman, 1973, for a thorough discussion). Basically, the availability heuristic leads people to make decisions by using information that can easily be brought to mind (i.e., information that is 'available'). This often leads to severe and systematic errors. This field of research also suggests that decision-makers do not necessarily use analytical approaches to evaluate the information content of available data or search for 'adequate information' (Nisbett and Ross 1980). For example, Tversky and Kahneman (1974) point out that one may assess the risk of heart attack among middle-aged people by recalling such occurrences among one's acquaintances even if it can be shown that it is an inappropriate basis for drawing such a conclusion. Obviously, for top managers, knowledge of the core business and the business they are most familiar with will be a significant source of available information. They tend to apply it to other businesses where it may or may not be appropriate (Das 1981). Research on cognitive processes suggests that the mind set and repertoire of tools that constitute the dominant logic are likely to be inappropriately applied by managers confronted with a 'different' business, and that there is significant 'learning' that precedes change in those biases. The difficulty of operating in diverse businesses which require multiple dominant logics is obvious.

STRATEGIC VARIETY AND THE DOMINANT LOGIC

The premises outlined above help us develop a framework for assessing the linkage between diversity and performance. Essentially they relate strategic variety amongst businesses in the firm, and changes in it, with the appropriateness of the dominant general management logic(s) that top managers in that firm use. We will examine in the rest of the paper the problems that diversified firms face in relating strategic variety and the dominant general management logic(s).

Strategic variety

Strategic variety in a diversified firm depends on the characteristics of the mix of business the firm is engaged in. During the past decade top managers have tended to reduce the strategic variety (not necessarily the number of district businesses) in the portfolio of the firm. This is accomplished, often, by divesting businesses that do not 'fit' – those that increase strategic variety. Many of the businesses divested are profitable (e.g., Sperry's sale of Vickers to concentrate on information technology, ITT's sale of its bakery division). Divesting businesses to get more 'focus' to the portfolio results from an implicit recognition that the demands on top management of strategic variety can be significant. Not all diversified firms have been proactive in reducing strategic variety. Some have been forced to divest businesses, after years of poor profit performance and an inability on their part to turn around the 'sick businesses'.

An alternative to the approach outlined above – reducing strategic variety by restricting the mix of businesses in the firm to those whose strategic characteristics are similar – is followed by firms like General Electric, Textron, or 3M. Typically, businesses with similar strategic characteristics tend to be grouped together, into 'sectors' for management purposes. As a result there is little strategic variety within a sector, but across sectors there can be significant differences. This approach reduces the strategic variety that top managers have to deal with by creating an intermediate level of general management. These group- or sector-level executives tend to manage the strategic direction of specific businesses within the sector. Conceptually, this arrangement explicitly recognizes the need to contain strategic variety for effective management. However, in practice, the role of sector executives and their relationship both with business-level managers and the top management of the firm can get unclear if top management of the firm attempts to directly influence the conduct of any one business or a group of businesses.

Changing strategic variety

So far we have considered how firms can contain strategic variety in a diversified firm, at a given point in time. But over time, even with an unchanging mix of businesses, the strategic variety can change. For example, the strategic characteristics of businesses can change due to changes in the structure of industries. The toy industry was changed, in a relatively short period of time, by the availability of inexpensive microprocessors. The combination of telecommunication and computers and deregulation is changing the financial services industry. Globalization has changed the nature of competition in several industries such as TV, hi-fi, autos, steel, machine tools, etc. As a result, even firms which do not ostensibly change the mix of businesses will have to cope with increasing strategic variety, as the underlying structural characteristics of businesses change. Top managers, as a result, must possess the ability to revise the dominant logic they used to manage those businesses. The inability of top managers both to identify changing structural characteristics of businesses and accept the need for change in dominant logic(s), may provide at least a partial explanation for the difficulties traditional businesses like steel, machine tools, and autos have faced during the past five years in the US.

An addition of a new business, either through internal development or acquisition, can also change the strategic variety within the firm. If the new business is distinctly different (e.g., General Motors' acquisition of EDS, or General Electric's acquisition of Utah International) the strategic variety it adds is easily recognized.

In such acquisitions, top managers also recognize that hasty attempts to impose the dominant logic of the firm on the acquired business may be dysfunctional. Often the acquired firm is 'left alone', at least for a time.

When a new business is created through internal development it is harder to recognize the different structural characteristics of that business compared to those in the current mix of businesses; more so if the new business is technologically not dissimilar to existing businesses. For example, the experience of the calculator, digital watch, and personal computer businesses at Texas Instruments illustrates the point. The dominant logic which worked so well for TI in the semiconductor business, when applied to the new business, led to failure. A dramatic contrast is the early recognition at IBM that the personal computer business was structurally quite distinct. This recognition resulted in the creation of an independent business unit for managing that business. It was not subject to the dominant logic of the mainframe business. As the PC business evolves, and as it takes on the characteristics of the mainframe business, at least in some applications and with some customer segments, IBM may reimpose the dominant logic of mainframes on that business.

To summarize, strategic variety in a diversified firm can change due to:

1 changes in the structural characteristics of the existing mix of businesses, or

Table 16.1 Nature of top management tasks in diversified firms

| | Sources of strategic variety | | |
| | | Addition of a new business | |
Top management orientation	Significant structural changes in core business	Similar to existing businesses	Dissimilar from existing businesses
Single dominant logic	(A) Revise the dominant logic	(B) No change required	(C) Create the capacity for Multiple dominant logic(s)
Multiple dominant logic(s)	(D) Revise the dominant logic applied to that business or regroup it under another sector	(E) Assign business to appropriate 'sector'	(F) Add to the variety of dominant logic(s)

2 changes in the mix of businesses caused by acquisitions or internal development.

In either case, top managers must explicitly examine the implications of changes in strategic variety. In other words, *major structural changes in an industry* have the same effect on the strategic variety of a firm as acquiring a new business.

The task of top management is to constantly re-examine its portfolio to ascertain if there are perceptible changes in the strategic variety as well as explicitly to assess the impact of new businesses on dominant logic(s) in the firm. The task of top management under various combinations of 'sources of strategic variety' and 'top management orientation' give us six possible combinations, as shown in Table 16.1. In a firm with a single dominant logic, if the nature of the core business changes significantly, then top managers will have to revise the dominant logic (A). If a new business is added, and is strategically similar (B), no change in dominant logic is needed. If, however, the new business is dissimilar, top managers have to create the capacity within the firm to cope with multiple dominant logics (C). In a firm operating with multiple dominant logics, if the nature of a significant business changes, then top managers may have to revise the dominant logic applied to that business or regroup it under a different 'sector' or 'group' (D). If the new business is strategically similar to one of the 'groups' or 'sectors' within the firm, then top managers may assign it to the appropriate sector (E). If the new business is dissimilar to the existing businesses, then top managers have to add variety to the dominant logics within the firm (F).

CONCLUSIONS

The concept of dominant general management logic and the role of top managers in understanding and managing the logic(s), are important aspects to be considered in the research on diversity and performance. There are several implications of including these concepts in the study of diversity and performance. We will list some:

Limits to diversity

We have argued that the 'real diversity' in a managerial sense in a firm does not arise from the variety in technologies or markets or by the number of district businesses *per se*, but from the strategic variety among businesses requiring a variety in the dominant logics used by top management. Further, the variety of dominant logics that a top management can handle depends on the composition of the team, and their experiences, as well as their attitude toward learning. These factors suggest that we ought to recognize that the limit to the diversity of businesses within a firm is determined by the strategic variety, and that the strategic variety that a firm can cope with is dependent on the composition of a top management team.

Undoubtedly, organization structure can help cope with increased strategic variety. One basic aspect of decentralization is to make decisions at the level where the proper expertise is available. In other words, the cognitive map is more likely to fit the strategic imperatives of the business. However, all decision-making cannot be decentralized. For example, resource allocation decisions *among* a firm's portfolio of businesses must be made. Furthermore, plans, strategies and budgets must be reviewed at the corporate level and managerial performance must be assessed. Hence organizational structure, although useful, is limited. It can attenuate the *intensity* of strategic variety that corporate-level management must deal with, but it cannot substitute for the need to handle strategic variety at the corporate level.

An alternative or supplementary approach is to reduce the strategic variety in the businesses of the firm – what has come to be known as 'focus' in the portfolio. An interesting variant on this is to impose a single strategic approach on each business. For example as Porter *et al.* (1983) discuss, Emerson Electric has a uniform goal across businesses of being the low-cost producer in each of its markets. Such an approach

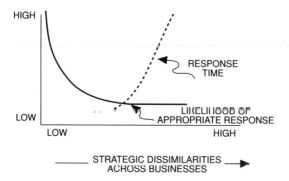

Figure 16.3 The diversity and performance

reduces strategic variety but may impose an inappropriate logic on a particular business. Interestingly, Emerson usually seeks to divest businesses that cannot meet this goal.

Ultimately many firms exceed the limits of organizational structure in attenuating the intensity of strategic variety and/or cannot reduce or limit strategic variety adequately. These firms face the reality of having to deal intensively with strategic variety at the corporate level and the necessity of developing multiple dominant logics if performance is to be sustained.

The bottom line is that each top management team at a given point in time has an inbuilt limit to the extent of diversity it can manage. Organizational structure and focus in the portfolio can help extend this limit but they cannot eliminate it.

Diversity and performance: the hidden costs

A high level of performance in a diversified firm requires the ability to 'respond fast' to competitor moves, as well as 'respond appropriately'. One of the implications of our thesis, so far, is that top managers are less likely to 'respond appropriately' to situations where the dominant logic is different, as well as not respond quickly enough, as they may be unable to interpret the meaning of information regarding unfamiliar businesses. The 'hidden costs' associated with diversifying into nonfamiliar businesses are shown schematically in Figure 16.3. These 'hidden costs' are not explicitly recognized when the overall business climate is very favorable. Problems surface when the newly acquired businesses (which are strategically dissimilar) encounter competitive problems or are faced with a profit crisis. Top managers find themselves unable to respond to the crisis under those circumstances (Hamermesh 1977).

Changing or adding dominant logics

The process of adding dominant logics is, given the previous discussion, obviously an important aspect in the management of diversified firms. Also, as the argument so far suggests, the process of changing dominant logics is important to any firm that encounters rapid change in the structure of the industries in which it competes. These issues revolve around the ability of the firm or its dominant coalition to learn. Fortunately, there is a small but growing literature on organizational learning (see Hedberg 1981, for an introduction and survey). This literature suggests ways in which organizations can change or add dominant logics.

First, let us consider the situation involved in changing the dominant logic of a (single-logic) firm. The explicit assumption here is that the structure of the core industry the firm competes in is or has changed significantly.

In general it appears (see March and Simon 1958; Downs 1967; Terreberrey 1968; Cyert and March 1963; Starbuck 1976; Hedberg 1973; Hedberg, Nystrom and Starbuck 1976) that changes in the ways organizations solve significant new problems (i.e., change dominant logics) are triggered by substantial problems or crises. Hedberg (1981) also suggests that opportunities or changes in key executives may also trigger learning, but here the evidence is small by comparison. (Key executive changes are often made in response to crises.) It would appear that in the overwhelming number of instances a crisis is needed to precipitate change (e.g., 'Why fix it if it is not broke?') Not only must there be a crisis but as Nystrom, Hedberg and Starbuck (1976) propose and illustrate, the initial response to the crisis is likely to be inappropriate. In other words the initial response is likely to draw on the now inappropriate but still current dominant logic. This, of course, provokes a deepening of the crisis and a search for other solutions. In other words survival is likely to become dependent on finding a new logic.

Given that the opportunity for learning has been elicited by a crisis (or other event) the organizational learning literature (e.g., Hedberg 1981) suggests that unlearning must occur to make way for new mental maps. Unlearning is simply the process by which firms eliminate old logics and behaviors and make room for new ones. Interestingly, the more successful organizations have been, the more difficult unlearning becomes (Argyris and Schon 1978; Starbuck and Hedberg 1977).

Given that these two preconditions, a precipitating crisis and a start of unlearning, have occurred, the stage is set for the kind of learning that can result in a new dominant logic. However, as Michael (1973) and Hedberg (1981) have observed, little is known about how organizations' cognitive structures are changed. Hence, the discussion *here must be largely speculative.* Hedberg (1981) makes four general suggestions: (1) making organizations more experimental; (2) regulating organizations' sensitivity to environmental changes to an optimal level (neither too low nor too high); (3) redesigning organizations' inner and outer environments; and (4) achieving a dynamic balance between stabilizing and destabilizing influences. Beyond these general areas the current authors suggest: (1) structuring the top management team to include individuals with significantly different experience bases; (2) encouraging top managers to enrich their experience bases through sabbaticals and educational experiences; (3) rehearsing as a management team for a broad range of future industry scenarios; (4) separating economic evaluation from manager evaluation so that executives can be rewarded for experimenting even when projects fail; and (5) legitimizing dissent. Furthermore, in an interesting article about managerial responses to changing environments, Kiesler and Sproul (1982) suggest developing schemas that incorporate the expectation of change as a fundamental component. Unfortunately, again the 'how to' remains largely undefined.

The discussion in this section so far has considered changing dominant logics, not adding new ones. Adding new logics implies retaining the old one and not unlearning it, but developing the ability to deal simultaneously with other logics. This generally falls beyond what has been studied in the organizational learning literature. Diversification is often not triggered by a crisis, and unlearning as described above is not desirable. It appears that what must occur is some kind of meta-learning in which the dominant coalition learns to simultaneously conceptualize different type businesses. Perhaps some sort of meta-logic evolves that specifies the necessity of, and rules for, picking between partially contradictory mental maps. Further research here is obviously needed.

The meaning of 'relatedness'

The concept of related or conglomerate diversification was typically based on an analysis of the technological and market characteristics. The view presented here suggests that we may have to develop a concept of relatedness based on the 'strategic similarities' of businesses and the cognitive composition of the top management team. In other words relatedness may be as much a cognitive concept as it is an economic and technical concept.

Future research

The concept of a dominant logic presents opportunities to deepen our understanding of the management of diversification and the relationships between diversity and performance. A first necessary step is to move beyond the purely conceptual stage to measurement of the construct, or in other words, to being able to specify just what a particular dominant logic actually is. The authors have had experience in trying to construct the dominant logic of a firm by in-depth interviewing of the top management team, and believe that useful results and insights can be achieved. However, such an approach, though useful as a consulting framework, lacks the rigor necessary to establishing general results. Furthermore, quantification is complicated by the cognitive nature of the dominant logic.

Decision-makers' descriptions of their own policies are often inaccurate (Hoffman 1960; Slovic 1969; Balke, Hammond and Meyer 1973). Similarly, stated policies and intentions often vary from what is actually used. Argyris and Schon (1974) describe this as the difference between 'espoused theories' and 'theories in use' that actually govern behavior. These researchers suggest that a person's theory in use cannot be obtained simply by asking for it. Creative questionnaires and analysis procedures, however, can be developed that elicit the true nature of the dominant logic. For example, the policy-capturing methodology (Slovic and Lichtenstein 1971; Slovic, Fischoff and Lichtenstein 1977) would seem to be a powerful approach to measuring a firm's dominant logic.

Another approach to establishing a firm's dominant logic could be through the use of historical analysis. As previous arguments have discussed, the dominant logic is developed as a result of the experiences of the key executives. Hence, delving into the industry and firm experience of these key individuals would seem to be a fruitful approach, especially when coupled with in-depth interviews of the individuals and their immediate subordinates.

A second important area for future research is the previously mentioned process of learning to use multiple dominant logics. The organizational learning literature deals primarily with changing cognitive maps. It does not deal with the process of learning to use multiple, partially contradictory maps. Some firms have obviously been able to solve this problem. Longitudinal clinical investigation is necessary to determine how.

REFERENCES

Allison, Graham J. *Essence of Decision: Explaining the Cuban Missile Crisis*. Little, Brown, Boston, MA, 1971.

Ansoff, H. Igor. *Corporate Strategy*. McGraw-Hill, New York, 1965.

Argyris, C. and D. A. Schon. *Theory in Practice: Increasing Professional Effectiveness*. Jossey-Bass, San Francisco, CA, 1974.

Argyris, C. and D. Schon. *Organizational Learning*. Addison-Wesley, Reading, MA, 1978.

Balke, W. M., K. R. Hammond and G. D. Meyer. 'An alternative approach to labor-management negotiations', *Administrative Science Quarterly*, **18**, 1973, pp. 311–27.

Bettis, R. A. 'Strategic portfolio management in the multibusiness firm: implementing the portfolio concept'. Unpublished doctoral dissertation, University of Michigan, 1979.

Bettis, R. and V. Mahajan. 'Risk/return performance of diversified firms', *Management Science*, **31**: 7, July 1985, pp. 785–99.

Bettis, R. A., W. K. Hall and C. K. Prahalad. 'Diversity and performance in the multibusiness firm', *National Proceedings of the American Institute for Decision Sciences*, 1978, pp. 210–12.

Bower, J. L. *Managing the Resource Allocation Process*. Irwin, Homewood, IL, 1972a.

——, 'Metamanagement: a technology and a philosophy'. Paper presented at the Winter meeting of AAAS, 20 November 1972b.

Chandler, Alfred D. *Strategy and Structure*. MIT Press, Cambridge, MA, 1962.

Channon, Derek. *The Strategy and Structure of British Enterprise*. Graduate School of Business Administration, Harvard University, Boston, 1973.

Cyert, R. and J. March. *A Behavioral Theory of the Firm*. Prentice Hall, Englewood Cliffs, NJ, 1963.

Das, Rajan. *Managing Diversification: The General Management Perspective*. Macmillan India, New Delhi, 1981.

Deal, Terrence E. and Allan A. Kennedy. *Corporate Cultures*. Addison-Wesley, Reading, MA, 1982.

de Groot, A. D. *Thought and Choice in Chess*. Mouton, The Hague, 1965.

Donaldson, G. and Jay Lorsch. *Decision Making at the Top*. Basic Books, New York, 1983.

Downs, A. *Inside Bureaucracy*. Little, Brown, Boston, MA, 1967.

Hambrick, D. C. 'Environmental scanning and organizational strategy', *Strategic Management Journal*, **3**, 1982, pp. 159–74.

Hamermesh, R. G. 'Responding to the divisional profit crisis'. Unpublished doctoral dissertation, Harvard Business School, 1977.

Haspeslagh, P. 'Portfolio planning: uses and limits', *Harvard Business Review*, January–February 1982, pp. 58–73.

Hedberg, B. 'Organizational stagnation and choice of strategy'. Working paper, International Institute of Management, Berlin, 1973.

——, 'How organizations learn and unlearn'. In Nystrom, P. and W. Starbuck (eds), *Handbook of Organizational Design*. Oxford University Press, Oxford, 1981.

Hedberg, B., P. Nystrom and W. Starbuck. 'Camping on seesaws: prescriptions for a self-designing organization', *Administrative Science Quarterly*, **21**, 1976, pp. 41–65.

Hofer, Charles W. and Dan Schendel. *Strategy Formulation: Analytical Concepts*. West, St Paul, MN, 1978.

Hoffman, P. 'The paramorphic representation of clinical judgment', *Psychological Bulletin*, **47**, 1960, pp. 116–31.

Huff, A. S. 'Industry influence on strategy reformulation', *Strategic Management Journal*, **3**, 1982, pp. 119–31.

Kiesler, S. and L. Sproul. 'Managerial response to changing environments: perspectives and problem sensing from social cognition', *Administrative Science Quarterly*, **37**, 1982, pp. 548–70.

Kuhn, Thomas S. *The Structure of Scientific Revolutions*, 2nd edn. University of Chicago Press, Chicago, IL, 1970.

March, J. and H. Simon. *Organizations*. Wiley, New York, 1958.

Michael, Donald N. *On Learning to Plan and Planning to Learn*. Jossey-Bass, San Francisco, CA, 1973.

Miles, R. H. *Coffin Nails and Corporate Strategies*. Prentice Hall, Englewood Cliffs, NJ, 1982.

Montgomery, Cynthia. 'Diversification, market structure and firm performance: an extension of Rumelt's model', Ph.D. dissertation, Purdue University, 1979.

Nathanson, Daniel and James Cassano. 'Organization, diversity, and performance', *Wharton Magazine*, Summer 1982, pp. 19–26.

Newell, A. and Herbert Simon. *Human Problem Solving*. Prentice-Hall, Englewood Cliffs, NJ, 1972.

Nisbett, R. and L. Ross. *Human Inference: Strategies and Shortcomings of Social Judgement*. Prentice-Hall, Englewood Cliffs, NJ, 1980.

Norman, D. *Memory and Attention*, 2nd edn. Wiley, New York, 1976.

Nystrom, P., B. Hedberg and W. Starbuck. 'Interacting processes as organizational designs'. In Kilman, R., L. Pondy and D. Slevin (eds) *The Management of Organization Design*. Elsevier, New York, 1976.

Ouchi, William G. *Theory Z*. Addison-Wesley, Reading, MA, 1981.

Pascale, Richard J. and Anthony G. Athos. *The Art of Japanese Management*. Simon and Schuster, New York, 1981.

Pavan, R. J. 'Strategy and structure of Italian enterprise'. Unpublished doctoral dissertation, Harvard Business School, 1972.

Peters, Thomas J. and Robert H. Waterman, Jr. *In Search of Excellence*. Harper and Row, New York, 1982.

Pooley, G. 'Strategy and structure of French enterprise'. Unpublished doctoral dissertation, Harvard Business School, 1972.

Porter, M. *Competitive Strategy*. The Free Press, New York, 1980.

Porter, M., D. Collis, J. DeBelina, J. Elsasser, J. Hornthal and R. Shearer. 'The chain saw industry in 1974'. In Porter, M. (ed.) *Cases in Competitive Strategy*. The Free Press, New York, 1983.

Prahalad, C. K. and Y. Doz. 'An approach to strategic control in MNCs', *Sloan Management Review*, Summer 1981, pp. 5–13.

Rumelt, Richard P. *Strategy, Structure, and Economic Performance*. Division of Research, Graduate School of Business Administration, Harvard University, 1974.

——, 'Diversity and profitability'. Paper MGL-51, Managerial Studies Center, Graduate School of Management, University of California, Los Angeles, 1977.

Schoeffler, Sidney, Robert D. Buzzell and Donald F. Heany. 'Impact of strategic planning on profit performance', *Harvard Business Review*, March–April 1974, pp. 137–45.

Simon, Herbert A. 'Information processing models of cognition', *Annual Review of Psychology*, **30**, 1979, pp. 363–96.

Skinner, B. F. *Science and Human Behavior*. Macmillan, New York, 1953.

Slovic, P. 'Analyzing the expert judge: a descriptive study of stockbroker's decision processes', *Journal of Applied Psychology*, **53**, 1969, pp. 255–63.

Slovic, P. and S. Lichtenstein. 'Comparison of Bayesian and regression approaches to the study of information processing in judgment', *Organizational Behavior and Human Performance*, **6**, 1971, pp. 649–744.

Slovic, P., B. Fischoff and S. Lichtenstein. 'Behavioral decision theory'. In Rosenzweig, R. and L. W. Porter (eds), *Annual Review of Psychology*. Annual Review, Palo Alto, CA, 1977, pp. 1 39.

Starbuck, W. 'Organizations and their environments'. In Dunnette, M. (ed.) *Handbook of Industrial and Organizational Psychology*. Rand McNally, Chicago, IL, 1976.

Starbuck, W. and B. Hedberg. 'Saving an organization from a stagnating environment'. In Thorelli, H. (ed.) *Strategy + Structure = Performance*. Indiana University Press, Bloomington, IN, 1977.

Suzuki, Y. 'The strategy and structure of top 100 Japanese industrial enterprises 1950–1970', *Strategic Management Journal*, **3**, 1980, pp. 265–91.

Terreberry, S. 'The evolution of organizational environments', *Administrative Science Quarterly*, **12**, 1968, pp. 590–613.

Thanheiser, H. 'Strategy and structure of German enterprise'. Unpublished doctoral dissertation, Harvard Business School, 1972.

Tversky, Amos and Daniel Kahneman. 'Availability: a heuristic for judging frequency and probability', *Cognitive Psychology*, **4**, 1973, pp. 207–32.

——, 'Judgment under uncertainty: heuristics and biases', *Science*, **185**, 1974, pp. 1124–31.

Weick, K. *The Social Psychology of Organizing*, 2nd edn. Addison-Wesley, Reading, MA, 1979.

Wrigley, Leonard. 'Divisional autonomy and diversification'. DBA dissertation, Harvard University, 1970.

Part VI

Developing a corporate strategy

Previous sections in this book have made it clear that corporate-level strategy for a multibusiness company is a fundamentally different subject from business-level strategy. Corporate-level strategy concerns the selection of businesses for inclusion in the corporate portfolio and decisions about how the corporate parent can influence its businesses in ways that will enhance their collective performance. This final section concerns processes and frameworks for developing a corporate-level strategy.

How a corporate-level strategy should be developed is a topic that has received relatively little attention in the literature on corporate strategy.[1] It is also frequently ignored by companies, which tend to concentrate their planning efforts on the development of business-level strategies. As a result, in many companies the corporate strategy is simply the aggregate of the businesses' strategies. Indeed, some authorities have questioned whether a corporate strategy can or should be more than the sum of the strategies of the businesses. Kenneth Andrews, one of the founders of the business policy course at Harvard Business School, expressed these doubts in his book, *The Concept of Corporate Strategy*, reflecting that,

> The overall common strategy of a highly diversified firm may be only the total of its divisional strategies. That it should be more than that is a matter for argument. To make it so puts heavy demands on the ability to conceptualise corporate purpose.[2]

Yet, if a corporate strategy is no more than the sum of its businesses' strategies, no value is added and there is no justification for the multibusiness company.

The authors cited in Parts II and III do provide advice and guidance that is relevant to the development of corporate-level strategy. Portfolio planning, value-based planning and the resource-based theory of the firm are all potentially helpful for decisions about which businesses to be in and how to allocate resources to them. The quest for synergy has implications both for what businesses should make up the portfolio and for how the corporate parent should influence them. However, none of these approaches provides a comprehensive framework for assessing the validity of a company's corporate-level strategy and for developing more convincing alternatives. In particular, they do not help companies to identify strategies that will avoid initiatives that will damage performance. As we have seen in Parts IV and V, this must be a key component of any framework for developing more successful corporate-level strategies.

The reading in this part is a chapter taken from Michael Goold, Andrew Campbell and Marcus Alexander's book, *Corporate-Level Strategy: Creating Value in the Multibusiness Company*. It focuses specifically on a practical framework that managers can use to test and refine their corporate strategy. The framework is based on the need for a fit between the characteristics and influence of the corporate parent and the needs and opportunities of the businesses. It also addresses explicitly the avoidance of the sort of misfits that lead to value destruction.

The starting point for the framework is the need to identify whether and how the corporate-level can add any value. But the ultimate goal of corporate strategy, it is argued, should be to add more value than other rival owners could. The criterion for assessing corporate strategy is therefore 'parenting advantage', just as the criterion for business strategy is competitive advantage. The parenting advantage criterion can be used to arrive at decisions concerning changes to the composition of the portfolio of businesses and concerning changes in the resources, competences and management processes of the corporate parent.

Goold, Campbell and Alexander's framework draws on many of the ideas discussed in earlier sections of the book. In particular, it encourages corporate-level managers to think through and analyse the economic rationale for their ownership of multiple businesses in terms of the added value they create, and it emphasizes the importance of the distinctive resources and skills that the corporate parent possesses. It proposes a basis for corporate-level strategy decisions that recognizes the vital role of the corporate parent, and its ability to create or to destroy value depending on the suitability of the influence it exercises on its different businesses.

NOTES AND REFERENCES

1 Since Igor Ansoff's book, *Corporate Strategy*, first published in 1965, there have been very few works devoted mainly to corporate-level strategy.
2 Andrews, Kenneth R. (1980) *The Concept of Corporate Strategy*, (Revised Edition) Richard D. Homewood, Illinois; D. Irwin, Inc., (first published 1965), p. 35.

ADDITIONAL READING

Andrews, Kenneth R. (1980) *The Concept of Corporate Strategy*, (Revised Edition) Richard D. Homewood, Illinois: Irwin, Inc., (first published 1965).

Explains the strategic planning process, developing the idea of matching corporate competences to environmental opportunity.

Ansoff, Igor (1965) *Corporate Strategy*, New York: McGraw-Hill

Analytical framework for developing a firm's strategy and especially for decisions on diversification.

Chapter 17

Developing a corporate strategy

Michael Goold, Andrew Campbell and *Marcus Alexander*

EDITORS' NOTE

The following selection is from Corporate-Level Strategy: Creating Value in the Multibusiness Company. *In the book, the authors develop the concept of parenting advantage as the guiding principle for corporate-level strategy. A parent should seek to gain parenting advantage – to create more value in its businesses than would be created than if those businesses were stand-alone entities, and also to create more value than if the businesses were owned by any other corporate parent. Goold, Campbell and Alexander argue that corporate strategy should identify how the company will achieve parenting advantage. In the selection included here, the authors explore how the concept of parenting advantage can help managers develop better corporate strategies.*

The prime criterion for corporate-level strategy decisions should be the impact the decision has on parenting advantage, just as the prime criterion for business-level strategy decisions is impact on competitive advantage. By providing a similarly clear criterion for corporate-level strategy decisions, we believe we can raise the quality of corporate strategies in the same way that competitive advantage thinking has raised the quality of business-level strategies.

Corporate strategy is about matching parenting characteristics with business characteristics in a way that leads to advantage now and in the future. Hence a thorough process for developing corporate strategy should involve four inputs:

- Understanding the characteristics of the parent.
- Understanding the characteristics of the businesses.
- Assessing the strengths and weaknesses of rival parents.
- Judging how all these factors may change in the future.

These four inputs are necessary for an analysis of parenting advantage on the basis of which a corporate strategy can be selected. The corporate strategy will have implications for which businesses to focus on (decisions about the portfolio) and what changes to make to the parent

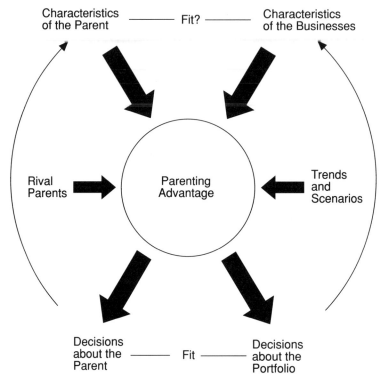

Figure 17.1 Corporate strategy framework

(decisions about the parent). Concerns about any one of these four inputs can provide both the motivation and the starting point for a review of the existing corporate strategy. (See Figure 17.1.)

By advocating this framework, we are not implying that corporate strategists need to do a comprehensive analysis every time they review their corporate strategies. We know that this is often unrealistic, not least because addressing all the points raised in this chapter involves a number of man-years of work. At any point in time, one of the four inputs may be the focus of attention. Sometimes, the company may be worried about a particularly threatening rival. At another time, concern may be focused on the size, cost, and bureaucratic influence of the parent. At another time, concern may be about changes in the environment of a particular business: Are the changes leading to a misfit between business characteristics and parenting characteristics? At yet another time, the focus may be on the long-term prospects for the company's existing heartland businesses. Each of the four inputs can, therefore, be the main focus of attention. The value of the comprehensive framework is that it helps managers keep all four inputs in mind, so that the implications of analysis of one input can be assessed in the light of the other inputs.

CHARACTERISTICS OF THE PARENT

There are different types of parenting characteristics – the parent's mental maps; structures, systems, and processes; functions, central services, and resources; people and skills; and decentralization contracts (Figure 17.2). By examining the parent through each of these five lenses we can gain an understanding of its parenting characteristics. The more that is understood about the parent and how it operates, the easier it is to judge what changes might be made to improve the parent, and which businesses will gain most from being owned by the parent.

Figure 17.3 identifies nine areas of analysis we have found useful in helping to understand the parent. We offer this full list as a menu from which corporate strategists can select to fill a gap in their understanding. Since each analysis can in itself be a substantial piece of work, managers will want to be clear about which element of the parent they are trying to understand better and why.

When it comes to making changes in the parenting approach, a detailed understanding of the characteristics the parent wants to change is essential. Hence time spent on detailed analysis can also be valuable in helping implement changes once a corporate strategy has been chosen. Initially, however, the strategist may want to make a rough assessment of parenting characteristics to provide an overview against which more detailed work can be targeted.

Interviews and workshops

A critical element of any analysis of parenting characteristics is discussion with managers. Every manager in the parent company can potentially provide useful information about the skills and resources in the parent, about how the relationships with businesses operate, and about the maps and predispositions that affect the way the parent behaves. Moreover, all the business managers who have contact with the parent also have useful information on these topics.

At a minimum, there should be discussions with senior line managers in the parent to understand their parenting maps. What are their objectives? Do they have any value creation insights? What parts of the existing parenting behavior are they most committed to? What do they think are the critical success factors of the businesses? It is also necessary to talk to some of the chief executives of the businesses to find out how they perceive the impact of the parent. What influence do they feel? What aspects of the parent do they find beneficial and what is unhelpful?

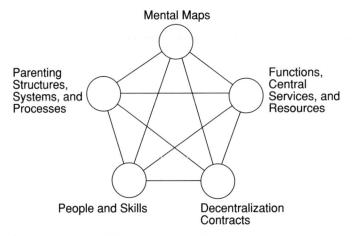

Mental Maps

Parenting Structures, Systems, and Processes

Functions, Central Services, and Resources

People and Skills

Decentralization Contracts

Figure 17.2 Characteristics of the parent

Parenting Characteristics

Analyses	Mental maps	Structure, processes, systems	Functions, central services, and resources	People and skills	Decentralization contracts
1. Interviews/ workshops	✔✔	✔	✔	✔	✔✔
2. Era analysis	✔✔	✔	✔	✔	✔
3. Values and behaviors audit	✔✔			✔	
4. Parenting roles audit		✔✔	✔	✔	✔
5. Processes and systems audit		✔✔		✔	✔
6. Linkage mechanisms audit		✔✔	✔	✔	✔
7. Function/ services audit		✔	✔✔	✔	
8. Policies audit		✔	✔✔		✔
9. Decentralization contracts	✔✔	✔✔	✔	✔	✔✔

Figure 17.3 Types of analysis

Era analysis

Unless a company has recently been through a radical change in management or portfolio composition, the roots of its existing parenting characteristics lie in the past. Moreover, all companies are continually changing and evolving. They are moving away from some historic parenting characteristics and toward some future characteristics. To understand the current characteristics, it is valuable to understand their roots and the way they have been developing. A corporate strategy era analysis is a useful tool for capturing this information. Table 17.1 is an era analysis of Grand Metropolitan. It summarizes the history of the company into four eras of corporate strategy, recording some of the main parenting characteristics in each era.

By understanding the different eras of corporate strategy, it is possible to develop a historical perspective on the present situation that explains particular behaviors, such as why the planning process is run in a given way or why the company is committed to decentralization.

Values and behaviors audit

When recording parenting characteristics it is often possible to overlook the impact of culture and norms of behavior. Unless the managers in the parent are actively pushing the parent's culture onto the businesses, it is easy to assume that it is not a major source of parenting influence. But business managers, eager to be recognized by parent managers and looking for opportunities for promotion, are influenced by the culture and norms of behavior in the parent.

Many companies try actively to manage these cultural signals, even writing them down into mission and philosophy statements such as Hewlett Packard's "HP way." In these cases, so long as the espoused philosophy is the philosophy in use, much of the analysis needed to understand the culture has already been done. In other companies, the culture is more implicit. In these organizations, recording the main behavior norms and the values associated with them can help to surface the culture, adding to the understanding of parenting characteristics.[1]

Parenting structure and roles audit

A parent organization structure chart is an important input to the analysis. It should identify all those organization units that are part of the parent and all those units that are businesses. In large parents, particularly organizations with matrix structures, different parts of the parent are playing different roles. In ABB, the region manager is playing a shareholder, performance-focused role, and the business area manager

Table 17.1 Grand Metropolitan era analysis

	1947–73	1973–80	1980–86	1986–93
Strategy	Buy property-backed assets that can produce enough cash flow to cover the cost of debt	Survive by generating the cash flow needed to cover interest	Diversify into the USA and services Rationalize Watney and Express Build IDV's brands and distribution	Declutter Acquire branded companies and revitalize IDV's brands and distribution Build IDV's brands and distribution
Opportunity	Many companies with valuable properties, sound cash flows, but low earnings and hence low share prices	Some of Grand Met's businesses overmanned	Some of Grand Met's businesses still overmanned IDV's brands underexploited internationally	Focus on businesses to which Grand Met can add most value Some branded companies need revitalizing Further exploit IDV brands and distribution network
Source of parenting value creation	Founder Maxwell Joseph's knowledge of property values Joseph relationships and reputation in the city Deal-making skills	Appointment of Allen Sheppard	"Light grip on the throat" and Sheppard's team Ability to internationalize IDV's brands	Ability to combine tight operating control with effective brand development
Parenting advantage?	Yes	?	Net disadvantage due to inappropriate diversification	Yes

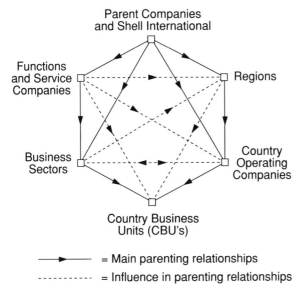

Figure 17.4 Parenting at Shell

is playing a global, strategically-focused role. In some companies, the matrix is even more complex. Figure 17.4 is a display of the organization matrix of Shell, probably the most complex company we researched. The matrix includes regions and functions as well as countries and business sectors. Each is playing a different role in the overall parenting of the country-based business units.

In other companies, there is a difference in roles for different layers in the hierarchy. In Cooper, a major role for the division is to create linkage value within the division, whereas the center's role is to Cooperize the division. In some companies, however, the audit reveals overlaps and duplications – situations where more than one part of the parent is seeking to do the same parenting job. Understanding the different roles is vital to understanding the parenting characteristics.[2]

Processes and systems audit

Four management systems are critical to the way parents create value – the human resource process, the budget process, the planning process, and the capital approval process.

Any detailed audit of parenting characteristics should involve an examination of these processes. A flow diagram detailing each step in the process and identifying the managers involved is a useful starting point. Discussions can then be held with the managers to find out how well the process operates and what influence the process has on the businesses. Each company's processes typically have strengths and weaknesses and suit one type of situation or problem better than another. An understanding of the process helps clarify which businesses benefit and which do not.

Linkage mechanisms audit

One of the sources of value is the way the parent influences the linkage relationships between business units. Much of the influence is informal, through line management. But there are also mechanisms such as committees, transfer pricing systems and project teams set up to increase the value gained from linkage relationships.

A detailed analysis can document each of these mechanisms and assess its impact. Exhibit 17.1 summarizes the questions that need to be asked as part of the linkage audit. The questions have been phrased as if each mechanism addressed a unique opportunity. More normally there is a cluster of reinforcing mechanisms that need to be taken together to make sense of the analysis. For example, a transfer pricing system may be part of a group of pricing mechanisms that involve a committee of marketing directors, a system of appeal and arbitration, and a whole series of exceptions and precedents that have developed informally over time.

Exhibit 17.1   Analyzing linkage opportunities

---

1 What would happen if there was no linkage mechanism and the units concerned were independent companies? This question helps to establish a base starting point for the analysis.
2 What value creation opportunities would be missed under the base starting point? This question helps to clarify the size and nature of the opportunities that the mechanism is addressing.
3 What blockages, if any, are responsible for opportunities being missed under the base starting point? Having a clear idea of the blockages that are creating the opportunity helps in selecting a mechanism.
4 How effective is this mechanism at releasing the value opportunity? The costs and benefits of the mechanism needs to be compared with the size of the opportunity.
5 Does this mechanism have any positive or negative side effects that need to be accounted for? This question is a prompt to think more widely about the impact of the mechanism.

Functions and services audit

Central functions and services are vital parts of the company's parenting characteristics. They can be divided into three areas: providing information and support to central managers; influencing the businesses through functional guidance; and providing services to the businesses. The first part of the audit is to break the functions down into these components. In some cases, this means splitting individual jobs across the three categories. In other cases, a whole department will fit in just one category. For example, a management development function consisting of one management development manager may be involved in all three activities. The manager may have an important role in advising the chief executive on appointments and helping to develop central managers; he or she may actively influence the quality of management development in the businesses; also, he or she may do projects for business managers, such as helping them recruit a management development manager or select a management course. An audit of this function would require the management development manager to allocate his or her time among the three activities.

The second part of the audit is to understand the needs of the "customer" for each of the three activities. What service levels does the chief executive want? What are the appropriate levels of functional guidance in this area? What services do the businesses say they need?

The third part of the audit is to judge the effectiveness of the function or service. This should be based on the views of the customers, an understanding of the activities, and an estimate of costs.[3]

Policies audit

A policies audit is a quick way of documenting some of the influences exerted by the parent. Policies can exist as part of functional influence, for example, health and safety policies or human resource policies. They also exist as part of the administrative and control fabric of the organization, for example, policies about planning or capital approval. An audit of policies should first identify them from manuals and other documents and then assess the impact of the policies on the performance of the businesses.

Many policies will be largely administrative having little effect on the businesses, but some will be important, influencing the way business managers behave. Policies that require common benefit or bonus packages across the businesses, for example, can reduce the ability of some businesses to recruit appropriate staff. In a detailed analysis, each policy should be examined for its impact on each business.

Decentralization contracts audit[4]

The other analyses will have helped define the parameters of the decentralization contracts as they are experienced by each business. However, it is helpful to summarize the decentralization contracts by attempting to articulate what powers are reserved for the parent and what are delegated to the businesses. Many of these will be defined in policy documents, the terms of reference for functions and committees, job descriptions, and the like. But these documents may not match well with the way in which the decentralization contracts work in practice. On what issues does the center take the prime initiative? When does the center expect to arbitrate over disagreements? What powers do the business managers have with regard to the tasks carried out by, and the staffing of, central functions? Under what circumstances does the center intervene in affairs normally delegated to the businesses? Answers to these questions help clarify the way the organization actually works.

Often it is not possible to get precise answers to these questions, both because there are too many issues to develop a complete picture and because the center normally reserves the right to become highly influential on anything that becomes critical to performance. However, broad answers to the questions, backed with a few illustrative examples, help to flesh out the decentralization contracts.

The cost of the parent

The final area of detailed analysis concerns costs. This is often harder to analyze than might be expected. Although it is normally possible to get a total figure for the parent, producing a breakdown by parenting activity is harder. Moreover, there is always a question of whether services paid for by the businesses should be viewed as a parent cost or a business cost.[5]

While it can be useful to have a detailed breakdown of cost by activity for the purpose of fine tuning a parent's effectiveness, we have not typically found detailed cost information to be a vital factor. This is partly because cost data does not usually throw much light on issues of fit or misfit. It is also because the indirect costs of the parent – time spent by business managers – are often much greater than the direct costs of the parent. We have plenty of examples of business managers saying that they have had to hire a planning manager or a health and safety expert to handle all the issues raised by the parent company planning team or health and safety department.

Alignment analysis

Once the parenting characteristics have been identified, it is useful to assess the degree to which they are well aligned in support of a consistent parenting approach. We have observed that the most successful companies have parenting characteristics that reinforce each other.

The structures, systems, and processes fit the mental maps; the functions and central services fit the decentralization contracts; and the people and skills provide the added ingredient that makes both the structure and the functions work well.

Frequently some parenting characteristics are out of line: the planning process may cut across the organization structure; a bonus system may undermine linkage initiatives; or a functional director may attempt to develop policies that interfere with the company's agreed decentralization contracts. In these circumstances, it is often possible to improve the corporate strategy just by improving the alignment between the parenting characteristics.

A simple way to test alignment is to use tools we have developed for classifying parenting style. Parenting style is a way of summarizing a company's parenting approach. All the parenting characteristics are relevant to a judgment about style. Once a style assessment has been made (Strategic Planning, Strategic Control, Financial Control), it is possible to identify parenting characteristics that do not fit well with the style.[6] These can then be the focus of change initiatives that will improve the alignment between parenting characteristics.

CHARACTERISTICS OF THE BUSINESSES

The corporate strategist needs to understand the businesses in the portfolio well enough to define the parenting opportunities in each business and judge whether each business fits or does not fit with the parent.

As an initial step, the scope and definition of each business unit needs to be established. It is sensible to start with the definitions currently employed within the company. Where the existing business unit definitions are unclear, a judgment may be needed.

Once a decision has been made about unit definitions, two sets of business characteristics can be analyzed for each unit: the parenting opportunities in the business, and the critical success factors of the business. As with parenting characteristics, detailed analysis of business characteristics is a major piece of work. Initially a first cut can be made of the business characteristics and further work carried out to provide additional detail where it is needed.

Parenting opportunities

Parenting opportunities can come from many sources. The business may be inappropriately defined, lack important skills, have an unsatisfactory strategy, or excessive overheads. The first step is to assess the performance of the business. Is the business performing as well as could be expected given its competitive position and market focus? If not, it has an improvement opportunity and may, therefore, be able to benefit from parenting influence of some sort.

The next step is to understand the nature of the parenting opportunities. This is essentially a creative analytical process. Exhibit 17.2 lists some factors we have found useful as prompts in analyzing opportunities. The focus is on the underlying conditions under which businesses are likely to have opportunities for improvement that are not being grasped by the business managers.

Exhibit 17.2   Understanding parenting opportunities

1 *Business Definition.*   Is the business defined so as to maximize its sources of competitive advantage?

2 *Business Size.*   Does the business suffer from problems related to being small (e.g., management succession, financial control skills) or big (e.g., bureaucracy, loss of motivation)?

3 *Management.*   Does the business have top-quality managers relative to its competitors? Are its managers focused on the right objectives/ambitions? Is the business dependent on attracting and retaining unusual people?

4 *Temptations.*   Does the nature of the business encourage managers to make mistakes (e.g., maturity often leads to excessive diversification; long product cycles can lead to excessive reliance on old products; cyclical swings can lead to too much investment during the upswing)?

5 *Linkages.*   Could this business effectively link with other businesses to improve efficiency or market position? Are the linkages complex or difficult to establish between the units concerned?

6 *Common Capabilities.*   Does this business have capabilities in common with other businesses that could be built, shared, and transferred between the businesses?

7 *Special Expertise.*   Could this business benefit from specialist or rare expertise that the parent possesses or could possess?

8 *External Relations.*   Does this business have difficult-to-manage external stakeholders (shareholders, government, unions, suppliers, etc.) that could be better managed by the parent company?

9 *Major Decisions.*   Does the business face difficult and infrequent decisions in which it lacks expertise (entry into China, major acquisitions, major capacity extensions)? Would it be difficult to get funding for major investments from external capital providers?

10 *Major Change.*   Is the business facing a need to make major changes for which its management has insufficient experience?

In some cases, there may be little improvement potential because the business is already benefiting from the parent's influence. In these situations, it is important to ask how the business would be affected if it was separated from the parent. Any loss of performance that would result from separation is a form of parenting opportunity.

The difficult task in analyzing parenting opportunities is to identify those areas of improvement that would be unlikely to happen without the parent's involvement. Most businesses are planning to improve their performance, and the majority of these plans are developed by and implemented by the managers within the businesses. Only some improvement plans require the influence of the parent: Only some improvement opportunities are parenting opportunities.

The third step in assessing parenting opportunities is to attempt to put a figure on the size of each area of opportunity. What would be the performance improvement if the opportunity was successfully addressed? In crude shareholder value terms, how much would the value of the business rise if the improvement was made? This assessment of the size of opportunities helps to rank order the businesses in terms of the potential value a parent could add.[7]

Critical success factors

The reverse of value creation is value destruction. Understanding the potential for value destruction involves understanding the businesses' critical success factors and judging whether any of the parenting characteristics are likely to misfit with the businesses. A business's critical success factors are the critical resources and capabilities needed to be a viable competitor in the market place.

The analysis should focus on those critical success factors that are likely to be influenced by the parent. One place to start is to understand the critical success factors that relate to the minimum parenting tasks – appointing senior managers, agreeing on and monitoring performance targets, authorizing major decisions, reacting to linkage disputes. What sort of managers are needed to make a success of this business? What are the main challenges facing the business and how should performance be measured? What is the nature of the major decisions, particularly capital expenditure decisions, facing the business? What areas of linkage exist with other businesses in the portfolio? By understanding the factors critical to success in each of these areas, it will be possible to judge whether any of the parenting characteristics will misfit in such a way as to destroy value.

The analysis, however, needs to go beyond a focus on success factors that relate to minimum parenting tasks. It should also include an assessment of the success factors for all areas of the business that the parent currently influences, or is likely to influence in a future corporate strategy. If the parent has a strong engineering function, then the success factors in engineering within the businesses need to be understood. If the parent is highly influential in public relations issues, then the success factors that relate to public relations need to be understood. The assessment of critical success factors is driven by the nature of the current and likely future parenting behavior.

Bedfellows analysis

The purpose of this analysis is to assess whether the businesses make natural bedfellows. Do the businesses have common features that suggest they should be parented by one parent company? Do they, for example, have parenting opportunities that are similar enough to benefit from one parent company? Do they have critical success factors that are similar? In most portfolios, there is a group of businesses with similar success factors and similar parenting opportunities. But there is often a large number of other businesses with different parenting opportunities or different success factors. It is valuable to identify the natural bedfellows – the ones with similar parenting opportunities and success factors – and distinguish them from the other businesses. A future corporate strategy is likely to build a heartland round the natural bedfellows.[8]

ASSESSING FIT

The review of corporate strategy may lead to changes either in the parent or in the portfolio of businesses. The assessment of current fit gives an important pointer to where changes are likely to be needed. Three fit tests can be used:

- Do the parent's perceptions of its opportunities to create value match the parenting opportunities in the businesses?
- Are any of the parent's characteristics particularly effective at addressing the parenting opportunities?
- Do any of the parent's characteristics fit poorly with the critical success factors?

In parents with a good fit, value is normally being created. Where the fit is poor, value is normally being destroyed. A number of different analyses can help assess the degree to which value is being created or destroyed.

- *Successes and Failures Analysis.* By identifying particular events and decisions in the company and grading them as successes or failures, it is often possible to see patterns. By assessing what contribution (if any) the parent has made to these events, it is possible to illuminate both the key parenting characteristics of the organization and the sorts of situations where value is created and destroyed. This is usually the analysis that yields most understanding of where and how the parent is creating value.
- *Performance of Businesses Relative to Direct Competitors.* Superior performance is only prima facie evidence of value creation by the parent

because it may be that the performance could have been achieved by the business on its own. Some assessment of the role of the parent in creating the performance is therefore also necessary.

- *Shareholder Value Analysis.*   The contribution to shareholder value, on a discounted cash flow (DCF) basis, of each business is an alternative method of measuring performance, and hence a second source of prima facie evidence of parenting added value. Once again, care must be taken, as this value may be entirely generated at the business level, with no contribution from the parent.
- *Value Gap Analysis.*   An analysis of what the businesses might be worth to a predator, who would be prepared to break up the company and sell the component parts separately, can indicate businesses in which the current parent appears to be creating relatively more or less value than alternative parents.
- *Discussions and Interviews with Managers in the Parent and in the Businesses.* Managers at all levels in the company will have views on whether value is being added or subtracted, and will be able to provide examples and anecdotes to support their views. Inevitably, these views will be somewhat subjective, but they provide an essential component of the assessment.

When the answers to the three fit questions are put together with the evidence from the five ways of assessing value creation, it is normally possible to reach conclusions about which businesses are benefiting from the parent's influence and which are being harmed by it. There are always grey areas: businesses about which it is hard to make judgments one way or the other. But the assessment can help explain where and why the parent is currently succeeding and failing.

It is important to remember that the assessment is based on historic data. A parent that has recently changed its characteristics will be difficult to assess. Businesses in changing environments will also be difficult to assess. However, where there is a reasonable history of stable parenting, it is possible to do highly detailed and valuable analysis. The vice president for corporate development of Emerson, Charlie Peters, who has completed a detailed assessment of fit at Emerson, argues that analysis of parenting characteristics, business characteristics, and fit should be pushed as far as possible:

It is important to work hard at identifying the sweet spot within your portfolio: those businesses where your parenting approach creates a particularly large amount of value. Based on my experience, this requires an enormous amount of detailed and rigorous analysis, and it pays back because the results are often counterintuitive.

RIVAL PARENT ANALYSIS

Rival parent analysis involves identifying, for each business, other parent companies that might add more value. The list of rival parents should include both direct competitors and other multibusiness companies whose parenting approach might be appropriate for the relevant business. For the companies identified as rival parents, a review of parenting characteristics and potential value creation, similar in concept to the appraisal described earlier in this chapter should be carried out.

Rival parent analysis is a vital component in assessing parenting advantage, but needs to take account of the long term. A snapshot analysis of a particular business at a point in time may indicate that a rival would add more (or less) value, whereas a longer view, or a view that takes account of synergies with other businesses, might reach the opposite conclusion. Rival parent analysis will highlight businesses in the portfolio that could be sold to more appropriate parents. In other words, it provides some guidance for portfolio options. It also provides guidance for parenting by helping identify alternative parenting approaches that work.

To start rival parent analysis, it is necessary to define a group of rival parents. These are companies that could be alternative parents of the businesses in the company's portfolio. For a large diversified company, the list of possible rival parents can be very long. But we have found it valuable to generate as full a list as possible before selecting which companies to analyze. Without a fairly full list, it is easy to choose obvious rivals and miss the creative benefit of identifying rival parents that have very different parenting characteristics and portfolios of businesses. For example, an oil company, such as Shell, can easily identify another oil company, such as Exxon, as a rival parent. It is also fairly clear that a minerals company, such as RTZ, is a rival parent for Shell's minerals businesses,[9] and that Dupont is a rival for Shell's chemicals businesses. It is less obvious that a diversified company, such as Hanson, is a rival for Shell's coal or chemical businesses, even though Hanson is one of the world's largest producers of coal and base chemicals.

We suggest four ways of developing names for the list of rival parents:

1 List all the obvious rivals: companies of similar size with similar portfolios of businesses.
2 For each business in the portfolio, list all the parents that own direct competitors to the business.
3 For each business in the portfolio, list all the companies that could have beneficial linkages with the business and note the parents that own these companies. Take particular care to note parents that own

similar businesses in different countries. These similar businesses often provide opportunities for skill and technology sharing.

4 For each business in the portfolio, consider the different types of value that could be added to the business (e.g., tight financial controls to improve cash flow, or linkages with sister companies in Europe), and describe the type of parents that could add this kind of value. Then identify companies that match this type.

Once the list of rival parents has been developed, the next step is to select the companies that will be analyzed in more detail. It will be impossible to do a full analysis of all the rival parents on the list. We suggest focusing on the most "obvious" rivals and then creating categories of less obvious rival parents, selecting one company to analyze from each category.

As with competitive analysis at the business level, rival parent analysis is a process of getting to know the rivals better and better, so that it is possible to use them as a benchmark of value creation. The benefits of this benchmarking are not limited to major strategy reviews. Like all benchmarking exercises, benefits can accrue in many small ways as ideas are gained for improving parenting influence. For example, one company in the electrical equipment industry noted that one of its rivals had less than a quarter of the number of managers in country head offices and yet appeared to be able to achieve as much country presence and coordination. By reverse engineering the country organization of this parent and understanding how the coordination was achieved, the first company was able to cut tens of millions of dollars from its country organizations. By decentralizing some of the functional tasks to businesses within the country and centralizing other activities to the corporate center, the country organization was able to focus on a few essential coordination activities such as liaising with the government, coordinating marketing to major customers, and coordinating graduate recruitment. Even these tasks were mainly led by the larger businesses, with the country organization providing some administrative support and impetus for action.

Most managers view rival parent analysis as a daunting task. Yet we can vouch for its value and practicality. Companies are not as secretive about their management philosophy as they are about their product technology. Normally accessible sources – company literature, ex-employees, recently sold businesses, direct contacts, studies by investment analysts, and other public sources – can provide considerable information. Moreover, it is often not necessary to devote more than a few days' work to each company to produce useful results. Table 17.2 displays the rival parent analysis carried out by one manufacturing company of its two most obvious rivals. The work took two days and the results can be

Table 17.2 Rival parent analysis – manufacturing

Company A	Company B
Financially driven	Strategically driven
Quick to pulll out of low profit investments	Long-term outlook
	Large "expatriate" group
Few "international" managers	International senior management group
Few nonnationals	
Authoritarian management style	Consensus management approach
Strong system	Discussion culture
Risk averse	Willingness to joint venture
Prefer equity control	Need for operational control

summarized on one page. Yet the implications are clear. Company A, a US-based company, is likely to be a better parent for certain kinds of businesses – for mature, US-based businesses with good cash flow potential. Company A is also likely to be better at rationalization opportunities. Company B, on the other hand, is likely to be a better parent for businesses with long investment lead times, such as technology-driven businesses, particularly those requiring complex global management structures and bold strategies. Even this simple analysis points to different sources of parenting advantage.

TRENDS AND SCENARIOS

All the analysis so far involves current or historic data. Yet really good corporate strategy options need to contain some vision: some view about how trends are evolving, about opportunities that will exist in ten years' time, about how the world is going to be. The danger with all analytically based approaches to strategy is that they are overinfluenced by historic data.

One of the methods for analyzing the future that has become widely respected is the scenarios technique.[10] The technique involves developing scenarios of two or more different and yet possible future worlds. These worlds represent different ways in which current trends and influences could move. They can be used to help the process of creating ideas about future sources of parenting advantage in three ways.

First, the scenario worlds can be used to judge which rival parents are likely to do well or badly in each scenario. This can help focus attention for further analysis of rival parents and contribute to the creation of parenting options. For example, a scenario that predicts a smooth transition to a common currency in Europe and the lowering of trade barriers worldwide may favor parent companies seeking to create value through internationalizing businesses. An opposite scenario may favor parent companies seeking to create value by linking businesses within national boundaries.

The second way to use scenarios is to compare the company's list of parenting characteristics against each scenario. Each parenting characteristic can be scored as positive, negative, or neutral against each scenario, giving a deeper understanding of the match between the company's parenting characteristics and the scenarios. This analysis also provides useful insights for developing parenting options.

The third use of scenarios is to generate different ways of adding value under the different scenarios. For example, a scenario that predicts an increase in retailer brands would also predict that a number of branded manufacturers will run into trouble by attempting to resist the trend. This suggests a parenting opportunity: buy companies with good product technology that are resisting the trend and change their strategy to be more supportive of the retailers. The insight would be the prediction that some companies will underperform because they will be locked into an outdated way of marketing. Assuming that other parents have not spotted the opportunity, the company ought to be able to buy companies with poor strategies and create value by redirecting their strategies.

Building a complete scenario is expensive and time-consuming because of the need to think through the impact of many different forces of influence. However, the alternative to scenario analysis – studying individual trends – has dangers. It can cause the analyst to overlook the impact an individual trend may have on the broader system. Frequently a seemingly obvious trend fails to emerge in the way predicted due to other factors in the system. The scenario approach attempts to look at the whole system and the total impact of all the trends. Individual trends analysis is most useful when it takes account of the likely influences of the broader system.

CHOOSING A CORPORATE STRATEGY

The previous sections of this chapter describe analyses and techniques for understanding the four inputs to corporate strategy development. This section is essentially about the creative part of corporate strategy development – the generation of options and strategies. It is also about the selection process: how to decide which strategy option is best for the company.

A useful starting point for option generation is to draw together the input analyses into an assessment of parenting advantage. In which businesses has the parent created more value than rival parents, and in which has it been inferior to rival parents? Is the company's parenting

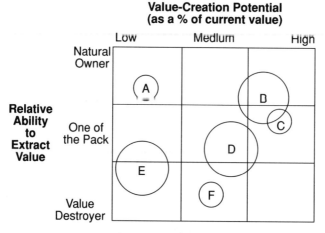

**Value-Creation Potential
(as a % of current value)**

Each circle represents a business in the
portfolio. Circle size is in proportion to the
current value of the business.

Figure 17.5 Parenting opportunity matrix

advantage in each business likely to increase or decrease in the future?
These assessments will not take account of changes to the corporate
strategy that may be made, but they provide the backdrop against which
changes need to be considered.

The assessment of parenting advantage can be plotted on a display
that also measures the potential for value creation in each business
(Figure 17.5). A "natural owner" is a parent that is at least as good or
better than rival parents: a natural owner has parenting advantage. "One
of the pack" is a parent that has no obvious disadvantages, but is not
clearly a "natural owner." A "value destroyer" is a parent that has clear
parenting weaknesses in exploiting the sources of value creation most
important for that business. Value creation potential is measured as a
percentage of current value. A "low" score would be an improvement
of less than 10 percent in the value of the business. A "medium" score
would be an improvement of 10 percent to 50 percent. A "high" score
would be an improvement over 50 percent.

A version of this matrix was first developed by the consultants
McKinsey & Company, in consulting work carried out with large
corporates in the late 1980s. Called the MACS framework (standing for
Market Activated Corporate Strategy), it has proved a useful way of
capturing both the nature of the parenting opportunities and the quality
of the existing parenting.[11] It provides a good backdrop for generating
options about which businesses should serve as a base for the corporate
strategy and what changes to make to parenting characteristics.

Generating corporate strategy options

No amount of analysis and understanding of parenting characteristics, business characteristics, rival parents, or trends in the environment will substitute for insight and creativity in the generation of corporate strategy options. It is a black art, and we do not wish to pretend that it is always possible to develop options that will give parenting advantage, or even options that will secure the company's future. There are situations in which we have been involved where the only solution appeared to be the dissolution of the company and the sale of the businesses to managers or rival parents. With this caveat, however, we have developed some approaches for aiding option generation and stimulating creativity. In particular, we have found it useful to generate parenting options as a separate exercise from portfolio options, and then to synthesize these two sets of options into three or four corporate strategy options.

Parenting options concern the ways in which the company aims to parent and create value in its businesses. Exhibit 17.3 summarizes a number of prompts we have found useful to the generation of parenting options. The skill in choosing options is to weave a path between being overambitious and not being ambitious enough. It is tempting to develop options modeled, for example, on ABB or BTR, when neither is a realistic ambition for the current parent. On the other hand, it is also possible to assume that all the current parent managers are immovable, making it hard to identify options that involve more than a minor change. Obviously, the parenting options must be realistic, taking account of the senior managers and their embedded values, beliefs, and

Exhibit 17.3   Prompts for developing parenting options

1 *Downsize, delayer, and decentralize.*   Many companies are improving their parenting by reducing value destruction.
2 *Encourage networking.*   Companies such as ABB, 3M, and Unilever are demonstrating that linkage benefits can be achieved at low cost through managed networking.
3 *Clarify the dominant process.*   Different options can be based on choosing different processes (e.g., budgeting, planning, or capital approval) as the dominant process.
4 *Focus on the dominant managers.*   Different options can be based on the different skill combinations that could be created by choosing different combinations of the senior team.
5 *Redefine division versus center roles.*   Companies frequently duplicate parenting tasks by doing them both in the division and the center.
6 *Build functional skills.*   Identify core skills that could be built through functional parenting.
7 *Build corporate development skills.*   Companies are frequently weak in acquisition, divestment, and venturing.

ways of working. Most substantive parenting options, however, will entail some people changes.

Portfolio options concern the sorts of businesses to have within the portfolio. They are often easier to develop than parenting options. The analysis of the existing parenting characteristics and business characteristics will have defined a group of businesses or a historic heartland that is likely to be the basis of most portfolio options. The challenge in option generation is to think of ways of extending, growing, or redefining the historic heartland. Exhibit 17.4 summarizes the prompts we have found useful when developing portfolio options.

The purpose of developing parenting options separate from portfolio options is to stimulate creativity. All parenting options have portfolio implications and vice versa. The process of developing the two sets of options helps break out of *status quo* thinking and can stimulate new combinations. Once the creative thinking is complete, the two lists need to be synthesized into three or four corporate strategy options, each of which can be described by a prospective parenting advantage statement.

The corporate strategist can also use the development of corporate strategy options to help the decision-making process. Frequently, senior management already has a strong view about a favored option, in which case additional options can be developed to provide refinement of the preferred option or a radical challenge to the current thinking. Sometimes senior managers are locked into a disagreement about the way forward, which may well have sparked the strategy review in the first place. In this case, the corporate strategy options should be chosen to illuminate the points of agreement and disagreement or establish a different logic for approaching the decision.

Exhibit 17.4   Prompts for developing portfolio options

1 *Mentally discard the misfits.*   The first step is to mentally cleanse the portfolio of clear misfits.
2 *Assume no size constraints.*   Avoid restricting options to ones that will make the company about the same size. Consider ones that will halve or double the size.
3 *Look for businesses with similar critical success factors.*   It is easier to develop distinctive parenting skills and gain a "feel" for businesses if the success factors are similar.
4 *Look for linkages.*   Look for businesses that share elements of the value chain, or have common skills.
5 *Be guided by scenarios.*   The danger is to choose a portfolio that fits the historic analysis, not the future opportunities.
6 *Try a zero-based approach.*   Assume the existing portfolio has been sold. The company now has a huge cash mountain to spend on new businesses.
7 *Consider a split or demerger.*   This is particularly relevant if the existing portfolio appears to have two or more heartlands.

Selecting a corporate strategy

The most important criterion for selecting a corporate strategy should be the degree to which the strategy will give parenting advantage now and in the future. Comparing the degree of advantage that is likely to result from one option against another is not easy. It requires detailed knowledge of the most threatening rivals, an understanding of the value creation opportunity, and management judgment. Nevertheless, we have found that the sort of analyses used to assess historical parenting fit can be brought to bear, and that the criterion is practical and can be used to distinguish between options.

Companies can have viable corporate strategies without a clear advantage over other parent companies. A company can create wealth and avoid hostile attentions so long as it is a "good" parent. Yet we believe strongly that the parenting advantage criterion is the best guide to help managers make better corporate strategy choices. If all the options are "good parent" options rather than "best parent" options, then management should choose the "best" good parent option.

There are two other criteria that can be used to refine the judgments about which option has the most parenting advantage. These criteria are only relevant when comparing options with similar degrees of parenting advantage.

1 *The Size of the Value Creation Opportunity.* In some situations, the parenting opportunity is limited: The businesses may only need a small amount of parenting influence and only offer the potential for a small increase in performance. This is often the case where separate national businesses share skills or technology, or where vertically linked businesses coordinate product flows. It is possible for a parent to have a clear advantage over other parents and yet still have only a small opportunity to create value. The increase in skill and technology sharing that the parent can create may be small, or the improvement in the coordination of product flows due to the parent may not make a substantial difference.

2 *The Intensity of the Rivalry between Parent Companies.* In some situations, parents are locked in a fierce battle for ownership of businesses. In the late 1980s, for example, Nestlé, Grand Metropolitan, Unilever, Procter & Gamble, Philip Morris, BSN, and other large food companies were competing vigorously to acquire major brands. The prices paid for companies such as Kraft, Rowntrees, Jacobs Suchard, Nabisco's European businesses, and Perrier were high, and probably resulted in most of the value creation opportunity being realized by the selling shareholders rather than the acquiring company. Even in situations where a company has an advantage, the rivalry between parents may be so

intense that the value creation opportunity for the buying company's shareholders is small. In these circumstances, it may be better to choose an alternative corporate strategy, where the degree of parenting advantage is similar but the parenting rivalry is less intense.

Taken together, these two criteria could result in a situation where the corporate strategy option with the most value creation potential is not the one with the highest degree of parenting advantage. However, we would still advise a company to focus on the option with the most parenting advantage. To choose to be a second-best parent, even in an area where there is currently room for both good and bad parents, is locking the company into a losing position in the long term.

In addition to the parenting advantage criterion, corporate strategists should consider implementation risk: the risks entailed in implementing changes to the parent or the portfolio. If the corporate strategy calls for the development of new and different parenting characteristics, or for extensive portfolio change, it may well be far from certain that it can be successfully implemented. In our experience, managers normally over-estimate their ability to change the parenting approach and to build new parenting skills and underestimate their ability to make portfolio changes.

Options with low implementation risk are preferable to ones with high risk. An option that has a lower level of parenting advantage and low risk may be preferable to one that has a high level of parenting advantage but requires developing important new parenting skills and making major portfolio changes. It can be preferable to choose a corporate strategy that builds on existing strengths rather than to reach for a bolder strategy with much higher risks.

The final criterion for choosing a strategy is the objectives and constraints of stakeholders – shareholders, customers, suppliers, employees, senior management, and others. The influence of customers and suppliers on the choice of corporate strategy is likely to be muted because their primary association with the company is through the businesses, not the parent. They therefore have less impact on the choice of parenting behavior or portfolio options. This does not mean that their objectives and constraints should be ignored, but rather that their influence is most strongly felt once the shape of the portfolio has been chosen.

Shareholders' objectives and constraints should be influential in choosing a corporate strategy. Shareholders want the value of the company to increase and hence the strategy that creates the most parenting advantage for the least risk will be the preferred option.

However, some shareholders may have specific requirements that need to be taken into account. How much risk do shareholders want to take? How important is stable earnings growth? Are shareholders prepared to support rights issues? What dividends do shareholders want? Do shareholders see the company as an engineering company or a consumer goods company? Many companies actively survey their shareholders to find out what they think and to seek answers to these questions. But shareholders change, making it necessary to update continuously the answers to the questions. Moreover, a change in corporate strategy may precipitate a change in the composition of shareholders; as one group of shareholders sells shares due to their discomfort with the strategy or the risk involved, another group will be buying the shares because of their comfort with the company's new direction. Our advice is to assume that shareholders are interested only in maximum long-term wealth creation, unless the company's particular shareholders have made different views clear to the company.

The employees and senior managers are another important stakeholder group. The majority of employees and managers work within the business units. Their objectives and constraints affect the choice of strategy both directly and through the risk of implementation. If the senior managers in the businesses do not support the proposed parenting approach, it is unlikely to be successful. But business managers and employees will change if the businesses change. Hence their needs are most relevant once the portfolio has been chosen.

The employees and managers working in the parent have a more direct influence on the choice of strategy. If these managers want a fast-growing, deal-oriented environment, it is inappropriate to choose a "back to the core" strategy. If the managers want the company to be a member of the Fortune 500, it may be inappropriate to choose a demerge strategy. Rather surprisingly, we have found that parent company managers are often reluctant to use their personal preferences as explicit criteria. They often claim to see themselves as "servants" of the company and hence believe that their personal preferences should, in some sense, be off limits. As professional managers, they feel they ought to choose a strategy uninfluenced by inner desires, ego needs, or personal ambitions.

In practice, we find that these personal preferences do emerge. But they are attributed to one of the other stakeholder groups. Managers say, "Our shareholders would be uncomfortable if we focused only on one business," when they mean "We would be uncomfortable." Or managers say, "Our shareholders require a 15 percent per annum growth in earnings per share," when they mean, "We want to be regarded as one of the best companies in the country and this means producing regular earnings growth of 15 percent per annum, like company X."

We feel that managers' personal ambitions, desires, fears, and constraints should be an explicit part of the screening process for choosing the best option, since they will be vital to the successful implementation of the new strategy. These desires will have inevitably influenced the selection of options, but it will aid the final decision if personal aspirations are made explicit. We would discourage managers from choosing an option that only meets personal aspirations and fails to meet any of the other criteria. But equally, we would discourage managers from choosing an option that meets all the other criteria, but leaves managers feeling uninspired and disappointed. It is the managers whose skills and hard work create the value. Unless their aspirations are met, they are unlikely to create an advantage over rivals.

DEFINING THE FUTURE CORPORATE STRATEGY

The final step in the process is to define the chosen corporate strategy in a form that can aid communication, guide decision making, and help to influence the mental maps of managers in the parent and in the businesses. This involves producing a parenting advantage statement (Exhibit 17.5).

The parenting advantage statement will list the main *value creation insights* on which the corporate strategy will be built. These insights will describe the nature of the improvement opportunities the parent will focus on, and the nature of the role the parent will take up in addressing the opportunities.

The parenting advantage statement will also describe the *distinctive parenting characteristics* around which the parenting approach will be designed. These distinctive parenting characteristics will address the value creation opportunities and will reinforce each other.

Finally, the statement will contain, in as much detail as possible, the *heartland* criteria. These criteria will describe the nature of the businesses that fit with the corporate strategy. The criteria will include industry, technology, or market descriptors; some descriptors that refer to the type of improvement potential that exists in the businesses; and some descriptors that define the type of business the parent has a feel for and, importantly, the type of business that should be avoided, where the parent's feel is inadequate.

A clear prospective parenting advantage statement is also the best starting point for the many implementation decisions that will be needed. It will help guide decisions about the portfolio and decisions about the parenting approach.

In addition to a parenting advantage statement, it is often also useful to reassess the company's objectives both in terms of its *strategic intent* (its ambitions expressed in competitive terms) and its *financial objectives*. These objectives will have been influential in the development of and selection between options. However, the objectives may have changed

Exhibit 17.5   Parenting advantage statement

Value Creation Insights	Insights about value creation: • Nature of the parenting opportunity. • Nature of the parent's role in addressing the opportunity.
Distinctive Parenting Characteristics	Parenting characteristics that will be at the center of the parenting approach, drawn from the following areas: • Mental maps. • Structures, systems, and processes. • Functions, central services, and resources. • People and skills. • Decentralization contracts.
Heartland Businesse	Criteria that define the type of business that is the focus of the strategy: • Industry, technology or market descriptors. • Type of parenting opportunities. • Critical success factor descriptors. • Negative descriptors.

in the process of choosing a corporate strategy and it will be useful to revisit them to clarify what the new objectives are. Many companies use this review of objectives to develop a new mission statement. Our research into mission statements suggests that it is better to delay the production of a new mission statement until the parent has had a few years of experience with the new strategy.[11] At this stage, therefore, we believe that statements of strategic intent and financial objectives are sufficient.

SUMMARY

We have shown how companies can set about reviewing their existing corporate strategy or developing a new one. We have provided a framework for thinking about the corporate strategy challenge. The framework provides a structured approach to the task, and suggests analyses and judgments that can be made to arrive at a preferred option. In practice, most companies do not develop strategies in this way. Strategies emerge out of experiments and initiatives driven by senior managers. We believe that our framework adds analytical rigor and rational structure to a process that we acknowledge is essentially experimental.

NOTES

1 A framework for understanding cultural values and their link to strategy is given in Andrew Campbell and Laura Nash, *A Sense of Mission*, Reading, MA: Addison-Wesley, 1993; Andrew Campbell, Marion Devine, and David Young, *A Sense of Mission*, London: Century Business and Economist Books, 1990.

2 For a fuller discussion see Michael Goold, Andrew Campbell and Marcus Alexander, *Corporate-Level Strategy*, New York: John Wiley & Sons, Inc., 1994, Appendix B.

3 See David Young and Michael Goold, *Effective Headquarters Staff*, London: Ashridge Strategic Management Centre, 1993, Section 5, for a fuller discussion of how to review and design headquarters staffs.

4 The decentralization contract between the parent and the business defines the issues over which the parent exerts influence and the issues which are normally decentralized to the business. A decentralization contract is partly defined by policies and rules, but it is also often implicit, based on mental maps and precedents.

5 David Young and Michael Goold, *Effective Headquarters Staff*, and *The Headquarters Fact Book*, London: Ashridge Strategic Management Centre, 1993. These volumes provide data on the size, structure, and cost of 107 UK-headquartered companies, and can provide some useful benchmarks.

6 A questionnaire (Style Questionnaire No. 1) has been developed to help assess the alignment of parenting characteristics. Copies can be ordered from the Ashridge Strategic Management Centre, 17 Portland Place, London W1N 3AF, England, Tel: +44-171-323-4422; Fax: +44-171-323-0903.

7 It is important that the analysis of parenting opportunities focus on the improvements that are due to the influence of the parent, and distinguish these from the improvements that would occur even if the parent was not involved. While in most cases this is a matter of judgment, a more scientific way to do this was described to us by Robin Buchanan, head of Bain & Co.'s London office. It involves developing a "full potential assessment" for each business based on an analysis of the market, industry structure, competitive strength and development potential. The assessment identifies a range of profit, cash flow and shareholder value figures, and defines the risks that would cause the business to be at the top of the range or near the bottom. By identifying which risks the parent organization can help manage, the particular contribution of the parent can be more easily identified.

8 A questionnaire (Style Questionnaire No. 2) has been developed to help assess whether businesses will respond best to a Strategic Planning, Strategic Control or Financial Control style. When different businesses need a parent with different styles they are unlikely to be viable bedfellows. Copies of the questionnaire can be ordered from Ashridge Strategic Management Centre, 17 Portland Place, London W1N 3AF, Tel: +44-171-323-4422; Fax: +44-171-323-0903.

9 Shell was considering divesting its mineral businesses at the time of writing.

10 A good description of this technique is provided by Peter Schwartz, *The Long View*, New York: Free Press, 1992.

11 See Michael Goold, Andrew Campbell and Marcus Alexander, *Corporate-Level Strategy*, New York: John Wiley & Sons, Inc., 1994 for another matrix for assessing businesses.

12 Refer to note 1, and *Do You Need A Mission Statement?* London: Economist Publications, Report No. 1208.

Index